Abortion Bibliography

for 1986

Abortion Bibliography

for 1986

Compiled by
Polly T. Goode

The Whitston Publishing Company
Troy, New York
1989

Library of Congress Catalog Card Number 72-78877

ISBN 0-87875-369-9

Printed in the United States of America

TABLE OF CONTENTS

Preface vii

List of Journals Cited ix

Subject Head Index xxvi

Books and Monographs 1

Periodical Literature 7

Author Index 220

PREFACE

This bibliography is the seventeenth in a series. It is a near complete bibliography of world literature surrounding the subject of abortion, one of the central social issues of our times. Entries earlier than 1986 coming to our attention after the 1985 volume are included here.

Beginning with the current volume, we are omitting the listing of periodical literature by title because of its very limited usefulness. Periodical literature is listed under all appropriate headings and is arranged alphabetically by title under each subject heading. A list of journals cited and a list of subject headings used in this bibliography are included in the preliminary pages.

The following bibliographies, indexes and abstracts have been searched in compiling this volume:

Access
Air University Library Index to Military Periodicals
AJN International Nursing Index
America: History and Life
American Humanities Index
American Reference Books Annual
Applied Science & Technology Index
Bibliographic Index
Biological Abstracts
Biological & Agricultural Index
British Humanities Index
Business Periodicals Index
C & P Abstracts
Canadian Education Index
Canadian Periodicals Index
Catholic Periodical & Literature Index
Communication Abstracts
Criminal Justice Abstracts
Criminal Justice Periodical Index
Criminology & Penology Abstracts
Cumulative Book Index
Current Index to Journals in Education
Dissertation Abstracts International A: Humanities and
Social Sciences
Dissertation Abstracts International B: The Sciences and
Engineering

Education Index
Environment Abstracts
Environment Index
Essay & General Literature Index
General Science Index
Higher Education Abstracts
Hospital Literature Index
Human Resources Abstracts
Humanities Index
Index Medicus
Index to Jewish Periodicals
Index to Legal Periodicals
Media Review Digest
Music Index
Nursing and Allied Health Literature
PAIS
PAIS Foreign Language Index
Philosopher's Index
Police Science Abstracts
Popular Periodical Index
Psychological Abstracts
Readers Guide to Periodical Literature
Religion Index One: Periodicals (from: Index to Religious
        Periodical Literature)
Religious & Theological Abstracts
Sage Family Studies Abstracts
Sage Urban Studies Abstracts
Social Sciences Index
Social Work Research & Abstracts
Sociological Abstracts
Studies on Women's Abstracts
Women's Studies Abstracts.

Polly T. Goode
Troy, New York

LIST OF JOURNALS CITED

AAOHN Journal
AARN Newsletter: Alberta Association of Registered Nurses Newsletter
Academe
Acta Anaesthesiologica Scandinavica
Acta Biomedica de l'Ateneo Parmense
Acta Dermato-Venereologica
Acta Endocrinologica
Acta Europaea Fertilitatis
Acta Gastroenterologica Belgica
Acta Geneticae Medicae et Gemellologiae
Acta Medica Hungarica
Acta Medica Iugoslavica
Acta Medica Polona
Acta Obstetricia et Gynecologica Scandinavica
Acta Paediatrica Scandinavica
Acta Pharmaceutica Hungarica
Acta Physiologica et Pharmacologica Bulgarica
Acta Universitatis Palackianae Olomucensis Facultatis Medicae
Acta Veterinaria Hungarica
Actas Urologicas Espanolas
Actualite
Ad Nurse
Adolescence
Advances in Prostaglandin and Thromboxane and Leukotriene Research
Advances in Psychosomatic Medicine
AFER: African Ecclesiastical Review
Africa
Africasia
Against the Current
AIDS Research
Akusherstvo i Ginekologiia
Albany Law Review
Alberta Report
Allergologia et Immunopathologia
Alternatives
America
American Bar Association Journal
American Economic Review
American Family Physican
American Health
American Journal of Clinical Oncology
American Journal of Clinical Pathology
American Journal of Comparative Law

American Journal of Epidemiology
American Journal of Hospice Care
American Journal of Industrial Medicine
American Journal of Medical Genetics
American Journal of Medicine
American Journal of Nursing
American Journal of Obstetrics and Gynecology
American Journal of Perinatology
American Journal of Public Health
American Journal of Reproductive Immunology and Microbiology
American Journal of Sociology
American Journal of Surgical Pathology
American Journal of Veterinary Research
American Mental Health Counselors Association Journal
American Naturalist
American Pharmacy
AMH
ANNA Journal : American Nephrology Nurses Association
Anaesthesia
Analog Science Fiction
Andrologia
Anesthesia and Analgesia
Anesthesiology
Annales de Chirurgie
Annales de Genetique
Annales Francaises d'Anesthesie et de Reanimation
Annali del Ospedale Maria Vittoria di Torino
Annali di Ostetricia Ginecologia Medicina Perinatale
Annali Italiani di Chirurgia
Annals of the Academy of Medicine, Singapore
Annals of the American Academy of Political and Social Science
Annals of Human Biology
Annals of Internal Medicine
ANPHI Papers: Academy of Nursing of the Philippines
ANS: Advances in Nursing Science
AORN Journal: Association of Operating Room Nurses Journal
Archiv fur Experimentelle Veterinaermedizin
Archiv fur Geschwulstforschung
Archiv fur Tierernahrung
Archives des Maladies du Coeur et des Vaisseaux
Archives for Dermatological Research
Archives of Andrology
Archives of Dermatological Research
Archives of Dermatology
Archives of Disease in Childhood
Archives of Gynecology
Archives of Internal Medicine
Archives of Sexual Behavior
Archives of Toxicology
Archives of Virology
Archivos Espanolese de Urologia
Arkhiv Anatomii, Gistologii i Embriologii
Arthritis and Rheumatism
Arzneimittel-Forschung
Asia-Oceania Journal of Obstetrics and Gynaecology

Asian Profile
Atherosclerosis
Atlantis
Australian and New Zealand Journal of Obstetrics and Gynaecology
Australian Clinical Review
Australian Family Physician
Australian Nurses' Journal
Australian Veterinary Journal
Behavorial and Neural Biology
Behavioral and Social Sciences Libarian
Beijing Review
Berkeley Journal of Sociology
Berliner und Munchener Tieraerztliche Wochenschrift
Biochemical and Biophysical Research Communications
Biology of Reproduction
BioScience
Birth
Birth Psychology Bulletin
Boletin-Asociacion Medica de Puerto Rico
Boletin de la Oficina Sanitaria Panamericana
Boston
Bratislavske Lekarske Listy
British Dental Journal
British Journal of Anaesthesia
British Journal of Cancer
British Journal of Clinical Psychology
British Journal of Hospital Medicine
British Journal of Industrial Medicine
British Journal of Obstetrics and Gynaecology
British Journal of Psychiatry
British Journal of Radiology
British Journal of Urology
British Medical Journal
British Poultry Science
British Veterinary Journal
Bulletin de l'Academie Nationale de Medecine
Bulletin of the American Academy of Psychiatry and the Law
Bulletin of the Atomic Scientists
Bulletin of Entomological Research
Business Week
Cahiers d'Anesthesiologie
California
California Nurse
Cambridge Law Journal
Canadian Anaesthetists Society Journal
Canadian Counsellor
Canadian Dimension
Canadian Historical Review
Canadian Journal of Family Law
Canadian Journal of Genetics and Cytology
Canadian Journal of Political Science
Canadian Journal of Public Health
Canadian Medical Association Journal
Canadian Nurse
Canadian Operating Room Nurses Journal

Canadian Review of Sociology and Anthropology
Cancer
Cancer Research
Capital University Law Review
Cardoza Law Review
Carta Mensal
Casopis Lekaru Ceskych
Catholic Lawyer
Cellular Immunology
Ceskoslovenska Gynekologie
Ceskoslovenska Psychiatrie
Changing Men
Changing Times
Chatelaine
Chemioterapia
Chemotherapy
Chen Tzu Yen Chiu
Chest
Child Abuse and Neglect
Child Development
Children Today
Chirurgia Italiana
Chirurgie Pediatrique
Christian Century
Christianity and Crisis
Christianity Today
Chronicle of Higher Education
Chung Hua Fu Chan Ko Tsa Chih
Chung Hua Hu Li Tsa Chih
Chung Kuo I Hsueh Ko Hsueh Yuan Hsueh Pao
Chung Kuo Yao Li Hsueh Pao
Chung Yao Tung Pao
Civil Liberties
Clinical and Experimental Hypertension
Clinical and Experimental Obstetrics and Gynecology
Clinical and Experimental Pharmacology and Physiology
Clinical and Investigative Medicine
Clinical Endocrinology
Clinical Genetics
Clinical Immunology and Immunopathology
Clinical Obstetrics and Gynaecology
Clinical Pharmacology and Therapeutics
Clinical Radiology
Clinical Reproduction and Fertility
Clinical Rheumatology
Clinical Science
Clinical Therapeutics
College Student Journal
Commonweal
Communiqu'elles
Community Medicine
Community Outlook
Concordia Journal
Congressional Quarterly Weekly Report
Connecticut Magazine

Connecticut Medicine
Conrad Grebel Review
Consensus
Conservative Digest
Contemporary Crises
Contraception
Contributions to Gynecology and Obstetrics
Cosmopolitan
Crime Control Digest
Criminal Law Monthly
Criminal Law Reporter: Court Decisions and Proceedings
Criminal Law Reporter: Opinions of the United States Supreme Court
Criminal Law Reporter: Supreme Court Proceedings
Criminal Law Review
Critical Social Research
Cross Currents
Curationis
Current Anthropology
Current History
Currents in Theology and Mission
Cytogenetics and Cell Genetics
DAI A: Dissertation Abstracts International: A. Humanities and Social Sciences
DAI B: Dissertation Abstracts International: B. Sciences and Engineering
Demography
Department of State Bulletin
Design News
Detroit College of Law Review
Deutsche Zeitschrift fuer Verdauungs-und Stoffwechselkrankheiten
Diabete et Metabolisme
Diagnostic Immunology
Dialogue
Discover
Draper Fund Report
Drug and Therapeutics Bulletin
Drug Intelligence and Clinical Pharmacy
DTW: Deutsche Tieraerztliche Wochenschrift
Duke Law Journal
East African Medical Journal
East West Journal
Ebony
Economic and Political Weekly
Economist
Ecumenist
Education and Treatment of Children
Eighteenth Century Life
Emergency Medicine
Environment
Enzyme
Equine Veterinary Journal
Ethics
Ethics and Medicine
European Journal of Obstetrics, Gynecology and Reproductive Biology
European Juornal of Pediatrics
Evaluation Review
Everywoman

Exceptional Parent
Experientia
Experimental and Clinical Endocrinology
Experimental and Molecular Pathology
Family and Community Health
Family Planning Perspectives
Family Relations
Far Eastern Economic Review
Farmaco
Farmakologiya i Toksikologiya
FDA Consumer
Fel'dsher i Akusherka
Feminist Issues
Feminist Studies
Fertility and Sterility
Florida State University Law Review
Focus
Folia Parasitologica
Food Technology
Forbes
Ford Foundation Report
Forecast for Home Economics
Fortschritte der Medizin
Fortschritte der Neurologie-Psychiatrie
Fortschritte der Ophthalmologie
Fortune
Free Inquiry in Creative Sociology
Frontiers
Fundamental and Applied Toxicology
Fundamentalist Journal
Futures
Futurist
Gastroenterology
Gay Comunity News
Geburtshilfe und Frauenheilkunde
Genetical Research
Genetics
Genetika
Genitourinary Medicine
Geographia Medica
Geographical Magazine
Ginecologia y Obstetricia de Mexico
Ginekologia Polska
Giornale di Clinica Medica
Glamour
Good Housekeeping
Governance
Guardian
Gut
Gynaekologische Rundschau
Gynakologe
Gynecologic and Obstetric Investigation
Gynecologic Oncology
Harefuah
Harpers

Harper's Bazaar
Harvard Law Review
Harvard Women's Law Journal
Hastings Center Report
Hautarzt
Health
Health and Social Work
Health Bulletin
Health Care for Women, International
Health Care Management Review
Health Education
Health Education Quarterly
Health Management Forum
Health Pac Bulletin
Health Values
Healthright
Healthsharing
Heresies
Herizons
Horizons
Hormone Research
Hospital Practice
Hospitals
Houston Journal of International Law
Howard Journal of Criminal Justice
Human Biology
Human Events
Human Genetics
Human Nutrition. Clinical Nutrition
Human Organization
Human Relations
Humanist
Hygie
IARC Scientific Publications
In These Times
Indian Journal of Experimental Biology
Indian Journal of Medical Research
Indian Journal of Pathology and Microbiology
Indian Journal of Pediatrics
Indian Journal of Public Health
Infirmiere Canadienne
Inside
Insight: The Washington Times
Intensive Care Nursing
Intercontinental Press
International Archives of Occupational and Environmental Health
International Family Planning Perspectives
International Journal for Vitamin and Nutrition Research
International Journal of Andrology
International Journal of Applied Philosophy
International Journal of Cancer
International Journal of Cardiology
International Journal of Clinical Pharmacology, Therapy and Toxicology
International Journal of Epidemiology
International Journal of Fertility

International Journal of Gynecological Pathology
International Journal of Gynaecology and Obstetrics
International Journal of Health Services
International Journal of Nursing Studies
International Journal of Psychoanalysis
International Journal of Women's Studies
International Migration Review
International Philosophical Quarterly
International Review of Cytology
International Surgery
International Viewpoint
Internationale Katholische Zeitschrift
International Wildlife
Irish Journal of Medical Science
Isis
Israel Journal of Medical Sciences
Issues in Mental Health Nursing
JAMA: Journal of the American Medical Association
Japanese Journal of Antibiotics
JCU: Journal of Clinical Ultrasound
JEN: Journal of Emergency Nursing
Jet
Jinrui Idengaku Zasshi
JOGN Nursing: Journal of Obstetric, Gynecologic and Neonatal Nursing
John Marshall Law Review
Jordemodern
Josanpu Zasshi
Journal de Chirurgie
Journal de Genetique Humaine
Journal de Gynecologie, Obstetrique et Biologie de la Reproduction
Journal for the Scientific Study of Religion
Journal of Abnormal Psychology
Journal of Adolescence
Journal of Adolescent Health Care
Journal of Advanced Nursing
Journal of Alcohol and Drug Education
Journal of Ambulatory Care Management
Journal of the American Academy of Dermatology
Journal of American College Health
Journal of the American College of Nutrition
Journal of the American Medical Women's Association
Journal of the American Paraplegia Society
Journal of American Studies
Journal of the American Veterinary Medical Association
Journal of Andrology
Journal of Animal Science
Journal of Applied Ecology
Journal of Applied Nutrition
Journal of Applied Philosophy
Journal of Applied Physiology
Journal of Applied Social Psychology
Journal of Applied Sociology
Journal of Asian Studies
Journal of the Association of Persons With Severe Handicaps
Journal of the Association of Physicians of India

Journal of Biomedical Materials Research
Journal of Biosocial Science
Journal of Christian Nursing
Journal of Chronic Diseases
Journal of Clinical Endocrinology and Metabolism
Journal of Clinical Pathology
Journal of Communication
Journal of Community Health
Journal of Comparative Family Studies
Journal of Comparative Psychology
Journal of Computor Assisted Tomography
Journal of Correctional Education
Journal of Counseling and Development
Journal of Counseling Psychology
Journal of Craniofacial Genetics and Developmental Biology
Journal of Criminal Justice
Journal of Cutaneous Pathology
Journal of Dairy Science
Journal of Endocrinology
Journal of Epidemiology and Community Health
Journal of Ethnopharmacology
Journal of Experimental Zoology
Journal of Family History
Journal of Family Law
Journal of Family Practice
Journal of Family Welfare
Journal of the Florida Medical Association
Journal of Geriatric Psychiatry
Journal of Gerontology
Journal of Health and Human Resources Administration
Jounral of Health and Social Behavior
Journal of Health Politics, Policy and Law
Journal of History
Journal of the History of Biology
Journal of Homosexuality
Journal of Hypertension
Journal of Immunology
Journal of Indian Anthropology
Journal of the Indian Medical Association
Journal of Laryngology and Otology
Journal of Lipid Research
Journal of Marriage and the Family
Journal of Mathematical Biology
Journal of the Medical Association of Georgia
Journal of the Medical Association of Thailand
Journal of Medical Ethics
Journal of Medical Genetics
Journal of Medical Philosophy
Journal of Medicinal Chemistry
Journal of the Mississippi State Medical Association
Journal of Neuroscience Nursing
Journal of Nurse-Midwifery
Journal of Nutrition
Journal of Obstetric, Gynecologic and Neonatal Nursing
Journal of Occupational Medicine

Journal of Ophthalmic Nursing and Technology
Journal of Pastoral Counseling
Journal of Pediatric Surgery
Journal of Pediatrics
Journal of Personality and Social Psychology
Journal of Pharmacokinetics and Biopharmaceutics
Journal of Police and Criminal Psychology
Journal of Postgraduate Medicine
Journal of Psychology
Journal of Psychosomatic Research
Journal of Public Health Policy
Journal of Reproduction and Fertility
Journal of Reproductive Immunology
Journal of Reproductive Medicine
Journal of Research in Crime and Delinquency
Journal of Rheumatology
Journal of the Royal College of General Practitioners
Journal of the Royal Society of Health
Journal of the Royal Society of Medicine
Journal of School Health
Journal of Sex and Marital Therapy
Journal of Sex Research
Journal of Social and Economic Studies
Journal of Social Work and Human Sexuality
Journal of Sociological Studies
Journal of the South African Veterinary Association
Journal of Steroid Biochemistry
Journal of Studies on Alcohol
Journal of Surgery and Oncology
Journal of the Tennessee Medical Association
Journal of Theoretical Biology
Journal of the Tongji Medical University
Journal of Toxicological Sciences
Journal of Toxicology and Environmental Health
Journal of Tropical Medicine and Hygiene
Journal of Tropical Pediatrics
Journal of Ultrasound in Medicine
Journal of Urology
Journal of Value Inquiry
Journal of Youth and Adolescence
Journalism History
Journalism Quarterly
JPMA: Journal of the Pakistan Medical Association
Jugoslavenska Ginekologija i Opstetricija
Jugoslavenska Ginekologija i Perinatolgi
Justice System Journal
Juvenile and Family Law Digest
Kango Gijutsu
Kango Tenbo
Katilolehti
Khirurgiia
Laboratory Animal Science
Ladies Home Journal
Lakartidningen
Lancet

Law Enforcement News
Legal Medicine
Life
Lijecnicki Vjesnik
Loyola of Los Angeles International and Comparative Law Journal
Lumen Vitae
Lutheran Forum
Maclean's
Mademoiselle
Marketing
Maternal-Child Nursing Journal
Maturitas
Mazingira
McCalls
MCN: American Journal of Maternal-Child Nursing
Mechanisms of Ageing and Development
Medecine Interne
Medical Biology
Medical Care
Medical Education
Medical Journal of Australia
Medical Oncology and Tumor Pharmacotherapy
Medicina Clinica
Medicine and Law
Medicine, Science and the Law
Medicinski Pregled
Meditsinskaia Radiologiia
Meditsinskaia Sestra
Metabolism
Midwife, Health Visitor and Community Nurse
Midwifery
Minerva Anestesiologica
Minerva Ginecologia
Minerva Medica
Minerva Psichiatrica
Minnesota Medicine
MMWR: Morbidity and Mortality Weekly Report
Mobius
Mobilizer
Monatsschrift fur Kinderheilkunde
Morphologiai es Igazsagugyi Orvosi Szemle
Mount Sinai Journal of Medicine
Ms
Multinational Monitor
Mutation Research
Narcotics Control Digest
Nation
National Catholic Reporter
National Now Times
National Review
National Women's Studies Association Perspectives
Nature
Nederlands Tijdschrift voor Geneeskunde
Neonatal Network
Neuroradiology

Neuroscience and Behavioral Physiology
New Age
New Directions for Women
New England Journal of Medicine
New Era Nursing Image International
New Jersey Medicine
New Jersey Nurse
New Republic
New Scientist
New Statesman
New York Times Magazine
New Zealand Medical Journal
New Zealand Nursing Journal
Newsweek
Nicaraguan Perspectives
Nippon Gan Chiryo Gakkai Shi
Nippon Hinyokika Gakkai Zasshi
Nippon Juigaku Zasshi
Nippon Sanka Fujinka Gakkai Zasshi
Nordisk Medicin
Northern Illinois University Law Review
Northwest Passage
Nurse Practitioner
Nurses Drug Alert
Nursing
Nursing Clinics of North America
Nursing Journal of India
Nursing Life
Nursing Management
Nursing Mirror
Nursing Mirror and Midwive's Journal
Nursing Outlook
Nursing Papers
Nursing Research
Nursing Times
Obstetrical and Gynecological Survey
Obstetrics and Gynecology
Oceans
Off Our Backs
Offentliche Gesundheitswesen
Oklahoma Observer
Oncology Nursing Forum
Onderstepoort Journal of Veterinary Research
Ontogenez
Open Road
Oral Surgery, Oral Medicine, Oral Pathology
Orvosi Hetilap
Out
Pacific Law Journal
Papua New Guinea Medical Journal
Paraplegia
Parents
Pathologe
Pediatric Annals
Pediatric Nursing

Pediatrics
Peptides
Perkins Journal
Pharmacotherapy
Pharmazie
Pharos
Phi Delta Kappa Fastbacks
Philosophical Quarterly
Philosophical Studies
Philosophy Today
Physiology and Behavior
Pielegniarka i Polozna
Planta Medica
Policy Review
Policy Studies Journal
Political Studies
Population
Population and Development Review
Population and Environment
Population and Environment: Behavioral and Social Issues
Population Bulletin
Population Reports
Population Research and Policy Review
Population Studies
Populi
Postgraduate Medical Journal
Postgraduate Medicine
Poultry Science
Practitioner
Prenatal Diagnosis
Present Tense
Presse Medicale
Prevention
Primary Care
Problemy Endokrinologii i Gormonoterapii
Proceedings of the National Academy of Sciences USA
Progress in Clinical and Biological Research
Progressive
Prostaglandins
Protect Yourself
Psychiatrie, Neurologie und Medizinische Psychologie, Beihefte
Psychiatry Research
Psychoanalytic Review
Psychological Bulletin
Psychological Reports
Psychology of Women Quarterly
Psychophysiology
Psychosomatics
Psychotherapie, Psychosomatik, Medizinische Psychologie
Public Citizen
Public Health
Public Health Reports
Public Health Reviews
Public Opinion
Public Opinion Quarterly

Quarterly Journal of Social Affairs
Quarterly Medical Review
Quarterly Review
Queen's Law Review
Radical America
Radiology
Readers Digest
Recent Progress in Hormone Research
Recent Results in Cancer Research
Recenti Progressi in Medicina
Reconciliation International
Reconciliation Quarterly
Redbook
Religious Studies
Research in Nursing and Health
Research in Veterinary Science
Resources for Feminist Research
Review of African Political Economy
Review of Public Data Use
Review of Religious Research
Reviews of Infectious Diseases
Revista Chilena de Obstetricia y Ginecologia
Revista de Enfermagen
Revista de la Facultad de Ciencias Medicas/Universidad Nacional de Cordoba
Revista Medica de Chile
Revista Paulista de Enfermagem
Revista Paulista de Medicina
Revue d'Elevage et de Medecine Veterinaire des Pays Tropicaux
Revue Francaise de Gynecologie et d'Obstetrique
Revue Neurologique
Rivista di Patologia Nervosa e Mentale
RN
RNAO News
Saint Louis
Saint Luke Journal
Salud Mental
Salud Publica de Mexico
Sangre
Scandinavian Journal of Psychology
Scandinavian Journal of Social Medicine
Schweizer Archiv fur Neurologie, Neurochirurgie und Psychiatrie
Schweizerische Medizinische Wochenschrift
Schweizerische Rundschau fur Medizin Praxis
Science
Science Digest
Science News
Science of the Total Environment
Scientific American
Scottish Journal of Theology
Scottish Medical Journal
Security Systems Digest
Seminars in Oncology Nursing
Seventeen
Sex Roles
Sexuality and Disability

Shih Yen Sheng Wu Hsueh Pao
Signs
Simply Living
Singapore Medical Journal
Social Affairs
Social Alternatives
Social Biology
Social Problems
Social Science and Medicine
Social Science Quarterly
Social Science Research
Social Theory and Practice
Social Work in Health Care
Socialist Review
Society
Sociological Focus
Sociological Perspectives
Sociology and Social Research
Sociology of Health and Illness
Soins. Gynecologie, Obstetrique, Puericulture, Pediatrie
Sojourners
Soundings
South African Medical Journal
Southern California Law Review
Southern Medical Journal
Southern University Law Review
Sovetskoe Zdravookhronenie
Soviet Medicine
Spare Rib
Srpski Arhiv za Celokupno Lekarstvo
SSU-Chuan i Hsueh Yuan Hsueh Pao
Statistics Bulletin of the Metropolitan Life Insurance Company
Statistics in Medicine
Steroids
Studies in Family Planning
Sunday Times
Surgery, Gynecology and Obstetrics
Taiwan I Hsueh Hui Tsa Chih
Technology Review
Teratology
Texas Medicine
Theological Studies
Theologische Quartalschrift
Therapeutische Umschau
Therapia Hungarica
Thrombosis and Haemostasis
Thrombosis Research
Tidsskrift for den Norske Laegeforening
Tierarztliche Praxis
Time
Times (London)
Times Higher Education Supplement
Tissue Antigens
Today's OR Nurse
Topics in Clinical Nursing

Toxicologic Pathology
Tradition
Transformation
Travel Holiday
Trial
Tropical Animal Health and Production
Tropical Doctor
TSF Bulletin
Tumori
Turkish Journal of Pediatrics
TV Guide
Ugeskrift for Laeger
Ulster Medical Journal
Ultrasound in Medicine and Biology
UN Chronicle
UN Fund for Population Activities Report
Union Medicale du Canada
University of Chicago Law Review
University of Dayton Law Review
University of Miami Law Review
University of Toronto Faculty of Law Review
Urologia Internationalis
Urologiia i Nefrologiia
Urology
US Agency for International Development Report
US News and World Report
USA Today
Utah Law Review
Vanderbilt Law Review
Venture
Vestnik Akademii Meditsinskikh Nauk SSSR
Veterinarno-Meditsinski Nauki
Veterinary Clinics of North America
Veterinary Microbiology
Veterinary Record
Virchows Archiv. Cell Pathology
Virginia Nurse
Vital Health Statistics
Vogue
Voprosy Meditsinskai Khimii
Voprosy Onkologii
Vutreshni Bolesti
Washington Law Review
Washington Monthly
Weekly Compilation of Presidential Documents
West European Politics
West Indian Medical Journal
Western Political Quarterly
WHO Bulletin
WHO Chronicle
Whole Earth Review
Wiadomosci Lekarskie
Wiener Klinische Wochenschrift
Wiener Medizinische Wochenschrift
Willamette Law Review

Wisconsin Medical Journal
Womanews
Women and Health
Women and Politics
Women and Therapy
Women's Review of Books
Women's Rights Law Reporter
Women's Studies Quarterly
Word and World
World Bank World Development Report
World Health
Worldwatch Paper
Yao Hsueh Hsueh Pao
Zahnaerztliche Munden und Kieferheilkunde mit Zentralblatt
Zeitschrift fur Aerztliche Fortbildung
Zeitschrift fur die Gesamte Strafrechtswissenschaft
Zeitschrift fur Gastroenterologie
Zeitschrift fur Geburtschilfe und Perinatologie
Zeitschrift fur Morphologie und Anthropologie
Zentralblatt fur Gynaekologie
Zhurnal Nevropatologii i Psikhiatrii

SUBJECT HEAD INDEX

Abortifacient Agents 7
Abortion—General 8
  Australia 12
  Bangladesh 12
  Canada 12
  England 13
  France 14
  Germany 14
  Great Britain 14
  Hungary 14
  India 14
  Ireland 15
  Italy 15
  Jordan 15
  Korea 15
  Netherlands 15
  Nicaragua 15
  Nigeria 16
  Norway 16
  Scotland 16
  Soviet Union 16
  Spain 16
  Sweden 16
  Taiwan 16
  Thailand 16
  United States 16
  Yucatan 19
Abortion—Advertising 19
Abortion—Attitudes 19
Abortion—Chemically Induced 22
Abortion—Complications 23
Abortion—Criminal 23
Abortion—Diagnosis 24
Abortion—Ethics
  See: Abortion—Attitudes
Abortion—Etiology 24
Abortion—Failed 27
Abortion—Habitual 27
Abortion—Habitual—Complications 30
Abortion—Habitual—Prevention and
  Control 30
Abortion—Habitual—Treatment 30

Abortion—History 31
Abortion—Incomplete 31
Abortion—Incomplete—
  Complications 32
Abortion—Incomplete—Diagnosis 32
Abortion—Induced 32
  See also: Abortion—Chemically
    Induced
Abortion—Induced—Complications 39
Abortion—Induced—Failed 40
Abortion—Laws and Legislation 40
Abortion—Legal 45
Abortion—Legal—Complications 47
Abortion—Literature 47
Abortion—Methods 47
Abortion—Missed 49
Abortion—Missed—Diagnosis 49
Abortion—Missed—Treatment 49
Abortion—Mortality and Mortality
  Statistics 49
Abortion—Nurses and Nursing 50
Abortion—Psychology and
  Psychiatry 50
Abortion—Research 52
Abortion—Septic 55
Abortion—Septic—Complications 56
Abortion—Sociology 56
Abortion—Spontaneous 56
  See also: Abruptio Placentae
Abortion—Spontaneous—Prevention
  and Control 59
Abortion—Statistics 59
Abortion—Therapeutic 60
Abortion—Therapeutic—
  Complications 61
Abortion—Threatened 61
Abortion—Threatened—
  Complications 62
Abortion—Threatened—Diagnosis 62
Abortion—Threatened—Prevention
  and Control 62
Abortion—Threatened—Treatment 62

Abortion—Veterinary 62
Abortion—Voluntary 66
Abortion and Civil Rights 67
Abortion and College Students 67
Abortion and Economics 67
Abortion and the ERA 67
Abortion and Feminism 67
Abortion and Hospitals 68
Abortion and Journalism 68
Abortion and Males 68
Abortion and Marriage 69
Abortion and NOW 69
Abortion and Parental Consent 69
Abortion and the Performing Arts 69
Abortion and Physicians 70
Abortion and Politics 70
Abortion and Religion 71
Abortion and Teens 74
Abortion and Women 75
Abortion Clinics 75
Abortion Counseling 77
Abortion Funding 77
Abortion Rights Groups 77
    See also: Pro-Choice Movement
Abruptio Placentae 79
Abruptio Placentae—Diagnosis 79
Abruptio Placentae—Etiology 80
Birth Control—General 80
    See also: Contraception
               Contraceptives
               Family Planning
  Africa 82
  Algeria 82
  Argentina 82
  Asia 82
  Australia 82
  Bangladesh 82
  Brazil 82
  China 83
  Developing Countries 83
  Egypt 84
  England 84
  Gambia 84
  Ghana 84
  Great Britain 84
  Guatemala 84
  Honduras 84
  Hungary 84
  India 85
  Ireland 85
  Israel 85
  Italy 85
  Ivory Coast 85
  Kenya 85
  Korea 85
  Namibia 85
  Nicaragua 85
  Nigeria 85
  Philippines 86
  Rwana 86
  Scotland 86
  Senegal 86
  South Africa 86
  Soviet Union 86
  Sri Lanka 86
  Swaziland 86
  Thailand 86
  Togo 86
  Tunisia 86
  Turkey 86
  Uganda 87
  United States 87
  Wales 88
  Western Samoa 88
  Yemen Arab Republic 88
Birth Control—Advertising 88
Birth Control—Attitudes 88
Birth Control—History 88
Birth Control—Laws and Legislation 88
Birth Control—Male 88
Birth Control—Methods 89
Birth Control—Psychology and
    Psychiatry 90
Birth Control—Research 90
Birth Control—Sociology 90
Birth Control—Statistics 90
Birth Control and Aging 90
Birth Control and Economics 90
Birth Control and Education 90
Birth Control and Feminism 91
Birth Control and Physicians 91
Birth Control and Politics 91
Birth Control and Religion 91
Birth Control and Teens 92
Birth Control and Women 93
Birth Control Clinics 94
  United States 94
Birth Control Failure 94
Birth Control Funding 95
Birth Control Programs 95
Conception—General 95
Conception—Laws and Legislation 95
Conception—Research 95
Contraception—General 95
    See also: Birth Control
               Contraceptives
               Family Planning
  Australia 98
  China 98
  Ghana 98
  Great Britain 98
  New Zealand 98
  Nigeria 98
  United States 98
Contraception—Complications 99
Contraception—Economics 99

Contraception—Education 99
Contraception—Female—Oral 99
Contraception—Male 99
Contraception—Methods 99
Contraception—Psychology and
    Psychiatry 100
Contraception—Research 101
Contraception—Veterinary 101
Contraception and College
    Students 101
Contraception and Physicians 101
Contraception and Religion 101
Contraception and Teens 102
Contraception and Women 103
Contraceptive Agents 103
    See also: Contraceptives
Contraceptive Agents—Female 104
    See also: Contraceptives—
        Female
Contraceptive Agents—Female—
    Complications 106
Contraceptive Agents—Female—
    Oral—Complications 107
Contraceptive Agents—Female—
    Research 107
Contraceptive Agents—Male 107
    See also: Contraceptives—Male
Contraceptive Agents—Male—
    Complications 108
Contraceptive Agents—Male—
    Research 108
Contraceptive Agents—Research 108
Contraceptives—General 108
    See also: Birth Control
        Contraception
        Contraceptive Agents
        Family Planning
Bangladesh 110
Brazil 110
Canada 110
China 111
Colombia 111
Costa Rica 111
Developing Countries 111
Egypt 111
Ghana 111
Great Britain 111
Hungary 112
India 112
Indonesia 112
Italy 112
Japan 112
Jordan 112
Korea 112
Kuwait 112
Mexico 113
Nigeria 113
Pakistan 113

Peru 113
Philippines 113
Puerto Rico 113
South Africa 113
Sudan 113
Thailand 113
United States 114
Zaire 114
Contraceptives—Advertising 114
Contraceptives—Attitudes 114
Contraceptives—Complications 115
Contraceptives—Counseling 115
Contraceptives—Education 115
Contraceptives—Female 116
    See also: Contraception—
        Female
Contraceptives—Female—
    Complications 116
Contraceptives—Female—Barrier 116
Contraceptives—Female—Barrier—
    Complications 117
Contraceptives—Female—
    Injected 117
Contraceptives—Female—IUD 117
Contraceptives—Female—IUD—
    Complications 118
Contraceptives—Female—Oral 119
Contraceptives—Female—Oral—
    Complications 126
Contraceptives—Female—Oral—
    Therapeutic Use 134
Contraceptives—Female—
    Postcoital 134
Contraceptives—Female—
    Postcoital—Complications 135
Contraceptives—Funding 135
Contraceptives—History 135
Contraceptives—Implanted 135
Contraceptives—Injected 135
Contraceptives—Injected—
    Complications 136
Contraceptives—Insurance 136
Contraceptives—Knowledge 136
Contraceptives—Laws and
    Legislation 136
Contraceptives—Male 136
    See also: Contraception—Male
Contraceptives—Male—Barrier 137
Contraceptives—Methods 137
Contraceptives—Oral 138
Contraceptives—Oral—
    Complications 140
Contraceptives—Oral—Therapeutic
    Use 141
Contraceptives—Postcoital—
    Complications 141
Contraceptives—Psychology and
    Psychiatry 141

Contraceptives—Research 142
Contraceptives—Sociology 144
Contraceptives—Statistics 144
Contraceptives and Aging 144
Contraceptives and Breastfeeding 144
Contraceptives and College
    Students 145
Contraceptives and Economics 145
Contraceptives and the Mentally
    Retarded 146
Contraceptives and Parental
    Consent 146
Contraceptives and Physicians 146
Contraceptives and Religion 146
Contraceptives and Teens 146
Contraceptives and Vitamins 148
Contraceptives and Women 148
Family Planning—General 149
    See also: Birth Control
               Contraception
               Contraceptives
    Africa 153
    Asia 153
    Australia 153
    Bangladesh 153
    Canada 153
    China 153
    Czechoslovakia 154
    Developing Countries 154
    Egypt 154
    England 154
    France 154
    Ghana 154
    Honduras 155
    India 155
    Indonesia 155
    Israel 155
    Jamaica 155
    Jordan 155
    Mexico 155
    Nepal 155
    New Guinea 156
    Nicaragua 156
    Nigeria 156
    Philippines 156
    Puerto Rico 156
    Senegal 157
    Singapore 157
    South Africa 157
    Taiwan 157
    Thailand 157
    Third World Countries 157
    United States 157
    Zaire 157
    Zimbabwe 158
Family Planning—Attitudes 158
Family Planning—Economics 158
Family Planning—Education 158

Family Planning—History 158
Family Planning—Laws and
    Legislation 158
Family Planning—Literature 159
Family Planning—Mortality and
    Mortality Statistics 159
Family Planning—Natural 159
Family Planning—Nurses and
    Nursing 159
Family Planning—Psychology and
    Psychiatry 159
Family Planning—Research 160
Family Planning—Sociology 160
Family Planning—Statistics 160
Family Planning and College
    Students 161
Family Planning and Feminism 161
Family Planning and Males 161
Family Planning and Physicians 161
Family Planning and Politics 161
Family Planning and Religion 161
Family Planning and Teens 161
Family Planning and Women 163
Family Planning Clinics 163
Family Planning Counseling 164
Family Planning Programs 164
    United States 166
Fertility—General 166
    Australia 170
    Bangladesh 170
    Bolivia 170
    Canada 171
    China 171
    Colombia 171
    Costa Rica 171
    Egypt 171
    Ghana 171
    India 171
    Ireland 171
    Israel 171
    Korea 171
    Kuwait 172
    Malaysia 172
    Mexico 172
    Nepal 172
    Nigeria 172
    Pakistan 172
    Philippines 172
    Poland 172
    Scotland 172
    Singapore 172
    Sri Lanka 173
    Sudan 173
    Surinam 173
    United States 173
Fertility—Female 173
Fertility—Male 174
Fertility—Research 175

Fertility—Statistics 181
Fertility Agents 181
Fertility Agents—Female 182
Fertility and Aging 182
Fertility and Teens 182
Hysterectomy—General 182
Hysterectomy—Complications 187
Hysterectomy—Economics 189
Hysterectomy—Methods 189
Hysterectomy—Nurses and
  Nursing 190
Hysterectomy—Psychology and
  Psychiatry 190
Hysterectomy—Sociology 191
Hysterectomy and Physicians 191
Planned Parenthood Federation
  of America 191
Population Control 191
Pro-Choice Movement 192
  See also: Abortion Rights Groups
Pro-Life Movement 192
Right to Life Movement
  See: Pro-Life Movement
Sex and Sexuality—General 193
Sex and Sexuality—College
  Students 195
Sex and Sexuality—Sociology 195
Sex and Sexuality—Teens 195
Sex Education 197
Sex Education and Children 198
Sex Education and College
  Students 198
Sex Education and the Handi-
  capped 198
Sex Education and the Teens 199
Sexually Transmitted Diseases 200
Sexually Transmitted Diseases—
  Prevention 200
Sterilization—General 200
  Australia 201
  Bangladesh 201
  British Columbia 201
  Canada 201
  Germany 201
  Mexico 201
  Nepal 202
  Puerto Rico 202
  Thailand 202
  United States 202
Sterilization—Attitudes 202
Sterilization—Complications 202
Sterilization—Counseling 202
Sterilization—Economics 203
Sterilization—Failure 203
Sterilization—Female 203
  See also: Sterilization—Tubal
Sterilization—Female—
  Complications 204

Sterilization—Induced 204
Sterilization—Laws and Legislation 204
Sterilization—Male 204
Sterilization—Methods 205
Sterilization—Nurses and Nursing 206
Sterilization—Psychology and
  Psychiatry 206
Sterilization—Research 207
Sterilization—Sociology 207
Sterilization—Statistics 208
Sterilization—Tubal 208
Sterilization—Tubal—
  Complications 211
Sterilization—Voluntary 212
Sterilization and Criminals 212
Sterilization and Hospitals 213
Sterilization and the Mentally
  Retarded 213
Sterilization and Parental Consent 213
Sterilization and Physicians 214
Sterilization and Teens 214
Sterilization and Women 214
Sterilization Failures 214
Sterilization Reversal 214
Vasectomy—General 216
Vasectomy—Complications 218
Vasectomy—Methods 218
Vasectomy—Psychology and
  Psychiatry 218
Vasectomy—Research 219
Vasectomy and Physicians 219

BOOKS AND MONOGRAPHS

ABORTION: JUDICIAL AND LEGISLATIVE CONTROL, UNITED STATES LIBRARY OF CONGRESS CONGRESSIONAL RESEARCH SERVICE REPORT IB74019, FEBRUARY 14, 1986. Washington: GPO, 1986.

ADOLESCENT REPRODUCTIVE HEALTH. New York: Gardner Press, 1985.

Ainsworth, M. FAMILY PLANNING PROGRAMS. Washington: The World Bank, 1985.

ARRESTING ABORTION. Westchester, IL: Crossway Books, 1985. Paper. $5.95.

Baker, D. BEYOND CHOICE. Portland, OR: Multnomah Press, 1985. $7.95.

Banerjee, K. STERILIZATION SYSTEMS. Westport, CT: Technomic, 1985.

Belcastro, P. A. THE BIRTH-CONTROL BOOK. Boston: Jones & Bartlett, 1986. Paper. $8.75.

Binns, Derrick St. Clair. A MULTIPLE REGRESSION ANALYSIS OF VARIABLES ASSOCIATED WITH THE USE OR NON-USE OF CONTRACEPTIVES BY TEENAGED BERMUDIAN HIGH SCHOOL STUDENTS. Ph.D. dissertation. Adelphi University, 1985. 126 pp.

Birdsall, N., editor. THE EFFECTS OF FAMILY PLANNING PROGRAMS ON FERTILITY IN THE DEVELOPING WORLD. World Bank Staff Working Papers, No. 667. Population and Development Series, No. 2. Washington, DC: The World Bank, 1985. 206 pp.

Bizem, Hinda-Rose. CHROMIUM STATUS: EFFECTS OF DEMOGRAPHIC CHARACTERISTICS, ORAL CONTRACEPTIVE AGENTS AND CHROMIUM SUPPLEMENTATION. Ph.D. dissertation. The University of Nebraska - Lincoln, 1985. 137 pp.

Cain, M. WOMEN'S STATUS AND FERTILITY IN DEVELOPING COUNTRIES: ON PREFERENCE AND ECONOMIC SECURITY. World Bank Staff Working Papers, No. 682. Population and Development Series, No. 7. Washington, DC: The World Bank, 1984. 68 pp.

Canada. Statistics Canada. Health Division. THERAPEUTIC ABORTIONS, 1985. Ottawa: The Division, 1986. Paper. 60 pp. Canada—$20.00; elsewhere—$21.50. ISSN 0700-138X.

Carrick, P. MEDICAL ETHICS IN ANTIQUITY. Reidel, 1985. $37.95; paper $15.95.

1

CHINA'S ONE-CHILD FAMILY POLICY. London: Macmillan Educ., 1985.

Christian, S. R. THE WOODLAND HILLS TRAGEDY. Westchester, IL: Crossway Books, 1985. Paper. $6.95.

Danda, A. K. FAMILY PLANNING. Delhi: Inter-India Publications., 1984. $25.00

Darabi, Katherine P., compiler. CHILDBEARING AMONG HISPANICS IN THE UNITED STATES: AN ANNOTATED BIBLIOGRAPHY. Westport, CT: Greenwood Press, 1987. xii+167 pp. $35.00. ISBN 0-313-25617-9.

Davis, Nanette J. FROM CRIME TO CHOICE: THE TRANSFORMATION OF ABOR-TION IN AMERICA. Westport, CT: Greenwood Press, 1985.

de Barella, Adriana. BIBLIOGRAFIA ANOTADA SOBRE POBLACION/PLANIFICA-CION FAMILIAR, COLOMBIA; COORDINACION Y EDICION. Colombia: Corpora-ción Centro Regional de Población, 1984. 284 pp.

De Blasi, Pasquale, Jr. MALE TEENAGERS AND CONTRACEPTIVE USE. Dr.S.W. dissertation. Columbia University, 1985.

Demeny, Paul. THE ECONOMIC RATIONALE OF FAMILY PLANNING PROGRAMS. New York: Population Council, 1987. 34 pp.

Derrick, C. TOO MANY PEOPLE. Ignatius Press, 1985. Paper.

Ervin, P. WOMEN EXPLOITED. Huntington, IN: Our Sunday Visitor, 1985. Paper. $6.95.

FAMILY PLANNING AS A SERVICE, WORLD BANK WORLD DEVELOPMENT RE-PORT 1984. Washington, DC: The World Bank, 1984. 127 pp.

Francome, Colin. ABORTION PRACTICE IN BRITAIN AND THE UNITED STATES. Winchester, MA: Allen & Unwin, 1986. 206 pp. $22.95; paper $11.95. ISBN 0-04-179004-9.

Goode, Polly T., compiler. ABORTION BIBLIOGRAPHY FOR 1981. Troy, NY: Whitston, 1983. 405 pp. $38.50.

—. ABORTION BIBLIOGRAPHY FOR 1982. Troy, NY: Whitston, 1984. 323 pp. $38.50.

—. ABORTION BIBLIOGRAPHY FOR 1983. Troy, NY: Whitston, 1985. 360 pp. $40.00.

—. ABORTION BIBLIOGRAPHY FOR 1984. Troy, NY: Whitston, 1986. 414 pp. $40.00.

—. ABORTION BIBLIOGRAPHY FOR 1985. Troy, NY: Whitston, 1987. 297 pp. $30.00.

Graber, Cynthia Volinsky. CONTRACEPTIVE USE IN ADOLESCENT FEMALES AND THE RELATION TO COGNITIVE DEVELOPMENTAL STATUS AND IDENTI-TY FORMATION. Ph.D. dissertation. Syracuse University, 1985.

Greenhalgh, Susan and John Bongaarts. FERTILITY POLICY IN CHINA: FUTURE OPTIONS. New York: Population Council, 1986. 31 pp.

Guttmacher, A. F. PREGNANCY, BIRTH AND FAMILY PLANNING. Revised edition. New York: Dutton, 1986. $18.95; paper $9.95.

2

HANDBOOK OF FAMILY PLANNING. New York: Churchill Livingstone, 1985. Paper.

Hermansen, J. KAREN'S CHOICE. Wheaton, IL: Tyndale House, 1985. Paper. $2.95.

Hoffacker, Paul, et al, editors. AUF LEBEN UND TOD: ABTREIBUNG IN DER DIS-KUSSION. 2d revised edition. Bastei-Lübbe, 1985. 250 pp. ISBN 3-404-60133-5.

Homans, Hilary, editor. THE SEXUAL POLITICS OF REPRODUCTION. Brookfield, VT: Gower, 1985.

Howe, L. K. MOMENTS ON MAPLE AVENUE. New York: Warner Books, 1986. Paper. $3.95.

Imber, J. B. ABORTION AND THE PRIVATE PRACTICE OF MEDICINE. New Haven: Yale University Press, 1986. $15.95.

THE INDONESIA CONTRACEPTIVE PREVALENCE SURVEY REPORT 1983: THE RESULTS OF SURVEYS IN FIVE CITIES, UNIVERSITY OF INDONESIA. United States Agency for International Development Report. Washington: GPO, 1984.

Jack, Mary Sue. THE RELATIONSHIP BETWEEN EGOCENTRISM AND CONTRA-CEPTIVE BEHAVIOR FOR ADOLESCENTS. Ph.D. dissertation. The University of Rochester, 1985. 163 pp.

John, Helen J. "Reflections on Autonomy and Abortion" in RESPECT AND CARE IN MEDICAL ETHICS, ed. by David H. Smith. Lanham, MD: University Press of America, 1984. pp. 277-300.

Jones, Elise F., et al. TEENAGE PREGNANCY IN INDUSTRIALIZED COUNTRIES: A STUDY. New Haven: Yale University Press, 1986. xiv+310 pp. $30.00. ISBN 0-300-03705-8.

Kaker, D. N. WOMEN AND FAMILY PLANNING. New York: Sterling Publishing, 1984.

Kangas, G. L. POPULATION DILEMMA. Baltimore: Arnold-Heinemann, 1985.

Kenny, Mary. ABORTION: THE WHOLE STORY. Quartet Books, 1986. 315 pp. ISBN 0-7043-2576-4.

Kenyon, Edwin. THE DILEMMA OF ABORTION. Winchester, MA: Faber & Faber, 1986. Paper. 283 pp. $14.95. ISBN 0-571-13935-3.

Kim, In-Chull. STUDIES ON THE SITE AND MECHANISM OF ANTIFERTILITY AC-TION OF GOSSYPOL. Ph.D. dissertation. University of Illinois at Chicago, Health Sciences Center, 1985. 148 pp.

La Joie, Karen Smith. ACCEPTANCE OF SEXUALITY AS A FACTOR IN OLDER ADOLESCENT FEMALES' KNOWLDGE OF REPRODUCTION AND USE OF CONTRACEPTION. Ph.D. dissertation. California School of Professional Psychology, Los Angeles, 1985. 118 pp.

Lawther, G. FAMILY PLANNING. Burbank, CA: Triangle Publishers, 1985.

Leslie, Norma June Streight. PREGNANCY AND DIVORCED SINGLE WOMEN: A STUDY OF THE VARIABLES WHICH AFFECT CONTRACEPTIVE USE AND

PREGNANCY OCCURRENCE IN DIVORCED WOMEN. Ph.D. dissertation. The University of Oklahoma Health Sciences Center, 1985. 236 pp.

Lewis, M. A. PRICING AND COST RECOVERY EXPERIENCE IN FAMILY PLANNING PROGRAMS. World Bank Staff Working Papers, No. 684. Population and Development Series, No. 9. Washington, DC: The World Bank, 1985. 75 pp.

LIFE, A GIFT OF GOD. St. Paul Eds., 1985.

Lotstra, H. ABORTION: THE CATHOLIC DEBATE IN AMERICA. New York: Irvington Publishers, 1985. $19.95.

Luker, K. ABORTION AND THE POLITICS OF MOTHERHOOD. Berkeley: University of California Press, 1985. Paper. $7.95.

McCormack, E. CUOMO VS. O'CONNOR. Commack, NY: Dolores Press, 1985. Paper. $8.95.

McDonnell, K. NOT AN EASY CHOICE. Toronto: Women's Press, 1984.

MALE FERTILITY AND ITS REGULATION. MTP Press, 1985.

Marshner, C. "Abortion: Once conceived, a Child Has the Right to be Born" in CURRENT CONTROVERSIES IN MARRIAGE AND FAMILY, ed. by H. Feldman and M. Feldman. Beverly Hills, CA: Sage Publications, 1985. pp. 203-211. $25.00/ $12.50.

Melton, Gary B., editor. ADOLESCENT ABORTION: PSYCHOLOGICAL AND LEGAL ISSUES. Report of the Interdivisional Committee on Adolescent Abortion, American Psychological Association. Lincoln: University of Nebraska Press, 1986. 152 pp. $17.50. ISBN 0-8032-3094-X.

Neaman, Lucile F., editor. WOMEN'S MEDICINE; A CROSS-CULTURAL STUDY OF INDIGENOUS FERTILITY REGULATION. New Brunswick, NJ: Rutgers University Press, 1985.

Neustatter, Angela, et al. MIXED FEELINGS: THE EXPERIENCE OF ABORTION. London: Pluto Press Ltg., 1986. 147 pp. ISBN 0-7453-0027-8.

New Jersey. General Assembly. Education Commission. PUBLIC HEARINGS: ASSEMBLY BILL 3345 (PROHIBITION OF CERTAIN SERVICES IN SCHOOL-BASED HEALTH FACILITIES): CAMDEN, NEW JERSEY, MAY 7, 1987. Trenton: The Commission, 1987. 188 pp.

New York State. Department of Health. INDUCED ABORTIONS RECORDED IN NEW YORK STATE, 1984; WITH FIVE YEAR SUMMARY, 1980-1984. Albany: The Department, n.d. Paper. 83 pp.

Ngin, Chor-Swang. REPRODUCTIVE DECISIONS AND CONTRACEPTIVE USE IN A CHINESE NEW VILLAGE IN MALAYSIA. Ph.D. dissertation. University of California, Davis, 1985. 169 pp.

Noonan, J. T., Jr. CONTRACEPTION. Enlarged Edition. Belknap Press, 1986.

THE POLICY AGENDA. World Bank World Development Report 1984. Washington, DC: The World Bank, 1984. 155 pp.

Popenoe, P. B. THE CONSERVATION OF THE FAMILY. New York: Garland, 1984. $32.00.

Riddle, R. Elizabeth Wassenberg. THE EFFECTS OF CONTRACEPTIVE INTENT, SOCIAL SUPPORT, CONJUGAL COMMUNICATION AND POWER, AND DE-SIRE FOR MORE CHILDREN ON CONTRACEPTIVE BEHAVIOR IN THE PHILIP-PINES. Dr.P.H. dissertation. University of California, Los Angeles, 1985. 178 pp.

Roe, Kathleen Marie. ABORTION WORK: A STUDY OF THE RELATIONSHIP BE-TWEEN PRIVATE TROUBLES AND PUBLIC ISSUES. Ph.D. dissertation. University of California, Berkeley, 1985. 494 pp.

Rubin, Eva R. ABORTION, POLITICS, AND THE COURTS: ROE V. WADE AND ITS AFTERMATH. Revised Edition. Westport, CT: Greenwood Press, 1987. x-254 pp. $35.00. ISBN 0-313-25614-4.

Schaeffer, F. A MODEST PROPOSAL FOR PEACE, PROSPERITY, AND HAPPI-NESS. Nashville: Thomas Nelson, 1984. Paper. $7.95.

Schmidt, Frederick Hugh. PRECLINICAL EVALUATION OF A LHRH ANTAGONIST, A POTENTIAL MALE CONTRACEPTIVE. Ph.D. dissertation. Rutgers University, The State University of New Jersey (Newark), 1986. 94 pp.

THE SEXUAL POLITICS OF REPRODUCTION. Brookfield, VT: Gower, 1985. $37.95.

Shapiro, T. M. POPULATION CONTROL POLITICS. Philadelphia: Temple University Press, 1985. $27.95.

SLOWING POPULATION GROWTH. World Bank World Development Report 1984. Washington, DC: The World Bank, 1984. 106 pp.

Snyder, Robin V. THE TWO WORLDS OF PUBLIC OPINION: MEDIA OPINION AND POLLED OPINION ON THE ABORTION ISSUE. Ph.D. dissertation. Rutgers University, The State University of New Jersey (New Brunswick), 1985. 228 pp.

Speckhard, Anne Catherine. THE PSYCHO-SOCIAL ASPECTS OF STRESS FOL-LOWING ABORTION. Ph.D. dissertation. University of Minnesota, 1985. 217 pp.

Spezialetti, Rosanne. BOVINE FETAL IMMUNOLOGY: A STUDY ON CONGENITAL SPIROCHETOSIS AND EPIZOOTIC BOVINE ABORTION. Ph.D. dissertation. University of California, Davis, 1985. 189 pp.

Spitzer, Robert J. THE RIGHT TO LIFE MOVEMENT AND THIRD PARTY POLITICS. Westport, CT: Greenwood Press, 1987. xii+154 pp. $29.95. ISBN 0-313-25390-0.

Staggenborg, Suzanne. PATTERNS OF COLLECTIVE ACTION IN THE ABORTION CONFLICT: AN ORGANIZATIONAL ANALYSIS OF THE PRO-CHOICE MOVE-MENT. Ph.D. dissertation. Northwestern University, 1985. 468 pp.

United Nations. Department of International Economic and Social Affairs. RECENT LEVELS AND TRENDS OF CONTRACEPTIVE USE AS ASSESSED IN 1983. New York: United Nations, 1984. 119 pp.

—. Department of International Economic and Social Affairs. REVIEW AND AP-PRAISAL OF THE WORLD POPULATION PLAN OF ACTION. New York: United Nations, 1986. Paper. vi+169 pp. $14.00. ISBN 92-1-151158-5.

United Nations Fund for Population Activities. INVENTORY OF POPULATION PRO-JECTS IN DEVELOPING COUNTRIES AROUND THE WORLD, 1985/86: MULTI-

LATERAL ASSISTANCE, BILATERAL ASSISTANCE, NON-GOVERNMENTAL
ORGANIZATION ASSISTANCE. New York: United Nations, 1987. Paper.
xi+826 pp. $20.00. ISBN 0-89714-050-8.

United States. National Center for Health Statistics. Vital and Health Care Statistics
Program. Division of Vital Statistics. CONTRACEPTIVE USE: UNITED STATES,
1982. Washington: GPO, 1986. Paper. iv+52 pp. United States—$2.75; else-
where—$3.45. ISBN 0-8406-0338-X.

Valliance, Theodore R., editor. VALUES AND ETHICS IN HUMAN DEVELOPMENT
PROFESSIONS. Dubuque Kendall/Hunt, 1984.

Van Dover, Leslie JoanWhite. INFLUENCE OF NURSE-CLIENT CONTRACTING ON
FAMILY PLANNING KNOWLEDGE AND BEHAVIORS IN A UNIVERSITY STU-
DENT POPULATION. Ph.D. dissertation. The University of Michigan, 1985. 148
pp.

Wennberg, R. N. LIFE IN THE BALANCE. Grand Rapids: Eerdmans, 1985. Paper.

Whicker, M. L. SEX ROLE CHANGES. New York: Praeger Publishers, 1986.
$27.95.

Wickwire, Karen S. THE USE OF A BEHAVIORAL INTERVENTION IN THE PRE-
PARATION OF PATIENTS FOR THE SURGICAL PROCEDURE INVOLVED IN
PREGNANCY TERMINATION. Ph.D. dissertation. University of Southern
Mississippi, 1985. 104 pp.

WOMEN'S MEDICINE. New Brunswick: Rutgers University Press, 1985. $28.00.

PERIODICAL LITERATURE

ABORTIFACIENT AGENTS

Absorption and elimination of a prostaglandin F analog, fenprostalene, in lactating dairy cows, by R. V. Tomlinson, et al. JOURNAL OF DAIRY SCIENCE 68(8): 2072-2077, August 1985.

Anti-implantation activity of the fruit of Lagenaria breviflora Robert, by A. A. Elujoba, et al. JOURNAL OF ETHNOPHARMACOLOGY 13(3):281-288, July 1985.

Application of orthogonal function spectrophotometry to the determination of total diterpene orthoesters in yuanhua (Daphne genkwa Sieb. et Zucc.) root injection, by M. Z. Wang, et al. YAO HSUEH HSUEH PAO 21(2):119-123, February 1986.

Breed differences in return to estrus after PGF2 alpha-induced abortions in swine, by D. L. Meeker, et al. JOURNAL OF ANIMAL SCIENCE 61(2):354-357, August 1985.

Cervical dilatation with meteneprost vaginal suppositories in first trimester abortion, by C. Somell, et al. CONTRACEPTION 33(2):189-194, February 1986.

Continuous extraovular prostaglandin F2 alpha instillation for second-trimester pregnancy termination, by J. Atad, et al. ISRAEL JOURNAL OF MEDICAL SCIENCES 21(12):935-939, December 1985.

Controlled release form of 16,16-dimethyl-trans-delta 2-PGE, methyl ester for early abortion, by I. T. Cameron, et al. CONTRACEPTION 33(2):121-125, February 1986.

Ectopic pregnancy among early abortion patients: does prostaglandin reduce the incidence?, by M. Borten, et al. PROSTAGLANDINS 30(6):891-905, December 1985.

Effects of epostane on progesterone synthesis in early human pregnancy, by L. Birgerson, et al. CONTRACEPTION 33(4):401-410, April 1986.

New non-hormonal antifertility drug DL 111-IT: I. Effects on testes and accessory glands of reproduction in male rats, by R. S. Prasad, et al. CONTRACEPTION 33(1):79-88, January 1986.

—: II. Effects on testicular hyaluronidase activity in male rats, by R. S. Prasad, et al. CONTRACEPTION 33(1):89-99, January 1986.

ABORTIFACIENT AGENTS (continued)

Preoperative cervix dilatation in first trimester pregnancy interruption using 9-deoxy-16, 16-dimethyl-9-methylene prostaglandin E2. A randomized double-blind study, by D. Brügger, et al. GEBURTSHILFE UND FRAUEN-HEILKUNDE 45(8):567-569, August 1985.

Preparation and properties of human chorionic gonadotropin antagonist for biological studies: antifertility effects in the female rat, by M. R. Sairam, et al. ACTA ENDOCRINOLOGICA 112(4):586-594, August 1986.

Prevention and treatment of DIC complicating Wirstroemia chamaedaphen Meisn. administration for mid-term labor induction, by G. S. Fan, et al. CHUNG KUO I HSUEH KO HSUEH YUAM HSUEH PAO 6(6):443-445, December 1984.

Production of monoclonal antidiotypic antibodies against trichosanthin-specific IgE by rat-mouse hybridomas, by Y. Y. Ji, et al. SHIH YEN SHEN WU HSUEH PAO 19(1):91-98, March 1986.

Status of the kallikrein-kinin system of the blood and level of endogenous prostaglandins after interruption of pregnancy during the second trimester using intra-amniotic administration of a hypertonic sodium chloride solution, by A. P. Nikonov. AKUSHERSTVO I GINEKOLOGIIA (1):60-62, January 1986.

Study of in vivo and in vitro responses to trichosanthin in the mouse, by M. Yeh, et al. SHIH YEN SHENG WU HSEUH PAO 19(1):81-90, March 1986.

Study of the mechanism of ONO-802 in the termination of early pregnancy by B model sonar monitoring, by L. L. Luo. CHUNG HUA FU CHAN KO TSA CHIH 20(4):240-242+, July 1985.

Synthesis of ent-17-(prop-1-ynyl-17 beta-hydroxy-11 beta-(4-(N,N-dimethyla-mino)-phenyl)-4,9-estradien-3-one, the antipode of RU-38 486, by E. Ottow, et al. STEROIDS 44(6):519-530, December 1984.

Transplacental passage of mifepristone [letter], by R. Frydman, et al. LANCET 2(8466):1252, November 30, 1985.

Treatment of women who have undergone chemically induced abortions, by M. S. Burnhill. JOURNAL OF REPRODUCTIVE MEDICINE 30(8):610-614, August 1985.

Value of an antiprogeseterone steroid in the treatment of extra-uterine pregnancy. Preliminary results, by F. X. Paris, et al. REVUE FRANCAISE DE GYNECOLOGIE ET D'OBSTETRIQUE 81(1):33-35, January 1986.

Woman's place is in the hospital (epostane), by A. Frater. NEW STATESMAN 111:8, June 6, 1986.

ABORTION—GENERAL
Abortion and medical discipline [letter], by V. Hadlow, et al. NEW ZEALAND MEDICAL JOURNAL 98(785):715, August 28, 1985.

Abortion and the two kingdoms, by D. R. Liefeld. CONCORDIA JOURNAL 12(6): 205-216, November 1986.

Abortion balloting spells danger. GUARDIAN 39(6):7, November 5, 1986.

Abortion cases, by M. E. Rust. AMERICAN BAR ASSOCIATION JOURNAL 72: 50-53, February 1986.

ABORTION—GENERAL (continued)

Abortion: a disputation, by P. Lushing. CARDOZO LAW REVIEW 8:243-283, December 1986.

Abortion foes ruled out-of-order, by J. Biehl. GUARDIAN 38(32):11, May 14, 1986.

Abortion in early pregnancy, by T. Mardesic. CESKOSLOVENSKA GYNEKOLO-GIE 51(6):447-448, July 1986.

Abortion: increasing the scope of tragedy? [letter], by E. J. Rzadki. CANADIAN MEDICAL ASSOCIATION JOURNAL 134(1):16-17, January 1, 1986.

Abortion liberalizing worldwide. OFF OUR BACKS 16(10):8, November 1986.

Abortion—a personal approach, by P. Mitchell. HERIZONS 4(4):44, June 1986.

Abortion: the politics of necessity and choice [review essay], by E. Fee, et al. FEMINIST STUDIES 12(2):361-373, Summer 1986.

Acts and omissions doctrine and abortion: reply to Dr. Toon [letter], by T. F. Murphy. JOURNAL OF MEDICAL ETHICS 12(1):53-54, March 1986.

Adoption vs. abortion, by E. Williams, et al. NEWSWEEK 107:39, April 28, 1986.

Between ourselves—reproductive freedom. OFF OUR BACKS 16(4):2, April 1986.

Birth control failure among patients with unwanted pregnancies: 1982-1984, by A. M. Sophocles, Jr., et al. JOURNAL OF FAMILY PRACTICE 22(1):45-48, January 1986.

Brain-life theory: towards a consistent biological definition of humanness, by J. M. Goldenring. JOURNAL OF MEDICAL ETHICS 11:198-204, December 1985.

Burns, abortions and dying declarations, by H. C. Frazier. MEDICINE AND LAW 5(5):431-440, 1986.

Case of Brave New People: a shadow and a hope [review], by S. C. Mott. TSF BULLETIN 10(2):27-31, November-December 1986.

Characterization of maternal antipaternal antibodies in secondary aborting women, by J. A. McIntyre, et al. CONTRIBUTIONS IN GYNECOLOGY AND OBSTETRICS 14:131-137, 1985.

Conflict over a past abortion as an influence on subsequent pregnancy risk, by L. Lemle. DAI: B 47(1), July 1986.

Consequences of treating the fetus as a human, by K. Kelly. WHOLE EARTH REVIEW 51:64, Summer 1986.

Curious case of abortion [letter], by P. G. Ney. NEW ZEALAND MEDICAL JOURNAL 98(785):716, August 28, 1985.

Cytogenetic analysis of early human abortuses after preparation of chromosomes directly from chorionic villi [letter], by I. Hansmann, et al. HUMAN GENETICS 72(2):189, February 1986.

Dearth of contraception fuels world abortion rate. NATIONAL CATHOLIC RE-PORTER 19:10, January 21, 1983.

Detection and interpretation of two different cell lines in triploid abortions, by I. A. Uchida, et al. CLINICAL GENETICS 28(6):489-494, December 1985.

Effect of consanguineous marriages on reproductive wastage, by S. A. Al-Awadi, et al. CLINICAL GENETICS 29(5):384-388, May 1986.

Epidemiological study of work with video screens and pregnancy outcome: I. A registry study, by A. Ericson, et al. AMERICAN JOURNAL OF INDUSTRIAL MEDICINE 9(5):447-457, 1986.

—: II. A case-control study, by A. Ericson, et al. AMERICAN JOURNAL OF IN-DUSTRIAL MEDICINE 9(5):459-475, 1986.

Evaluation of ultrasonography and hormonal monitoring in early abortion, by G. Y. Qian. CHUNG HUA FU CHAN KO TSA CHIH 21(1):22-24+, January 1986.

Fetal experimentation: protocols, propriety and parameters. QUEEN'S LAW JOURNAL 11:166-197, Fall 1985.

Fetal mortality in sibships of cases with neural tube defects, by A. D. Sadovnick, et al. CLINICAL GENETICS 29(5):409-412, May 1986.

Finding a better way: excerpt from *If I should die before I wake,* 1986, by J. Simpson. FUNDAMENTALIST JOURNAL 5(3):20-24, March 1986.

Flock at odds with its shepherds [news], by C. Low, et al. INSIGHT: THE WASH-INGTON TIMES 2(30):8-13, July 28, 1986.

Foetal bleeding in the first and second trimester uterine haemorrhage, by S. V. Parulekar, et al. JOURNAL OF POSTGRADUATE MEDICINE 31(1):43-45, January 1985.

For the "poor mute mothers"? Margaret Sanger and *The Woman Rebel,* by L. Masel-Walters. JOURNALISM HISTORY 11(1-2):3-10+, 1984.

Global study on abortion. NATIONAL NOW TIMES 19(5):8, October 1986.

Haptoglobin typing in abortion in the first trimester, by S. Nikschick, et al. ZEN-TRALBLATT FUR GYNAEKOLOGIE 108(4):251-253, 1986.

Herbal abortifacts. OPEN ROAD 20:13, Fall 1986.

Human chorionic gonadotropin in early normal and pathologic pregnancy. Discordant levels in peripheral maternal blood and blood from the uterine and abdominal cavities, by J. A. Steier, et al. AMERICAN JOURNAL OF OBSTET-RICS AND GYNECOLOGY 154(5):1091-1094, May 1986.

I crossed over, by P. Simpson. SAINT LOUIS 13(83):14, March 1986.

Immunologic factors and failed pregnancy, by J. E. Jirásek. CASOPIS LEKARU CESKYCH 125(23):697-701, June 6, 1986.

Indices of steroid hormones and free amino acids in the fetoplacental system in abortion, by P. P. Grigorenko. AKUSHERSTVO I GINEKOLOGIIA (12):41-43, December 1985.

International family planning. HOUSTON JOURNAL OF INTERNATIONAL LAW 8:155-173, Autumn 1985.

Is abortion the issue? (Harper's symposium). HARPERS 273:35-43, July 1986.

Lead content in abortion material from urban women in early pregnancy, by P. Borella, et al. INTERNATIONAL ARCHIVES OF OCCUPATIONAL AND ENVIRONMENTAL HEALTH 57(2):93-99, 1986.

Leader is excommunicated [news]. CHRISTIANITY TODAY 30(4):54, March 7, 1986.

Leptospira hazard to humans. VETERINARY RECORD 119:541, November 29, 1986.

Letter to my sisters, by M. Ann. WOMEN AND THERAPY 4(4):1, Winter 1985.

Live and let live and die when you must, by J. R. Nelson. PERKINS JOURNAL 39(3):334-337, July 1986.

Maternal antibodies to paternal B-lymphocytes in normal and abnormal pregnancy, by D. A. Power, et al. AMERICAN JOURNAL OF REPRODUCTIVE IMMUNOLOGY AND MICROBIOLOGY 10(1):10-13, January 1986.

Mr. Pawley's fetal mistake, by L. Byfield. ALBERTA REPORT 13:12, April 14, 1986.

Natural law evolution, and the question of personhood, by T. H. Milby. QUARTERLY REVIEW 6(2):39-47, Summer 1986.

No ultimatum [news]. CHRISTIAN CENTURY 103(11):321, April 2, 1986.

Non-negotiable demand, by C. M. Musil. NATIONAL WOMEN'S STUDIES ASSOCIATION PERSPECTIVES 4:1-2, Summer 1986.

Now if Paddy the publisher himself were to get pregnant, by T. Byfield. ALBERTA REPORT 13:60, March 17, 1986.

Pregnant coypus opt for male offspring. NEW SCIENTIST 111:29, September 4, 1986.

Progesterone antagonism: science and society, by W. F. Crowley, Jr. NEW ENGLAND JOURNAL OF MEDICINE 315:1607-1608, December 18, 1986.

Prostaglandins in the fetal circulation following maternal ingestion of a prostaglandin synthetase inhibitor during mid-pregnancy, by I. Z. MacKenzie, et al. INTERNATIONAL JOURNAL OF GYNAECOLOGY AND OBSTETRICS 23(6):455-458, December 1985.

Seasonal variation in conception and various pregnancy outcomes, by C. W. Warren, et al. SOCIAL BIOLOGY 33:116-126, Spring-Summer 1986.

Selective abortion and the diagnosis of fetal damage: issues and concerns, by L. G. Cohen. JOURNAL OF THE ASSOCIATION OF PERSONS WITH SEVERE HANDICAPS 11:188-195, Fall 1986.

Sisters do it for themselves, by G. Farley. GUARDIAN 38(29):1, April 23, 1986.

ABORTION—GENERAL (continued)

Stitch in time . . . cervical incompetence, by P. A. Hillard. PARENTS 61(10):210+, October 1986.

Strasser on dependence, reliance, and need, by M. Davis. PHILOSOPHICAL QUARTERLY 36:384-391, July 1986.

Summer on abortion, by R. Weitz, et al. DIALOGUE 24(4):671-699, Winter 1985.

Test-tube women: what future for motherhood?, by L. Paltrow. WOMEN'S RIGHTS LAW REPORTER 8(4):303, Fall 1985.

To make a seamless garment use a single piece of cloth, by C. E. Gudorf. CROSS CURRENTS 34:473-491, Winter 1984-1985.

Uncertain futures, by A. Asch. WOMEN'S REVIEW OF BOOKS 4(2):16, November 1986.

What is life? [letter], by M. A. Yuille. NATURE 317(6035):281, September 26-October 2, 1985.

When life begins. ECONOMIST 301:15-16, November 15, 1986.

When a pregnant woman endangers her fetus—a commentary [case studies], by B. K. Rothman. HASTINGS CENTER REPORT 16:25, February 1986.

Whither the womb? Myths, machines, and mothers, by A. F. D'Adamo, et al. FRONTIERS 9(1):72-79, 1986.

Who shall live? Who shall die?, by E. Gilson. PRESENT TENSE 10:21-25, Spring 1983.

World at a glance: population, growth, military spending, "quality of life," and abortion politics. BULLETIN OF THE ATOMIC SCIENTSTS 42(4):17-19, April 1986.

World population crisis. BULLETIN OF THE ATOMIC SCIENTISTS 42(4):13-19, April 1986.

Wrongful life [case notes]. JOURNAL OF FAMILY LAW 23(4):646-649, 1984-1985.

AUSTRALIA
High incidence of preterm births and early losses in pregnancy after in vitro fertilisation. Australian in vitro fertilisation collaborative group. BRITISH MEDICAL JOURNAL 291(6503):1160-1163, October 26, 1985.

Overview: the history of contraception and abortion in Australia, by D. Wyndham. HEALTHRIGHT 5:9-11, November 1985.

BANGLADESH
Induced abortion in a rural area of Bangladesh, by A. R. Khan, et al. STUDIES IN FAMILY PLANNING 17(2):95-99, March-April 1986.

CANADA
Abortion by the ballot box: Fort McMurray's plebiscite on feticide is a Canadian first, by B. Henker. ALBERTA REPORT 13:12, April 28, 1986.

ABORTION—GENERAL (continued)

CANADA (continued)
Abortion coalition in Quebec pushes legalization, by K. Herland. HERIZONS 4(4):10, June 1986.

Abortion controversy (Alberta doctors protest ban on extra billing), by C. Barrett. MACLEAN'S 99:8, December 22, 1986.

Abortion on the docket (H. Morgentaler's challenge), by S. Aikenhead. MAC-LEAN'S 99:56-57, October 20, 1986.

Battleground Fort McMurray: the campaigns are set for Canada's first abortion plebiscite, by R. Umezawa. ALBERTA REPORT 13:12, August 25, 1986.

Canada: abortion law fight. OFF OUR BACKS 17(7):4, July 1986.

Canada—interview with abortion rights campaigner. INTERNATIONAL VIEW-POINT 99:28, May 19, 1986.

Canadian abortion law, by R. M. Ferri. CATHOLIC LAWYER 30:336-363, Summer 1986.

Choosing to abort: pro-life loses in Fort McMurray's referendum, by L. Slobodian. ALBERTA REPORT 13:50-51, November 3, 1986.

Cytogenetic studies in spontaneous abortion: the Calgary experience, by C. C. Lin, et al. CANADIAN JOURNAL OF GENETICS AND CYTOLOGY 27(5):565-570, October 1985.

Fort McMurray's choice, by C. Milner, et al. ALBERTA REPORT 13:30, January 6, 1986.

Montreal Pregnancy Study: an investigation of very early pregnancies, by A. Lippman, et al. CANADIAN JOURNAL OF PUBLIC HEALTH 77(suppl 1):157-163, May-June 1986.

Montreal rally on abortion rights. INTERCONTINENTAL PRESS 24(5):143, March 10, 1986.

Pro-choices cry foul: Saskatchewan feminists accuse a minister of making abortions difficult, by L. Cohen. ALBERTA REPORT 13:22, April 21, 1986.

Pro-lifers subpoena a mayor: but Calgary's Klein appeals to quash the ploy, by G. Siegfried. ALBERTA REPORT 13:35-36, August 18, 1986.

Vancouver tribunal condemns abortion laws, by G. Lang. HERIZONS 4(3):11, April 1986.

Voice for the unborn: the abortion law is tested in (Saskatchewan) appeal court, by L. Cohen. ALBERTA REPORT 13:21-22, December 30, 1985.

ENGLAND
Introduction to the history and present state of the law relating to abortion in England, by C. R. Fradd. ETHICS AND MEDICINE 1(4):60-64, 1985.

ABORTION—GENERAL (continued)

FRANCE
Abortion law reform in France, by D. M. Stetson. JOURNAL OF COMPARA-
TIVE FAMILY STUDIES 17(3):277-290, Autumn 1986.

Pregnancy and unwanted children after failure of sterilization and voluntary
termination of pregnancy. I. Disconcerting French and foreign jurisprudence, by J. H. Soutoul, et al. JOURNAL DE GYNECOLOGIE, OB-
STETRIQUE ET BIOLOGIE DE LA REPRODUCTION 15(3):273-279,
1986.

GERMANY
Abortion according to paragraph 218ff. of the German penal code and life
support of premature infants from the viewpoint of the pediatrician, by H.
von Voss. MONATSSCHRIFT FUR KINDERHEILKUNDE 134(5):232-
239, May 1986.

German euthanasia programme [letter]. NEW ZEALAND MEDICAL JOUR-
NAL 98(791):1019, November 27, 1985.

Medical letters must also be read. . . ! Consequences of a risky intervention
not considered—decision of the German federal court. FORTSCHRITTE
DER MEDIZIN 104(11):64, March 20, 1986.

West Germany—feminism and the unions, by S. Engert. INTERNATIONAL
VIEWPOINT 94:19, March 10, 1986.

GREAT BRITAIN
Aftercare following miscarriage . . . extending the role of the community mid-
wife, by S. Arber. MIDWIFE, HEALTH VISITOR AND COMMUNITY
NURSE 21(12):432+, December 1985.

"Alas! poor Yorick," I knew him ex utero: the regulation of embryo and fetal
experimentation and disposal in England and the United States, by N. P.
Terry. VANDERBILT LAW REVIEW 39:419-470, April 1986.

Political implications of attitudes to abortion in Britain, by J. Chapman. WEST
EUROPEAN POLITICS 9(1):7-31, 1986.

Pre-natal injury, homicide and the draft criminal code, by J. Temkin. CAM-
BRIDGE LAW JOURNAL 45:414-429, November 1986.

Pro-choice or pro-life, by J. South. NEW STATESMAN 110:10-12+, November 15, 1985.

HUNGARY
Impact of abortion policy on prematurity in Hungary, by Z. Makoi. ACTA
PAEDIATRICA SCANDINAVICA 319:84-88, 1985.

INDIA
Has the MTP (Medical Terminationof Pregnancy) Act in India proved beneficial?, by M. L. Solapurkar, et al. JOURNAL OF FAMILY WELFARE 31:
46-52, March 1985.

India makes sure of baby boys. . . . NEW SCIENTIST 112:8-9, December 25,
1986+.

India: move to stop sex-test abortion, by R. Rao. NATURE 324:202, November 20, 1986.

INDIA (continued)
India's unborn brides, by E. Silver. GUARDIAN November 14, 1986, p. 17.

Rampant female foeticide in India, by P. Darshini. ISIS 11:1, September 1986.

IRELAND
Birth control and abortion in Ireland, by N. Dosterom. HERIZONS 4(2):13, March 1986.

Ireland: clinic sued . . . condoms debates, by N. Bythe. OFF OUR BACKS 16(1):10, January 1986.

Ireland—Sinn Fein debates abortion policy, by T. Gorton. INTERNATIONAL VIEWPOINT 110:25, December 8, 1986.

Regulation of fertility in Belgrade, by M. Husar, et al. SRPSKI ARHIV ZA CELOKUPNO LEKARSTVO 113(7):601-609, July 1985.

Social change and moral politics: the Irish Constitutional Referendum 1983, by B. Girvin. POLITICAL STUDIES 34:61-81, March 1986.

ITALY
Characteristics of women undergoing induced abortion: results of a case-control study from Northern Italy, by C. La Vecchia, et al. CONTRACEP-TION 32(6):637-649, December 1985.

JORDAN
Serodiagnosis of toxoplasma gondii in habitually aborting women and other adults from North Jordan, by S.K. Abdel-Hafez, et al. FOLIA PARASITOLOGICA 33(1):7-13, 1986.

KOREA
Rejected sex of Korea, by T. Selassie. SPARE RIB 172:49, November 1986.

NETHERLANDS
Initial Dutch experiences with early pregnancy interruption using the antipro-gesterone agent mifepriston, by H. A. Vervest, et al. NEDERLANDS TIJDSCHRIFT VOOR GENEESKUNDE 129(35):1680-1683, August 31, 1985.

NICARAGUA
Abortion in Nicaragua: an emerging issue, by S. Sangree, et al. MS 14:25, June 1986.

Nicaragua: abortion laws criticized. OFF OUR BACKS 17(7):4, July 1986.

Nicaragua—debate on abortion rights, by C. Jaquith. INTERCONTINENTAL PRESS 24(1):4, January 13, 1986.

Nicaragua—debate on abortion rights continues. INTERNATIONAL VIEW-POINT 102:28, June 30, 1986.

Nicaragua—legalization of abortion discussed, by C. Jaquith. INTERCON-TINENTAL PRESS 24(3):63, February 10, 1986.

Nicaragua's minister of health Dora Maria Tellex, by R. Rolon, et al. NICARA-GUAN PERSPECTIVES 12:36, Summer 1986.

NIGERIA

Control of reproduction: principle—Nigeria, by R. Pittin. REVIEW OF AFRICAN POLITICAL ECONOMY 35:40, May 1986.

Offering an alternative to illegal abortion in Nigeria, by T. O. Odejide. NEW ERA NURSING IMAGE INTERNATIONAL 2(2):39-42, 1986.

NORWAY

Induced abortions and births. Trends in seven counties, Norway, 1972-1983, by F. E. Skjeldestad. SCANDINAVIAN JOURNAL OF SOCIAL MEDICINE 14(2):61-66, 1986.

SCOTLAND

Cytogenetic analysis in 100 spontaneous abortions in North-East Scotland, by S. E. Procter, et al. CLINICAL GENETICS 29(2):101-103, February 1986.

SOVIET UNION

Soviet birth control: a majority prefers abortion. DISCOVER 7:8, April 1986.

SPAIN

Spain—nation at war over abortion, by R. MacKay. GUARDIAN 11:15, December 10, 1986.

Spanish state—the women's movement on the rise. INTERNATIONAL VIEWPOINT 94:17, March 10, 1986.

SWEDEN

Conference report: Feminist International Network of Resistance to Reproductive and Genetic Engineering, Sweden, July 1985, by S. Brodribb. RESOURCES FOR FEMINIST RESEARCH 14:54-55, 1985.

TAIWAN

Induced abortion: reported and observed practice in Taiwan, by J. F. Wang. HEALTH CARE FOR WOMEN, INTERNATIONAL 6(5-6):383-404, 1985.

THAILAND

Abortion: an attitude study of professional staff at Ramathibodi Hospital, by W. Phuapradit, et al. JOURNAL OF THE MEDICAL ASSOCIATION OF THAILAND 69(1):22-27, January 1986.

UNITED STATES

Abortion-clinic bombing: the war on sex, by S. Schneider. MADEMOISELLE 92:172-173+, April 1986.

Abortion in Louisiana: the applicability of R.S. 14:87 to a non-licensed physician. SOUTHERN UNIVERSITY LAW REVIEW 11:103-112, Spring 1985.

Abortion in the United States: politics or policy?, by C. Djerassi. BULLETIN OF THE ATOMIC SCIENTISTS 42:38-41, April 1986.

Advertising abortion during the 1830s and 1840s: Madame Restell builds a business, by M. Olasky. JOURNAL OF HISTORY 13:49-55, Summer 1986.

UNITED STATES (continued)

"Alas! poor Yorick," I knew him ex utero: the regulation of embryo and fetal experimentation and disposal in England and the United States, by N. P. Terry. VANDERBILT LAW REVIEW 39:419-470, April 1986.

City of Akron v. Akron Center for Reproductive Health, Inc. state decision prevales, but for how long? UNIVERSITY OF MIAMI LAW REVIEW 38:921-938, September 1984.

Comparison of complication rates in first trimester abortions performed by physician assistants and physicians, by M. A. Freedman, et al. AMERICAN JOURNAL OF PUBLIC HEALTH 76(5):550-556, May 1986.

Crossover in newspaper coverage of abortion from murder to liberation, by M. N. Olasky, et al. JOURNALISM QUARTERLY 63:31-37, Spring 1986.

Ecology of abortions in the United States since 1973: a replication and extension. POPULATION AND ENVIRONMENT 7(3):137, Fall 1984.

Economic model of teenage pregnancy decision-making, by A. Leibowitz, et al. DEMOGRAPHY 23:67-77, February 1986.

Family planning: abort it. ECONOMIST 297:37-38, November 9, 1985.

Guardians ad litem—for fetus—New Jersey. JUVENILE AND FAMILY LAW DIGEST 18(2):93-95, February 1986.

How planned parenthood won in Arkansas (ran two controversial commercials against abortion referendum). HUMAN EVENTS 46:5, November 22, 1986.

Husband notification for abortion in Utah: a patronizing problem. UTAH LAW REVIEW 1986:609-628, 1986.

Leads from the MMWR. Rubella vaccination during pregnancy—United States, 1971-1985. JAMA 255(21):2867+, June 6, 1986.

Massachusetts anti-abortion measure put on ballot. NATIONAL NOW TIMES 19(3):5, May 1986.

Massachusetts to vote on anti-abortion referendum, by K. Westheimer. GAY COMMUNITY NEWS 13(42):3, May 17, 1986.

Maternal deaths associated with barbiturate anesthetics—New York City. MMWR 35(37):579-582+, September 19, 1986.

Minnesota judge strikes down notification law, by M. Specktor. GUARDIAN 39(13):4, December 24, 1986.

Mitres in mischief, church, politics and tax. ECONOMIST 299:24, May 17, 1986.

My church threw me out (executive director of Planned Parenthood of Rhode Island excommunicated by Catholic Church), ed. by M. Orth, et al. REDBOOK 167:14+, June 1986.

No legal impediment: access to abortion in the United States, by A. S. Cohan. JOURNAL OF AMERICAN STUDIES 20:189-205, August 1986.

ABORTION—GENERAL (continued)

UNITED STATES (continued)
Ohio adopts an abortion notification statute. UNIVERSITY OF DAYTON LAW REVIEW 12:205-241, Fall 1986.

Opposing abortion clinics: a New York Times 1971 crusade, by M. N. Olasky. JOURNALISM QUARTERLY 63:305-310+, Summer 1986.

Parental consent for abortion: impact of the Massachusetts law, by V. G. Cartoof, et al. AMERICAN JOURNAL OF PUBLIC HEALTH 76(4):397-400, April 1986.

Pasadena, Texas, officers told not to work at abortion centers. CRIME CONTROL DIGEST 19(46):8, November 18, 1985.

People vote on abortion funding: Colorado and Washington. FAMILY PLANNING PERSPECTIVES 17(4):155, July-August 1985.

Portrait of American women who obtain abortions, by S. K. Henshaw, et al. FAMILY PLANNING PERSPECTIVES 17(2):90-96, March-April 1985.

Prevalence and trends in oral contraceptive use in premenopausal females ages 12-54 years, United States, 1971-1980, by R. Russell-Briefel, et al. AMERICAN JOURNAL OF PUBLIC HEALTH 75(10):1173-1176, October 1985.

Prevalence of chlamydia trachomatis and other micro-organisms in women seeking abortions in Pittsburgh, Pennsylvania, United States of America, by A. J. Amortegul, et al. GENITOURINARY MEDICINE 62(2):88-92, April 1986.

Public policy and adolescent sexual behavior in the United States, by M. L. Finkel, et al. SOCIAL BIOLOGY 30:140-150, Summer 1983.

Rubella vaccination during pregnancy—United States, 1971-1985. MMWR 35(17):275-276+, May 2, 1986.

Should parents be notified of their minor daughter's abortion? A pregnant question for Florida legislators. FLORIDA STATE UNIVERSITY LAW REVIEW 14:719-743, Fall 1986.

State laws and the provision of family planning and abortion services in 1985, by T. Sollom, et al. FAMILY PLANNING PERSPECTIVES 17(6):262-266, November-December 1985.

Supreme Court throws out Illinois abortion case. OFF OUR BACKS 16(6):9, June 1986.

Teen pregnancy in New Orleans: factors that differentiate teens who deliver, abort, and successfully contracept, by E. Landry, et al. JOURNAL OF YOUTH AND ADOLESCENCE 15(3):259-274, June 1986.

Tracking the intractable: a survey on the abortion controversy [review article], by J. J. Kelly. CROSS CURRENTS 35:212-218, Summer-Fall 1985.

25,000 in United States abortion rights march, by P. Liyama. INTERCONTINENTAL PRESS 24(7):214, April 7, 1986,

ABORTION—GENERAL (continued)

UNITED STATES (continued)
United States Supreme Court 1985-1986 term: abortion. CRIMINAL LAW REPORTER: SUPREME COURT PROCEEDINGS 39(24):4165-4167, September 17, 1986.

Virginia mothers can sue doctors in failed abortions. JET 70:7, May 19, 1986.

We are the majority, say LA marchers, by R. Hippler. GUARDIAN 38(25):11, March 26, 1986.

YUCATAN
Incomplete abortion: characteristics of the patients treated in the O'Horan Hospital of Mérida, Yúcatan, by T. E. Canto de Cetina, et al. SALUD PUBLICA DE MEXICO 27(6):507-513, November-December 1985.

ABORTION—ADVERTISING
Advertising abortion during the 1830s and 1840s: Madame Restell builds a business, by M. Olasky. JOURNAL OF HISTORY 13:49-55, Summer 1986.

Solomon and Ruth needed [controversy over abortion advertisement signed by Catholic religious]. AMERICA 154:42-43, January 25, 1986.

Truth in advertising, please ("abortion rights" ads). AMERICA 154:1, January 4-11, 1986.

ABORTION—ATTITUDES
Abortion: an attitude study of professional staff at Ramathibodi Hospital, by W. Phuapradit, et al. JOURNAL OF THE MEDICAL ASSOCIATION OF THAILAND 69(1):22-27, January 1986.

Abortion attitudes and performance among male and female obstetrician-gynecologists, by C. S. Weisman, et al. FAMILY PLANNING PERSPECTIVES 18(2):67-73, March-April 1986.

Abortion: a case study in ethical decision making, by R. C. Crossman. CONSENSUS 11(4):5-13, October 1985.

Abortion: a look at our Christian roots, by E. K. Jesaitis. NATIONAL CATHOLIC REPORTER 19:7, January 21, 1983.

Abortion: a moral choice, by C. Hewyard. FRONTIERS 9(1):42-45, 1986.

Abortion of the silent scream (correlation between antiabortion movement and votes of legislators on human pain, suffering and violence), by J. W. Prescott. HUMANIST 46:10-17+, September-October 1986.

Abortion, pluralism, feminism (discussion of April 11, 1986 article, the fetus and fundamental rights), by J. C. Callahan. COMMONWEAL 113:338-342, June 6, 1986.

Analysis of nursing students' attitude toward bioethics (3). Attitude toward induced abortion, by O. Nakayama, et al. KANGO TENBO 11(5):492-497, April 1986.

Are you for RU-486?, by T. Kaye. NEW REPUBLIC 194;13-15, January 27, 1986.

ABORTION—ATTITUDES (continued)

Attitudes of mothers of children with Down syndrome concerning amniocentesis, abortion, and prenatal genetic counseling techniques, by T. E. Elkins, et al. OBSTETRICS AND GYNECOLOGY 68(2):181-184, August 1986.

Baccalaureate nursing students' attitudes toward abortion, by M. C. Smith. DAI: A 47(3), September 1986.

Chicago church acts against a former member who performs abortions (Moody Church confronts Dr. A. Bickham). CHRISTIANITY TODAY 30:63+, February 7, 1986.

Comment on Tooley's *Abortion and Infanticide* [review article], by M. Tushnet, et al. ETHICS 96(2):350-355, January 1986.

ERA and the abortion controversy: a case of dissonance reduction, by L. Bolce, et al. SOCIAL SCIENCE QUARTERLY 67:299-314, June 1986.

Ethics of life and death (mercy killing, nuclear war, abortion), by J. J. Haldane. SCOTTISH JOURNAL OF THEOLOGY 38(4):603-611, 1985.

Fathers and fetuses, by G. W. Harris, Jr. ETHICS 96:594-603, April 1986.

Feelings about abortion: an insider's view, by J. Wainer. HEALTHRIGHT 5(1):23-25, November 1985.

Fetus as a person, by C. Olds. BIRTH PSYCHOLOGY BULLETIN 6(2):21-26, Fall 1985.

Genesis and abortion: an exegetical test of a biblical warrant in ethics, by W. S. Kurz. THEOLOGICAL STUDIES 47(4):668-680, December 1986.

How technology is reframing the abortion debate, by D. Callahan. HASTINGS CENTER REPORT 16(1):33-42, February 1986.

Humanity, personhood, and abortion, by A. C. Ray. INTERNATIONAL PHILO-SOPHICAL QUARTERLY 25:233-245, 1985.

Influence of maternal attitudes on urban, black teens' decisions about abortion v delivery, by E. Freeman, et al. JOURNAL OF REPRODUCTIVE MEDICINE 30(10):731-735, October 1985.

Inquiry into the moral prerogatives of the potential human life, by O. A. Cvitanic. PHAROS 49(2):13-17, Spring 1986.

Is the old right now new?, by N. Thornton. SOCIAL ALTERNATIVES 5(4):6, November 1986.

Kantian argument against abortion, by H. J. Gensler. PHILOSOPHICAL STUDIES 49:83-98, January 1986.

Metaethical framework of anti-abortion rhetoric, by R. A. Lake. SIGNS 11:478-499, Spring 1986.

Moral absolutism and abortion: Alan Donagan on the hysterectomy and cranio-tomy cases, by T. Reynolds. ETHICS 95(4):866-873, July 1985.

Moral community of persons, by S. M. Jordan. PHILOSOPHY TODAY 30:108-118, Summer 1986.

Moral dilemma: two views [letter], by D. M. Pedulla. POSTGRADUATE MEDICINE 79(6):34-35, May 1, 1986.

Moral theory and oral standing: a reply to Woods and Soles, by L. W. Sumner. DIALOGUE 24:691-699, Winter 1985.

Not killing, by R. Aitken. WHOLE EARTH REVIEW 51:63, Summer 1986.

Nuns deny Vatican claim (signers of statement supporting abortion rights). CHRISTIAN CENTURY 103(24):704, August 13-20, 1986.

On being pregnant, by M. Pellauer. CHRISTIANITY AND CRISIS 46:228-230, July 14, 1986.

Opinions regarding abortion among male Nigerian undergraduate students in the United States, by A. Adebayo, et al. SOCIAL BIOLOGY 32(1-2):132-135, Spring-Summer 1985.

Philosophy and the morality of abortion, by J. Baker. JOURNAL OF APPLIED PHILOSOPHY 2(2):261-270, October 1985.

Political implications of attitudes to abortion in Britain, by J. Chapman. WEST EUROPEAN POLITICS 9(1):7-31, 1986.

Prenatal diagnosis and female abortion: a case study in medical law and ethics, by B. M. Dickens. JOURNAL OF MEDICAL ETHICS 12:143-144, September 1986.

Problem of abortion: a complex bio-medical moral issue [editorial], by J. M. Gessell. SAINT LUKE JOURNAL 29(2):83-86, March 1986.

Pro-life or pro-choice: is there a credible alternative?, by S. Andre. SOCIAL THEORY AND PRACTICE 12:223-240, Summer 1986.

Public opinion and the legalization of abortion, by T. F. Hartnagel, et al. CANADIAN REVIEW OF SOCIOLOGY AND ANTHROPOLOGY 22:427-430, August 1985; 22(3):411-430, 1985.

Right to life and the restoration of the American republic, by L. Lehrman. NATIONAL REVIEW 38:25-28, August 29, 1986.

Rules of practice in Paul Ramsey's medical ethics, by R. W. Jones. PERKINS JOURNAL 39(1):34-43, January 1986.

Search for gender differences on fertility-related attitudes: questioning the relevance of sociobiology theory for understanding social psychological aspects of human reproduction, by D. Granberg, et al. PSYCHOLOGY OF WOMEN QUARTERLY 9(4):431-437, December 1985.

Selling chastity—the sly new attack on your sexual freedom (prolife pregnancy-testing centers masquerading as abortion clinics), by S. Bolotin. VOGUE 176:482-483+, March 1986.

Should abortion be legal? Two contrasting views, by J. C. Willke, et al. SEVENTEEN 45:86-87+, January 1986.

Social basis of antifeminism: religious networks and culture, by J. L. Himmelstein. JOURNAL FOR THE SCIENTIFIC STUDY OF RELIGION 25(1):1-15, March 1986.

Sociology, ideology, and the abortion issue: a content analysis of family sociology texts, by R. J. Adamek. JOURNAL OF APPLIED SOCIOLOGY 2(1):43-56, 1985.

Souls on ice (frozen embryo transfer and the dilemma of abortion), by M. K. Blakely. VOGUE 176:346+, September 1986.

Startling fount of healing (use of cells taken from aborted human fetuses), by K. McAuliffe. US NEWS AND WORLD REPORT 101:68-70, November 3, 1986.

Teaching about abortion as a public issue, by P. B. Richard. WOMEN'S STUDIES QUARTERLY 12(4):27-30, Winter 1984.

Three abortion theorists: a critical appreciation, by J. W. Anderson. DAI: A 47(4), October 1986.

Tracking the intractable: a survey on the abortion controversy [review article], by J. J. Kelly. CROSS CURRENTS 35:212-218, Summer-Fall 1985.

Trends in public attitudes toward legal abortion, 1972-1978, by S. A. Moldanado. RESEARCH IN NURSING AND HEALTH 8(3):219-225, September 1985.

Understanding the abortion debate, by K. Glen. SOCIALIST REVIEW 89:51, September 1986.

Why abortion is a human rights issue, by J. Kemp. CONSERVATIVE DIGEST 12:39+, August 1986.

Women and abortion: attitudes, social networks, decision-making, by G. Faria, et al. SOCIAL WORK IN HEALTH CARE 11(1):85-96, Fall 1985.

ABORTION—CHEMICALLY INDUCED
Abortions among dental personnel exposed to nitrous oxide [letter], by H. C. Schuyt, et al. ANAESTHESIA 41(1):82-83, January 1986.

Assay of polychlorobiphenyls in human blood in relation to epidemiological studies, by V. Leoni, et al. FARMACO 41(8):245-254, August 1986.

Bovine abortion and death associated with consumption of aflatoxin-contaminated peanuts, by A. C. Ray, et al. JOURNAL OF THE AMERICAN VETERINARY MEDICAL ASSOCIATION 188(10):1187-1188, May 15, 1986.

Caffeine consumption during pregnancy and association with late spontaneous abortion, by W. Srisuphan, et al. AMERICAN JOURNAL OF OBSTETRICS AND GYNECOLOGY 154(1):14-20, January 1986.

Equine abortion and chloral hydrate [letter], by W. E. Allen. VETERINARY RECORD 118(14):407, April 5, 1986.

Evaluation of chromosomal damage in males exposed to Agent Orange and their families, by C. I. Kaye, et al. JOURNAL OF CRANIOFACIAL GENETICS AND DEVELOPMENTAL BIOLOGY 1:259-265, 1985.

ABORTION—CHEMICALLY INDUCED (continued)

Exposure to anesthetic gases and reproductive outcome. A review of the epidemiologic literature, by T. N. Tannenbaum, et al. JOURNAL OF OCCUPA-
TIONAL MEDICINE 27(9):659-668, September 1985.

On the embryotoxic effects of benzene and its alkyl derivatives in mice, rats and
rabbits, by G. Ungváry, et al. ARCHIVES OF TOXICOLOGY 8:425-430, 1985.

Possible dioxin poisoning in cattle, by F. G. Davies, et al. VETERINARY RECORD
117(9):207, August 31, 1985.

Reconception of mares following termination of pregnancy with prostaglandin
F2 alpha before and after day 35 of pregnancy, by B. L. Penzhorn, et al.
EQUINE VETERINARY JOURNAL 18(3):215-217, May 1986.

Reproductive toxicity of ovulation induction, by A. R. Scialli. FERTILITY AND
STERILITY 45(3):315-323, March 1986.

Spontaneous abortions among women employed in the plastics industry, by M.
L. Lindbohm, et al. AMERICAN JOURNAL OF INDUSTRIAL MEDICINE
8(6):579-586, 1985.

Treatment of women who have undergone chemically induced abortions, by M.
S. Burnhill. JOURNAL OF REPRODUCTIVE MEDICINE 30(8):610-614,
August 1985.

Vaginal spermicides and spontaneous abortion of known karyotype, by B. Strobino, et al. AMERICAN JOURNAL OF EPIDEMIOLOGY 123(3):431-443,
March 1986.

ABORTION—COMPLICATIONS
Abortion before first live birth and risk of breast cancer, by O. C. Hadjimichael, et
al. BRITISH JOURNAL OF CANCER 53(2):281-284, February 1986.

Acute endometritis and salpino-oophoritis following an artifical abortion, by A. P.
Kiriushchenkov. FEL'DSHER I AKUSHERKA 50(7):58-61, July 1985.

Influence of pregnancy, birth and abortion on the evolution of systemic lupus
erythematosus, by S. Mitu, et al. MEDECINE INTERNE 24(1):55-60, January-
March 1986.

Low birth weight in pregnancies following induced abortion: no evidence for an
association, by M. B. Bracken, et al. AMERICAN JOURNAL OF EPIDEMI-
OLOGY 123(4):604-613, April 1986.

ABORTION—CRIMINAL
Cluster of abortion deaths at a single facility, by M. E. Kafrissen, et al. OBSTET-
RICS AND GYNECOLOGY 68(3):387-389, September 1986.

Illegal abortion: an attempt to assess its cost to the health services and its incidence in the community, by I. Figà-Talamanca, et al. INTERNATIONAL
JOURNAL OF HEALTH SERVICES 16(3):375-389, 1986.

Incidence of major abdominal surgery after septic abortion—an indicator of complications due to illegal abortion, by A. Richards, et al. SOUTH AFRICAN
MEDICAL JOURNAL 68(11):799-800, November 23, 1985.

Offering an alternative to illegal abortion in Nigeria, by T. O. Odejide. NEW ERA
NURSING IMAGE INTERNATIONAL 2(2):39-42, 1986.

ABORTION—CRIMINAL (continued)

Role of abortion in control of global population growth, by S. D. Mumford, et al. CLINICAL OBSTETRICS AND GYNAECOLOGY 13(1):19-31, March 1986.

ABORTION—DIAGNOSIS
Human pregnancy failure [letter], by T. Lind, et al. LANCET 1(8472):91-92, January 11, 1986.

ABORTION—ETHICS
See: Abortion—Attitudes

ABORTION—ETIOLOGY
Abortion and perinatal sepsis associated with campylobacter infection, by A. E. Simor, et al. REVIEWS OF INFECTIOUS DISEASES 8(3):397-402, May-June 1986.

Abortion of twins following chloral hydrate anesthesia in a mare, by J. U. Akpokodje, et al. VETERINARY RECORD 118(11):306, March 15, 1986.

Abortions that fail, by A. M. Kaunitz, et al. OBSTETRICS AND GYNECOLOGY 66(4):533-537, October 1985.

Analysis of abortions, by A. Sziachta, et al. WIADOMOSCI LEKARSKIE 38(15): 1055-1059, August 1, 1985.

Association of endometriosis and spontaneous abortion: effect of control group selection, by D. A. Metzger, et al. FERTILITY AND STERILITY 45(1):18-22, January 1986.

Chorioamniotic infections following diagnostic amniocentesis in the second trimester, by U. Siekmann, et al. ZEITSCHRIFT FUR GEBURTSCHILFE UND PERINATOLOGIE 189(3):119-124, May-June 1985.

Chromosomal factors in repeated foetal loss, by L. Singhania, et al. JOURNAL OF THE INDIAN MEDICAL ASSOCIATION 83(5):168-169, May 1985.

Collagen synthesis in the cells obtained from speciments of human spontaneous abortion with abnormal chromosomes, by V. I. Kukharenko, et al. AKUSHER-STVO I GINEKOLOGIIA (6):63-64, June 1986.

Conference at the Salpêtriére, October 1984. Cerebral infarction, abortions and presence of circulating anticoagulant, by G. Herreman, et al. REVUE NEU-ROLOGIQUE 141(12):822-826, 1985.

Congenital spirochetosis in calves: association with epizootic bovine abortion, by J. W. Osebold, et al. JOURNAL OF THE AMERICAN VETERINARY MEDI-CAL ASSOCIATION 188(4):371-376, February 15, 1986.

Demonstration in Hungary of Q fever associated with abortion in cattle and sheep, by M. Rády, et al. ACTA VETERINARIA HUNGARICA 33(3-4):169-176, 1985.

Effects of cesarean section on fertility and abortions, by E. Hemminki. JOURNAL OF REPRODUCTIVE MEDICINE 31(7):620-624, July 1986.

Epizootiologic investigations on a sheep farm with toxoplasma gondii-induced abortions, by J. P. Dubey, et al. JOURNAL OF THE AMERICAN VETERI-NARY MEDICAL ASSOCIATION 188(2):155-158, January 15, 1986.

ABORTION—ETIOLOGY (continued)

Etiologic factors in habitual spontaneous abortions in the first pregnancy trimester, by O. Sadovsky, et al. BRATISLAVSKE LEKARSKE LISTY 85(1):90-96, January 1986.

Fetal death in early pregnancy due to electric current, by R. Jaffe, et al. ACTA OBSTETRICIA ET GYNECOLOGICA SCANDINAVICA 65(3):283, 1986.

Formation of amniotic bands as a result of early rupture of the amniotic sac, by K. Csécsei, et al. MORPHOLOGIAI ES IGAZSAGUGYI ORVOSI SZEMLE 26(2): 119-122, April 1986.

Frequency of infertility and abortion in cows infected with tritrichomonas foetus var. brisbane, by B. L. Clark, et al. AUSTRALIAN VETERINARY JOURNAL 63(1):31-32, January 1986.

Glycemic control and spontaneous abortion in insulin-dependent diabetic women, by M. Miodovnik, et al. OBSTETRICS AND GYNECOLOGY 68(3):366-369, September 1986.

Induced abortion and the chromosomal characteristics of subsequent miscarriages (spontaneous abortion), by J. Kline, et al. AMERICAN JOURNAL OF EPIDEMIOLOGY 123(6):1066-1079, June 1986.

Lupus anticoagulant: a place for pre-pregnancy treatment? [letter], by R. G. Farquharson, et al. LANCET 2(8459):842-843, October 12, 1985.

Lupus anticoagulant, thrombosis, and fetal loss [editorial], by D. I. Feinstein. NEW ENGLAND JOURNAL OF MEDICINE 313(21):1348-1350, November 21, 1985.

Luteal phase defects in repeated abortion, by J. A. Vanrell, et al. INTERNATIONAL JOURNAL OF GYNAECOLOGY AND OBSTETRICS 24(2):111-115, April 1986.

Methodology of epidemiological studies of the problems of perinatal medicine, by S. I. Sleptsova. AKUSHERSTVO I GINEKOLOGIIA (6):9-13, June 1986.

Miscarriage and its implications, by A. Oakely. MIDWIFE, HEALTH VISITOR AND COMMUNITY NURSE 22(4):123-124+, April 1986.

Müllerian abnormalities in fertile women and recurrent aborters, by J. A. Portuondo, et al. JOURNAL OF REPRODUCTIVE MEDICINE 31(7):616-619, July 1986.

Nature and significance of spontaneous abortions, by E. Engel, et al. SCHWEIZERISCHE RUNDSCHAU FUR MEDIZIN PRAXIS 74(12):304-309, March 19, 1985.

Pathomorphology and genetics in early pregnancy, by H. Göcke, et al. PATHOLOGE 6(5):249-259, September 1985.

Pregnant women and chlamydia infection [letter], by R. G. Eddy, et al. VETERINARY RECORD 118(18):519, May 3, 1986.

Prolonged hypoparathyroidism presenting eventually as second trimester abortion, by R. Eastell, et al. BRITISH MEDICAL JOURNAL 291(6500):955-956, October 5, 1985.

Randomised controlled trial of genetic amniocentesis in 4606 low-risk women, by A. Tabor, et al. LANCET 1(8493):1287-1293, June 7, 1986.

Relation between various characteristics of the semen and the occurrence of conception and unfavorable outcome of pregnancy in women with menstrual cycle disorders, by A. Krzeminski, et al. WIADOMOSCI LEKARSKIE 38(18): 1283-1289, September 15, 1985.

Relationship between abortion in the first pregnancy and development of pregnancy-induced hypertension in the subsequent pregnancy, by D. M. Strickland, et al. AMERICAN JOURNAL OF OBSTETRICS AND GYNECOLOGY 154(1):146-148, January 1986.

Risk of late first and second trimester miscarriage after induced abortion, by M. B. Bracken, et al. AMERICAN JOURNAL OF PERINATOLOGY 3(2):84-91, April 1986.

Role of hormonal disorders in the pathogenesis of abortion, by G. R. Rakhmatuilaeva. PROBLEMY ENDOKRINOLOGII I GORMONOTERAPII 32(1):77-81, January-February 1986.

Safety of chorionic villus sampling [letter], by M. J. Keirse, et al. LANCET 2(8467):1312, December 7, 1985.

Serodiagnosis of toxoplasma gondii in habitually aborting women and other adults from North Jordan, by S. K. Abdel-Hafez, et al. FOLIA PARASITOLOGICA 33(1):7-13, 1986.

Spontaneous abortion after amniocentesis in women with a history of spontaneous abortion, by S. M. Esrig, et al. PRENATAL DIAGNOSIS 5(5):321-328, September-October 1985.

Spontaneous abortion and interpregnancy interval, by C. C. Hebert, et al. EUROPEAN JOURNAL OF OBSTETRICS, GYNECOLOGY AND REPRODUCTIVE BIOLOGY 22(3):125-132, July 1986.

Striking association between lupus anticoagulant and fetal loss in systemic lupus erythematosus patients [letter], by R. H. Derksen, et al. ARTHRITIS AND RHEUMATISM 29(5):695-696, May 1986.

Thrombosis, recurrent abortions and intrauterine foetal death in a patient with lupus anticoagulant, by L. Altomonte, et al. CLINICAL RHEUMATOLOGY 4(4):455-457, December 1985.

Transferrin and infertility: genetic-clinical study. Preliminary note, by G. Del Porto, et al. MINERVA GINECOLOGIA 37(12):731-734, December 1985.

Typhoid fever complicating pregnancy, by R. Amster, et al. ACTA OBSTETRICIA ET GYNECOLOGICA SCANDINAVICA 64(8):685-686, 1985.

Uterine myoma initiating a spontaneous abortion, by A. P. Kiriushchenkov. FEL'DSHER I AKUSHERKA 50(11):50-54, November 1985.

"Villi test", safe, rapid and reliable. NEDERLANDS TIJDSCHRIFT VOOR GENEESKUNDE 130(1):36-37, January 4, 1986.

Zinc deficiency is not a cause for abortion, congenital abnormality and small-for-gestational age infant in Chinese women, by A. Ghosh, et al. BRITISH JOUR-

ABORTION—ETIOLOGY (continued)

NAL OF OBSTETRICS AND GYNAECOLOGY 92(9):886-891, September 1985.

ABORTION—FAILED
Liability of the physician in a legal but failed abortion for social reasons, by G. H. Schlund. GEBURTSHILFE UND FRAUENHEILKUNDE 45(9):674-676, September 1985.

Pricing the "burden" of a child: a mother gets $10,000 after a failed abortion saves twins she now loves, by D. Philip. ALBERTA REPORT 13:41-42, July 14, 1986.

Virginia mothers can sue doctors in failed abortions. JET 70:7, May 19, 1986.

ABORTION—HABITUAL
Antibody responses in secondary aborting women: effect of inhibitors in blood, by J. A. McIntyre, et al. AMERICAN JOURNAL OF REPRODUCTIVE IMMUNOLOGY AND MICROBIOLOGY 9(4):113-118, December 1985.

Cerebral infarction, lupus anticoagulant, and habitual abortion [letter], by J. S. Greenspoon. JAMA 255(16):2164, April 25, 1986.

Changes in the serum concentrations of the alpha and beta fractions of chorionic gonadotropin in women with habitual abortions and skin grafts, by Ts. Despodova, et al. AKUSHERSTVO I GINEKOLOGIIA 25(2):48-54, 1986.

Changes in the serum levels of alpha fetoproteins during pregnancy in women with habitual abortions and skin grafts, by Ts. Espodova, et al. AKUSHERSTVO I GINEKOLOGIIA 25(1):19-26, 1986.

Characteristics of the endometrial estrogen-receptor system in women with habitual abortion and uterine hypoplasia, by N. D. Fanchenko, et al. AKUSHERSTVO I GINEKOLOGIIA (10):56-57, October 1985.

Characteristics of women with recurrent spontaneous abortions and women with favorable reproductive histories, by B. Strobino, et al. AMERICAN JOURNAL OF PUBLIC HEALTH 76(8):986-991, August 1986.

Chromosomal factors in repeated foetal loss, by L. Singhania, et al. JOURNAL OF THE INDIAN MEDICAL ASSOCIATION 83(5):168-169, May 1985.

Chromosome abnormalities in couples with habitual spontaneous abortions, by L. Zergollern, et al. ACTA MEDICA IUGOSLAVICA 39(3):147-170, 1985.

Circulating antisperm antibodies in recurrently aborting women, by G. G. Haas, Jr., et al. FERTILITY AND STERILITY 45(2):209-215, February 1986.

Clinical value of research in chronic spontaneous abortion, by J. A. McIntyre, et al. AMERICAN JOURNAL OF REPRODUCTIVE IMMUNOLOGY AND MICROBIOLOGY 10(3):121-126, March 1986.

Complex balanced translation [letter], by G. Del Porto, et al. MINERVA GINECOLOGIA 38(1-2):101-102, January-February 1986.

Computer model for the study of segregation in reciprocal translocation carriers: application to 20 new cases, by M. A. De Arce, et al. AMERICAN JOURNAL OF MEDICAL GENETICS 24(3):519-525, July 1986.

ABORTION—HABITUAL (continued)

Conference at the Salpêtriére, October 1984. Cerebral infarction, abortions and presence of circulating anticoagulant, by G. Herreman, et al. REVUE NEU-ROLOGIQUE 141(12):822-826, 1985.

Cytogenetic aspects of habitual abortion, by G. Del Porto, et al. MINERVA GINECOLOGIA 38(3):119-125, March 1986.

Dermatoglyphic findings in families with spontaneous abortions, by M. Kuklík, et al. CASOPIS LEKARU CESKYCH 125(8):240-244, February 21, 1986.

Etiologic factors in habitual spontaneous abortions in the first pregnancy trimester, by O. Sadovsky, et al. BRATISLAVSKE LEKARSKE LISTY 85(1):90-96, January 1986.

Familial complex autosomal translocations involving chromosomes 7, 8, and 9 exhibiting male and female transmission with segregation and recombination, by S. Walker, et al. JOURNAL OF MEDICAL GENETICS 22(6):484-491, December 1985.

Genetic and clinical study of a family with abnormal hemoglobin Hb D Punjab 121 beta Glu—Gln, by IuE. Dubrova, et al. GENETIKA 21(11):1918-1920, November 1985.

Histocompatibility in Italian couples with recurrent spontaneous abortions of unknown origin and with normal fertility, by M. Vanoli, et al. TISSUE ANTIGENS 26(4):227-233, October 1985.

Histomorphological, histoenzymatic and ultrastructural changes in the placenta in pregnant women with habitual abortions and skin grafts, by Ts. Despodova, et al. AKUSHERSTVO I GINEKOLOGIIA 25(1):15-19, 1986.

HLA system and habitual spontaneous abortions, by E. Persitz, et al. HARE-FUAH 110(1):33-36, January 1, 1986.

Immunoglobulins in the serum of pregnant women with habitual abortions and skin grafts, by Ts. Despodova, et al. AKUSHERSTVO I GINEKOLOGIIA 25(3):13-19, 1986.

Immunologic indices in habitual abortion, by G. G. Dzhvebenava, et al. AKU-SHERSTVO I GINEKOLOGIIA (1):41-43, January 1986.

Immunological disorders of coagulation in habitual abortion. Prospective study, by P. Edelman, et al. PRESSE MEDICALE 15(21):961-964, May 24, 1986.

Importance of the marriage structure in predicting abortion, by L. V. Antipenskaia, et al. GENETIKA 22(1):158-163, January 1986.

Indication status of chromosome analysis in the diagnostic evaluation of recurrent abortions, by M. Brackertz, et al. ZEITSCHRIFT FUR GEBURTSCHILFE UND PERINATOLOGIE 189(6):249-254, November-December 1985.

Inhibitors of complement-mediated cytotoxicity in normal and secondary aborters sera, by D. S. Torry, et al. AMERICAN JOURNAL OF REPRODUCTIVE IM-MUNOLOGY AND MICROBIOLOGY 10(2):53-57, February 1986.

Luteal phase defects in repeated abortion, by J. A. Vanrell, et al. INTERNA-TIONAL JOURNAL OF GYNAECOLOGY AND OBSTETRICS 24(2):111-115, April 1986.

Menarcheal age and habitual miscarriage: evidence for an association, by M. B. Bracken, et al. ANNALS OF HUMAN BIOLOGY 12(6):525-531, November-December 1985.

Nature and significance of spontaneous abortions, by E. Engel, et al. SCHWEI-ZERISCHE RUNDSCHAU FUR MEDIZIN PRAXIS 74(12):304-309, March 19, 1985.

New horizons in the diagnosis, evaluation and therapy of recurrent spontaneous abortion, by A. E. Beer. CLINICAL OBSTETRICS AND GYNAECOLOGY 13(1):115-124, March 1986.

Phenotypic and functional evaluation of suppressor cells in normal pregnancy and in chronic aborters, by T. M. Fiddes. CELLULAR IMMUNOLOGY 97(2): 407-418, February 1986.

Population-genetical study of differential fertility in human (based on an example of habitual abortion). I. Approach to the problem and analysis of morpho-physiological and demographic traits, by IuP. Altukhov, et al. GENETIKA 22(7):1207-1212, July 1986.

Population genetics study of the differential fertility in urban populations, by A. N. Kucher, et al. GENETIKA 22(2):304-311, February 1986.

Pregnancy wastage associated with paracentric inversion of chromosome 13, by B. G. Bateman, et al. JOURNAL OF MEDICAL GENETICS 23(4):370, August 1986.

Primary chronic abortion, preeclampsia, idiopathic intrauterine growth retardation, hydatidiform mole, and choriocarcinoma: a unifying concept, by C. A. La-barrere, et al. AMERICAN JOURNAL OF REPRODUCTIVE IMMUNOLOGY AND MICROBIOLOGY 10(4):156-157, April 1986.

Recurrent abortion with lupus anticoagulant,and pre-eclampsia: a common final pathway for two different diseases? Case report, by G. Gregorini, et al. BRITISH JOURNAL OF OBSTETRICS AND GYNAECOLOGY 93(2):194-196, February 1986.

Recurrent pregnancy losses and parental chromosome abnormalities [review], by A. T. Tharapel, et al. BRITISH JOURNAL OF OBSTETRIC AND GYNAE-COLOGY 92(9):899-914, September 1985.

Repeated abortion associated with a lupus-type circulating anticoagulant [letter], by I. Arribas Gómez, et al. SANGRE 31(3):369-370, 1986.

Reproductive risk of paracentric inversion carriers: report of two unrelated cases with paracentric inversion of the long arm of chromosome 3, by R. Kasai, et al. JINRUI IDENGAKU ZASSHI 30(2):57-67, June 1985.

Resectoscopic management of müllerian fusion defects, by A. H. DeCherney, et al. FERTILITY AND STERILITY 45(5):726-728, May 1986.

Role of chromosome aberrations in recurrent abortion: a study of 269 balanced translocations, by M. Campana, et al. AMERICAN JOURNAL OF MEDICAL GENETICS 24(2):341-356, June 1986.

ABORTION—HABITUAL (continued)

Self concept of women with negative obstetrical histories and after gynecological operations for neoplasma, by E. Michalek, et al. GINEKOLOGIA POLSKA 56(11):691-698, November 1985.

Serodiagnosis of toxoplasma gondii in habitually aborting women and other adults from North Jordan, by S. K. Abdel-Hafez, et al. FOLIA PARASITOL-OGICA 33(1):7-13, 1986.

Spontaneous abortion after amniocentesis in women with a history of spontaneous abortion, by S. M. Esrig, et al. PRENATAL DIAGNOSIS 5(5):321-328, September-October 1985.

Spontaneous recurrent fetal wastage and autoimmune abnormalities: a study of fourteen cases, by J. P. Clauvel, et al. CLINICAL IMMUNOLOGY AND IM-MUNOPATHOLOGY 39(3):523-530, June 1986.

Transferrin and infertility: genetic-clinical study. Preliminary note, by G. Del Porto, et al. MINERVA GINECOLOGIA 37(12):731-734, December 1985.

Translocation mosaicism in a woman having multiple miscarriages, by L. J. Sciorra, et al. AMERICAN JOURNAL OF MEDICAL GENETICS 22(3):615-617, November 1985.

Unusual translocation 46,XX,t(14;17)(q33.2;p11,2) in a woman with recurrent spontaneous abortions, by E. Calzolari, et al. HUMAN GENETICS 71(2):181, 1985.

XY translocation in a woman with dyschondrosteosis and sterility, by R. Youlton, et al. REVISTA MEDICA DE CHILE 113(3):228-230, March 1985.

ABORTION—HABITUAL—COMPLICATIONS
Anticardiolipin syndrome, by G. R. Hughes, et al. JOURNAL OF RHEUMA-TOLOGY 13(3):486-489, June 1986.

IgM gammopathy and the lupus anticoagulant syndrome in habitual aborters [letter], by G. Finazzi, et al. JAMA 255(1):39, January 3, 1986.

Prostacyclin deficiency in a young woman with recurrent thrombosis, by J. G. Lanham, et al. BRITISH MEDICAL JOURNAL 292(6518):435-436, February 15, 1986.

ABORTION—HABITUAL—PREVENTION AND CONTROL
Prevention of habitual abortion by buffycoat transfusions, by H. Neumeyer, et al. ZEITSCHRIFT FUR GEBURTSCHILFE UND PERINATOLOGIE 189(5):197-201, September-October 1985.

Thrombocythaemia and recurrent late abortions: normal outcome of pregnancies after antiaggregatory treatment . Case report, by W. Snethlage, et al. BRIT-ISH JOURNAL OF OBSTETRICS AND GYNAECOLOGY 93(4):386-388, April 1986.

ABORTION—HABITUAL—TREATMENT
Blood transfusions for recurrent abortion: is the treatment worse than the disease? [letter], by J. A. Hill, et al. FERTILITY AND STERILITY 46(1):152-154, July 1986.

ABORTION—HABITUAL—TREATMENT (continued)

Blood transfusions generate/increase previously absent/weak blocking antibody in women with habitual abortion, by A. M. Unander, et al. FERTILITY AND STERILITY 44(6):766-771, December 1985.

Hypothesis: blocking factors and human pregnancy: an alternative explanation for the success of lymphocyte transfusion therapy in abortion-prone women, by M. Davies. AMERICAN JOURNAL OF REPRODUCTIVE IMMUNOLOGY AND MICROBIOLOGY 10(2):58-63, February 1986.

Idiopathic habitual abortions (role of immunity), by M. F. Reznikoff-Etievant, et al. BULLETIN DE L'ACADEMIE NATIONALE DE MEDECINE 170(1):23-31, Janaury 1986.

Immunologic testing and immunotherapy in recurrent spontaneous abortion, by J. A. McIntyre, et al. OBSTETRICS AND GYNECOLOGY 67(2):169-175, February 1986.

Immunotherapy of habitual abortion, by Y. Yagami. KANGO GIJUTSU 31(11): 1505-1506, August 1985.

Laboratory and clinical aspects of research in chronic spontaneous abortion, by J. A. McIntyre, et al. DIAGNOSTIC IMMUNOLOGY 3(4):163-170, 1985.

New horizons in the diagnosis, evaluation and therapy of recurrent spontaneous abortion, by A. E. Beer. CLINICAL OBSTETRICS AND GYNAECOLOGY 13(1):115-124, March 1986.

Our experience in treating habitual abortions by skin grafts, by Ts. Despodova. AKUSHERSTVO I GINEKOLOGIIA 25(2):42-48, 1986.

Production of blocking antibodies by vaccination with husband's lymphocytes in unexplained recurrent aborters: the role in successful pregnancy, by K. Takakuwa, et al. AMERICAN JOURNAL OF REPRODUCTIVE IMMUNOLOGY AND MICROBIOLOGY 10(1):1-9, January 1986.

Transfusions of leukocyte-rich erythrocyte concentrates: a successful treatment in selected cases of habitual abortion, by A. M. Unander, et al. AMERICAN JOURNAL OF OBSTETRICS AND GYNECOLOGY 154(3):516-520, March 1986.

Treatment of habitual abortion with human chorionic gonadotropin: results of open and placebo-controlled studies, by R. F. Harrison. EUROPEAN JOURNAL OF OBSTETRICS, GYNECOLOGY AND REPRODUCTIVE BIOLOGY 20(3):159-168, September 1985.

Use of ultrasound in the management of repeated abortions, by M. Mahran, et al. ULTRASOUND IN MEDICINE AND BIOLOGY (suppl 2):101-104, 1983.

ABORTION—HISTORY
Induced abortion: we could do better, by A. Valette. SOINS. GYNECOLOGIE, OBSTETRIQUE, PUERICULTURE, PEDIATRIE (55):31-47, December 1985.

"Secrets of generation display'd": *Aristole's master-piece* in 18th century England (sexual advice literature), by R. Porter. EIGHTEENTH CENTURY LIFE 9(3):1-21, May 1985.

ABORTION—INCOMPLETE
Glycemic control and spontaneous abortion in insulin-dependent diabetic wo-

ABORTION—INCOMPLETE (continued)

men, by M. Miodovnik, et al. OBSTETRICS AND GYNECOLOGY 68(3):366-369, September 1986.

Identification of chorion villi abortio specimens, by B. Lindahl, et al. OBSTETRICS AND GYNECOLOGY 67(1):79-81, January 1986.

Incomplete abortion: characteristics of the patients treated in the O'Horan Hospital of Mérida, Yúcatan, by T. E. Canto de Cetina, et al. SALUD PUBLICA DE MEXICO 27(6):507-513, November-December 1985.

Malimplantation caused by trophoblastic insufficiency resulting in failure of gestation following in vitro fertilization-embryo transfer, by L. Nebel, et al. CONTRIBUTIONS TO GYNECOLOGY AND OBSTETRICS 14:170-175, 1985.

Outcome of subsequent pregnancies following antibiotic therapy after primary or multiple spontaneous abortions, by A. Toth, et al. SURGERY, GYNECOLOGY AND OBSTETRICS 163(3):243-250, September 1986.

ABORTION—INCOMPLETE—COMPLICATIONS
Features of the status of the hemostatic system during post-abortion endometritis, by Z. A. Nakimova. AKUSHERSTVO I GINEKOLOGIIA (1):70-72, January 1986.

ABORTION—INCOMPLETE—DIAGNOSIS
Echographic monitoring of pathologic pregnancy in the first trimester: threatened abortion, by S. Donadio, et al. MINERVA GINECOLOGIA 37(9):475-477, September 1985.

Immunohistochemical demonstration of placental hormones in the diagnosis of uterine versus ectopic pregnancy, by E. Angel, et al. AMERICAN JOURNAL OF CLINICAL PATHOLOGY 84(6):705-709, December 1985.

Sonographic demonstration of post-abortion intrauterine osseous tissue, by P. Bourgouin, et al. JOURNAL OF ULTRASOUND IN MEDICINE 4(9):507-509, September 1985.

ABORTION—INDUCED
See also: Abortion—Chemically Induced

Abortion and the man. Psychological and psychopathological manifestations in the face of lost fatherhood, by P. Benvenuti, et al. RIVISTA DI PATOLOGIA NERVOSA E MENTALE 104(6):255-268, November-December 1983.

Abortion: an attitude study of professional staff at Ramathibodi Hospital, by W. Phuapradit, et al. JOURNAL OF THE MEDICAL ASSOCIATION OF THAILAND 69(1):22-27, January 1986.

Abortion attitudes and performance among male and female obstetrician-gynecologists, by C. S. Weisman, et al. FAMILY PLANNING PERSPEC-TIVES 18(2):67-73, March-April 1986.

Abortion counseling, by R. Kubota. CALIFORNIA NURSE 82(1):4-5, February 1986.

Abortion counselling—a new component of medical care, by U. Landy. CLINICAL OBSTETRICS AND GYNAECOLOGY 13(1):33-41, March 1986.

Abortion in the second trimester using carboprost tromethamine, by B. Beric, et al. JUGOSLOVENSKA GINEKOLGIA PERINATOLGI 25(5-6):103-109, September-December 1985.

Abortion: an issue that won't go away [letter]. CANADIAN MEDICAL ASSOCIA-TION JOURNAL 134(8):868-869+, April 15, 1986.

Abortion: the new debate, by D. Callahan. PRIMARY CARE 13(2):255-262, June 1986.

Abortion: the teenage patient and the OR nurse, by T. Howard. CANADIAN NURSE 81(10):28-30, November 1985.

Acts and omissions doctrine and abortion [letter], by P. D. Toon. JOURNAL OF MEDICAL ETHICS 11(4):217, December 1985.

Acute endometritis and salpino-oophoritis following an artifical abortion, by A. P. Kiriushchenkov. FEL'DSHER I AKUSHERKA 50(7):58-61, July 1985.

Adjustment to abortion in marital relations, by B. Wimmer-Puchinger. GYNA-KOLOGE 19(1):33-36, March 1986.

AFP and HbF determination in maternal blood as a parameter of fetomaternal microtransfusion in interventions of the pregnant uterus, by B. Alsheimer, et al. GEBURTSHILFE UND FRAUENHEILKUNDE 45(10):727-730, October 1985.

Analysis of nursing students' attitude toward bioethics (3). Attitude toward in-duced abortion, by O. Nakayama, et al. KANGO TENBO 11(5):492-497, April 1986.

Attempted conversion of twin to singleton pregnancy in two mares with asso-ciated changes in plasma oestrone sulphate concentrations, by J. H. Hyland, et al. AUSTRALIAN VETERINARY JOURNAL 62(12):406-409, December 1985.

Attitudes of mothers of children with Down syndrome concerning amniocentesis, abortion, and prenatal genetic counseling techniques, by T. E. Elkins, et al. OBSTETRICS AND GYNECOLOGY 68(2):181-184, August 1986.

Breed differences in return to estrus after PGF2 alpha-induced abortions in swine, by D. L. Meeker, et al. JOURNAL OF ANIMAL SCIENCE 61(2):354-357, August 1985.

Cervical dilatation with meteneprost vaginal suppositories in first trimester abor-tion, by C. Somell, et al. CONTRACEPTION 33(2):189-194, February 1986.

Cervical dilatation with prostaglandin F2 alpha for first trimester abortion, by P. K. Ntrajan, et al. SOUTHERN MEDICAL JOURNAL 79(7):830-831, July 1986.

Characteristics of women undergoing induced abortion: results of a case-control study from Northern Italy, by C. La Vecchia, et al. CONTRACEPTION 32(6): 637-649, December 1985.

Chorionic biopsy and increased anxiety [letter], by P. R. Wyatt. LANCET 2(8467): 1312-1313, December 7, 1985.

ABORTION—INDUCED (continued)

Continuous extraovular prostaglandin F2 alpha instillation for second-trimester pregnancy termination, by J. Atad, et al. ISRAEL JOURNAL OF MEDICAL SCIENCES 21(12):935-939, December 1985.

Cross-cultural history of abortion, by R. N. Shain. CLINICAL OBSTETRICS AND GYNAECOLOGY 13(1):1-17, March 1986.

Dilemma of wrongful birth, wrongful life [interview by Bill Trent], by B. M. Dickens. CANADIAN MEDICAL ASSOCIATION JOURNAL 133(12):1238-1240, December 15, 1985.

Disappearance of human chorionic gonadotropin from plasma and urine following induced abortion, by B. van der Lugt, et al. ACTA OBSTETRICIA ET GYNECOLOGICA SCANDINAVICA 64(7):547-552, 1985.

Down syndrome and abortion [letter]. REVISTA PAULISTA DE MEDICINA 103(5):267-278, September-October 1985.

Early pregnancy interruption with a single PGF2 alpha 15-methyl-analogue vaginal suppository, by M. Borten, et al. JOURNAL OF REPRODUCTIVE MEDICINE 30(10):741-744, October 1985.

Ectopic pregnancy among early abortion patients: does prostaglandin reduce the incidence?, by M. Borten, et al. PROSTAGLANDINS 30(6):891-905, December 1985.

Effect of induced abortion on prematurity. Analysis of the period from 1979 to 1984, by J. Deutinger, et al. WIENER MEDIZINISCHE WOCHENSCHRIFT 135(13-14):329-332, July 31, 1985.

Effect of induced and spontaneous abortions on sex ratio and various characteristics of the female reproductive functions, by A. I. Taptunova, et al. AKUSHERSTVO I GINEKOLOGIIA (10):43-45, October 1985.

Enflurane for the voluntary interruption of pregnancy, by D. Safran, et al. CAHIERS D'ANESTHESIOLOGIE 33(7):603-605, November 1985.

Evaluation of blood loss during suction termination of pregnancy: ketamine compared with methohexitone, by N. R. Coad, et al. ACTA ANAESTHESIOLOGICA SCANDINAVICA 30(3):253-255, April 1986.

Expenditures for reproduction-related health care, by V. R. Fuchs, et al. JAMA 255(1):76-81, January 3, 1986.

Experimental studies on the antifertility properties of Arachniodes exilis, by G. Y. Yao. CHUNG YAO TUNG PAO 10(9):40-41, September 1985.

Features of the status of the hemostatic system during post-abortion endometritis, by Z. A. Nakimova. AKUSHERSTVO I GINEKOLOGIIA (1):70-72, January 1986.

Fetal rights. The first Belfast Royal Maternity Hospital Perinatal Lecture, by J. H. Pinkerton. ULSTER MEDICAL JOURNAL 54(1):30-40, April 1985.

Fetal tibia retained in uterine cavity for eight years after legal aboration, by H. J. Ingerslev, et al. ACTA OBSTETRICIA ET GYNECOLOGICA SCANDINAVICA 65(4):371-372, 1986.

Incidence of biological intravascular coagulation in legal induced abortions, by S. Boudaoud, et al. ANNALES FRANCAISES D'ANESTHESIE ET DE RE-ANIMATION 5(1):5-9, 1986.

Induced abortion and fertility, by T. Frejka. FAMILY PLANNING PERSPECTIVES 17(5):230-234, September-October 1985.

Induced abortion and risk of secondary infertility, by K. Dinto. DAI: B 47(2), August 1986.

Induced abortion in a rural area of Bangladesh, by A. R. Khan, et al. STUDIES IN FAMILY PLANNING 17(2):95-99, March-April 1986.

Induced abortion: reported and observed practice in Taiwan, by J. F. Wang. HEALTH CARE FOR WOMEN, INTERNATIONAL 6(5-6):383-404, 1985.

Induced abortion: we could do better, by A. Valette. SOINS. GYNECOLOGIE, OBSTETRIQUE, PUERICULTURE, PEDIATRIE (55):31-47, December 1985.

Induced abortions and births. Trends in seven counties, Norway, 1972-1983, by F. E. Skjeldestad. SCANDINAVIAN JOURNAL OF SOCIAL MEDICINE 14(2): 61-66, 1986.

Influence of different prostaglandin applications on cervical rheology, by L. Spätling, et al. INTERNATIONAL JOURNAL OF GYNAECOLOGY AND OBSTETRICS 23(5):369-376, October 1985.

Initial Dutch experiences with early pregnancy interruption using the antipro-gesterone agent mifepriston, by H. A. Vervest, et al. NEDERLANDS TIJDSCHRIFT VOOR GENEESKUNDE 129(35):1680-1683, August 31, 1985.

Intense emotional reactions with induced abortion, by C. Vivier. INFIRMIERE CANADIENNE 27(11):19, December 1985.

IUD insertion following induced abortion, by L. Querido, et al. CONTRACEPTION 31(6):603-610, June 1985.

Low birth weight in pregnancies following induced abortion: no evidence for an association, by M. B. Bracken, et al. AMERICAN JOURNAL OF EPIDEMI-OLOGY 123(4):604-613, April 1986.

Man: an axiological analysis from a Christian perspective, by R. Adams. ANPHI PAPERS 20(1-2):15-21, January-June 1985.

Maternal deaths associated with barbiturate anesthetics—New York City. MMWR 35(37):579-582+, September 19, 1986.

Maternal deaths related to abortions in Sweden, 1931-1980, by U. Högberg, et al. GYNECOLOGIC AND OBSTETRIC INVESTIGATION 20(4):169-178, 1985.

Mid-gestational abortion for medical or genetic indications, by W. F. Rayburn, et al. CLINICAL OBSTETRICS AND GYNAECOLOGY 13(10:71-82, March 1986.

Midtrimester abortion by intracervical prostaglandin E2, by S. Stampe Sørensen, et al. EUROPEAN JOURNAL OF OBSTETRICS, GYNECOLOGY AND RE-PRODUCTIVE BIOLOGY 21(3):165-171, March 1986.

Midtrimester abortion with Laminaria and vacuum evacuation on a teaching service, by A. M. Altman, et al. JOURNAL OF REPRODUCTIVE MEDICINE 30(8):601-606, August 1985.

Midtrimester artificial abortion using 16, 16-dimethyl-trans-delta 2-PGE1 methyl ester (Preglandin), laminaria tents and continuous epidural anesthesia, by I. Fuchi, et al. ASIA-OCEANIA JOURNAL OF OBSTETRICS AND GYNAE-COLOGY 11(3):377-385, September 1985.

Miscarriage or abortion [letter], by R. W. Beard, et al. LANCET 2(8464):1122-1123, November 16, 1985.

Occurrence of molar pregnancy in patients undergoing elective abortion: comparison with other clinical presentations, by B. H. Yuen, et al. AMERICAN JOURNAL OF OBSTETRICS AND GYNECOLOGY 154(2):273-276, February 1986.

Outpatient termination of pregnancy: halothane or alfentanil-supplemented anaesthesia, by K. M. Collins, et al. BRITISH JOURNAL OF ANAESTHESIA 57(12):1226-1231, December 1985.

Partial termination of a quintuplet pregnancy, by P.Lopes, et al. ZEITSCHRIFT FUR GEBURTSCHILFE UND PERINATOLOGIE 189(5):239-240, September-October 1985.

Perceived credibility of a "neutral" abortion-related message and its sponsor, by M. Spadafora, et al. JOURNAL OF PSYCHOLOGY 120(2):137-141, March 1986.

Portrait of American women who obtain abortions, by S. K. Henshaw, et al. FAMILY PLANNING PERSPECTIVES 17(2):90-96, March-April 1985.

Possibilities of general anesthesia in mini-abortion, by J. Posluch, et al. CESKO-SLOVENSKA GYNEKOLOGIE 51(6):427-429, July 1986.

Pregnancy and induced abortion among teenagers, by S. Tado. JOSANPU ZASSHI 39(11):1003, November 1985.

Pregnancy and unwanted children after failure of sterilization and voluntary termination of pregnancy. I. Disconcerting French and foreign jurisprudence, by J. H. Soutoul, et al. JOURNAL DE GYNECOLOGIE, OBSTETRIQUE ET BIOLOGIE DE LA REPRODUCTION 15(3):273-279, 1986.

Pregnancy interfering action of LHRH and anti-LHRH, by C. Das, et al. JOURNAL OF STEROID BIOCHEMISTRY 23(5B):803-806, November 1985.

Pregnancy termination: techniques, risks, and complications and their management, by R. G. Castadot. FERTILITY AND STERILITY 45(1):5-17, January 1986.

Pregnancy with a malformed fetus interrupted in the 22d week of gestation, by G. Zdravkovic, et al. SRPSKI ARHIV ZA CELOKUPNO LEKARSTVO 113(3): 259-264, March 1985.

ABORTION—INDUCED (continued)

Preliminary results with the antiprogestational compound RU-486 (mifepristone) for interruption of early pregnancy, by H. A. Vervest, et al. FERTILITY AND STERILITY 44(5):627-632, November 1985.

Preoperative cervical dilatation for first trimester induced abortion: comparison of two prostaglandin analogues, by W. T. Mao, et al. CONTRACEPTION 33(2): 195-201, February 1986.

Preoperative cervix dilatation in first trimester pregnancy interruption using 9-deoxy-16, 16-dimethyl-9-methylene prostaglandin E2. A randomized double-blind study, by D. Brügger, et al. GEBURTSHILFE UND FRAUEN-HEILKUNDE 45(8):567-569, August 1985.

Preoperative dilatation of the cervix uteri by vaginal application of 9-deoxo-16, 16-dimethyl-9-methylene PGE2 in pregnancy interruption during the first trimester. double-blind clinical study, by A. Friedli, et al. JOURNAL DE GYNE-COLOGIE, OBSTETRIQUE ET BIOLOGIE DE LA REPRODUCTION 15(2): 215-221, 1986.

Preparation of the cervix: hydrophilic and prostaglandin dilators, by P. D. Darney. CLINICAL OBSTETRICS AND GYNAECOLOGY 13(1):43-51, March 1986.

Prevention of infection with metronidazole in abortion induced by PFG2 alpha, by G. Koinzer, et al. ZENTRALBLATT FUR GYNAEKOLOGIE 108(3):163-166, 1986.

Progesterone receptor blockage. Effect on uterine contractility and early pregnancy, by M. Bygdeman, et al. CONTRACEPTION 32(1):45-51, July 1985.

Propofol ("Diprivan") infusion as main agent for day case surgery, by B. McLeod, et al. POSTGRADUATE MEDICAL JOURNAL (61 suppl 3):105-107, 1985.

Psychiatric admissions and choice of abortion, by P. K. Andersen, et al. STATISTICS IN MEDICINE 5(3):243-253, May-June 1986.

Psychiatric aspects of pregnancy termination, by A. Lazarus, et al. CLINICAL OBSTETRICS AND GYNAECOLOGY 13(1):125-134, March 1986.

Psychological factors related to post-abortion "subtle" contraceptive unreliability, by P. Lehtinen, et al. SCANDINAVIAN JOURNAL OF PSYCHOLOGY 26(3): 277-284, 1985.

Psychological sequelae of abortion based on fetal indications, by A. von Gontard. MONATSSCHRIFT FUR KINDERHEILKUNDE 134(3):150-157, March 1986.

Psychoreactivity in voluntary abortion, by M. P. Graziani. MINERVA PSICHI-ATRICA 26(2):193-200, April-June 1985.

Regulation of fertility in Belgrade, by M. Husar, et al. SRPSKI ARHIV ZA CELOKUPNO LEKARSTVO 113(7):601-609, July 1985.

Right to life?. KATILOLEHTI 91(1):18-23, February 1986.

Right to live with pain, by L. Morin. INFIRMIERE CANADIENNE 27(11):17-18, December 1985.

Risk factors for resuction with postabortal syndrome in first trimester induced abortion, by S. W. Bagley. DAI: B 47(2), August 1986.

Safety of local versus general anesthesia for second-trimester dilatation and evacuation abortion, by H. T. MacKay, et al. OBSTETRICS AND GYNE-COLOGY 66(5):661-665, November 1985.

Selective termination in quintuplet pregnancy during first trimester [letter], by H. H. Kanhai, et al. LANCET 1(8495):1447, June 21, 1986.

Single abortion—multiple abortions, a comparison, by P. Goebel. PSYCHO-THERAPIE, PSYCHOSOMATIK, MEDIZINISCHE PSYCHOLOGIE 36(2):83-88, February 1986.

Status of the kallikrein-kinin system of the blood and level of endogenous prostaglandins after interruption of pregnancy during the second trimester using intra-amniotic administration of a hypertonic sodium chloride solution, by A. P. Nikonov. AKUSHERSTVO I GINEKOLOGIIA (1):60-62, January 1986.

Study of the mechanism of ONO-802 in the termination of early pregnancy by B model sonar monitoring, by L. L. Luo. CHUNG HUA FU CHAN KO TSA CHIH 20(4):240-242+, July 1985.

Surgical techniques of uterine evacuation in first- and second-trimester abortion, by P. G. Stubblefield. CLINICAL OBSTETRICS AND GYNAECOLOGY 13(1):53-70, March 1986.

Termination of pregnancy. CLINICAL OBSTETRICS AND GYNAECOLOGY 13(1):1-160, March 1986.

Termination of pregnancy in the second trimester by the modified Manstein method, by J. Tomásek, et al. CESKOSLOVENSKA GYNEKOLOGIE 51(3):141-146, April 1986.

Trends in induced legal abortion morbidity and mortality, by N. J. Binkin. I CLINICAL OBSTETRICS AND GYNAECOLOGY 13(1):83-93, March 1986.

Trends in public attitudes toward legal abortion, 1972-1978, by S. A. Moldanado. RESEARCH IN NURSING AND HEALTH 8(3):219-225, September 1985.

Unplanned pregnancy, by J. Nuthall. NEW ZEALAND NURSING JOURNAL 79(7):11-15, July 1986.

Upholding the sanctity of life [letter]. CANADIAN MEDICAL ASSOCIATION JOURNAL 134(8):866+, April 15, 1986.

Use of an emulsion formulation of propofol ("Diprivan") in intravenous anaesthesia for termination of pregnancy. A comparison with methohexitone, by J. M. Cundy, et al. POSTGRADUATE MEDICAL JOURNAL (61 suppl 3):129-131, 1985.

Vacuum-aspiration of uterine contents after a missed menstrual period, by I. M. Bloshanskii, et al. AKUSHERSTVO I GINEKOLOGIIA (7):55-58, July 1985.

Value of premedication and a preoperative informative talk, by B. Ek, et al. LAKARTIDNINGEN 82(38):3153-3155, September 18, 1985.

Why me? Second trimester abortion, by A. Neidhardt. AMERICAN JOURNAL OF NURSING 86(10):1133-1135, October 1986.

ABORTION—INDUCED (continued)

Women and abortion: attitudes, social networks, decision-making, by G. Faria, et al. SOCIAL WORK IN HEALTH CARE 11(1):85-96, Fall 1985.

Your hands: lethal or life saving?, by M. James. NURSING JOURNAL OF INDIA 77(8):213, August 1986.

ABORTION—INDUCED—COMPLICATIONS

Accidental intra-myometrial injection of hypertonic saline, by S. V. Parulekar, et al. JOURNAL OF POSTGRADUATE MEDICINE 32(1):51-53, January 1986.

Choriocarcinoma following M.T.P., by A. Sen Gupta, et al. JOURNAL OF THE INDIAN MEDICAL ASSOCIATION 82(7):255-256, July 1984.

Comparison of complication rates in first trimester abortions performed by physician assistants and physicians, by M. A. Freedman, et al. AMERICAN JOURNAL OF PUBLIC HEALTH 76(5):550-556, May 1986.

Does the hygroscopic property of the laminaria tent imply a risk for ascending infection in legal abortions? A microbiological study, by G. R. Evaldson, et al. ACTA OBSTETRICIA ET GYNECOLOGICA SCANDINAVICA 65(3):257-261, 1986.

Effects of artifical abortion, by U. Dudziak. PIELEGNIARKA I POLOZNA (9):5-6, 1985.

Effects of mid-trimester induced abortion on the subsequent pregnancy, by M. J. Seller, et al. PRENATAL DIAGNOSIS 5(6):375-380, November-December 1985.

Impact of abortion on subsequent fecundity, by C. J. Hogue. CLINICAL OBSTETRICS AND GYNAECOLOGY 13(1):95-103, March 1986.

Induced abortion and the chromosomal characteristics of subsequent miscarriages (spontaneous abortion), by J. Kline, et al. AMERICAN JOURNAL OF EPIDEMIOLOGY 123(6):1066-1079, June 1986.

Intestinal injuries following induced abortion, by D. A. Imoedemhe, et al. INTERNATIONAL JOURNAL OF GYNAECOLOGY AND OBSTETRICS 22(4):303-306, August 1984.

Prevention and treatment of DIC complicating Wirstroemia chamaedaphen Meisn. administration for mid-term labor induction, by G. S. Fan, et al. CHUNG KUO I HSUEH KO HSUEH YUAM HSUEH PAO 6(6):443-445, December 1984.

Rare late complication of first trimester induced abortion requiring hysterectomy-subinvolution of the placental bed [case report], by E. T. Lee, et al. BRITISH JOURNAL OF OBSTETRICS AND GYNAECOLOGY 93(7):777-781, July 1986.

Risk managment in pregnancy termination, by M. S. Burnhill. CLINICAL OBSTETRICS AND GYNAECOLOGY 13(1):145-156, March 1986.

Risk of late first and second trimester miscarriage after induced abortion, by M. B. Bracken, et al. AMERICAN JOURNAL OF PERINATOLOGY 3(2):84-91, April 1986.

ABORTION—INDUCED—COMPLICATIONS (continued)

Risks of preterm delivery and small-for-gestational age infants following abortion: a population study, by R. M. Pickering, et al. BRITISH JOURNAL OF OBSTETRICS AND GYNAECOLOGY 92(11):1106-1112, November 1985.

Sequelae of induced first-trimester abortion. A prospective study assessing the role of postabortal pelvic inflammatory disease and prophylactic antibiotics, by L. Heisterberg, et al. AMERICAN JOURNAL OF OBSTETRICS AND GYNECOLOGY 155(1):76-80, July 1986.

Study of traumatic amenorrhea and ovarian function, by Z. L. Wu, et al. SSU-CHUAN I HSUEH YUAN HSUEH PAO 16(4):347-350, December 1985.

Treatment of women who have undergone chemically induced abortions, by M. S. Burnhill. JOURNAL OF REPRODUCTIVE MEDICINE 30(8):610-614, August 1985.

Ultrasonic scanning after the legal termination of pregnancy with complications, by H. Refn. UGESKRIFT FOR LAEGER 148(22):1341-1342, May 26, 1986.

Uterine rupture following intramuscular injection of Carboprost in midtrimester pregnancy termination [letter], by S. N. Tripathy. JOURNAL OF THE INDIAN MEDICAL ASSOCIATION 83(9):328, September 1985.

ABORTION—INDUCED—FAILED
Pregnancy proceeding to term following failed induced abortion, by H. J. Doppenberg, et al. NEDERLANDS TIJDSCHRIFT VOOR GENEESKUNDE 130(25):1158-1160, June 21, 1986.

ABORTION—LAWS AND LEGISLATION
Abortion. CRIMINAL LAW REPORTER: OPINIONS OF THE UNITED STATES SUPREME COURT 39(5):3054-3061, April 30, 1986; 39(11):3137-3160, June 11, 1986; also in JOURNAL OF FAMILY LAW 24(4):699-706, June 1986.

—[case notes]. JOURNAL OF FAMILY LAW 23(4):619-625, 1984-1985; 24(1): 73-84, 1985-1986.

Abortion according to paragraph 218ff. of the German penal code and life support of premature infants from the viewpoint of the pediatrician, by H. von Voss. MONATSSCHRIFT FUR KINDERHEILKUNDE 134(5):232-239, May 1986.

Abortion and the Supreme Court: why legislative motive matters, by L. H. Glantz. AMERICAN JOURNAL OF PUBLIC HEALTH 76:1452-1455, December 1986.

Abortion controversy (Alberta doctors protest ban on extra billing), by C. Barrett. MACLEAN'S 99:8, December 22, 1986.

Abortion funding (Supreme Court decision). CHRISTIAN CENTURY 103:1144-1145, December 17, 1986.

Abortion in Louisiana: the applicability of R.S. 14:87 to a non-licensed physician. SOUTHERN UNIVERSITY LAW REVIEW 11:103-112, Spring 1985.

Abortion in Nicaragua: an emerging issue, by S. Sangree, et al. MS 14:25, June 1986.

Abortion in the United States: politics or policy?, by C. Djerassi. BULLETIN OF THE ATOMIC SCIENTISTS 42:38-41, April 1986.

Abortion—(1) it is unconstitutional for a state to require unemancipated minors and incompetents to wait twenty-four hours after parental notification before having an abortion. (2) a state statute concerning parental notice in abortion is enjoined until the state supreme court promulgates rules assuring the expeditious and confidential disposition of the judicial hearings which allow a mature minor or an immature minor whose best interests require an abortion to forego the state's parental notice requirement. Zbaraz v. Hartigan. JOURNAL OF FAMILY LAW 24:699-706, June 1986.

Abortion: L.A. restrictions downed, by P. Reidinger. AMERICAN BAR ASSOCIATION JOURNAL October 1, 1986, p. 93.

Abortion law reform in France, by D. M. Stetson. JOURNAL OF COMPARATIVE FAMILY STUDIES 17(3):277-290, Autumn 1986.

Abortion 1986: state constitutional perspectives, by J. M. Healey. CONNECTICUT MEDICINE 50(6):417, June 1986; 50(7):491, July 1986.

Abortion of the silent scream (correlation between antiabortion movement and votes of legislators on human pain, suffering and violence), by J. W. Prescott. HUMANIST 46:10-17+, September-October 1986.

Abortion on the docket (H. Morgentaler's challenge), by S. Aikenhead. MACLEAN'S 99:56-57, October 20, 1986.

Amicus brief (Richard Thornburg v. American College of Obstetricians and Gynecologists), by L. Paltrow. WOMEN'S RIGHTS LAW REPORTER 9:3-24, Winter 1986.

Another abortion ruling, by E. Goodman. OKLAHOMA OBSERVER 15:17, July 10/25, 1983.

Arguments over abortion delay civil rights bill (news; Civil Rights Restoration Act), by K. A. Lawton. CHRISTIANITY TODAY 30(8):46-47, May 16, 1986.

Banning abortion: an analysis of Senate votes on a bimodal issue, by R. A. Strickland, et al. WOMEN AND POLITICS 6:41-56, Spring 1986.

Canada: abortion law fight. OFF OUR BACKS 17(7):4, July 1986.

Canadian abortion law, by R. M. Ferri. CATHOLIC LAWYER 30:336-363, Summer 1986.

Church and state (federal judge fines Catholic Church for refusing to turn over documents on its antiabortion campaign), by R. N. Ostling. TIME 127:19, May 19, 1986.

City of Akron v. Akron Center for Reproductive Health, Inc. state decision prevales, but for how long? UNIVERSITY OF MIAMI LAW REVIEW 38:921-938, September 1984.

Compelling governmental interests jurisprudence of the Burger Court: a new perspective on Roe v. Wade. ALBANY LAW REVIEW 50:675-723, Spring 1986.

Court renews abortion rights, strikes "Baby Doe" regulations, by E. Witt. CON-GRESSIONAL QUARTERLY WEEKLY REPORT 44:1334-1336, June 14, 1986.

Crimes/offenses. CRIMINAL LAW MONTHLY 5(8):4, January 1986.

Dear Bob, you should stand alone (R. Packwood's stand on abortion rights), by W. F. Buckley. NATIONAL REVIEW 38:63, April 25, 1986.

Ecology of abortions in the United States since 1973: a replication and extension. POPULATION AND ENVIRONMENT 7(3):137, Fall 1984.

Examination of proposals for a human life amendment, by J. Bopp. CAPITAL UNIVERSITY LAW REVIEW 15:415-474, Spring 1986.

Get beyond labels (controversy over federal funding of family planning clinics), by N. Amidei. COMMONWEAL 113:37-38, January 31, 1986.

Has the MTP (Medical Terminationof Pregnancy) Act in India proved beneficial?, by M. L. Solapurkar, et al. JOURNAL OF FAMILY WELFARE 31:46-52, March 1985.

Henry's in the high court: abortionist Morgentaler is defended on constitutional grounds, by D. Jenish. ALBERTA REPORT 13:9-10, October 20, 1986.

High Court strikes down abortion restrictions, rules on handicapped infants, by K. A. Lawton. CHRISTIANITY TODAY 30(10):38-39, July 11, 1986.

House of Lords rules DHSS guidance on contraception lawful, by D. Brahams. LANCET 2(8461):959-960, October 26, 1985.

Impact of the Hyde Amendment on Congress: effects of single issue politics on legislative dysfunction June 1977-June 1978, by S. J. Tolchin. WOMEN AND POLITICS 5:91-106, September 1985.

India: move to stop sex-test abortion, by R. Rao. NATURE 324:202, November 20, 1986.

International comparison of abortion law and practice. Comparative legal notes on the current policy discussion. ZEITSCHRIFT FUR DIE GESAMTE STRA-FRECHTSWISSENSCHAFT 97(4):1043-1073, 1985.

Introduction to the history and present state of the law relating to abortion in England, by C. R. Fradd. ETHICS AND MEDICINE 1(4):60-64, 1985.

Is abortion a civil right [editorial], by D. E. Anderson. CHRISTIANITY AND CRISIS 46(5):103-105, April 7, 1986.

Is "Roe v. Wade" on last legs: one High Court vacancy could tip balance (another strict constructionist could tip balance in favor of abortionists). HUMAN EVENTS 46:1+, June 21, 1986.

Jimenez rally to target abortion vote, by S. Poggi. GAY COMMUNITY NEWS 14(9):1, September 14, 1986.

June, bioethics and the Supreme Court, by M. A. Gardell. JOURNAL OF MEDI-CAL PHILOSOPHY 11:285-290, August 1986.

Legislation proposed to restrict wrongful-life suits, by B. Steinbock. HASTINGS CENTER REPORT 16:19, April 1986.

Massachusetts anti-abortion measure put on ballot. NATIONAL NOW TIMES 19(3):5, May 1986.

Massachusetts to vote on anti-abortion referendum, by K. Westheimer. GAY COMMUNITY NEWS 13(42):3, May 17, 1986.

Minnesota judge strikes down notification law, by M. Specktor. GUARDIAN 39(13):4, December 24, 1986.

Morgan (Katzenbach v. Morgan, 86 S. Ct. 1717) "power" and the forced recon- sideration of constitutional decisions, by S. L. Carter. UNIVERSITY OF CHICAGO LAW REVIEW 53:819-863, Summer 1986.

Nicaragua: abortion laws criticized. OFF OUR BACKS 17(7):4, July 1986.

Nicaragua—legalization of abortion discussed, by C. Jaquith. INTERCON- TINENTAL PRESS 24(3):63, February 10, 1986.

1986 Supreme Court cases on womens rights. NATIONAL NOW TIMES 19(4):7, July 1986.

No legal impediment: access to abortion in the United States, by A. S. Cohan. JOURNAL OF AMERICAN STUDIES 20:189-205, August 1986.

Of fathers, fetuses, and fairy tales, by C. Levine. HASTINGS CENTER REPORT 16:2, October 1986.

Of laws, not men. NATION 242(4):100, February 1, 1986.

Parental consent for abortion: impact of the Massachusetts law, by V. G. Cartoof, et al. AMERICAN JOURNAL OF PUBLIC HEALTH 76(4):397-400, April 1986.

Pregnant teens must make own choices on abortion. JET 70:24, July 14, 1986.

Pre-natal injury, homicide and the draft criminal code, by J. Temkin. CAMBRIDGE LAW JOURNAL 45:414-429, November 1986.

Privacy, abortion, and judicial review: haunted by the ghost of Lochner, by H. Garfield. WASHINGTON LAW REVIEW 61:293-365, April 1986.

Public opinion and the legalization of abortion, by T. F. Hartnagel, et al. CANAD- IAN REVIEW OF SOCIOLOGY AND ANTHROPOLOGY 22:427-430, August 1985; 22(3):411-430, 1985.

Reason, revelation and liberal justice: reflections on George Grant's analysis of Roe v. Wade, by W. Mathie. CANADIAN JOURNAL OF POLITICAL SCIENCE 19:443-455, September 1986.

Reform of Penal Code Paragraph 218 and its consequences from the viewpoint of the Department of Public Health, by K. Hollstein. OFFENTLICHE GE- SUNDHEITSWESEN 47(8):386-391, August 1985.

Reproductive rights for a more humane world , by F. Wattleton. HUMANIST 46:5- 7+, July-August 1986.

Roe v Wade: 15 years later, by S. Poggi. GAY COMMUNITY NEWS 13(29):1, February 8, 1986.

Roe v Wade reaffirmed, by D. O. Stewart. AMERICAN BAR ASSOCIATION JOURNAL 72:41, August 1, 1986.

Roe v Wade reaffirmed, again, by G. J. Annas. HASTINGS CENTER REPORT 16(5):26-27, October 1986.

Shalom and the unborn, by M. J. Gorman. TRADITION 3(1):26-33, 1986; also in TRANSFORMATION 3(1):26-32+, January-March 1986.

Should medical technology dictate a woman's right to choose?, by N. K. Rhoden. TECHNOLOGY REVIEW 89:21-22, April 1986.

Social change and moral politics: the Irish Constitutional Referendum 1983, by B. Girvin. POLITICAL STUDIES 34:61-81, March 1986.

State abortion bills. OFF OUR BACKS 16(4):7, April 1986; 16(5):5, May 1986; 16(6):9, June 1986; 17(7):6, July 1986.

State laws and the provision of family planning and abortion services in 1985, by T. Sollom, et al. FAMILY PLANNING PERSPECTIVES 17(6):262-266, November-December 1985.

Supreme Court backs abortion. OFF OUR BACKS 17(8):8, August 1986.

Supreme Court preview, by B. K. Repa. AMERICAN BAR ASSOCIATION JOURNAL 76:117, January 1, 1986.

Supreme Court—rulings remove restrictions on abortion. NATIONAL CATHOLIC REPORTER 19:6, July 1, 1983.

Supreme Court throws out Illinois abortion case. OFF OUR BACKS 16(6):9, June 1986.

Supreme Court upholds ruling against a law restricting abortion [news]. CHRISTIANITY TODAY 30(9):43, June 13, 1986.

Supreme Court weighs abortion case [news], by M. Mawyer. FUNDAMENTALIST JOURNAL 5(1):68-69, January 1986.

Tactic of legal reform: learning from the recent past, by C. Davies, et al. HOWARD JOURNAL OF CRIMINAL JUSTICE 25(1):25-32, February 1986.

United States Supreme Court 1985-1986 term: abortion. CRIMINAL LAW REPORTER: SUPREME COURT PROCEEDINGS 39(24):4165-4167, September 17, 1986.

Using state constitutions to expand public funding for abortions: throwing away the carrot with the stick, by E. Relkin, et al. WOMEN'S RIGHTS LAW REPORTER 9:27-88, Winter 1986.

Vancouver tribunal condemns abortion laws, by G. Lang. HERIZONS 4(3):11, April 1986.

Virginia mothers can sue doctors in failed abortions. JET 70:7, May 19, 1986.

Voice for the unborn: the abortion law is tested in (Saskatchewan) appeal court, by L. Cohen. ALBERTA REPORT 13:21-22, December 30, 1985.

ABORTION—LEGAL

Abortion [letter], by P. Ney. NEW ZEALAND MEDICAL JOURNAL 98(790):965, November 13, 1985.

Abortion according to paragraph 218ff. of the German penal code and life support of premature infants from the viewpoint of the pediatrician, by H. von Voss. MONATSSCHRIFT FUR KINDERHEILKUNDE 134(5):232-239, May 1986.

Abortion: alternatives, objectivity and statistics [letter]. CANADIAN MEDICAL ASSOCIATION JOURNAL 134(3):215-216, February 1, 1986.

Abortion: medical perspectives and problems, by C. C. John. PHAROS 48(4):31-34, Fall 1985.

Abortion 1986: state constitutional perspectives, by J. M. Healey. CONNECTICUT MEDICINE 50(6):417, June 1986; 50(7):491, July 1986.

Abortion of thinking, by P. de Bellefeuille. CANADIAN MEDICAL ASSOCIATION JOURNAL 134(2):115+, January 15, 1986.

Antiabortion movement and Babe Jane Doe, by C. Paige, et al. JOURNAL OF HEALTH POLITICS, POLICY AND LAW 11(2):255-269, Summer 1986.

Characteristics of women undergoing induced abortion: results of a case-control study from Northern Italy, by C. La Vecchia, et al. CONTRACEPTION 32(6): 637-649, December 1985.

Contraception before and after legal abortions, by A. Tollan. TIDSSKRIFT FOR DEN NORSKE LAEGEFORENING 105(31):2199-2201, November 10, 1985.

Contraception a year after voluntary interruption of pregnancy, by O. Chevrant-Breton, et al. REVUE FRANCAISE DE GYNECOLOGIE ET D'OBSTETRIQUE 81(2):67-69, February 1986.

Contraceptive care and family planning: a correction [letter], by J. McCracken. JOURNAL OF THE ROYAL COLLEGE OF GENERAL PRACTITIONERS 36(285):179, April 1986.

Current status of actions for wrongful life and wrongful birth, by S. Taub. LEGAL MEDICINE 1985, pp. 180-195.

Deliveries and abortions 1980-1984, by L. B. Knudsen. UGESKRIFT FOR LAEGER 148(15):923-924, April 7, 1986.

Ethical and legal problems posed by the prenatal diagnosis of abnormalities. Legal aspects, by D. Thouvenin. CHIRURGIE PEDIATRIQUE 26(2):67-75, 1985.

—. Medical data, by J. M. Thoulon, et al. CHIRURGIE PEDIATRIQUE 26(2):57-61, 1985.

Evaluation of intramuscular suprostone and vacuum aspiration for termination of early pregnancy, by S. Prasad, et al. CONTRACEPTION 32(5):429-435, November 1985.

Fetal tibia retained in uterine cavity for eight years after legal aboration, by H. J. Ingerslev, et al. ACTA OBSTETRICIA ET GYNECOLOGICA SCANDINAVICA 65(4):371-372, 1986.

German euthanasia programme [letter]. NEW ZEALAND MEDICAL JOURNAL 98(791):1019, November 27, 1985.

How technology is reframing the abortion debate, by D. Callahan. HASTINGS CENTER REPORT 16(1):33-42, February 1986.

Hypocrisy of abortion [letter], by S. M. Lena. CANADIAN MEDICAL ASSOCIATION JOURNAL 133(8):731, October 15, 1985.

Impact of abortion policy on prematurity in Hungary, by Z. Makoi. ACTA PAEDIATRICA SCANDINAVICA 319:84-88, 1985.

Incidence of biological intravascular coagulation in legal induced abortions, by S. Boudaoud, et al. ANNALES FRANCAISES D'ANESTHESIE ET DE RE-ANIMATION 5(1):5-9, 1986.

Is routine ultrasound before termination of pregnancy worthwhile?, by Y. Jarallah, et al. SCOTTISH MEDICAL JOURNAL 30(4):232-233, October 1985.

Is voluntary abortion to be regarded now as a contraceptive?, by F. Corongiu, et al. ANNALI DEL OSPEDALE MARIA VITTORIA DI TORINO 27(7-12):260-270, July-December 1984.

Legal aspects of abortion practice, by E. B. Goldman. CLINICAL OBSTETRICS AND GYNAECOLOGY 13(1):135-143, March 1986.

Legally induced abortion in 1984, by L. B. Knudsen, et al. UGESKRIFT FOR LAEGER 148(6):353-355, February 3, 1986.

Liability of the physician in a legal but failed abortion for social reasons, by G. H. Schlund. GEBURTSHILFE UND FRAUENHEILKUNDE 45(9):674-676, September 1985.

Medical letters must also be read. . . ! Consequences of a risky intervention not considered—decision of the German federal court. FORTSCHRITTE DER MEDIZIN 104(11):64, March 20, 1986.

Morgentaler: the debate continues [letter]. CANADIAN MEDICAL ASSOCIATION JOURNAL 134(3):212, February 1, 1986.

New life: God's call—human responsibility, by J. G. Ziegler. GEBURTSHILFE UND FRAUENHEILKUNDE 45(10):739-748, October 1985.

On the abortion issue [letter], by H. S. Jonas. PHAROS 49(1):37-38, Winter 1986.

Perinatal ethics [letter], by W. J. Watson. OBSTETRICS AND GYNECOLOGY 68(1):141-142, July 1986.

Policy-making: a CMA raison d'être [letter], by G. Ponsford. CANADIAN MEDICAL ASSOCIATION JOURNAL 134(7):701+, April 1, 1986.

Problems caused by the therapeutic interruption of pregnancy. Apropos of 120 cases observed from 1976 to 1983, by C. Dognin, et al. REVUE FRAN-

ABORTION—LEGAL (continued)

CAISE DE GYNECOLOGIE ET D'OBSTETRIQUE 80(1):33-38, January 1985.

Reform of Penal Code Paragraph 218 and its consequences from the viewpoint of the Department of Public Health, by K. Hollstein. OFFENTLICHE GE-SUNDHEITSWESEN 47(8):386-391, August 1985.

Regional prospective study of psychiatric sequelae of legal abortion, by W. Barnett, et al. FORTSCHRITTE DER NEUROLOGIE-PSYCHIATRIE 54(4): 106-118, April 1986.

Role of abortion in control of global population growth, by S. D. Mumford, et al. CLINICAL OBSTETRICS AND GYNAECOLOGY 13(1):19-31, March 1986.

Rubella as the reason for termination of pregnancy after the 12th week of pregnancy, by M. Bitsch, et al. UGESKRIFT FOR LAEGER 148(33):2113-2115, August 11, 1986.

Selected Jewish views of life and medical practice, by J. J. Lindenthal, et al. NEW JERSEY MEDICINE 82(10):795-799, October 1985.

Trends in induced legal abortion morbidity and mortality, by N. J. Binkin. I CLINICAL OBSTETRICS AND GYNAECOLOGY 13(1):83-93, March 1986.

Trends in public attitudes toward legal abortion, 1972-1978, by S. A. Moldanado. RESEARCH IN NURSING AND HEALTH 8(3):219-225, September 1985.

Various pharmacologic combinations in anesthesia for voluntary abortions in day hospitals, by F. Ciri, et al. MINERVA ANESTESIOLOGICA 52(1-2):15-18, January-February 1986.

Wrongful life cases and the courts, by M. S. Henifin. WOMEN AND HEALTH 11(2):97-102, Summer 1986.

ABORTION—LEGAL—COMPLICATIONS
Complications of legal abortion, by H. H. Bräutigam. THERAPEUTISCHE UMSCHAU 43(5):356-364, May 1986.

ABORTION—LITERATURE
Exposure to anesthetic gases and reproductive outcome. A review of the epidemiologic literature, by T. N. Tannenbaum, et al. JOURNAL OF OCCUPATIONAL MEDICINE 27(9):659-668, September 1985.

Making the choice: 1927 (excerpt from Hills Like White Elephants), by E. Hemingway. HARPERS 273:41, July 1986.

"Secrets of generation display'd": *Aristole's master-piece* in 18th century England (sexual advice literature), by R. Porter. EIGHTEENTH CENTURY LIFE 9(3):1-21, May 1985.

ABORTION—METHODS
Abortion pill, by S. Clements. EVERYWOMAN 9:11, 1985.

Continuous extraovular prostaglandin F2 alpha instillation for second-trimester pregnancy termination, by J. Atad, et al. ISRAEL JOURNAL OF MEDICAL SCIENCES 21(12):935-939, December 1985.

Ectopic pregnancy among early abortion patients: does prostaglandin reduce the incidence?, by M. Borten, et al. PROSTAGLANDINS 30(6):891-905, December 1985.

Evaluation of intramuscular suprostone and vacuum aspiration for termination of early pregnancy, by S. Prasad, et al. CONTRACEPTION 32(5):429-435, November 1985.

Induction of labour with mifepristone after intrauterine fetal death [letter], by D. Cabrol, et al. LANCET 2(8462):1019, November 2, 1985.

Method for first trimester selective abortion in multiple pregnancy, by Y. Dumez, et al. CONTRIBUTIONS TO GYNECOLOGY AND OBSTETRICS 15:50-53, 1986.

Midtrimester abortion with Laminaria and vacuum evacuation on a teaching service, by A. M. Altman, et al. JOURNAL OF REPRODUCTIVE MEDICINE 30(8):601-606, August 1985.

Partial termination of a quintuplet pregnancy, by P. Lopes, et al. ZEITSCHRIFT FUR GEBURTSCHILFE UND PERINATOLOGIE 189(5):239-240, September-October 1985.

Preoperative cervical dilatation for first trimester induced abortion: comparison of two prostaglandin analogues, by W. T. Mao, et al. CONTRACEPTION 33(2): 195-201, February 1986.

Preoperative dilatation of the cervix uteri by vaginal application of 9-deoxo-16, 16-dimethyl-9-methylene PGE2 in pregnancy interruption during the first trimester. Double-blind clinical study, by A. Friedli, et al. JOURNAL DE GYNE-COLOGIE, OBSTETRIQUE ET BIOLOGIE DE LA REPRODUCTION 15(2): 215-221, 1986.

Preparation of the cervix: hydrophilic and prostaglandin dilators, by P. D. Darney. CLINICAL OBSTETRICS AND GYNAECOLOGY 13(1):43-51, March 1986.

Relief of pain in first-trimester abortion [letter], by S. Trupin. AMERICAN JOUR-NAL OF OBSTETRICS AND GYNECOLOGY 153(5):591, November 1, 1985.

Second trimester abortion by dilatation and evacuation, by J. Wainer. HEALTH-RIGHT 5:13-16, May 1986.

Study of the mechanism of ONO-802 in the termination of early pregnancy by B model sonar monitoring, by L. L. Luo. CHUNG HUA FU CHAN KO TSA CHIH 20(4):240-242+, July 1985.

Surgical techniques of uterine evacuation in first- and second-trimester abortion, by P. G. Stubblefield. CLINICAL OBSTETRICS AND GYNAECOLOGY 13(1): 53-70, March 1986.

Technique for mid-trimester termination of pregnancies with severe oligo-hydramnios, by A. Abramson, et al. JOURNAL OF ULTRASOUND IN MEDI-CINE 4(10):551-552, October 1985.

Techniques for termination of pregnancy in the second trimester, by I. S. Fraser. HEALTHRIGHT 5:33-36, November 1985.

ABORTION—METHODS (continued)

Termination of early pregnancy by the progesterone antagonist RU 486 (mifepristone), by B. Couzinet, et al. NEW ENGLAND JOURNAL OF MEDICINE 315:1565-1570, December 18, 1986.

Termination of pregnancy in the second trimester by the modified Manstein method, by J. Tomásek, et al. CESKOSLOVENSKA GYNEKOLOGIE 51(3):141-146, April 1986.

Vacuum-aspiration of uterine contents after a missed menstrual period, by I. M. Bloshanskii, et al. AKUSHERSTVO I GINEKOLOGIIA (7):55-58, July 1985.

ABORTION—MISSED
Abortions that fail, by A. M. Kaunitz, et al. OBSTETRICS AND GYNECOLOGY 66(4):533-537, October 1985..

Lupus anticoagulant: a place for pre-pregnancy treatment? [letter], by R. G. Farquharson, et al. LANCET 2(8459):842-843, October 12, 1985.

Missed abortion, and later spontaneous abortion, in pregnancies clinically normal at 7-12 week, by I. R. McFadyen. EUROPEAN JOURNAL OF OBSTETRICS, GYNECOLOGY AND REPRODUCTIVE BIOLOGY 20(6):381-384, December 1985.

Serum concentration of pregnancy-specific beta 1-glycoprotein in missed abortion, by N. Radikov, et al. AKUSHERSTVO I GINEKOLOGIIA 24(5):7-11, 1985.

ABORTION—MISSED—DIAGNOSIS
Diagnostic significance of various endocrine shifts in missed abortion, by I. A. Salov. AKUSHERSTVO I GINEKOLOGIIA (9):68-69, August 1985.

Echographic monitoring of pathologic pregnancy in the first trimester: threatened abortion, by S. Donadio, et al. MINERVA GINECOLOGIA 37(9):475-477, September 1985.

Yolk sac sign: sonographic appearance of the fetal yolk sac in missed abortion, by S. R. Hurwitz. JOURNAL OF ULTRASOUND IN MEDICINE 5(8):435-438, August 1986.

ABORTION—MISSED—TREATMENT
Induction of labour and termination of missed abortions with enzaprost, by M. Farkas, et al. THERAPIA HUNGARICA 31(1):31-38, 1983.

ABORTION—MORTALITY AND MORTALITY STATISTICS
Age, period and cohort effects on maternal mortality: alinear logit model, by E. J. C. Tu, et al. SOCIAL BIOLOGY 30:400-412, Winter 1983.

Cluster of abortion deaths at a single facility, by M. E. Kafrissen, et al. OBSTETRICS AND GYNECOLOGY 68(3):387-389, September 1986.

Maternal deaths associated with barbiturate anesthetics—New York City. MMWR 35(37):579-582+, September 19, 1986.

Maternal deaths related to abortions in Sweden, 1931-1980, by U. Högberg, et al. GYNECOLOGIC AND OBSTETRIC INVESTIGATION 20(4):169-178, 1985.

ABORTION—MORTALITY AND MORTALITY STATISTICS (continued)

Trends in induced legal abortion morbidity and mortality, by N. J. Binkin. I CLINI-
CAL OBSTETRICS AND GYNAECOLOGY 13(1):83-93, March 1986.

ABORTION—NURSES AND NURSING
Abortion counseling, by R. Kubota. CALIFORNIA NURSE 82(1):4-5, February
1986.

Abortion: the teenage patient and the OR nurse, by T. Howard. CANADIAN
NURSE 81(10):28-30, November 1985.

Aftercare following miscarriage . . . extending the role of the community midwife,
by S. Arber. MIDWIFE, HEALTH VISITOR AND COMMUNITY NURSE 21(12):
432+, December 1985.

Analysis of nursing students' attitude toward bioethics (3). Attitude toward induced abortion, by O. Nakayama, et al. KANGO TENBO 11(5):492-497, April
1986.

Antineoplastic drugs and spontaneous abortion in nurses [letter]. NEW
ENGLAND JOURNAL OF MEDICINE 314(16):1048-1051, April 17, 1986.

Baccalaureate nursing students' attitudes toward abortion, by M. C. Smith. DAI: A
47(3), September 1986.

Caring in the instance of unexpected early pregnancy loss, by K. M. Swanson-
Kauffman. TOPICS IN CLINICAL NURSING 8(2):37-46, July 1986.

Combined qualitative methodology for nursing research . . . the human experience of miscarriage, by K. M. Swanson-Kauffman. ANS 8(3):58-69, April
1986.

Nurses ease pain in perinatal losses, by M. Taggert. NEW JERSEY NURSE
16(4):10, July-August 1986.

Nurses speak out on teens and abortion, by M. Allen. CANADIAN NURSE
81(10):31-32, November 1985.

RCM supplement. "You can always try for another" [interview by Gill Crabbe], by
E. Proctor, et al. NURSING TIMES 82(28):71, July 9-15, 1986.

ABORTION—PSYCHOLOGY AND PSYCHIATRY
Abortion and the man. Psychological and psychopathological manifestations in
the face of lost fatherhood, by P. Benvenuti, et al. RIVISTA DI PATOLOGIA
NERVOSA E MENTALE 104(6):255-268, November-December 1983.

Abortion counseling, by R. Kubota. CALIFORNIA NURSE 82(1):4-5, February
1986.

Abortion counselling—a new component of medical care, by U. Landy. CLINICAL
OBSTETRICS AND GYNAECOLOGY 13(1):33-41, March 1986.

Adjustment to abortion in marital relations, by B. Wimmer-Puchinger. GYNA-
KOLOGE 19(1):33-36, March 1986.

Attitudes of mothers of children with Down syndrome concerning amniocentesis,
abortion, and prenatal genetic counseling techniques, by T. E. Elkins, et al.
OBSTETRICS AND GYNECOLOGY 68(2):181-184, August 1986.

Clinic (male reaction), by M. Blumenthal. NEW YORK TIMES MAGAZINE November 2, 1986.

Combined qualitative methodology for nursing research . . . the human experience of miscarriage, by K. M. Swanson-Kauffman. ANS 8(3):58-69, April 1986.

Comparison of two interventions to assist men who accompany their partners for abortions, by R. A. Karesky. DAI: B, 47(4), October 1986.

Contraception a year after voluntary interruption of pregnancy, by O. Chevrant-Breton, et al. REVUE FRANCAISE DE GYNECOLOGIE ET D'OBSTETRIQUE 81(2):67-69, February 1986.

Correlational and predictive study of depression in women following abortion, by P. L. Sowards. DAI: B 47(4), October 1986.

Differences in self-concept and locus of control among women who seek abortions. AMERICAN MENTAL HEALTH COUNSELORS ASSOCIATION JOURNAL 8(1):4-11, January 1986.

Early pregnancy loss in the infertile couple, by N. A. Bowers. JOGN NURSING 14(6 suppl):55S-57S, November-December 1985.

Exploratory study of the miscarriage experience, by M. H. Hutti. HEALTH CARE FOR WOMEN, INTERNATIONAL 7(5):371-389, 1986.

Healing a hidden grief, by B. Rush. JOURNAL OF CHRISTIAN NURSING 3(3):10-11, Summer 1986.

Induced abortion: reported and observed practice in Taiwan, by J. F. Wang. HEALTH CARE FOR WOMEN, INTERNATIONAL 6(5-6):383-404, 1985.

Intense emotional reactions with induced abortion, by C. Vivier. INFIRMIERE CANADIENNE 27(11):19, December 1985.

Involuntary pregnancy loss research and the implications for nursing, by K. S. Reed. ISSUES IN MENTAL HEALTH NURSING 6(3-4):209-217, 1984.

Man: an axiological analysis from a Christian perspective, by R. Adams. ANPHI PAPERS 20(1-2):15-21, January-June 1985.

Miscarriage and its implications, by A. Oakely. MIDWIFE, HEALTH VISITOR AND COMMUNITY NURSE 22(4):123-124+, April 1986.

Perinatal grief and loss [an overview], by S. L. Gardner, et al. NEONATAL NETWORK 5(2):7-15, October 1986.

Psychiatric admissions and choice of abortion, by P. K. Andersen, et al. STATISTICS IN MEDICINE 5(3):243-253, May-June 1986.

Psychiatric aspects of pregnancy termination, by A. Lazarus, et al. CLINICAL OBSTETRICS AND GYNAECOLOGY 13(1):125-134, March 1986.

Psychological factors related to post-abortion "subtle" contraceptive unreliability, by P. Lehtinen, et al. SCANDINAVIAN JOURNAL OF PSYCHOLOGY 26(3):277-284, 1985.

Psychological sequelae of abortion based on fetal indications, by A. von Gontard. MONATSSCHRIFT FUR KINDERHEILKUNDE 134(3):150-157, March 1986.

Psychoreactivity in voluntary abortion, by M. P. Graziani. MINERVA PSICHI-ATRICA 26(2):193-200, April-June 1985.

Psychosexual aspects of abortion, by C. López Elizondo. SALUD MENTAL 5(1): 20-23, Spring 1982.

Reflections on a miscarriage . . . one couple's psychological and emotional re-sponses, by S. B. Hardin, et al. MATERNAL-CHILD NURSING JOURNAL 15(1):23-30, Spring 1986.

Regional prospective study of psychiatric sequelae of legal abortion, by W. Barnett, et al. FORTSCHRITTE DER NEUROLOGIE-PSYCHIATRIE 54(4): 106-118, April 1986.

Right to live with pain, by L. Morin. INFIRMIERE CANADIENNE 27(11):17-18, December 1985.

Self concept of women with negative obstetrical histories and after gynecological operations for neoplasma, by E. Michalek, et al. GINEKOLOGIA POLSKA 56(11):691-698, November 1985.

Single abortion—multiple abortions, a comparison, by P. Goebel. PSYCHO-THERAPIE, PSYCHOSOMATIK, MEDIZINISCHE PSYCHOLOGIE 36(2):83-88, February 1986.

Why me? Second trimester abortion, by A. Neidhardt. AMERICAN JOURNAL OF NURSING 86(10):1133-1135, October 1986.

Women and abortion: attitudes, social networks, decision-making, by G. Faria, et al. SOCIAL WORK IN HEALTH CARE 11(1):85-96, Fall 1985.

"You can always try for another" . . . community midwives, by E. Proctor, et al. NURSING TIMES 82(29):RCM Suppl:71, July 9-15, 1986.

Your hands: lethal or life saving?, by M. James. NURSING JOURNAL OF INDIA 77(8):213, August 1986.

ABORTION—RESEARCH
Abortion and early neonatal death of kids attributed to intrauterine yersinia pseudotuberculosis infection, by S. T. Witte, et al. JOURNAL OF THE AMERICAN VETERINARY MEDICAL ASSOCIATION 187(8):834, October 15, 1985.

Abortion and the politics of social research. BERKELEY JOURNAL OF SOCI-OLOGY 31:183, 1986.

Abortion in sheep caused by a nonclassified, anaerobic, flagellated bacterium, by C. A. Kirkbride, et al. AMERICAN JOURNAL OF VETERINARY RESEARCH 47(2):259-262, February 1986.

Abortion of twins following chloral hydrate anesthesia in a mare, by J. U. Akpo-kodje, et al. VETERINARY RECORD 118(11):306, March 15, 1986.

Abortion: toward a standard based upon clinical medical signs of life and death, by J. E. Kennedy, et al. JOURNAL OF FAMILY LAW 23(4):545-563, 1984-1985.

Absorption and elimination of a prostaglandin F analog, fenprostalene, in lactating dairy cows, by R. V. Tomlinson, et al. JOURNAL OF DAIRY SCIENCE 68(8): 2072-2077, August 1985.

Acinetobacter calcoaceticus in three cases of late abortion in water buffaloes, by A. M. Das, et al. VETERINARY RECORD 118(8):214, February 22, 1986.

Active suppression of host-vs-graft reaction in pregnant mice. VII. Spontaneous abortion of allogeneic CBA/J x DBA/2 fetuses in the uterus of CBA/J mice correlates with deficient non-T suppressor cell activity, by D. A. Clark, et al. JOURNAL OF IMMUNOLOGY 136(5):1668-1675, March 1, 1986.

"Alas! poor Yorick," I knew him ex utero: the regulation of embryo and fetal experimentation and disposal in England and the United States, by N. P. Terry. VANDERBILT LAW REVIEW 39:419-470, April 1986.

Attempted conversion of twin to singleton pregnancy in two mares with associated changes in plasma oestrone sulphate concentrations, by J. H. Hyland, et al. AUSTRALIAN VETERINARY JOURNAL 62(12):406-409, December 1985.

Bovine abortion and death associated with consumption of aflatoxin-contaminated peanuts, by A. C. Ray, et al. JOURNAL OF THE AMERICAN VETERINARY MEDICAL ASSOCIATION 188(10):1187-1188, May 15, 1986.

Bovine abortion associated with bacillus licheniformis, by G. Mitchell, et al. AUSTRALIAN VETERINARY JOURNAL 63(5):160-161, May 1986.

Bovine abortion caused by Bacillus cereus, by J. Schuh, et al. JOURNAL OF THE AMERICAN VETERINARY MEDICAL ASSOCIATION 187(10):1047-1048, November 15, 1985.

Bovine chlamydial abortion: serodiagnosis by modified complement-fixation and indirect inclusion fluorescence tests and enzyme-linked immunosorbent assay, by J. A. Perez-Martinez, et al. AMERICAN JOURNAL OF VETERINARY RESEARCH 47(7):1501-1506, July 1986.

Bovine embryo transfer pregnancies. I. Abortion rates and characteristics of calves, by K. K. King, et al. JOURNAL OF ANIMAL SCIENCE 61(4):747-757, October 1985.

Demonstration in Hungary of Q fever associated with abortion in cattle and sheep, by M. Rády, et al. ACTA VETERINARIA HUNGARICA 33(3-4):169-176, 1985.

Enzyme activities in amniotic fluid and maternal blood in sheep, before and after induced foetal death and abortion, by A. R. Mohamed, et al. BRITISH VETERINARY JOURNAL 141(5):498-506, September-October 1985.

Epizootiologic investigations on a sheep farm with toxoplasma gondii-induced abortions, by J. P. Dubey, et al. JOURNAL OF THE AMERICAN VETERINARY MEDICAL ASSOCIATION 188(2):155-158, January 15, 1986.

Equine abortion and chloral hydrate [letter], by W. E. Allen. VETERINARY RECORD 118(14):407, April 5, 1986.

Equine herpesvirus type 1 abortion in an onager and suspected herpesvirus myelitis in a zebra, by R. J. Montali, et al. JOURNAL OF THE AMERICAN VETERINARY MEDICAL ASSOCIATION 187(11):1248-1249, December 1, 1985.

Experimental infection of pregnant ewes with listeria monocytogenes, by M. Gitter, et al. VETERINARY RECORD 118(21):575-578, May 24, 1986.

Failure of strange females to cause pregnancy block in collared lemmings, dicrostonyx groenlandicus, by R. J. Brooks, et al. BEHAVIORAL AND NEURAL BIOLOGY 44(3):485-491, November 1985.

Field studies on the efficacy of a long acting preparation of oxytetracycline in controlling outbreaks of enzootic abortion of sheep, by A. Greig, et al. VETERINARY RECORD 117(24):627-628, December 14, 1985.

Haemophilus somnus infection of cattle—results of bacteriological study with special reference to abortion substrates, by H. Kiupel, et al. ARCHIV FUR EXPERIMENTELLE VETERINAERMEDIZIN 40(2):164-169, March 1986.

Immunofluorescence and cell culture techniques in the diagnosis of viral infection of aborted bovine fetuses, by M. H. Lucas, et al. VETERINARY RECORD 118(9):242-243, March 1, 1986.

Influence of a genetic difference confined to mutation of H-2K on the incidence of pregnancy block in mice, by K. Yamazaki, et al. PROCEEDINGS OF THE NATIONAL ACADEMY OF SCIENCES USA 83(3):740-741, February 1986.

Isolation of leptospires from the genital tract and kidneys of aborted sows, by W. A. Ellis, et al. VETERINARY RECORD 118(11):294-295, March 15, 1986.

Isolation of Rift Valley fevor virus from cattle abortions in Tanzania, by A. Kondela, et al. TROPICAL ANIMAL HEALTH AND PRODUCTION 17(3):185-186, August 1985.

Mycoplasma bovis abortion of cows following experimental infection, by H. Bocklisch, et al. ARCHIV FUR EXPERIMENTELLE VETERINAERMEDIZIN 40(1):48-55, January 1986.

Mycoplasma infection—factors interfering in toxicologic experiments on reproduction, by N. C. Juhr. BERLINER UND MUNCHENER TIERAERZTLICHE WOCHENSCHRIFT 99(2):37-41, February 1, 1986.

Mycoplasmas recovered from bovine genitalis, aborted foetuses and placentas in the Republic of South Africa, by C. J. Trichard, et al. ONDERSTEPOORT JOURNAL OF VETERINARY RESEARCH 52(2):105-110, June 1985

Necrosis and abscessation of placental sites in a Pekingese bitch, by B. L. Penzhorn. JOURNAL OF THE SOUTH AFRICAN VETERINARY ASSOCIATION 56(3):135-136, September 1985.

New non-hormonal antifertility drug DL 111-IT: I. Effects on testes and accessory glands of reproduction in male rats, by R. S. Prasad, et al. CONTRACEPTION 33(1):79-88, January 1986.

ABORTION—RESEARCH (continued)

—: II. Effects on testicular hyaluronidase activity in male rats, by R. S. Prasad, et al. CONTRACEPTION 33(1):89-99, January 1986.

New productive technology: some implications for the abortion issue, by C. Overall. JOURNAL OF VALUE INQUIRY 19:279-292, 1985.

On the embryotoxic effects of benzene and its alkyl derivatives in mice, rats and rabbits, by G. Ungváry, et al. ARCHIVES OF TOXICOLOGY 8:425-430, 1985.

Ovine enzootic abortion: experimental studies of immune responses, by M. Dawson, et al. RESEARCH IN VETERINARY SCIENCE 40(1):59-64, January 1986.

Porcine abortion caused by Bacillus sp., by C. A. Kirkbride, et al. JOURNAL OF THE AMERICAN VETERINARY MEDICAL ASSOCIATION 188(9):1060-1061, May 1, 1986.

Pregnant women and chlamydia infection [letter]. VETERINARY RECORD 118(21):594-595, May 24, 1986.

Toxicity of calotropis procera. Effect of a calotropis procera-based feed on embryonic and neonatal mortality in laboratory mice, by B. Faye. REVUE D'ELEVAGE ET DE MEDECINE VETERINAIRE DES PAYS TROPICAUX 38(1):72-75, 1985.

Trypanosoma evansi infection in buffaloes in North-East Thailand. II. Abortions, by K. F. Löhr, et al. TROPICAL ANIMAL HEALTH AND PRODUCTION 18(2): 103-108, May 1986.

ABORTION—SEPTIC
Abortion in sheep caused by a nonclassified, anaerobic, flagellated bacterium, by C. A. Kirkbride, et al. AMERICAN JOURNAL OF VETERINARY RESEARCH 47(2):259-262, February 1986.

Bovine abortion caused by Bacillus cereus, by J. Schuh, et al. JOURNAL OF THE AMERICAN VETERINARY MEDICAL ASSOCIATION 187(10):1047-1048, November 15, 1985.

Chorioamniotic infections following diagnostic amniocentesis in the second trimester, by U. Siekmann, et al. ZEITSCHRIFT FUR GEBURTSCHILFE UND PERINATOLOGIE 189(3):119-124, May-June 1985.

Clinical aspects and diagnosis of a miscarriage of herpetic etiology, by G. I. Gerasimovich, et al. AKUSHERSTVO I GINEKOLOGIIA (8):63-64, August 1985.

Flow-through method of ultraviolet irradiation of the blood in the complex treatment of patients with suppurative and inflammatory complications and renal insufficiency, by A. M. Sazonov, et al. SOVIET MEDICINE (3):37-42, 1986.

Incidence of major abdominal surgery after septic abortion—an indicator of complications due to illegal abortion, by A. Richards, et al. SOUTH AFRICAN MEDICAL JOURNAL 68(11):799-800, November 23, 1985.

Outbreak of bovine abortion attributed to ergot poisoning, by W. T. Appleyard. VETERINARY RECORD 118(2):48-49, January 11, 1986.

ABORTION—SEPTIC (continued)

Porcine abortion caused by Bacillus sp., by C. A. Kirkbride, et al. JOURNAL OF THE AMERICAN VETERINARY MEDICAL ASSOCIATION 188(9):1060-1061, May 1, 1986.

Surgical management of diffuse peritonitis complicating obstetric/gynecologic infections, by M. E. Rivlin, et al. OBSTETRICS AND GYNECOLOGY 67(5): 652-656, May 1986.

Typhoid fever complicating pregnancy, by R. Amster, et al. ACTA OBSTETRICIA ET GYNECOLOGICA SCANDINAVICA 64(8):685-686, 1985.

ABORTION—SEPTIC—COMPLICATIONS
Septic abortion complicated by rhinocerebral phycomycosis (mucormycosis) [a case report], by P. M. Shweni, et al. SOUTH AFRICAN MEDICAL JOURNAL 69(8):515-516, April 12, 1986.

Status of immunological and nonspecific reactivity in patients with acute renal failure in obstetrical and gynecological pathology, by M. I. Sorokina, et al. AKUSHERSTVO I GINEKOLOGIIA (7):42-45, July 1985.

Tricuspid valve endocarditis following septic abortion, by S. S. Vaidya, et al. JOURNAL OF THE ASSOCIATION OF PHYSICIANS OF INDIA 34(2):147, February 1986.

ABORTION—SOCIOLOGY
Abortion and the politics of social research. BERKELEY JOURNAL OF SOCI-OLOGY 31:183, 1986.

Combined qualitative methodology for nursing research . . . the human experi-ence of miscarriage, by K. M. Swanson-Kauffman. ANS 8(3):58-69, April 1986.

Reconstructing gender in America: self-definition and social action among abortion activists, by F. D. Ginsberg. DAI: A 47(3), September 1986.

Reflections on a miscarriage . . . one couple's psychological and emotional re-sponses, by S. B. Hardin, et al. MATERNAL-CHILD NURSING JOURNAL 15(1):23-30, Spring 1986.

Social change and moral politics: the Irish Constitutional Referendum 1983, by B. Girvin. POLITICAL STUDIES 34:61-81, March 1986.

Sociology, ideology, and the abortion issue: a content analysis of family sociology texts, by R. J. Adamek. JOURNAL OF APPLIED SOCIOLOGY 2(1):43-56, 1985.

Women and abortion: attitudes, social networks, decision-making, by G. Faria, et al. SOCIAL WORK IN HEALTH CARE 11(1):85-96, Fall 1985.

ABORTION—SPONTANEOUS
See also: Abruptio Placentae

Antineoplastic drugs and spontaneous abortion in nurses [letter]. NEW ENGLAND JOURNAL OF MEDICINE 314(16):1048-1051, April 17, 1986.

Association of endometriosis and spontaneous abortion: effect of control group selection, by D. A. Metzger, et al. FERTILITY AND STERILITY 45(1):18-22, January 1986.

Basis for the use of immunodepressants in treating women suffering from miscarriages, by S. D. Bulienko, et al. AKUSHERSTVO I GINEKOLOGIIA (8):41-44, August 1985.

Cardiac malformations in spontaneous abortions, by L. M. Gerlis. INTERNATIONAL JOURNAL OF CARDIOLOGY 7(1):29-46, January 1985.

Clinical value of research in chronic spontaneous abortion, by J. A. McIntyre, et al. AMERICAN JOURNAL OF REPRODUCTIVE IMMUNOLOGY AND MICROBIOLOGY 10(3):121-126, March 1986.

Collagen synthesis in the cells obtained from specimens of human spontaneous abortion with abnormal chromosomes, by V. I. Kukharenko, et al. AKUSHERSTVO I GINEKOLOGIIA (6):63-64, June 1986.

Cusum test of homogeneity with an application in spontaneous abortion epidemiology, by B. Levin, et al. STATISTICS IN MEDICINE 4(4):469-488, October-December 1985.

Cytogenetic analysis in 100 spontaneous abortions in North-East Scotland, by S. E. Procter, et al. CLINICAL GENETICS 29(2):101-103, February 1986.

Cytogenetic studies in spontaneous abortion: the Calgary experience, by C. C. Lin, et al. CANADIAN JOURNAL OF GENETICS AND CYTOLOGY 27(5):565-570, October 1985.

Cytogenetics of recurrent spontaneous aborters, by S. P. McManus, et al. IRISH JOURNAL OF MEDICAL SCIENCE 155(7):216-220, July 1986.

Effect of induced and spontaneous abortions on sex ratio and various characteristics of the female reproductive functions, by A. I. Taptunova, et al. AKUSHERSTVO I GINEKOLOGIIA (10):43-45, October 1985.

Elevated maternal glycohemoglobin in early pregnancy and spontaneous abortion among insulin-dependent diabetic women, by M. Miodovnik, et al. AMERICAN JOURNAL OF OBSTETRICS AND GYNECOLOGY 153(4):439-442, October 15, 1985.

Evaluation of karyotypes of married couples in cases of spontaneous abortion, by J. Brycz-Witkowska, et al. GINEKOLOGIA POLSKA 56(3):127-131, March 1985.

Evaluation of the risk of spontaneous abortion at various stages of pregnancy. Study of overall risk and of normal ultrasound pregnancy, by D. Oberweis, et al. JOURNAL DE GYNECOLOGIE,OBSTETRIQUE ET BIOLOGIE DE LA REPRODUCTION 14(5):563-566, 1985.

Glycemic control and spontaneous abortion in insulin-dependent diabetic women, by M. Miodovnik, et al. OBSTETRICS AND GYNECOLOGY 68(3):366-369, September 1986.

Hormonal treatment of spontaneous abortions—our experience, by A. Katsulov, et al. AKUSHERSTVO I GINEKOLOGIIA 24(6):1-4, 1985.

Importance of nutrition for women with clinical signs of spontaneous abortion, by I. Vasileva. AKUSHERSTVO I GINEKOLOGIIA 25(1):37-44, 1986.

ABORTION—SPONTANEOUS (continued)

Incipient spontaneous abortion, by T. P. Barkhatova. FEL'DSHER I AKU-SHERKA 50(8):38-42, August 1985.

Influence of the length of the human Y chromosome on spontaneous abortions. A prospective study in family lines with inherited polymorphic Y chromosomes, by P. Genest, et al. ANNALES DE GENETIQUE 28(3):143-148, 1985.

Missed abortion, and later spontaneous abortion, in pregnancies clinically normal at 7-12 week, by I. R. McFadyen. EUROPEAN JOURNAL OF OBSTETRICS, GYNECOLOGY AND REPRODUCTIVE BIOLOGY 20(6):381-384, December 1985.

Outcome of subsequent pregnancies following antibiotic therapy after primary or multiple spontaneous abortions, by A. Toth, et al. SURGERY, GYNECOLOGY AND OBSTETRICS 163(3):243-250, September 1986.

Rapid cytogenetic diagnosis of early spontaneous abortions [letter], by B. Eiben, et al. LANCET 1(8492):1273-1274, May 31, 1986.

Reproductive health of working women: spontaneous abortions and congenital malformations, by M. L. Lindbohm, et al. PUBLIC HEALTH REVIEWS 13(1-2):55-87, 1985.

Self-reported data on spontaneous abortions compared with data obtained by computer linkage with the hospital registry, by L. Z. Heidam, et al. SCANDI-NAVIAN JOURNAL OF SOCIAL MEDICINE 13(4):159-163, 1985.

Self-sterility MHC polymorphism, and spontaneous abortion, by T. G. Wegmann. CONTRIBUTIONS TO GYNECOLOGY AND OBSTETRICS 14:16-22, 1985.

Spontaneous abortion, by J. J. Laferia. CLINICAL OBSTETRICS AND GYNAE-COLOGY 13(1):105-114, March 1986.

Spontaneous abortion after amniocentesis in women with a history of spontaneous abortion, by S. M. Esrig, et al. PRENATAL DIAGNOSIS 5(5):321-328, September-October 1985.

Spontaneous abortion and interpregnancy interval, by C. C. Hebert, et al. EURO-PEAN JOURNAL OF OBSTETRICS, GYNECOLOGY AND REPRODUCTIVE BIOLOGY 22(3):125-132, July 1986.

Spontaneous abortion and pregnancy outcome after normal first-trimester ultra-sound examination, by R. D. Wilson, et al. OBSTETRICS AND GYNE-COLOGY 67(3):352-355, March 1986.

Spontaneous abortions among women employed in the plastics industry, by M. L. Lindbohm, et al. AMERICAN JOURNAL OF INDUSTRIAL MEDICINE 8(6):579-586, 1985.

Spontaneous abortions among women working in the pharmaceutical industry, by H. Taskinen, et al. BRITISH JOURNAL OF INDUSTRIAL MEDICINE 43(3):199-205, March 1986.

Thyroxine-binding globulin in spontaneous abortion, by L. Skjöldebrand, et al. GYNECOLOGIC AND OBSTETRIC INVESTIGATION 21(4):187-192, 1986.

ABORTION—SPONTANEOUS (continued)

Uterine myoma initiating a spontaneous abortion, by A. P. Kiriushchenkov. FEL'DSHER I AKUSHERKA 50(11):50-54, November 1985.

Vaginal spermicides and spontaneous abortion of known karyotype, by B. Strobino, et al. AMERICAN JOURNAL OF EPIDEMIOLOGY 123(3):431-443, March 1986.

ABORTION—SPONTANEOUS—PREVENTION AND CONTROL
Decreased abortions in HMG-induced pregnancies with prophylactic progesterone therapy, by J. H. Check, et al. INTERNATIONAL JOURNAL OF FERTILITY 30(3):45-47, 1985.

Effect of partusisten administered to pregnant women with uterine hemorrhage caused by placenta praevia on the prolongation of pregnancy, by L. Sozanski, et al. GINEKOLOGIA POLSKA 56(12):754-758, December 1985.

Evidence of improved pregnancy outcome with diethylstilbestrol (DES) treatment of women with previous pregnancy failures: a retrospective analysis, by H. W. Horne, Jr. JOURNAL OF CHRONIC DISEASES 38(10):873-880, 1985.

Place of elective cerclage operation for cervical incompetence during pregnancy, by V. Deshpande, et al. JOURNAL OF POSTGRADUATE MEDICINE 31(3): 155-157, July 1985.

Prevention of miscarriage, by T. I. Kuznetsova. FEL'DSHER I AKUSHERKA 50(7):6-8, July 1985.

Risk of fetal anomalies as a result of preogesterone therapy during pregnancy, by J. H. Check, et al. FERTILITY AND STERILITY 45(4):575-577, April 1986.

ABORTION—STATISTICS
Abortion: alternatives, objectivity and statistics [letter]. CANADIAN MEDICAL ASSOCIATION JOURNAL 134(3):215-216, February 1, 1986.

Abortion rate in A.I.D. and semen characteristics: a study of 1345 pregnancies, by D. Schwartz, et al. ANDROLOGIA 18(3):292-298, May-June 1986.

Abortion ten years later—1.5 million yearly; backers, foes polarized, by J. T. Beifuss. NATIONAL CATHOLIC REPORTER 19:1+, January 21, 1983.

Comparison of complication rates in first trimester abortions performed by physician assistants and physicians, by M. A. Freedman, et al. AMERICAN JOURNAL OF PUBLIC HEALTH 76(5):550-556, May 1986.

Deliveries and abortions 1980-1984, by L. B. Knudsen. UGESKRIFT FOR LAEGER 148(15):923-924, April 7, 1986.

Ecology of abortions in the United States since 1973: a replication and extension. POPULATION AND ENVIRONMENT 7(3):137, Fall 1984.

Effect of induced abortion on prematurity. Analysis of the period from 1979 to 1984, by J. Deutinger, et al. WIENER MEDIZINISCHE WOCHENSCHRIFT 135(13-14):329-332, July 31, 1985.

Medical value of examining tissue from therapeutic abortions: an analysis of 13,477 cases, by F. W. Kiel. BRITISH JOURNAL OF OBSTETRICS AND GYNAECOLOGY 93(6):594-596, June 1986.

ABORTION—STATISTICS (continued)

Miscarriage rate in women aged 35 years or more, by B. Gustavii. CONTRIBU-
TIONS TO GYNECOLOGY AND OBSTETRICS 15:45-49, 1986.

Randomised controlled trial of genetic amniocentesis in 4606 low-risk women, by
A. Tabor, et al. LANCET 1(8493):1287-1293, June 7, 1986.

Self-reported data on spontaneous abortions compared with data obtained by
computer linkage with the hospital registry, by L. Z. Heidam, et al. SCANDI-
NAVIAN JOURNAL OF SOCIAL MEDICINE 13(4):159-163, 1985.

ABORTION—THERAPEUTIC

Abortion 1986: state constitutional perspectives, by J. M. Healey. CONNEC-
TICUT MEDICINE 50(6):417, June 1986; 50(7):491, July 1986.

Cervical dilatation with sulprostone prior to vacuum aspiration. A two-dose, randomized study, by N. J. Christensen. CONTRACEPTION 32(4):359-365,
October 1985.

Chlamydia trachomatis infection in unmarried women seeking abortions, by P.
Chaudhuri, et al. GENITOURINARY MEDICINE 62(1):17-18, February 1986.

Evaluation of 100 autopsies performed in the maternity service of the Hôtel-Dieu
in Lyon during an 18 month period, by M. P. Cordier, et al. JOURNAL DE
GENETIQUE HUMAINE 33(3-4):294-300, September 1985.

Induction of labour with mifepristone after intrauterine fetal death [letter], by D.
Cabrol, et al. LANCET 2(8462):1019, November 2, 1985.

Interruption of first trimester human pregnancy following Epostane therapy. Effect of prostaglandin E2 pessaries, by M. A. Webster, et al. BRITISH JOUR-
NAL OF OBSTETRICS AND GYNAECOLOGY 92(9):963-968, September
1985.

Late terminations of pregnancy following second trimester amniocentesis, by J.
Timothy, et al. BRITISH JOURNAL OF OBSTETRICS AND GYNAECOLOGY
93(4):343-347, April 1986.

Medical value of examining tissue from therapeutic abortions: an analysis of
13,477 cases, by F. W. Kiel. BRITISH JOURNAL OF OBSTETRICS AND
GYNAECOLOGY 93(6):594-596, June 1986.

Method for first trimester selective abortion in multiple pregnancy, by Y. Dumez,
et al. CONTRIBUTIONS TO GYNECOLOGY AND OBSTETRICS 15:50-53,
1986.

Mid-trimester termination of pregnancies with severe oligohydramnios [letter], by
J. D. Stephens. JOURNAL OF ULTRASOUND IN MEDICINE 5(8):470,
August 1986.

Morphological study of the removed fetus after therapeutic abortion for echographic anomalies (apropos of 42 cases), by F. Serville, et al. JOURNAL DE
GENETIQUE HUMAINE 33(3-4):301-312, September 1985.

New trends in the management of Rh factor isoimmunization, by A. García
Alonso, et al. GINECOLOGIA Y OBSTETRICIA DE MEXICO 53:291-295,
November 1985.

ABORTION—THERAPEUTIC (continued)

Problems caused by the therapeutic interruption of pregnancy. Apropos of 120 cases observed from 1976 to 1983, by C. Dognin, et al. REVUE FRAN-CAISE DE GYNECOLOGIE ET D'OBSTETRIQUE 80(1):33-38, January 1985.

Relief of pain in first-trimester abortion [letter], by S. Trupin. AMERICAN JOUR-NAL OF OBSTETRICS AND GYNECOLOGY 153(5):591, November 1, 1985.

Retention of products of conception after therapeutic abortion, by E. R. Wiebe. CANADIAN MEDICAL ASSOCIATION JOURNAL 134(5):505, March 1, 1986.

Return of ovulation after evacuation of hydatidiform moles, by P. C. Ho, et al. AMERICAN JOURNAL OF OBSTETRICS AND GYNECOLOGY 153(6):538-542, November 15, 1985.

Role of H2 receptor antagonist premedication in pregnant day care patients, by J. G. Stock, et al. CANADIAN ANAESTHETISTS SOCIETY JOURNAL 32(5): 463-467, September 1985.

Spontaneous abortion and pregnancy outcome afer normal first-trimester ultra-sound examination, by R. D. Wilson, et al. OBSTETRICS AND GYNE-COLOGY 67(3):352-355, March 1986.

Subtle differences on abortion [letter], by M. A. Vojtecky. AMERICAN JOURNAL OF PUBLIC HEALTH 76(2):204, February 1986.

Technique for mid-trimester termination of pregnancies with severe oligo-hydramnios, by A. Abramson, et al. JOURNAL OF ULTRASOUND IN MEDI-CINE 4(10):551-552, October 1985.

Toward the disappearance of therapeutic abortions, by E. Hervet. BULLETIN DE L'ACADEMIE NATIONALE DE MEDECINE 169(5):587-595, May 1985.

ABORTION—THERAPEUTIC—COMPLICATIONS
Real-time ultrasound diagnosis of bleeding uterine perforation during therapeutic abortion, by E. Shalev, et al. JCU 14(1):66-67, January 1986.

Sonographic demonstration of post-abortion intrauterine osseous tissue, by P. Bourgouin, et al. JOURNAL OF ULTRASOUND IN MEDICINE 4(9):507-509, September 1985.

ABORTION—THREATENED
Beta-1-glycoprotein determination in normal and disturbed pregnancy, by K. Sterzik, et al. INTERNATIONAL JOURNAL OF GYNAECOLOGY AND OB-STETRICS 24(1):65-68, February 1986.

Evidence of improved pregnancy outcome with diethylstilbestrol (DES) treatment of women with previous pregnancy failures: a retrospective analysis, by H. W. Horne, Jr. JOURNAL OF CHRONIC DISEASES 38(10):873-880, 1985.

Monitoring trophoblast-specific-beta-1-globulin (SP1) and alpha 2-glycoprotein (SP3) in women with risk pregnancies, by L. Mikulíková, et al. CESKOSLO-VENSKA GYNEKOLOGIE 50(9):640-644, November 1985.

Prognostic significance of fetal size in early diabetic (and normal?) pregnancy and in threatened abortion, by J. F. Pedersen, et al. ULTRASOUND IN MEDICINE AND BIOLOGY 2(suppl):573-576, 1983.

ABORTION—THREATENED (continued)

Threatened abortion: sonographic distinction of normal and abnormal gestation sacs [letter], by A. V. Cadkin, et al. RADIOLOGY 160(2):567-568, August 1986.

ABORTION—THREATENED—COMPLICATIONS
Pathogenesis and correction of disorders of the sympathetic-adrenal and immune systems in abortion, by E. T. Mikhailenko, et al. AKUSHERSTVO I GINEKOLOGIIA (8):44-46, August 1985.

Risk of birth of children with developmental defects in women with threatened abortion, by L. D. Rybalkina, et al. AKUSHERSTVO GINEKOLOGIIA (3):48-50, 1986.

ABORTION—THREATENED—DIAGNOSIS
Echographic monitoring of pathologic pregnancy in the first trimester: threatened abortion, by S. Donadio, et al. MINERVA GINECOLOGIA 37(9):475-477, September 1985.

Prognostic value of ultrasound, HCG and progesterone in threatened abortion, by B. C. Eriksen, et al. JCU 14(1):3-9, January 1986.

Threatened abortion: sonographic distinction of normal and abnormal gestation sacs, by D. A. Nyberg, et al. RADIOLOGY 158(2):397-400, February 1986.

Threatened premature labor, by T. P. Barkhatova. FEL'DSHER I AKUSHERKA 50(9):46-50, September 1985.

Usefulness of determining the HCG level by the passive hemagglutination inhibition test and Prognosticon All-in hemagglutination test in pathology of early pregnancy, by B. Berlinski, et al. WIADOMOSCI LEKARSKIE 38(23): 1641-1643, December 1, 1985.

ABORTION—THREATENED—PREVENTION AND CONTROL
Results of clinical use of prostaglandin synthesis inhibitors in the complex treatment of threatened premature-interruption of pregnancy, by N. V. Khachapuridze. AKUSHERSTVO I GINEKOLOGIIA (1):38-41, January 1986.

ABORTION—THREATENED—TREATMENT
Clinical management for abortion in early gestational weeks, by Y. Sagara. NIPPON SANKA FUJINKA GAKKAI ZASSHI 38(2):267-272, February 1986.

Clinical tests in obstetrics. 12. Diagnosis of threatened abortion, by M. Ishii. JOSANPU ZASSHI 39(12):1011-1014, December 1985.

Vaginal flora during supportive therapy using a pessary in pregnancy, by I. Havlík, et al. CESKOSLOVENSKA GYNEKOLOGIE 51(4):258-259, May 1986.

ABORTION—VETERINARY
Abortion and early neonatal death of kids attributed to intrauterine yersinia pseudotuberculosis infection, by S. T. Witte, et al. JOURNAL OF THE AMERICAN VETERINARY MEDICAL ASSOCIATION 187(8):834, October 15, 1985.

Abortion of twins following chloral hydrate anesthesia in a mare, by J. U. Akpokodje, et al. VETERINARY RECORD 118(11):306, March 15, 1986.

ABORTION—VETERINARY (continued)

Absorption and elimination of a prostaglandin F analog, fenprostalene, in lactating dairy cows, by R. V. Tomlinson, et al. JOURNAL OF DAIRY SCIENCE 68(8): 2072-2077, August 1985.

Acinetobacter calcoaceticus in three cases of late abortion in water buffaloes, by A. M. Das, et al. VETERINARY RECORD 118(8):214, February 22, 1986.

Attempted conversion of twin to singleton pregnancy in two mares with associated changes in plasma oestrone sulphate concentrations, by J. H. Hyland, et al. AUSTRALIAN VETERINARY JOURNAL 62(12):406-409, December 1985.

Bovine abortion and death associated with consumption of aflatoxin-contaminated peanuts, by A. C. Ray, et al. JOURNAL OF THE AMERICAN VETERINARY MEDICAL ASSOCIATION 188(10):1187-1188, May 15, 1986.

Bovine abortion associated with bacillus licheniformis, by G. Mitchell, et al. AUSTRALIAN VETERINARY JOURNAL 63(5):160-161, May 1986.

Bovine abortion caused by Bacillus cereus, by J. Schuh, et al. JOURNAL OF THE AMERICAN VETERINARY MEDICAL ASSOCIATION 187(10):1047-1048, November 15, 1985.

Bovine chlamydial abortion: serodiagnosis by modified complement-fixation and indirect inclusion fluorescence tests and enzyme-linked immunosorbent assay, by J. A. Perez-Martinez, et al. AMERICAN JOURNAL OF VETERINARY RESEARCH 47(7):1501-1506, July 1986.

Bovine embryo transfer pregnancies. I. Abortion rates and characteristics of calves, by K. K. King, et al. JOURNAL OF ANIMAL SCIENCE 61(4):747-757, October 1985.

Bovine leptospirosis: some clinical features of serovar hardjo infection, by W. A. Ellis, et al. VETERINARY RECORD 117(5):101-104, August 3, 1985.

Breed differences in return to estrus after PGF2 alpha-induced abortions in swine, by D. L. Meeker, et al. JOURNAL OF ANIMAL SCIENCE 61(2):354-357, August 1985.

Chlamydia isolated from abortion in sheep, by J. T. Seaman. AUSTRALIAN VETERINARY JOURNAL 62(12):436, December 1985.

Chondrifying fibrosarcoma in the abdominal cavity of a bovine aborted fetus, by S. Sato, et al. NIPPON JUIGAKU ZASSHI 48(1):173-175, February 1986.

Congenital spirochetosis in calves: association with epizootic bovine abortion, by J. W. Osebold, et al. JOURNAL OF THE AMERICAN VETERINARY MEDICAL ASSOCIATION 188(4):371-376, February 15, 1986.

Demonstration in Hungary of Q fever associated with abortion in cattle and sheep, by M. Rády, et al. ACTA VETERINARIA HUNGARICA 33(3-4):169-176, 1985.

Distinguishing between ovine abortion and ovine arthritis chlamydia psittaci isolaets with specific monoclonal antibodies, by W. J. DeLong, et al. AMERICAN JOURNAL OF VETERINARY RESEARCH 47(7):1520-1523, July 1986.

Enzyme activities in amniotic fluid and maternal blood in sheep, before and after induced foetal death and abortion, by A. R. Mohamed, et al. BRITISH VETERINARY JOURNAL 141(5):498-506, September-October 1985.

Epizootiologic investigations on a sheep farm with toxoplasma gondii-induced abortions, by J. P. Dubey, et al. JOURNAL OF THE AMERICAN VETERINARY MEDICAL ASSOCIATION 188(2):155-158, January 15, 1986.

Equine abortion and chloral hydrate [letter], by W. E. Allen. VETERINARY RECORD 118(14):407, April 5, 1986.

Equine herpesvirus type 1 abortion in an onager and suspected herpesvirus myelitis in a zebra, by R. J. Montali, et al. JOURNAL OF THE AMERICAN VETERINARY MEDICAL ASSOCIATION 187(11):1248-1249, December 1, 1985.

Equine herpesvirus type 1 (EHV-1) induced abortions and paralysis in a Lipizzaner stud: a contribution to the classification of equine herpesviruses, by S. I. Howdhury, et al. ARCHIVES OF VIROLOGY 90(3-4):273-288, 1986.

Experimental infection of pregnant ewes with listeria monocytogenes, by M. Gitter, et al. VETERINARY RECORD 118(21):575-578, May 24, 1986.

Failure of strange females to cause pregnancy block in collared lemmings, dicrostonyx groenlandicus, by R. J. Brooks, et al. BEHAVIORAL AND NEURAL BIOLOGY 44(3):485-491, November 1985.

Field studies on the efficacy of a long acting preparation of oxytetracycline in controlling outbreaks of enzootic abortion of sheep, by A. Greig, et al. VETERINARY RECORD 117(24):627-628, December 14, 1985.

Frequency of infertility and abortion in cows infected with tritrichomonas foetus var. brisbane, by B. L. Clark, et al. AUSTRALIAN VETERINARY JOURNAL 63(1):31-32, January 1986.

Haemophilus somnus infection of cattle—results of bacteriological study with special reference to abortion substrates, by H. Kiupel, et al. ARCHIV FUR EXPERIMENTELLE VETERINAERMEDIZIN 40(2):164-169, March 1986.

Herd problem of abortions and malformed calves attributed to bovine viral diarrhea, by C. E. Ross, et al. JOURNAL OF THE AMERICAN VETERINARY MEDICAL ASSOCIATION 188(6):618-619, March 15, 1986.

Immunofluorescence and cell culture techniques in the diagnosis of viral infection of aborted bovine fetuses, by M. H. Lucas, et al. VETERINARY RECORD 118(9):242-243, March 1, 1986.

Isolation of leptospires from the genital tract and kidneys of aborted sows, by W. A. Ellis, et al. VETERINARY RECORD 118(11):294-295, March 15, 1986.

Isolation of Rift Valley fevor virus from cattle abortions in Tanzania, by A. Kondela, et al. TROPICAL ANIMAL HEALTH AND PRODUCTION 17(3):185-186, August 1985.

Leptospires in pig urogenital tracts and fetuses, by W. A. Ellis, et al. VETERINARY RECORD 117(3):66-67, July 20, 1985.

Mycoplasma bovis abortion of cows following experimental infection, by H. Bocklisch, et al. ARCHIV FUR EXPERIMENTELLE VETERINAERMEDIZIN 40(1):48-55, January 1986.

Mycoplasma infection—factors interfering in toxicologic experiments on reproduction, by N. C. Juhr. BERLINER UND MUNCHENER TIERAERZTLICHE WOCHENSCHRIFT 99(2):37-41, February 1, 1986.

Mycoplasmas recovered from bovine genitalis, aborted foetuses and placentas in the Republic of South Africa, by C. J. Trichard, et al. ONDERSTEPOORT JOURNAL OF VETERINARY RESEARCH 52(2):105-110, June 1985.

Necrosis and abscessation of placental sites in a Pekingese bitch, by B. L. Penzhorn. JOURNAL OF THE SOUTH AFRICAN VETERINARY ASSOCIATION 56(3):135-136, September 1985.

Outbreak of bovine abortion attributed to ergot poisoning, by W. T. Appleyard. VETERINARY RECORD 118(2):48-49, January 11, 1986.

Outbreak of toxoplasma gondii abortion, mummification and perinatal death in goats, by G. H. Nurse, et al. AUSTRALIAN VETERINARY JOURNAL 63(1): 27-29, January 1986.

Ovine abortion associated with campylobacter jejuni, by K. S. Diker, et al. VETERINARY RECORD 118(11):307, March 15, 1986.

Ovine enzootic abortion: experimental studies of immune responses, by M. Dawson, et al. RESEARCH IN VETERINARY SCIENCE 40(1):59-64, January 1986.

Ovine enzootic abortion: field observations on naturally acquired and vaccine-elicited delayed type hypersensitivity to chlamydia psittaci (ovis), by A. J. Wilsmore, et al. VETERINARY RECORD 118(12):331-332, March 22, 1986.

Porcine abortion caused by Bacillus sp., by C. A. Kirkbride, et al. JOURNAL OF THE AMERICAN VETERINARY MEDICAL ASSOCIATION 188(9):1060-1061, May 1, 1986.

Possible correlations between preventive foot-and-mouth disease vaccination and abortion in cattle, by D. Ahlers, et al. DTW 92(10):423-428, October 8, 1985.

Possible dioxin poisoning in cattle, by F. G. Davies, et al. VETERINARY RECORD 117(9):207, August 31, 1985.

Potential danger to pregnant women of Chlamydia psittaci from sheep, by D. Buxton. VETERINARY RECORD 118(18):510-511, May 3, 1986.

Pregnant women and chlamydia infection [letter]. VETERINARY RECORD 118(21):594-595, May 24, 1986.

—, by R. G. Eddy, et al. VETERINARY RECORD 118(18):519, May 3, 1986.

Prevalence of leptospira infection in aborted pigs in Northern Ireland, by W. A. Ellis, et al. VETERINARY RECORD 118(3):63-65, January 19, 1986.

Rapid detection of chlamydia psittaci in vaginal swabs of aborted ewes and goats by enzyme linked immunosorbent assay (ELISA), by A. Souriau, et al. VETERINARY MICROBIOLOGY 11(3):251-259, March 1986.

Reconception of mares following termination of pregnancy with prostaglandin F2 alpha before and after day 35 of pregnancy, by B. L. Penzhorn, et al. EQUINE VETERINARY JOURNAL 18(3):215-217, May 1986.

Reduced progesterone and altered cotyledonary prostaglandin values induced by locoweed (astragalus lentiginosus) in sheep, by L. C. Ellis, et al. AMERICAN JOURNAL OF VETERINARY RESEARCH 46(9):1903-1907, September 1985.

Selective abortion of entire litters in the coypu: adaptive control of offspring production in relation to quality and sex, by L. M. Gosling. AMERICAN NATURALIST 127:777-795, June 1986.

Serum hormone patterns during abortion in the Bolivian squirrel monkey, by E. J. Diamond, et al. LABORATORY ANIMAL SCIENCE 35(6):619-623, December 1985.

Significance of the histologic study of the chorion for establishing the causes of cattle abortions, by J. von Sandersieben, et al. DTW 92(10):419-423, October 8, 1985.

Significance of leptospiral titres associated with bovine abortion, by J. K. Elder, et al. AUSTRALIAN VETERINARY JOURNAL 62(8):258-262, August 1985.

Toxicity of calotropis procera. Effect of a calotropis procera-based feed on embryonic and neonatal mortality in laboratory mice, by B. Faye. REVUE D'ELEVAGE ET DE MEDECINE VETERINAIRE DES PAYS TROPICAUX 38(1):72-75, 1985.

Toxoplasma gondii-induced abortion in dairy goats, by J. P. Dubey, et al. JOURNAL OF THE AMERICAN VETERINARY MEDICAL ASSOCIATION 188(2): 159-162, January 15, 1986.

Toxoplasma-like sporozoa in an aborted equine fetus, by J. P. Dubey, et al. JOURNAL OF THE AMERICAN VETERINARY MEDICAL ASSOCIATION 188(11):1312-1313, June 1, 1986.

Trypanosoma evansi infection in buffaloes in North-East Thailand. II. Abortions, by K. F. Löhr, et al. TROPICAL ANIMAL HEALTH AND PRODUCTION 18(2): 103-108, May 1986.

Vaccination against leptospiral abortion and renal carriage [letter], by E. S. Broughton, et al. VETERINARY RECORD 118(7):190-191, February 15, 1986.

Yersinia enterocolitica associated with third trimester abortion in buffaloes, by A. M. Das, et al. TROPICAL ANIMAL HEALTH AND PRODUCTION 18(2):109-112, May 1986.

ABORTION—VOLUNTARY
Various pharmacologic combinations in anesthesia for voluntary abortions in day hospitals, by F. Ciri, et al. MINERVA ANESTESIOLOGICA 52(1-2):15-18, January-February 1986.

ABORTION AND CIVIL RIGHTS

Arguments over abortion delay civil rights bill (news; Civil Rights Restoration Act), by K. A. Lawton. CHRISTIANITY TODAY 30(8):46-47, May 16, 1986.

Is abortion a civil right [editorial], by D. E. Anderson. CHRISTIANITY AND CRISIS 46(5):103-105, April 7, 1986.

ABORTION AND COLLEGE STUDENTS
Opinions regarding abortion among male Nigerian undergraduate students in the United States, by A. Adebayo, et al. SOCIAL BIOLOGY 32(1-2):132-135, Spring-Summer 1985.

Students join march for abortion rights. CHRONICLE OF HIGHER EDUCATION 32:33, March 19, 1986.

ABORTION AND ECONOMICS
Abortion economics, by D. A. Farber. NEW REPUBLIC 195:15-16, July 14-21, 1986.

Abortion 1986: state constitutional perspectives, by J. M. Healey. CONNECTI-CUT MEDICINE 50(6):417, June 1986; 50(7):491, July 1986.

Abortion tax deductions must be halted (parents get dependency exemption if aborted child lives briefly before it dies), by W. Carney. HUMAN EVENTS 46:15, March 22, 1986.

Economic model of teenage pregnancy decision-making, by A. Leibowitz, et al. DEMOGRAPHY 23:67-77, February 1986.

Expenditures for reproduction-related health care, by V. R. Fuchs, et al. JAMA 255(1):76-81, January 3, 1986.

Legal aspects of abortion practice, by E. B. Goldman. CLINICAL OBSTETRICS AND GYNAECOLOGY 13(1):135-143, March 1986.

ABORTION AND THE ERA
ERA and the abortion controversy: a case of dissonance reduction, by L. Bolce, et al. SOCIAL SCIENCE QUARTERLY 67:299-314, June 1986.

ABORTION AND FEMINISM
Abortion, pluralism, feminism (discussion of April 11, 1986 article, the fetus and fundamental rights), by J. C. Callahan. COMMONWEAL 113:338-342, June 6, 1986.

Conference report: Feminist International Network of Resistance to Reproductive and Genetic Engineering, Sweden, July 1985, by S. Brodribb. RE-SOURCES FOR FEMINIST RESEARCH 14:54-55, 1985.

Feminists must humanize abortion demands, by V. Moghadam. GUARDIAN 38(41):23, August 6, 1986.

Not an easy choice: feminist reexamines abortion, by K. McDonnell. WHOLE EARTH REVIEW 51:58-62, Summer 1986.

NOW backs investigation of legal action, by G. Wilde. NATIONAL NOW TIMES 19(3):1, May 1986.

NOW moves for Federal injunction—anti-abortion. NATIONAL NOW TIMES 19(4):3, July 1986.

ABORTION AND FEMINISM (continued)

Precarious unity of feminist theory and practice: the praxis of abortion. UNIVER-
SITY OF TORONTO FACULTY OF LAW REVIEW 44:85-108, Spring 1986.

Pro-choices cry foul: Saskatchewan feminists accuse a minister of making abortions difficult, by L. Cohen. ALBERTA REPORT 13:22, April 21, 1986.

Spanish state—the women's movement on the rise. INTERNATIONAL VIEW-
POINT 94:17, March 10, 1986.

To preserve and protect life: a Christian feminist perspective on abortion, by G. E.
Soley. SOJOURNERS 15(9):34-37, October 1986.

West Germany—feminism and the unions, by S. Engert. INTERNATIONAL
VIEWPOINT 94:19, March 10, 1986.

ABORTION AND HOSPITALS
Abortion: an attitude study of professional staff at Ramathibodi Hospital, by W.
Phuapradit, et al. JOURNAL OF THE MEDICAL ASSOCIATION OF THAI-
LAND 69(1):22-27, January 1986.

Effects of waste anaesthetic gases, by C. Wilson, et al. CANADIAN OPERATING
ROOM NURSES JOURNAL 3(6):13+, December 1985.

Hospitals: new targets of antiabortion violence?, by B. McCormick, HOSPITALS
60(5):109, March 5, 1986.

Incomplete abortion: characteristics of the patients treated in the O'Horan Hospital of Mérida, Yúcatan, by T. E. Canto de Cetina, et al. SALUD PUBLICA DE
MEXICO 27(6):507-513, November-December 1985.

Self-reported data on spontaneous abortions compared with data obtained by
computer linkage with the hospital registry, by L. Z. Heidam, et al. SCANDI-
NAVIAN JOURNAL OF SOCIAL MEDICINE 13(4):159-163, 1985.

Various pharmacologic combinations in anesthesia for voluntary abortions in day
hospitals, by F. Ciri, et al. MINERVA ANESTESIOLOGICA 52(1-2):15-18,
January-February 1986.

ABORTION AND JOURNALISM
Crossover in newspaper coverage of abortion from murder to liberation, by M. N.
Olasky, et al. JOURNALISM QUARTERLY 63:31-37, Spring 1986.

ABORTION AND MALES
Abortion and the man. Psychological and psychopathological manifestations in
the face of lost fatherhood, by P. Benvenuti, et al. RIVISTA DI PATOLOGIA
NERVOSA E MENTALE 104(6):255-268, November-December 1983.

Clinic (male reaction), by M. Blumenthal. NEW YORK TIMES MAGAZINE November 2, 1986.

Comparison of two interventions to assist men who accompany their partners for
abortions, by R. A. Karesky. DAI: B, 47(4), October 1986.

Fathers and fetuses, by G. W. Harris, Jr. ETHICS 96:594-603, April 1986.

Of fathers, fetuses, and fairy tales, by C. Levine. HASTINGS CENTER REPORT
16:2, October 1986.

ABORTION AND MALES (continued)

Opinions regarding abortion among male Nigerian undergraduate students in the United States, by A. Adebayo, et al. SOCIAL BIOLOGY 32(1-2):132-135, Spring-Summer 1985.

ABORTION AND MARRIAGE
Adjustment to abortion in marital relations, by B. Wimmer-Puchinger. GYNA-KOLOGE 19(1):33-36, March 1986.

Husband notification for abortion in Utah: a patronizing problem. UTAH LAW RE-VIEW 1986:609-628, 1986.

Importance of the marriage structure in predicting abortion, by L. V. Antipenskaia, et al. GENETIKA 22(1):158-163, January 1986.

Reflections on a miscarriage . . . one couple's psychological and emotional re-sponses, by S. B. Hardin, et al. MATERNAL-CHILD NURSING JOURNAL 15(1):23-30, Spring 1986.

ABORTION AND NOW
Labor union women join NOW for abortion rights, by A. Morrell. INTERNATIONAL VIEWPOINT 94:16, March 10, 1986.

NOW backs investigation of legal action, by G. Wilde. NATIONAL NOW TIMES 19(3):1, May 1986.

NOW moves for Federal injunction—anti-abortion. NATIONAL NOW TIMES 19(4):3, July 1986.

ABORTION AND PARENTAL CONSENT
Abortion—(1) it is unconstitutional for a state to require unemancipated minors and incompetents to wait twenty-four hours after parental notification before having an abortion. (2) a state statute concerning parental notice in abortion is enjoined until the state supreme court promulgates rules assuring the ex-peditious and confidential disposition of the judicial hearings which allow a mature minor or an immature minor whose best interests require an abortion to forego the state's parental notice requirement. Zbaraz v. Hartigan. JOUR-NAL OF FAMILY LAW 24:699-706, June 1986.

Ohio adopts an abortion notification statute. UNIVERSITY OF DAYTON LAW REVIEW 12:205-241, Fall 1986.

Parental consent for abortion: impact of the Massachusetts law, by V. G. Cartoof, et al. AMERICAN JOURNAL OF PUBLIC HEALTH 76(4):397-400, April 1986.

Should parents be notified of their minor daughter's abortion? A pregnant ques-tion for Florida legislators. FLORIDA STATE UNIVERSITY LAW REVIEW 14: 719-743, Fall 1986.

Zbaraz v. Hartigan: mandatory twenty-four hour waiting period after parental notification unconstitutionally burdens a minor's abortion decision. JOHN MARSHALL LAW REVIEW 19:1071-1086, Summer 1986.

ABORTION AND THE PERFORMING ARTS
Answering silent scream (Patricia Jaworski's pro choice audio cassette answers the film), by E. Doerr. HUMANIST 46:37, May-June 1986.

ABORTION AND THE PERFORMING ARTS (continued)

Fetus as spaceman (views of Rossalind Petchesky on The Silent Scream), by A. Hornaday. MS 14:82+, March 1986.

ABORTION AND PHYSICIANS
Abortion attitudes and performance among male and female obstetrician-gynecologists, by C. S. Weisman, et al. FAMILY PLANNING PERSPEC-TIVES 18(2):67-73, March-April 1986.

Abortion controversy (Alberta doctors protest ban on extra billing), by C. Barrett. MACLEAN'S 99:8, December 22, 1986.

Abortion in Louisiana: the applicability of R.S. 14:87 to a non-licensed physician. SOUTHERN UNIVERSITY LAW REVIEW 11:103-112, Spring 1985.

Availability of reproductive health services from United States private physicians, by M. T. Orr, et al. FAMILY PLANNING PERSPECTIVES 17(2):63-69, March-April 1985.

Comparison of complication rates in first trimester abortions performed by physician assistants and physicians, by M. A. Freedman, et al. AMERICAN JOURNAL OF PUBLIC HEALTH 76(5):550-556, May 1986.

Liability of the physician in a legal but failed abortion for social reasons, by G. H. Schlund. GEBURTSHILFE UND FRAUENHEILKUNDE 45(9):674-676, September 1985.

New pro-choice doctor steps forward, by L. Lathrop. HERIZONS 4(3):9, April 1986.

Thornburgh v. American College of Obstetricians and Gynecologists. DETROIT COLLEGE OF LAW REVIEW 1986:1263-1290, Winter 1986.

Virginia mothers can sue doctors in failed abortions. JET 70:7, May 19, 1986.

Why I changed my mind: a Christian gynaecologist explains his reasons for saying "no" to abortions, by P. Armon. ETHICS AND MEDICINE 1(3):47-48, 1985.

ABORTION AND POLITICS
Abortion and the conscience of the nation, by R. Reagan. CATHOLIC LAWYER 30:99-106, Spring 1986.

Abortion in the United States: politics or policy?, by C. Djerassi. BULLETIN OF THE ATOMIC SCIENTISTS 42:38-41, April 1986.

Anomaly in political perception, by D. Granberg. PUBLIC OPINION QUARTERLY 49:504-516, Winter 1985.

ARM wins suit (news; abortion rights mobilization charge that United States Catholic Conference had illegal political activities). CHRISTIAN CENTURY 103(5):112-113, February 5-12, 1986.

Democratic morality, by R. J. Neuhaus. NATIONAL REVIEW 38:47, July 18, 1986.

GLDC snubs Dukakis at abortion rights rally, by K. Kahn. GAY COMMUNITY NEWS 13(29):1, February 8, 1986.

Human rights and institutional process: abortion policy in six nations, by J. E. Lennertz. POLICY STUDIES JOURNAL 15:147-157, September 1986.

Impact of the Hyde Amendment on Congress: effects of single issue politics on legislative dysfunction June 1977-June 1978, by S. J. Tolchin. WOMEN AND POLITICS 5:91-106, September 1985.

Kowtowing to Dukakas. GAY COMMUNITY NEWS 13(27):4, January 25, 1986.

Lawyers are at odds with Reagan Administration on abortion, by L. R. Reskin. AMERICAN BAR ASSOCIATION JOURNAL 76:42, January 1, 1986.

Marching on Washington: I didn't dare hope this one would matter, by S. Dworkin. MS 14:86, June 1986.

Mitres in mischief, church, politics and tax. ECONOMIST 299:24, May 17, 1986.

1986 election report, by C. Douglas. OFF OUR BACKS 16(11):1, December 1986.

Political implications of attitudes to abortion in Britain, by J. Chapman. WEST EUROPEAN POLITICS 9(1):7-31, 1986.

Reagan justice department handed defeat. NATIONAL NOW TIMES 19(3):3, May 1986.

ABORTION AND RELIGION

Abortion and the sexual agenda, by S. Callahan. COMMONWEAL 113:232-238, April 25, 1986.

Abortion-clinic bombing: the war on sex, by S. Schneider. MADEMOISELLE 92:172-173+, April 1986.

Abortion: focus on conflict (questions concerning when life begins, quality of life, shape of family, and role of women in society), by R. J. Ohrstedt. CURRENTS IN THEOLOGY AND MISSION 13(3):132-142, June 1986.

Abortion: how should women decide [forum], ed. by V. Lindermayer. CHRISTI- ANITY AND CRISIS 46(10):227-250, July 14, 1986.

Abortion: a look at our Christian roots, by E. K. Jesaitis. NATIONAL CATHOLIC REPORTER 19:7, January 21, 1983.

Abortion of the silent scream (correlation between antiabortion movement and votes of legislators on human pain, suffering and violence), by J. W. Prescott. HUMANIST 46:10-17+, September-October 1986.

Abortion, pluralism, feminism (discussion of April 11, 1986 article, the fetus and fundamental rights), by J. C. Callahan. COMMONWEAL 113:338-342, June 6, 1986.

Academic freedom and the abortion issue: four incidents at Catholic institutions. ACADEME 72(suppl):13a, July-August 1986.

Are you for RU-486?, by T. Kaye. NEW REPUBLIC 194;13-15, January 27, 1986.

ARM wins suit (news; abortion rights mobilization charge that United States Catholic Conference had illegal political activities). CHRISTIAN CENTURY 103(5):112-113, February 5-12, 1986.

Black judge increases penalty against bishops (pro-choice group vs. Catholic Church's abortion stand). JET 70:8, May 26, 1986.

Catholicism and modernity [editorial], by D. C. Maguire. HORIZON 13(2):355-370, Fall 1986.

Chicago church acts against a former member who performs abortions (Moody Church confronts Dr. A. Bickham). CHRISTIANITY TODAY 30:63+, February 7, 1986.

Christian action: third approach to abortion, by G. B. Wilson. NATIONAL CATHO-LIC REPORTER 19:4, January 21, 1983.

Church and state (federal judge fines Catholic Church for refusing to turn over documents on its antiabortion campaign), by R. N. Ostling. TIME 127:19, May 19, 1986.

Churches on abortion, ed. by T. Ryan. ECUMENISM 83:1-28, September 1986.

Clinics of deception (pro life pregnancy testing centers masquerade as abortion clinics), by M. D. Uehling. NEWSWEEK 108:20, September 1, 1986.

Comparison of church statements on abortion; pt. 2: a working tool, by R. Fortin. ECUMENISM 84:23-36, December 1986.

Democratic morality, by R. J. Neuhaus. NATIONAL REVIEW 38:47, July 18, 1986.

Dissenting Catholics take pro-choice stand, by B. Yuill. NATIONAL CATHOLIC REPORTER 19:25, February 11, 1983.

Euthanasia, liberty, and religion [review article], by J. Ladd. ETHICS 93(1):129-138, October 1982.

Fetus and fundamental rights (Catholic Church), by J. C. Callahan. COMMON-WEAL 113:203-209, April 11, 1986.

Genesis and abortion: an exegetical test of a biblical warrant in ethics, by W. S. Kurz. THEOLOGICAL STUDIES 47(4):668-680, December 1986.

G.O.P. litmus test (right wing support for antiabortion positions). TIME 127:31, June 23, 1986.

Inside a right-to-life mind, by J. A. Hennessee. MADEMOISELLE 92:173+, April 1986.

Man: an axiological analysis from a Christian perspective, by R. Adams. ANPHI PAPERS 20(1-2):15-21, January-June 1985.

Maureen's choice: McTeer's new abortion job is disgusting to pro-lifers. AL-BERTA REPORT 13:46-47, February 10, 1986.

Mitres in mischief, church, politics and tax. ECONOMIST 299:24, May 17, 1986.

ABORTION AND RELIGION (continued)

Moral discourse in the church: a process politicized: how do and should Lutherans address social ethics?, by P. Nelson. LUTHERAN FORUM 20(1):19-21, 1986.

More ads, no more bombs. AMERICA 154:82-83, February 8, 1986.

My church threw me out (executive director of Planned Parenthood of Rhode Island excommunicated by Catholic Church), ed. by M. Orth, et al. REDBOOK 167:14+, June 1986.

Not killing, by R. Aitken. WHOLE EARTH REVIEW 51:63, Summer 1986.

Nuns deny Vatican claim [signers of statement supporting abortion rights). CHRISTIAN CENTURY 103(24):704, August 13-20, 1986.

Nuns' expulsion urged [news]. CHRISTIAN CENTURY 103(10):288, March 19-26, 1986.

On being pregnant, by M. Pellauer. CHRISTIANITY AND CRISIS 46:228-230, July 14, 1986.

Perils of apostasy: Maureen McTeer courts R. C. excommunication, by L. Byfield. ALBERTA REPORT 13:26-27, June 9, 1986.

Prolife leaders say 1986 has been a very good year, by R. Frame. CHRISTIANITY TODAY 30:30-31, November 21, 1986.

Right to life and the restoration of the American republic, by L. Lehrman. NATIONAL REVIEW 38:25-28, August 29, 1986.

Selected Jewish views of life and medical practice, by J. J. Lindenthal, et al. NEW JERSEY MEDICINE 82(10):795-799, October 1985.

Selling chastity—the sly new attack on your sexual freedom (prolife pregnancy-testing centers masquerading as abortion clinics), by S. Bolotin. VOGUE 176:482-483+, March 1986.

Should abortion be legal? Two contrasting views, by J. C. Willke, et al. SEVENTEEN 45:86-87+, January 1986.

Social basis of antifeminism: religious networks and culture, by J. L. Himmelstein. JOURNAL FOR THE SCIENTIFIC STUDY OF RELIGION 25(1):1-15, March 1986.

Solomon and Ruth needed (controversy over abortion advertisement signed by Catholic religious). AMERICA 154:42-43, January 25, 1986.

Souls on ice (frozen embryo transfer and the dilemma of abortion), by M. K. Blakely. VOGUE 176:346+, September 1986.

Startling fount of healing (use of cells taken from aborted human fetuses), by K. McAuliffe. US NEWS AND WORLD REPORT 101:68-70, November 3, 1986.

Support from superiors (superiors of nuns facing dismissal by the Vatican for signing a statement on abortion). CHRISTIAN CENTURY 103(4):87, January 29, 1986.

ABORTION AND RELIGION (continued)

Supporting choice: Christian responsibilities [editorial], by G. Hovey. CHRIS-
TIANITY AND CRISIS 46(3):51-53, March 3, 1986.

To preserve and protect life: a Christian feminist perspective on abortion, by G. E.
Soley. SOJOURNERS 15(9):34-37, October 1986.

Truth in advertising, please ("abortion rights" ads). AMERICA 154:1, January 4-
11, 1986.

Vatican clears three more (news; nuns faced with expulsion for signing statement; abortion). CHRISTIAN CENTURY 103(9):265, March 12, 1986.

Vatican two refuses to bow to Rome's will. NATIONAL NOW TIMES 19(4):4, July
1986.

Vatican's battered wives (nuns who signed ad questioning Catholic unity on
abortion), by J. Gramick. CHRISTIAN CENTURY 103:17-20, January 1-8,
1986.

Where have all the babies gone?, by K. Menehan. CHRISTIANITY TODAY
29(15):26-29, 1985.

Why I changed my mind: a Christian gynaecologist explains his reasons for saying
"no" to abortions, by P. Armon. ETHICS AND MEDICINE 1(3):47-48, 1985.

ABORTION AND TEENS

Abortion: the teenage patient and the OR nurse, by T. Howard. CANADIAN
NURSE 81(10):28-30, November 1985.

Denise's decision (teenager's abortion), by C. McCall. LIFE 9:72-74+, March
1986.

Economic model of teenage pregnancy decision-making, by A. Leibowitz, et al.
DEMOGRAPHY 23:67-77, February 1986.

Influence of maternal attitudes on urban, black teens' decisions about abortion v
delivery, by E. Freeman, et al. JOURNAL OF REPRODUCTIVE MEDICINE
30(10):731-735, October 1985.

Nurses speak out on teens and abortion, by M. Allen. CANADIAN NURSE
81(10):31-32, November 1985.

Pregnancy and induced abortion among teenagers, by S. Tado. JOSANPU
ZASSHI 39(11):1003, November 1985.

Pregnant teens must make own choices on abortion. JET 70:24, July 14, 1986.

Public policy and adolescent sexual behavior in the United States, by M. L.
Finkel, et al. SOCIAL BIOLOGY 30:140-150, Summer 1983.

Should parents be notified of their minor daughter's abortion? A pregnant question for Florida legislators. FLORIDA STATE UNIVERSITY LAW REVIEW 14:
719-743, Fall 1986.

Teen pregnancy in New Orleans: factors that differentiate teens who deliver,
abort, and successfully contracept, by E. Landry, et al. JOURNAL OF YOUTH
AND ADOLESCENCE 15(3):259-274, June 1986.

ABORTION AND TEENS (continued)

Teenagers talk about sex, pregnancy and contraception, by E. E. Kiser. FAMILY PLANNING PERSPECTIVES 17(2):83-90, March-April 1985.

What can government do to prevent teen pregnancy [interview], by J. A. Gasper. CHRISTIANITY TODAY 30(1):50-53, January 17, 1986.

Zbaraz v. Hartigan: mandatory twenty-four hour waiting period after parental notification unconstitutionally burdens a minor's abortion decision. JOHN MARSHALL LAW REVIEW 19:1071-1086, Summer 1986.

ABORTION AND WOMEN
Abortion and the politics of motherhood, by A. Rose. ATLANTIS 11(1):158, Fall 1985.

Abortion: focus on conflict (questions concerning when life begins, quality of life, shape of family, and role of women in society), by R. J. Ohrstedt. CURRENTS IN THEOLOGY AND MISSION 13(3):132-142, June 1986.

Abortion: how should women decide [forum], ed. by V. Lindermayer. CHRISTI-ANITY AND CRISIS 46(10):227-250, July 14, 1986.

Differences in self-concept and locus of control among women who seek abortions. AMERICAN MENTAL HEALTH COUNSELORS ASSOCIATION JOURNAL 8(1):4-11, January 1986.

Hierarchy's values don't value women, by E. Bader. GUARDIAN 39(12):2, December 17, 1986.

Labor union women join NOW for abortion rights, by A. Morrell. INTERNATIONAL VIEWPOINT 94:16, March 10, 1986.

Update on Women. NEW DIRECTIONS FOR WOMEN 15(2):18, March 1986.

"Women, power, and sex in the 21st century"—opening remarks, by B. Cicatelli. FRONTIERS 9(1):1-2, 1986.

Women's freedom, women's power, by L. Gordon. RADICAL AMERICA 19(6): 31, November 1986.

Women's media project, by J. Campbell. NATIONAL NOW TIMES 19(3):6, May 1986.

ABORTION CLINICS
Abolition of abortion services at Ste-Therese. COMMUNIQU'ELLES 12(1):8, January 1986.

Abortion-clinic bombing: the war on sex, by S. Schneider. MADEMOISELLE 92: 172-173+, April 1986.

Abortion foes use clinical subterfuge, by J. Gold. IN THESE TIMES 10(25):4, May 21, 1986.

Abortion rights, by E. Bader. GUARDIAN 39(10):4, December 3, 1986.

Bombers arond town, by J. Berck. WOMANEWS 7(2):16, February 1986.

Bombing clinics harms pro-life cause, by H. B. Gow. HUMAN EVENTS 46:13+, March 22, 1986.

ABORTION CLINICS (continued)

Bombing people not property. OFF OUR BACKS 16(1):18, January 1986.

Canada—interview with abortion rights campaigner. INTERNATIONAL VIEW-POINT 99:28, May 19, 1986.

Choice update—still ain't satisfied, by S. Newmann. HERIZONS 4(1):14, January 1986.

Clinic bombing continues. OFF OUR BACKS 16(2):6, February 1986.

Clinic (male reaction), by M. Blumenthal. NEW YORK TIMES MAGAZINE November 2, 1986.

Clinics of deception (pro life pregnancy testing centers masquerade as abortion clinics), by M. D. Uehling. NEWSWEEK 108:20, September 1, 1986.

Cluster of abortion deaths at a single facility, by M. E. Kafrissen, et al. OBSTETRICS AND GYNECOLOGY 68(3):387-389, September 1986.

Commitment greater than fear, by E. Bader. GUARDIAN 39(7):2, November 12, 1986.

Fake clinic hauled into court, by E. Bader. GUARDIAN 39(6):2, November 5, 1986.

Ireland: clinic sued . . . condoms debates, by N. Bythe. OFF OUR BACKS 16(1): 10, January 1986.

New pro-choice doctor steps forward, by L. Lathrop. HERIZONS 4(3):9, April 1986.

New RICO twist: damaged abortion clinic sues, by N. Blodgett. AMERICAN BAR ASSOCIATION JOURNAL 76:26, January 1, 1986.

NOW backs investigation of legal action, by G. Wilde. NATIONAL NOW TIMES 19(3):1, May 1986.

NOW moves for Federal injunction—anti-abortion. NATIONAL NOW TIMES 19(4):3, July 1986.

Opposing abortion clinics: a New York Times 1971 crusade, by M. N. Olasky. JOURNALISM QUARTERLY 63:305-310+, Summer 1986.

Preterm settles decade-long union dispute, by J. Ogletree. GAY COMMUNITY NEWS 13(41):3, May 3, 1986.

Pro-lifers give birth to phony abortion clinics, by M. Neuberger. WOMANEWS 8:1, September 1986.

Protesters harass abortion clinic, by S. Burke. OUT 4(9):1, July 1986.

Selling chastity—the sly new attack on your sexual freedom (prolife pregnancy-testing centers masquerading as abortion clinics), by S. Bolotin. VOGUE 176:482-483+, March 1986.

Terror and harrassment charged in clinic case, by D. Mathiason. GUARDIAN 38(23):7, March 12, 1986.

ABORTION CLINICS (continued)

Unholy water (abortionists who bomb clinics) [editorial], by S. Schmidt. ANALOG SCIENCE FICTION 106:4+, July 1986.

Update on Women. NEW DIRECTIONS FOR WOMEN 15(2):18, March 1986.

ABORTION COUNSELING
Abortion counseling, by R. Kubota. CALIFORNIA NURSE 82(1):4-5, February 1986.

Abortion counselling—a new component of medical care, by U. Landy. CLINICAL OBSTETRICS AND GYNAECOLOGY 13(1):33-41, March 1986.

ABORTION FUNDING
Abortion funding (Supreme Court decision). CHRISTIAN CENTURY 103:1144-1145, December 17, 1986.

Examining abortion funding policy arguments: an attempt to recast the debate, by L. F. Goldstein. WOMEN AND POLITICS 5:41-63, Summer-Fall 1985.

Fund aids poor women seeking abortions, by C. Black. GUARDIAN 38(41):5, August 6, 1986.

Get beyond labels (controversy over federal funding of family planning clinics), by N. Amidei. COMMONWEAL 113:37-38, January 31, 1986.

People vote on abortion funding: Colorado and Washington. FAMILY PLANNING PERSPECTIVES 17(4):155, July-August 1985.

Public funding of contraceptive, sterilization and abortion services, 1983, by R. B. Gold, et al. FAMILY PLANNING PERSPECTIVES 17:25-29, January-February 1985.

—, 1985, by R. B. Gold, et al. FAMILY PLANNING PERSPECTIVES 18:259-264, November-December 1986.

Understanding the abortion debate, by K. Glen. SOCIALIST REVIEW 89:51, September 1986.

Using state constitutions to expand public funding for abortions: throwing away the carrot with the stick, by E. Relkin, et al. WOMEN'S RIGHTS LAW RE-PORTER 9:27-88, Winter 1986.

Voters decide on abortion. OFF OUR BACKS 16(10):10, November 1986.

ABORTION RIGHTS GROUPS
See also: Pro-Choice Movement

Abolition of abortion services at Ste-Therese. COMMUNIQU'ELLES 12(1):8, January 1986.

Abortion coalition in Quebec pushes legalization, by K. Herland. HERIZONS 4(4):10, June 1986.

Abortion rights actions scheduled, by S. Craine. INTERCONTINENTAL PRESS 24(1):7, January 13, 1986.

Abortion rights: contested terrain, by D. Freeley. AGAINST THE CURRENT 1(3):3, May 1986.

ABORTION RIGHTS GROUPS (continued)

Abortion rights fight grows. INTERCONTINENTAL PRESS 24(5):143, March 10, 1986.

Abortion rights marches take on "Church and State". GAY COMMUNITY NEWS 14(15):1, October 28, 1986.

Abortion rights win narrow victory, by J. Biehl. GUARDIAN 38(38):3, June 25, 1986.

Abortion rights withstand heat, by S. Poggi. GAY COMMUNITY NEWS 14(17):3, November 9, 1986.

ARM wins suit (news; abortion rights mobilization charge that United States Catholic Conference had illegal political activities). CHRISTIAN CENTURY 103(5):112-113, February 5-12, 1986.

Biggest demonstration ever for abortion rights. INTERNATIONAL VIEWPOINT 96:28, April 7, 1986.

Choice group says no to lesbians, gay men, by K. Westheimer. GAY COMMUNITY NEWS 13(43):3, May 24, 1986.

Choosing to abort: pro-life loses in Fort McMurray's referendum, by L. Slobodian. ALBERTA REPORT 13:50-51, November 3, 1986.

Coalition work in the pro-choice movement: organizational and environmental opportunities and obstacles, by S. Staggenborg. SOCIAL PROBLEMS 33:374-390, June 1986.

Defend our gains and move forward [interview]. AGAINST THE CURRENT 1(3):7, May 1986.

Homophobia in what's left of the left, by S. Poggi. GAY COMMUNITY NEWS 13(45):2, June 7, 1986.

In favor of the right to abortion [letter]. CIVIL LIBERTIES 358:12, Summer 1986.

Jerry Falwell meets the Sisters of Justice, by B. Khan. OFF OUR BACKS 16(2): 15, February 1986.

March for women's lives. NORTHWEST PASSAGE 26(8):12, April 1986.

Montreal rally on abortion rights. INTERCONTINENTAL PRESS 24(5):143, March 10, 1986.

Of laws, not men. NATION 242(4):100, February 1, 1986.

On the march for choice, by L. Hart. NEW DIRECTIONS FOR WOMEN 15:1, May-June 1986.

100,000 march for women's lives, by E. Bader. GUARDIAN 38(24):1, March 19, 1986.

125,000 march for women's lives, by D. Kulp. OFF OUR BACKS 16:1, April 1986.

150,000 turn out for abortion rights march, by J. McKnight. GAY COMMUNITY NEWS 13(36):1, March 29, 1986.

ABORTION RIGHTS GROUPS (continued)

Rights studied, defended. NEW DIRECTIONS FOR WOMEN 15(2):4, March 1986.

Roe v Wade: 15 years later, by S. Poggi. GAY COMMUNITY NEWS 13(29):1, February 8, 1986.

Students join march for abortion rights. CHRONICLE OF HIGHER EDUCATION 32:33, March 19, 1986.

25,000 in United States abortion rights march, by P. Liyama. INTERCON-TINENTAL PRESS 24(7):214, April 7, 1986,

United States—100,000 march for abortion rights, by C. Wagner. INTER-CONTINENTAL PRESS 24(6):200, March 24, 1986.

Women of color mobilize for abortion rights. NATIONAL NOW TIMES 18(8):3, February 1986.

ABRUPTIO PLACENTAE
Association of prolonged, preterm premature rupture of the membranes and abruptio placentae, by D. M. Nelson, et al. JOURNAL OF REPRODUCTIVE MEDICINE 31(4):249-253, April 1986.

Comparison of blood levels of vitamin A, beta-carotene and vitamin E in abruptio placentae with normal pregnancy, by S. C. Sharma, et al. INTERNATIONAL JOURNAL FOR VITAMIN AND NUTRITION RESEARCH 56(1):3-9, 1986.

Incidence and recurrence rate of abruptio placentae in Sweden, by M. Kåregård, et al. OBSTETRICS AND GYNECOLOGY 67(4):523-528, April 1986.

Peripheral placental separation: a possible relationship to premature labor, B. A. Harris, Jr., et al. OBSTETRICS AND GYNECOLOGY 66(6):774-778, December 1985.

Placental laceration and stillbirth following motor vehicle accident with legal ramifications, by M. M. Nichols, et al. TEXAS MEDICINE 82(3):26-28, March 1986.

Profile of intra-partum and post-partum aspects of ante-partum haemorrhage from Punwani Maternity Hospital, Nairobi, by Y. P. Bansal. EAST AFRICAN MEDI-CAL JOURNAL 62(11):807-812, November 1985.

Use of heparin in the combination therapy of parturients having undergone pre-mature detachment of a normally positioned placenta, by G. Akmuradova, et al. AKUSHERSTVO I GINEKOLOGIIA (6):53-56, June 1985.

ABRUPTIO PLACENTAE—DIAGNOSIS
Abruptio placentae, by A. Katsulov, et al. AKUSHERSTVO I GINEKOLOGIIA 25(1):78-86, 1986.

Abruptio placentae: apparent thickening of the placenta caused by hyperechoic retroplacental clot, by M. C. Mintz, et al. JOURNAL OF ULTRASOUND IN MEDICINE 5(7):411-413, July 1986.

Characteristics of the clinical picture, hemostatic system and procedures for managing pregnancy and labor in premature detachment of a normally situ-ated placenta, by A. N. Strizhakov, et al. AKUSHERSTVO I GINEKOLOGIIA (8):28-31, August 1985.

ABRUPTIO PLACENTAE—DIAGNOSIS (continued)

Clinico-morphological aspects of the premature detachment of a normally situated placenta, by N. B. Kramarskaia. AKUSHERSTVO I GINEKOLOGIIA (3):59-63, March 1986.

Early placental abruption diagnosed by ultrasound, by A. Csongrády, et al. ORVOSI HETILAP 126(40):247-32475, October 6, 1985.

Placental abruption and subchorionic hemorrhage in the first half of pregnancy: United States appearance and clinical outcome, by E. E. Sauerbrei, et al. RADIOLOGY 160(1):109-112, July 1986.

ABRUPTIO PLACENTAE—ETIOLOGY
Chronic ureaplasma urealyticum amnionitis associated with abruptio placentae, by W. Foulon, et al. OBSTETRICS AND GYNECOLOGY 68(2):280-282, August 1986.

BIRTH CONTROL—GENERAL
See also: Contraception
            Contraceptives
            Family Planning

Birth control: vanishing options, by A. Toufexis, et al. TIME 128(9):78, September 1, 1986.

Birth control: what you need to know [pictorial], by D. Edmondson. PARENTS 61(10):156-158+, October 1986.

Birth control: what's now, what's next?, by P. Gadsby. GOOD HOUSEKEEPING 203(5):323, November 1986.

Birth dearth (with dialogue), by B. J. Wattenberg, et al. PUBLIC OPINION 8:6-20+, December 1985+.

Brain birth: a proposal for defining when a fetus is entitled to human life status. SOUTHERN CALIFORNIA LAW REVIEW 59:1061-1078, July 1986.

Case and comment: aiding and abetting, by S. Herbert, et al. CRIMINAL LAW REVIEW February 1986, pp. 113-118.

Contraceptive knowledge and use of birth control as a function of sex guilt, by C. Berger, et al. INTERNATIONAL JOURNAL OF WOMEN'S STUDIES 8(1):72-79, January-February 1985.

Desire for a child and birth control, by M. Guy. LUMEN VITAE 41(2):188-204, 1986.

Entry into marriage and parenthood by young men and women: the influence of family background, by R. T. Michael, et al. DEMOGRAPHY 22(4):515-544, November 1985.

Family planning before birth—and after, by J. Bermel. HASTINGS CENTER REPORT 16:2, June 1986.

Fecundability and the frequency of marital intercourse: new models incorporating the ageing of gametes, by R. G. Potter, et al. POPULATION STUDIES 40(1): 159-170, March 1986.

BIRTH CONTROL—GENERAL (continued)

Fertility decision making among young mothers, by S. K. Dunn. DAI: A 46(11): 3396A, May 1986.

Fertility rights, by L. B. Ackerman. SCIENCE 7:55-56, January-February 1986.

Gillick defeated but have we seen last of her? SPARE RIB 161:43, December 1985.

Heading your way: five-year birth control, by J. Glass. HARPERS BAZAAR 119: 105+, June 1986.

House panel hears how prescription drugs get diverted. NARCOTICS CONTROL DIGEST 16(15):4-5, July 23, 1986.

Hunger must not be, by Z. Nightingale. HUMANIST 46:20-21+, January-February 1986.

Illegitimacy—we ignore the roots, by S. Tyler. SAINT LOUIS 12(81):14, January 1986.

International family planning. HOUSTON JOURNAL OF INTERNATIONAL LAW 8:155-173, Autumn 1985.

Issues in contraceptive development. POPULATION 15:1, May 1985.

Keep taking the pill (we think). NEW SCIENTIST 111:21, September 25, 1986.

Medical care. JOURNAL OF FAMILY LAW 24(4):747-748, June 1986.

Multilevel effects of socioeconomic development and family planning programs on children never born, by B. Entwisle, et al. AMERICAN JOURNAL OF SOCIOLOGY 91:616-649, November 1985.

Natural alternative, by N. Cameron. HERIZONS 4(6):39, September 1986.

"Natural" control of fertility, by E. Basker. SOCIOLOGY OF HEALTH AND ILLNESS 8(1):3-25, March 1986.

Plato redivivus (eugenic program of *Republic* 5 and modern population control practices), by H. J. Vogt. THEOLOGISCHE QUARTALSCHRIFT 166(1):56-58, 1986.

Population control plan takes heat. EAST WEST JOURNAL 16(10):11, October 1986.

Risky business of birth control (liability suits), by C. Skrzycki. US NEWS AND WORLD REPORT 100:42-43, May 26, 1986.

Rural-urban differentials in marital fertility in four muslim populations, by S. Admad. JOURNAL OF BIOSOCIAL SCIENCE 17(2):157-166, 1985.

Sexuality, contraception and health: birth control. LADIES HOME JOURNAL 103(8):54+, August 1986.

Sida, ce que font les chinois, by D. Gascon. ACTUALITE 11:150-151, October 1986.

BIRTH CONTROL—GENERAL (continued)

Sociology, ideology, and the abortion issue: a content analysis of family sociology texts, by R. J. Adamek. JOURNAL OF APPLIED SOCIOLOGY 2(1):43-56, 1985.

Summer on abortion, by R. Weitz, et al. DIALOGUE 24(4):671-699, Winter 1985.

Torts. JOURNAL OF FAMILY LAW 24(2):390, 1985-1986.

Towards smaller families: the crucial role of the private sector. DRAPER FUND REPORT December 1986, pp. 1-32.

Vaginal sponges and TSS. TRIAL 21(12):87-89, December 1985.

Value of children, family welfare and communication strategy: some observations, by K. K. Verma. JOURNAL OF SOCIAL AND ECONOMIC STUDIES 1(3): 287-296, July-September 1984.

Women's freedom, women's power, by L. Gordon. RADICAL AMERICA 19(6): 31, November 1986.

AFRICA
Africa and the limits to growth, by R. U. Light. HUMANIST 46:27-29+, July-August 1986.

Population control urged, by Y. Rusheng. BEIJING REVIEW 29:13, June 2, 1986.

Search for a fair deal. AFRICA (179):60+, July 1986.

ALGERIA
Population policy compendium: Algeria, UN Department of International Economic and Social Affairs. UN FUND FOR POPULATION ACTIVITIES REPORT June 1985.

ARGENTINA
Argentina "in democracy" feminism 1985, by N. Sternbach. OFF OUR BACKS 16(1):6, January 1986.

ASIA
Averting crisis in Asia?, by L.-J. Cho. BULLETIN OF THE ATOMIC SCIENTISTS 42:30-33, April 1986.

South Asia's family planning schedule, by Y. Kureishi. INSIDE 10(47):47, November 1986.

AUSTRALIA
Australia claims lead in race for unisex pill, by J. Ford. NEW SCIENTIST 110:21, May 8, 1986.

BANGLADESH
Influence of female education, labor force participation, and age at marriage on fertility behavior in Bangladesh, by R. H. Chaudhury. SOCIAL BIOLOGY 31(1-2):59-74, Spring-Summer 1984.

BRAZIL
Problema populacional brasileiro e pobreza, by G. de Paiva. CARTA MENSAL 31:37-47, April 1985.

BIRTH CONTROL—GENERAL (continued)

CHINA
Alternative to the one-child policy in China. POPULATION AND DEVELOP-
MENT REVIEW 11(4):585, December 1985.

China: a nation in ferment (interview with J. D. Hair), by J. Strohm. INTERNA-
TIONAL WILDLIFE 16:44-49, March-April 1986.

China's side, by M. Morain. HUMANIST 46:29-30, September-October 1986.

Family planning in China, by J. K. Kallgren. CURRENT HISTORY 85:269-
272+, September 1986.

Marriage and fertility in China: a graphical analysis, by Z. Yi, et al. POPULA-
TION AND DEVELOPMENT REVIEW 11(4):721-736, December 1985.

Mosher sues Stanford, by B. J. Culliton. SCIENCE 234:280, October 17, 1
986.

No slackening in family planning, by X. Yang. BEIJING REVIEW 29:6-7, March
10, 1986.

Politics, power and prevention: the People's Republic of China case, by E. H.
Johnson. JOURNAL OF CRIMINAL JUSTICE 14(5):449-457, September-October 1986.

Redirection of the Chinese family: ramifications of minimal reproduction, by H.
Y. Tien. ASIAN PROFILE 14:305-313, August 1986.

Reducing China's one billion. MAZINGIRA 894):17, 1985.

Return of the baby killers, by J. Mirsky. NEW STATESMAN 111:19-20, March
21, 1986.

— (link between female infanticide and one-child family policy), by J. Mirsky.
NEW STATESMAN March 21, 1986, pp. 19-20.

UNFPA executive director expresses "deep distress" at impending cut in
United States contribution (disagreement concerning family planning
program). UN CHRONICLE 22:53, September 1985.

Who lost China? (disagreement over family planning program). SCIENTIFIC
AMERICAN 255:54D-55, November 1986.

DEVELOPING COUNTRIES
Births and economic growth. FUTURIST 20:56, September-October 1986.

Contraception—the next 25 years, by J. A. Loraine. FUTURES 18:526-535,
August 1986.

Directive language, by M. Morain. HUMANIST 46:29, September-October
1986.

How to get the poor some help, by G. Richards. HUMANIST 46:19-22+,
March-April 1986.

Imperialism and the pill (cultural and biological imperialism implicit in United
States population control efforts), by T. Bethell. NATIONAL REVIEW
38:38-40, March 14, 1986.

83

BIRTH CONTROL—GENERAL (continued)

DEVELOPING COUNTRIES (continued)
International family planning, by M. P. McPherson. DEPARTMENT OF
STATE BULLETIN 86:43-45, March 1986.

International scene, by M. Morain. HUMANIST 46:33-34, November-
December 1986.

Multilevel dependence of contraceptive use on socioeconomic development
and family planning program strength, by B. Entwisle, et al.
DEMOGRAPHY 23(2):199-216, May 1986.

Population growth and economic development (with editorial comment by
Alan McGowan), by S. H. Preston. ENVIRONMENT 28(inside cover):6-
9+, March 1986.

Population update, by M. Morain. HUMANIST 46:31-32, July-August 1986+.

Worldwide challenge, by M. Morain. HUMANIST 46:31-32, July-August
1986.

EGYPT
Reflections on recent levels and trends of fertility and ortality in Egypt, by B.
Bucht, et al. POPULATION STUDIES 40(1):101-113, March 1986.

Rumor, misinformation and oral contraceptive use in Egypt, by J. DeClerque,
et al. SOCIAL SCIENCE AND MEDICINE 23(1):83-92, 1986.

ENGLAND
Morning-after pill OK (news; rape victims; ruling by Roman Catholic bishops of
England and Wales). CHRISTIAN CENTURY 103(20):577, June 18-25,
1986.

GAMBIA
Population policy compendium: Gambia, UN Department of International Eco-
nomic and Social Affairs. UN FUND FOR POPULATION ACTIVITIES RE-
PORT May 1985.

GHANA
Fertility and family planning in Accra, by G. B. Fosu. JOURNAL OF BIO-
SOCIAL SCIENCE 18(1):11-22, January 1986.

GREAT BRITAIN
How conservative are British attitudes to reproduction?, by J. Simons.
QUARTERLY JOURNAL OF SOCIAL AFFAIRS 2(1):41-54, 1986.

GUATEMALA
Population policy compendium: Guatemala, UN Department of International
Economic and Social Affairs. UN FUND FOR POPULATION ACTIVITIES
REPORT May 1985.

HONDURAS
Population policy compendium: Honduras, UN Department of International
Economic and Social Affairs. UN FUND FOR POPULATION ACTIVITIES
REPORT August 1985.

HUNGARY
Social demography of Hungarian villages in the eighteenth and nineteenth

BIRTH CONTROL—GENERAL (continued)

HUNGARY (continued)
centuries (with special attention to Sárpilis, 1792-1804), by R. Andorka, et al. JOURNAL OF FAMILY HISTORY 11(2):169-192, 1986.

INDIA
Health, fertility, and society in India: microstudies and macrostudies [review article], by B. D. Miller. JOURNAL OF ASIAN STUDIES 45:1027-1036, November 1986.

IRELAND
Birth control and abortion in Ireland, by N. Dosterom. HERIZONS 4(2):13, March 1986.

ISRAEL
How does fertility relate to religiosity: survey evidence from Israel, by S. Neuman, et al. SOCIOLOGY AND SOCIAL RESEARCH 70:178-180, January 1986.

Radio and family planning in Israel: letters to broadcastears, by R. Shtarkshall, et al. JOURNAL OF COMMUNICATION 35:69-81, Spring 1985.

ITALY
Oral contraceptives in a southern Italian community, by M. A. Korovkin. CURRENT ANTHROPOLOGY 27:80-83, February 1986.

IVORY COAST
Population policy compendium: Ivory Coast, UN Department of International Economic and Social Affairs. UN FUND FOR POPULATION ACTIVITIES REPORT July 1985.

KENYA
Fanisi's choice, by J. Tierney. SCIENCE 7:26-42, January-February 1986.

Milked. ECONOMIST 298:41, March 22, 1986.

Population policy compendium: Kenya, UN Department of International Economic and Social Affairs. UN FUND FOR POPULATION ACTIVITIES REPORT July 1985.

State of the species, cont. (discussion of January-February 1986 article, Fanisi's choice), by T. Tierney. SCIENCE 7:13-15, May 1986.

KOREA
Evaluation of contraceptive history data in the Republic of Korea, by A. R. Pebley, et al. STUDIES IN FAMILY PLANNING 17(1):22-35, January-February 1986.

NAMIBIA
Politics of population control in Namibia, by J. Lindsay. REVIEW OF AFRICAN POLITICAL ECONOMY 36:58, September 1986.

NICARAGUA
Population policy compendium: Nicaragua, UN Department of International Economic and Social Affairs. UN FUND FOR POPULATION ACTIVITIES REPORT October 1985.

NIGERIA
Changing pattern of post-partum sexual abstinence in a Nigerian rural

BIRTH CONTROL—GENERAL (continued)

NIGERIA (continued)
    community, by A. E. Isenalumhe, et al. SOCIAL SCIENCE AND MEDI-
    CINE 23(7):683-686, 1986.

    Control of reproduction: principle—Nigeria, by R. Pittin. REVIEW OF
    AFRICAN POLITICAL ECONOMY 35:40, May 1986.

PHILIPPINES
    Evaluating the effects of optimally distributed public programs: child health
    and family planning interventions (Laguna province), by M. R. Rosen-
    zweig, et al. AMERICAN ECONOMIC REVIEW 76:470-482, June 1986.

RWANDA
    Plans for Rwanda, by S. Surkes. GEOGRAPHICAL MAGAZINE 58:168-169,
    April 1986.

SCOTLAND
    Pre-term foetal life times in Scotland, by R. M. Pickering, et al. POPULATION
    STUDIES 40(1):115-127, March 1986.

    Victorian values and the fertility decline: the case of Scotland, by D. Kemmer.
    CRITICAL SOCIAL RESEARCH 2(1):1-31, Winter 1986.

SENEGAL
    Vanguard family planning acceptors in Senegal, by D. Nichols, et al. STUD-
    IES IN FAMILY PLANNING 16(5):271-278, September-October 1985.

SOUTH AFRICA
    South Africa: crimes against women. AFRICA (170):70-71, October 1985.

SOVIET UNION
    Soviet birth control: a majority prefers abortion. DISCOVER 7:8, April 1986.

SRI LANKA
    Environmental and other factors influencing fertility in Sri Lanka, by D. F. S.
    Fernando. JOURNAL OF BIOSOCIAL SCIENCE 18(2):209-214, April
    1986.

SWAZILAND
    Population policy compendium: Swaziland, UN Department of International
    Economic and Social Affairs. UN FUND FOR POPULATION ACTIVITIES
    REPORT March 1985.

THAILAND
    Fun and games. WORLD HEALTH March 1986, pp. 20-21.

TOGO
    Population policy compendium: Togo, UN Department of International
    Economic and Social Affairs. UN FUND FOR POPULATION ACTIVITIES
    REPORT July 1985.

TUNISIA
    Effects of socioeconomic development upon a model of women's fertility de-
    cision making in a Tunisian Community, by C. D. Miller. DAI: A 46(10):
    3164A, April 1986.

TURKEY
    Too many young Turks. ECONOMIST 300:43, August 23, 1986.

BIRTH CONTROL—GENERAL (continued)

UGANDA
Population policy compendium: Uganda, UN Department of International
Economic and Social Affairs. UN FUND FOR POPULATION ACTIVITIES
REPORT July 1985.

UNITED STATES
Adoption of fertility limitation in an American frontier population: an analysis
and simulation of socio-religious subgroups (Mormans), by D. L. Anderton, et al. SOCIAL BIOLOGY 31(1-2):140-159, Spring-Summer 1984.

Contraceptive practices among female heroin addicts, by N. Ralph, et al.
AMERICAN JOURNAL OF PUBLIC HEALTH 76(8):1016-1017, August
1986; Discussion 76:1460, December 1986.

Decision to terminate childbearing: differences in preoperative ambivalence
between tubal ligation women and vasectomy wives, by R. N. Shain, et al.
SOCIAL BIOLOGY 31(1-2):40-58, Spring-Summer 1984.

Estimates of pregnancies and pregnancy rates for the United States, 1976-
1981, by S. J. Ventura, et al. PUBLIC HEALTH REPORTS 100:31-33,
January-February 1985.

Family planning: abort it. ECONOMIST 297:37-38, November 9, 1985.

Modern contraceptive practice in rural Appalachia, by G. A. Gairola, et al.
AMERICAN JOURNAL OF PUBLIC HEALTH 76(8):1004-1008, August
1986.

Paths to adolescent parenthood: implications for prevention, by L. H. Flick.
PUBLIC HEALTH REPORTS 101(2):132-147, March-April 1986.

Public policy and public opinion toward sex education and birth control for
teenagers, by P. A. Reichelt. JOURNAL OF APPLIED SOCIAL PSY-
CHOLOGY 16(2):95-106, 1986.

Religion and fertility in the United States: the importance of marriage patterns
and Hispanic origin, by W. D. Mosher, et al. DEMOGRAPHY 23:367-379,
August 1986.

Reproductive rights for a more humane world , by F. Wattleton. HUMANIST
46:5-7+, July-August 1986.

School-based health clinics: an idea whose time has come? (clinic of
Chicago's DuSable High School), by R. L. Frame. CHRISTIANITY TODAY
30(4):42-44, March 7, 1986.

Screening the vasectomy applicant: reassessing the importance of eligibility
criteria, by J. Uhlman, et al. SOCIAL BIOLOGY 33:102-108, Spring-
Summer 1986.

Source of service and visit rate of family planning services: United States,
1982, by W. D. Mosher, et al. PUBLIC HEALTH REPORTS 101(4):405-
416, July-August 1986.

Teen pregnancy in New Orleans: factors that differentiate teens who deliver,
abort, and successfully contracept, by E. Landry, et al. JOURNAL OF
YOUTH AND ADOLESCENCE 15(3):259-274, June 1986.

BIRTH CONTROL—GENERAL (continued)

WALES
Morning-after pill OK (news; rape victims; ruling by Roman Catholic bishops of England and Wales). CHRISTIAN CENTURY 103(20):577, June 18-25, 1986.

WESTERN SAMOA
Discriminant analysis as a method for differentiating potential acceptors of family planning: Western Samoa, by L. P. Gans, et al. HUMAN ORGANIZATION 44:228-233, Fall 1985.

YEMEN ARAB REPUBLIC
Population policy compendium: Yemen Arab Republic, UN Department of International Economic and Social Affairs. UN FUND FOR POPULATION ACTIVITIES REPORT July 1985.

BIRTH CONTROL—ADVERTISING
New update: change urged in ad policy on birth control, by R. Zacks. TV GUIDE 34:41+, October 25, 1986.

BIRTH CONTROL—ATTITUDES
Artificial birth control: an impasse revisited, by N. J. Rigall. THEOLOGICAL STUDIES 47:681-690, December 1986.

Attitudes of women of reproductive age to in vitro fertilization and embryo research, by E. M. Aler, et al. JOURNAL OF BIOSOCIAL SCIENCE 18(2):155-167, April 1986.

Comment on Tooley's *Abortion and Infanticide* [review article], by M. Tushnet, et al. ETHICS 96(2):350-355, January 1986.

How conservative are British attitudes to reproduction?, by J. Simons. QUARTERLY JOURNAL OF SOCIAL AFFAIRS 2(1):41-54, 1986.

Papa don't preach (controversy surrounding school-based clinics). NATION 243(13):396-397, October 25, 1986.

BIRTH CONTROL—HISTORY
Historical look at a contemporary question: the cervical cap, by J. A. Zimmet, et al. HEALTH EDUCATION 17:53-57, October-November 1986.

Social demography of Hungarian villages in the eighteenth and nineteenth centuries (with special attention to Sárpilis, 1792-1804), by R. Andorka, et al. JOURNAL OF FAMILY HISTORY 11(2):169-192, 1986.

BIRTH CONTROL—LAWS AND LEGISLATION
Artificial reproduction techniques, fertility regulation: the challenge of contemporary family law, by P. F. Silva-Ruiz. AMERICAN JOURNAL OF COMPARATIVE LAW 34(suppl):125-140, 1986.

Court upholds ortho damages, by P. Kelly. MULTINATIONAL MONITOR 8(1):18, December 1986.

BIRTH CONTROL—MALE
Husbands' sex-role preferences and contraceptive intentions: the case of the male pill, by W. Marsiglio. SEX ROLES 12(5-6):655-663, March 1985.

Sex and male responsibility, by P. Grant. GLAMOUR 84:314, March 1986.

Comparison of census and family planning program data on contraceptive pre-valence, Indonesia, by K. Streatfield. STUDIES IN FAMILY PLANNING 16(6 pt 1):342-349, November-December 1985.

Comparison of 1970 and 1980 survey findings on family planning in India, by M. E. Khan, et al. STUDIES IN FAMILY PLANNING 16(6 pt 1):312-320, Novem-ber-December 1985.

Contraceptive social marketing: lessons from experience. POPULATION RE-PORTS 13(3):773, July-August 1985.

Contraceptive use, amenorrhea, and breastfeeding in postpartum women, by V. H. Laukaran, et al. STUDIES IN FAMILY PLANNING 16(6 pt 1):293-301, November-December 1985.

Contraceptive use in Canada, 1984, by T. R. Balakrishnan, et al. FAMILY PLANNING PERSPECTIVES 17(5):209-215, September-October 1985.

Evaluation of contraceptive history data in the Republic of Korea, by A. R. Pebley, et al. STUDIES IN FAMILY PLANNING 17(1):22-35, January-February 1986.

Fertility and family planning surveys: [update]. POPULATION REPORTS (8): M289-M348, September-October 1985; 13(4):289, September-October 1985.

Immunological methods of birth control, by M. Sh. Verbitskii. VESTNIK AKA-DEMII MEDITSINSKIKH NAUK SSSR (1):28-36, 1986.

Individual vs. group education in family planning clinics, by J. H. Johnson. FAMILY PLANNING PERSPECTIVES 17(6):255-259, November-December 1985.

Infant feeding practices, postpartum amenorrhea, and contraceptive use in Thailand, by J. Knodel, et al. STUDIES IN FAMILY PLANNING 16(6 pt 1):302-311, November-December 1985.

Issues in contraceptive development. POPULATION 15:1, May 1985.

Maintaining family planning acceptance levels through development incentives in Northeastern Thailand, by J. Stoeckel, et al. STUDIES IN FAMILY PLANNING 17(1):36-43, January-February 1986.

Next contraceptive revolution, by L. E. Atkinson, et al. FAMILY PLANNING PER-SPECTIVES 18(1):19-26, January-February 1986.

Teenagers talk about sex, pregnancy and contraception, by E. E. Kiser. FAMILY PLANNING PERSPECTIVES 17(2):83-90, March-April 1985.

Under the skin (birth-control method). SCIENTIFIC AMERICAN 255:78+, October 1986.

Vanguard family planning acceptors in Senegal, by D. Nichols, et al. STUDIES IN FAMILY PLANNING 16(5):271-278, September-October 1985.

Worldwide trends in funding for contraceptive research and evaluation, by L. E. Atkinson, et al. FAMILY PLANNING PERSPECTIVES 17(5):196-199+, September-October 1985.

BIRTH CONTROL—PSYCHOLOGY AND PSYCHIATRY

Contraceptive knowledge and use of birth control as a function of sex guilt, by C. Berger, et al. INTERNATIONAL JOURNAL OF WOMEN'S STUDIES 8(1):72-79, January-February 1985.

BIRTH CONTROL—RESEARCH

Attitudes of women of reproductive age to in vitro fertilization and embryo research, by E. M. Aler, et al. JOURNAL OF BIOSOCIAL SCIENCE 18(2):155-167, April 1986.

Conference report: Feminist International Network of Resistance to Reproductive and Genetic Engineering, Sweden, July 1985, by S. Brodribb. RESOURCES FOR FEMINIST RESEARCH 14:54-55, 1985.

Contraceptive vaccine moves up from baboons to humans, by D. MacKenzie. NEW SCIENTIST 109:21, February 27, 1986.

Downfall of absent professor, by G. Maslen. TIMES HIGHER EDUCATION SUPPLEMENT 727:10, October 10, 1986.

Next contraceptive revolution, by L. E. Atkinson, et al. FAMILY PLANNING PERSPECTIVES 18(1):19-26, January-February 1986.

One step closer to a pill for men. NEW SCIENTIST 110:28, June 5, 1986.

Worldwide trends in funding for contraceptive research and evaluation, by L. E. Atkinson, et al. FAMILY PLANNING PERSPECTIVES 17(5):196-199+, September-October 1985.

BIRTH CONTROL—SOCIOLOGY

Effects of socioeconomic development upon a model of women's fertility decision making in a Tunisian Community, by C. D. Miller. DAI: A 46(10):3164A, April 1986.

Environmental and other factors influencing fertility in Sri Lanka, by D. F. S. Fernando. JOURNAL OF BIOSOCIAL SCIENCE 18(2):209-214, April 1986.

Teenage fertility, socioeconomic status and infant mortality, by M. E. Miller, et al. JOURNAL OF BIOSOCIAL SCIENCE 17(2):147-155, 1985.

BIRTH CONTROL—STATISTICS

Determinants of parity distribution: a cross-national analysis of the effects of modernization on fertility, by K. Trent. DAI: A 46(10):3164-A, April 1986.

Gallup survey uncovers birth control misconceptions. AMERICAN FAMILY PHYSICIAN 33:296+, April 1986.

BIRTH CONTROL AND AGING

Ageing gamete in relation to birth control failures and Down syndrome, by P. H. Jongbloet. EUROPEAN JOURNAL OF PEDIATRICS 144(4):343-347, November 1985.

BIRTH CONTROL AND ECONOMICS

Effects of socioeconomic development upon a model of women's fertility decision making in a Tunisian Community, by C. D. Miller. DAI: A 46(10):3164A, April 1986.

BIRTH CONTROL AND EDUCATION

Birth control at school: pass or fail? EBONY 41:37-38+, October 1986.

BIRTH CONTROL AND EDUCATION (continued)

Birth-control clinics in schools? (interview with L. Zabin and L. Maher). US NEWS AND WORLD REPORT 101:82, September 29, 1986.

Birth control: what you need toknow [pictorial], by D. Edmondson. PARENTS 61(10):156-158+, October 1986.

Education chief blasts birth control in schools (views of W. Bennett). JET 70:22, May 5, 1986.

BIRTH CONTROL AND FEMINISM
Argentina "in democracy" feminism 1985, by N. Sternbach. OFF OUR BACKS 16(1):6, January 1986.

Feminist movements and changes in sex roles: the influence of technology, by J. J. Kronenfeld, et al. SOCIOLOGICAL FOCUS 19(1):47-60, 1986.

BIRTH CONTROL AND PHYSICIANS
Doctors' attitude towards family planning, by A. Chandani. JOURNAL OF SOCI-OLOGICAL STUDIES 1(1):155-162, January 1986.

BIRTH CONTROL AND POLITICS
Impact of birth control as women in politics, by J. J. Kronenfeld, et al. FREE IN-QUIRY IN CREATIVE SOCIOLOGY 14(1):27-32, May 1986.

Politics of population control in Namibia, by J. Lindsay. REVIEW OF AFRICAN POLITICAL ECONOMY 36:58, September 1986.

Politics, power and prevention: the People's Republic of China case, by E. H. Johnson. JOURNAL OF CRIMINAL JUSTICE 14(5):449-457, September-October 1986.

BIRTH CONTROL AND RELIGION
Adoption of fertility limitation in an American frontier population: an analysis and simulation of socio-religious subgroups (Mormans), by D. L. Anderton, et al. SOCIAL BIOLOGY 31(1-2):140-159, Spring-Summer 1984.

Artificial birth control: an impasse revisited, by N. J. Rigall. THEOLOGICAL STUDIES 47:681-690, December 1986.

Birth-control clinics in schools? (interview with L. Zabin and L. Maher). US NEWS AND WORLD REPORT 101:82, September 29, 1986.

Catholic physician, the contraception issue and the three questions of ethics, by J. O'Donohoe. JOURNAL OF PASTORAL COUNSELING 18(1):34-46, 1983.

Cleric on a collision course with Vatican over orthodoxy [news], by C. Low. INSIGHT: THE WASHINGTON TIMES 2(30):14-15, July 28, 1986.

Comparison of church statements on abortion; pt. 2: a working tool, by R. Fortin. ECUMENISM 84:23-36, December 1986.

Contraception and prescriptive infallibility, by G. L. Hallett. THEOLOGICAL STUDIES 43:629-650, December 1982; Discussion 47:134-145, March 1986.

Infallibility and contraception: a reply to Garth Hallett, by G. Grisez. THEO-LOGISCHE QUARTALSCHRIFT 47(1):134-145, March 1986.

BIRTH CONTROL AND RELIGION (continued)

Interpreting change in American Catholicism: the river and the floodgate, by D. R. Hoge. REVIEW OF RELIGIOUS RESEARCH 27(4):289-299, June 1986.

Morning-after pill OK (news; rape victims; ruling by Roman Catholic bishops of England and Wales). CHRISTIAN CENTURY 103(20):577, June 18-25, 1986.

Natural regulation of fertility, a responsibility of today's church?, by M. C. D'Ursel. LUMEN VITAE 41(2):205-215, 1986.

Papa don't preach (controversy surrounding school-based clinics). NATION 243(13):396-397, October 25, 1986.

Religion and fertility in the United States: the importance of marriage patterns and Hispanic origin, by W. D. Mosher, et al. DEMOGRAPHY 23:367-379, August 1986.

School-based health clinics: an idea whose time has come? (clinic of Chicago's DuSable High School), by R. L. Frame. CHRISTIANITY TODAY 30(4):42-44, March 7, 1986.

Teen-age contraception (suit against DuSable High School birth control clinic in Chicago). CHRISTIANITY TODAY 103:1064, November 26, 1986.

Wrongful birth concept gains acceptance, by G. Oliver. NATIONAL CATHOLIC REPORTER 19:2, February 4 1983.

BIRTH CONTROL AND TEENS

Birth control at school: pass or fail? EBONY 41:37-38+, October 1986.

Birth-control clinics in schools? (interview with L. Zabin and L. Maher). US NEWS AND WORLD REPORT 101:82, September 29, 1986.

Call to tame the genie of teen sex (recommendations of National Research Council panel), by S. McBee. US NEWS AND WORLD REPORT 101:8, December 22, 1986.

Doing something about teenage pregnancy [editorial]. FAMILY PLANNING PER-SPECTIVES 17:52, March-April 1985.

Education chief blasts birth control in schools (views of W. Bennett). JET 70:22, May 5, 1986.

Ethnicity and fertility: the fertility expectations and family size of Mexican-American and Anglo adolescents and adults, husbands and wives, by A. M. Sorenson. DAI: A 12(1):3872A, June 1986.

Evaluation of a pregnancy prevention program for urban teenagers, by L. S. Zabin, et al. FAMILY PLANNING PERSPECTIVES 18(3):119-126, May-June 1986.

Paths to adolescent parenthood: implications for prevention, by L. H. Flick. PUBLIC HEALTH REPORTS 101(2):132-147, March-April 1986.

Perceptions of sexual responsibility: do young men and women agree?, by M. K. Sheehan, et al. PEDIATRIC NURSING 12(1):17-21, January-February 1986.

BIRTH CONTROL AND TEENS (continued)

Policy by pathology (high school birth control clinics), by R. J. Neuhaus. NA-TIONAL REVIEW 38:46, December 5, 1986.

Public policy and public opinion toward sex education and birth control for teenagers, by P. A. Reichelt. JOURNAL OF APPLIED SOCIAL PSY-CHOLOGY 16(2):95-106, 1986.

School-based health clinics: an idea whose time has come? (clinic of Chicago's DuSable High School), by R. L. Frame. CHRISTIANITY TODAY 30(4):42-44, March 7, 1986.

—: a new approach to preventing adolescent pregnancy, by J. Dryfoos. FAMILY PLANNING PERSPECTIVES 17(2):70-82, March-April 1985.

Teen pregnancy in New Orleans: factors that differentiate teens who deliver, abort, and successfully contracept, by E. Landry, et al. JOURNAL OF YOUTH AND ADOLESCENCE 15(3):259-274, June 1986.

Teen-age contraception (suit against DuSable High School birth control clinic in Chicago). CHRISTIANITY TODAY 103:1064, November 26, 1986.

Teenage fertility, socioeconomic status and infant mortality, by M. E. Miller, et al. JOURNAL OF BIOSOCIAL SCIENCE 17(2):147-155, 1985.

What can government do to prevent teen pregnancy [interview], by J. A. Gasper. CHRISTIANITY TODAY 30(1):50-53, January 17, 1986.

Who has the right to advise children on birth control?, by P. Gerber, et al. MEDICAL JOURNAL OF AUSTRALIA 144(8):419-423, April 14 1986.

Why not birth control in the school?, by E. Bader. GUARDIAN 39(4):2, October 22, 1986.

BIRTH CONTROL AND WOMEN
Attitudes of women of reproductive age to in vitro fertilization and embryo re-search, by E. M. Aler, et al. JOURNAL OF BIOSOCIAL SCIENCE 18(2):155-167, April 1986.

Birth control improved status of women: expert. JET 69:8, January 27, 1986.

Development of a decision aid for women choosing a method of birth control, by E. M. Wall. JOURNAL OF FAMILY PRACTICE 21(5):351-355, November 1985.

Effects of socioeconomic development upon a model of women's fertility de-cision making in a Tunisian Community, by C. D. Miller. DAI: A 46(10):3164A, April 1986.

How women really feel about birth control. LADIES HOME JOURNAL 103:545, August 1986.

Impact of birth control as women in politics, by J. J. Kronenfeld, et al. FREE IN-QUIRY IN CREATIVE SOCIOLOGY 14(1):27-32, May 1986.

South Africa: crimes against women. AFRICA (170):70-71, October 1985.

Why smart women are stupid about birth control, by P. Span. GLAMOUR 84:252-253+, November 1986.

BIRTH CONTROL CLINICS

Birth control at school: pass or fail? EBONY 41:37-38+, October 1986.

Birth-control clinics in schools? (interview with L. Zabin and L. Maher). US NEWS AND WORLD REPORT 101:82, September 29, 1986.

Call to tame the genie of teen sex (recommendations of National Research Council panel), by S. McBee. US NEWS AND WORLD REPORT 101:8, December 22, 1986.

Choice of contraception in connection with the closing of a contraception clinic. Results of an anonymous questionnaire answered by 401 women, by M. Dueholm, et al. UGESKRIFT FOR LAEGER 147(48):3940-3946, November 25, 1985.

Criteria for selective screening for Chlamydia trachomatis infection in women attending family planning clinics, by H. H. Handsfield, et al. JAMA 255:1730-1734, April 4, 1986.

Education chief blasts birth control in schools (views of W. Bennett). JET 70:22, May 5, 1986.

Motivations for adolescents' first visit to a family planning clinic, ed. by D. B. Schwartz, et al. ADOLESCENCE 21:535-545, Fall 1986.

Papa don't preach (controversy surrounding school-based clinics). NATION 243(13):396-397, October 25, 1986.

Policy by pathology (high school birth control clinics), by R. J. Neuhaus. NATIONAL REVIEW 38:46, December 5, 1986.

School-based health clinics: an idea whose time has come? (clinic of Chicago's DuSable High School), by R. L. Frame. CHRISTIANITY TODAY 30(4):42-44, March 7, 1986.

—: a new approach to preventing adolescent pregnancy, by J. Dryfoos. FAMILY PLANNING PERSPECTIVES 17(2):70-82, March-April 1985.

School for scandal: birth control clinics, by J. Ruby. OFF OUR BACKS 16(11):2, December 1986.

Source of service and visit rate of family planning services: United States, 1982, by W. D. Mosher, et al. PUBLIC HEALTH REPORTS 101(4):405-416, July-August 1986.

What can government do to prevent teen pregnancy [interview], by J. A. Gasper. CHRISTIANITY TODAY 30(1):50-53, January 17, 1986.

UNITED STATES
Teen-age contraception (suit against DuSable High School birth control clinic in Chicago). CHRISTIANITY TODAY 103:1064, November 26, 1986.

BIRTH CONTROL FAILURE
Birth control failure among patients with unwanted pregnancies: 1982-1984, by A. M. Sophocles, Jr., et al. JOURNAL OF FAMILY PRACTICE 22(1):45-48, January 1986.

BIRTH CONTROL FAILURE (continued)

Birth control failure (resulting from incorrect use of oral contraceptives, foam, rhythm, condoms, etc.), by A. M. Sophocles, Jr. AMERICAN FAMILY PHYSICIAN 34:101-106, October 1986.

BIRTH CONTROL FUNDING
AID withholds U.N. population funds, by C. Holden. SCIENCE 233:1147, September 12, 1986.

BIRTH CONTROL PROGRAMS
Contraceptive social marketing: lessons from experience. POPULATION REPORTS 13(3):773, July-August 1985.

CONCEPTION—GENERAL
Products of conception: the social context of reproductive choices, by B. K. Rothman. JOURNAL OF MEDICAL ETHICS 11:188-192, December 1985.

CONCEPTION—LAWS AND LEGISLATION
Remaking conception and pregnancy: how the laws influence reproductive technology, by L. B. Andrews. FRONTIERS 9(1):36-40, 1986.

CONCEPTION—RESEARCH
Remaking conception and pregnancy: how the laws influence reproductive technology, by L. B. Andrews. FRONTIERS 9(1):36-40, 1986.

CONTRACEPTION—GENERAL
See also: Birth Control
             Contraceptives
             Family Planning

Acceptance of contraceptive practice by grandmultiparae in Benin City, Nigeria, by A. E. Omu, et al. INTERNATIONAL JOURNAL OF GYNAECOLOGY AND OBSTETRICS 24(2):145-150, April 1986.

Alcohol use, sexual intercourse, and contraception: an exploratory study, by B. J. Flanigan, et al. JOURNAL OF ALCOHOL AND DRUG EDUCATION 31:6-40, Spring 1986.

Birth control: vanishing options, by A. Toufexis, et al. TIME 128(9):78, September 1, 1986.

Breast feeding, fertility and child health: a review of international issues . . . the contraceptive effect of breast feeding, by M. J. Houston. JOURNAL OF ADVANCED NURSING 11(1):35-40, January 1986.

Business as usual, by J. Rachlin. WOMEN'S REVIEW OF BOOKS 4(2):7, November 1986.

Cold hands, conception and contraception, by C. Roberts, et al. NEW SCIENTIST 105:22, January 10, 1985.

Comparisons of the potential utility of LHRH agonists and antagonists for fertility control, by B. H. Vickery. JOURNAL OF STEROID BIOCHEMISTRY 23(5B): 779-791, November 1985.

Complications of contraception. ECONOMIST 298:68-69+, January 4 1986.

Contraception and control, by E. Bader. GUARDIAN 38(24):8, March 29, 1986.

CONTRACEPTION—GENERAL (continued)

Contraception before and after legal abortions, by A. Tollan. TIDSSKRIFT FOR DEN NORSKE LAEGEFORENING 105(31):2199-2201, November 10, 1985.

Contraception choices now. CHANGING TIMES 40:121-127, November 1986.

Contraception for the older woman [review], by E. Weisberg. CLINICAL REPRODUCTION AND FERTILITY 3(2):115-123, June 1985.

Contraception in context, by R. M. Gillespie, et al. FRONTIERS 9(1):3-8 1986.

Contraception in female adolescents. Point of view of a gynecologist, by A. Romagny. REVUE FRANCAISE DE GYNECOLOGIE ET D'OBSTETRIQUE 81(5):279-281, May 1986.

Contraception: what's ahead, by P. L. McIntosh. VOGUE 176:532, October 1986.

Contraception: you can get it if you really want, by R. Shapiro. NURSING TIMES 81(44):18, October 30-November 5, 1985.

Contraceptive care and family planning: a correction [letter], by J. McCracken. JOURNAL OF THE ROYAL COLLEGE OF GENERAL PRACTITIONERS 36(285):179, April 1986.

Contraceptive care and family planning in an urban general practice, by J. S. McCracken. JOURNAL OF THE ROYAL COLLEGE OF GENERAL PRACTITIONERS 36(282):13-16, January 1986.

Contraceptives: on hold. Liability fears are cutting off research, by M. Clark, et al. NEWSWEEK 107(18):68, May 5, 1986.

Current principles of regulation of the reproductive function in women, by I. A. Manuilova. AKUSHERSTVO I GINEKOLOGIIA (7):49-52, July 1985.

Dearth of contraception fuels world abortion rate. NATIONAL CATHOLIC REPORTER 19:10, January 21, 1983.

Exploitation of animal mobility [news], by P. D. Moore. NATURE 317(6035):288-289, September 26-October 2, 1985.

Factors affecting the choice of nonpermanent contraceptive methods among married women, by M. MacDowell, et al. SOCIAL BIOLOGY 31(3-4):222-231, Fall-Winter 1984.

Family planning: taking precautions, by C. Clifford. NURSING TIMES 82(38):55-56+, September 17-23, 1986.

Future of contraception, by D. Edmondson. PARENTS 61(10):257-258+, October 1986.

Immaculate contraception, by N. Friedman. CALIFORNIA 8:52+, August 1983.

Inquiry into the moral prerogatives of the potential human life, by O. A. Cvitanic. PHAROS 49(2):13-17, Spring 1986.

Medico-social aspects of contraception [editorial], by A. da C. Bastos. REVISTA PAULISTA DE MEDICINA 104(1):3-4, January-February 1986.

CONTRACEPTION—GENERAL (continued)

Modern contraceptive practice in rural Appalachia, by G. A. Gairola, et al. AMERI-CAN JOURNAL OF PUBLIC HEALTH 76(8):1004-1008, August 1986.

Multilevel dependence of contraceptive use on socioeconomic development and family planning program strength, by B. Entwisle, et al. DEMOGRAPHY 23(2):199-216, May 1986.

Next contraceptive revolution, by L. E. Atkinson, et al. FAMILY PLANNING PER-SPECTIVES 18(1):19-26, January-February 1986.

Non-cross-reactivity of antibodies to murine LDH-C4 with LDH-A4 and LDH-B4, by Z.-G. Liang, et al. JOURNAL OF EXPERIMENTAL ZOOLOGY 240:377-384, December 1986.

Population status and fertility control worldwide, by F. Havránek. CESKOSLO-VENSKA GYNEKOLOGIE 51(2):116-119, March 1986.

Postpartum sexuality and contraception, by J. Richters. HEALTHRIGHT 5(2):25-27, February 1986.

Prepregnancy counseling and contraception in the insulin-dependent diabetic patient, by J. M. Steel. CLINICAL OBSTETRICS AND GYNECOLOGY 28(3):553-566, September 1985.

Production of monoclonal antibodies to porcine zona pellucida and their in-hibition of sperm penetration through human zona pellucida in vitro, by T. Mori, et al. JOURNAL OF REPRODUCTIVE IMMUNOLOGY 8(1):1-11, August 1985.

Racial differences in the perception of contraception option attributes, by R. J. McDermott, et al. HEALTH EDUCATION 17:9-14, December 1986-January 1987.

Reversible contraception for the 1980s, by D. A. Grimes. JAMA 255(1):69-75, January 3, 1986.

Role of self-efficacy in achieving health behavior change. HEALTH EDUCATION QUARTERLY 13(1):73-92, Spring 1986.

RU 486—an antiprogestational compound, by L. Wray. HEALTHRIGHT 5:37-38, November 1985.

Searching for ideal contraceptives. SOCIETY 23(1):41-43, November-December 1985.

Sexuality, contraception and health: birth control. LADIES HOME JOURNAL 103(8):54+, August 1986.

—: the sexual stages of marriage. LADIES HOME JOURNAL 103(8):51-53, August 1986.

Sweeter side of life: a review of diabetes and its effects on pregnancy, by M. A. Crichton, et al. MIDWIFERY 1(4):195-206, December 1985.

Teenage pregnancy [editorial], by J. K. Bury. BRITISH JOURNAL OF OBSTET-RICS AND GYNAECOLOGY 92(11):1081-1083, November 1985.

CONTRACEPTION—GENERAL (continued)

Victoria Gillick and the age of consent: a transatlantic view, by H. E. Emson. CANADIAN MEDICAL ASSOCIATION JOURNAL 134(4):319-320, February 15, 1986.

What's new in contraception?, by S. L. Camp, et al. USA TODAY 114:88-92, May 1986.

Why isn't contraception better?, by O. S. Nordberg. PARENTS 61(10):161+, October 1986.

AUSTRALIA
Overview: the history of contraception and abortion in Australia, by D. Wyndham. HEALTHRIGHT 5:9-11, November 1985.

CHINA
Women's health care and the workplace in the People's Republic of China, by P. Elder, et al. JOURNAL OF NURSE-MIDWIFERY 31(4):182-188, July-August 1986.

GHANA
Fertility and family planning in Accra, by G. B. Fosu. JOURNAL OF BIO-SOCIAL SCIENCE 18(1):11-22, January 1986.

GREAT BRITAIN
House of Lords rules DHSS guidance on contraception lawful, by D. Brahams. LANCET 2(8461):959-960, October 26, 1985.

NEW ZEALAND
New Zealand contraception and health study: design and preliminary report, by New Zealand Contraception and Health Study Group. NEW ZEALAND MEDICAL JOURNAL 99(800):283-286, April 23, 1986.

NIGERIA
Use of contraceptives for birth spacing in a Nigerian city, by G. A. Oni, et al. STUDIES IN FAMILY PLANNING 17(4):165-171, July-August 1986.

UNITED STATES
Adolescents' values, sexuality, and contraception in a rural New York county, by N. McCormick, et al. ADOLESCENCE 20(78):385-395, Summer 1985.

Effects of formal sex education on adolescent intercourse, contraception and pregnancy in the United States, by D. A. Dawson. DAI: A 47(4), October 1986.

End of IUD marketing in the United States: what does it mean for American women?, by J. D. Forrest. FAMILY PLANNING PERSPECTIVES 18(2): 52-55+, March-April 1986.

Sex-education needs and interests of high school students in a rural New York county, by N. McCormick, et al. ADOLESCENCE 20(79):581-592, Fall 1985.

Teen pregnancy in New Orleans: factors that differentiate teens who deliver, abort, and successfully contracept, by E. Landry, et al. JOURNAL OF YOUTH AND ADOLESCENCE 15(3):259-274, June 1986.

Two o-clock: contraception. ECONOMIST November 15, 1986, pp. 41-42.

CONTRACEPTION—COMPLICATIONS

Complications on contraception. ECONOMIST 298:68-69+, January 4, 1986.

CONTRACEPTION—ECONOMICS

Do contraceptive prices affect demand?, by M. A. Lewis. STUDIES IN FAMILY PLANNING 17(3):126-135, May-June 1986.

CONTRACEPTION—EDUCATION

Care of postpartum adolescents, by S. Fullar. MCN 11(6):398-403, November-December 1986.

Group discussion on contraceptive issues, by B. A. Rienzo. HEALTH EDUCA-TION 16(4):52-53, August-September 1985.

CONTRACEPTION—FEMALE—ORAL

Second look at the pill, by J. Ismach. AMH 5:47+, July-August 1986.

CONTRACEPTION—MALE

Gonadotrophin-releasing hormone agonists for new approaches to contraception in man, by S. J. Nillius. WIENER KLINISCHE WOCHENSCHRIFT 97(23):865-873, December 6, 1985.

Implications of treatment on sex knowledge, sex attitudes and contraception of sexual liberal/conservative males, by L. M. Haverstock. DAI: A 47(3), September 1986.

CONTRACEPTION—METHODS

Adolescent facing contraception: methods, by M. R. Herrero Martin, et al. RE-VISTA DE ENFERMAGEN 9(95):40-48, June 1986.

Choice of contraception in connection with the closing of a contraception clinic. Results of an anonymous questionnaire answered by 401 women, by M. Dueholm, et al. UGESKRIFT FOR LAEGER 147(48):3940-3946, November 25, 1985.

Contraception for the older woman [review], by E. Weisberg. CLINICAL REPRO-DUCTION AND FERTILITY 3(2):115-123, June 1985.

Contraception in female adolescents. Point of view of a pediatrician, by P. Berlier. REVUE FRANCAISE DE GYNECOLOGIE ET D'OBSTETRIQUE 81(5):275-277, May 1986.

Contraception in male monkeys by intra-vas deferens injection of a pH lowering polymer, by S. K. Guha, et al. CONTRACEPTION 32(1):109-118, July 1985.

Contraception in the mentally handicapped, by L. Beck. FORTSCHRITTE DER MEDIZIN 103(30):739, August 15, 1985.

Contraceptive methods for adolescents, by Y. Salomon-Bernard. SOINS. GYNECOLOGIE, OBSTETRIQUE, PUERICULTURE, PEDITRIE (53):3, October 1985.

Contraceptive practices among female heroin addicts, by N. Ralph, et al. AMERICAN JOURNAL OF PUBLIC HEALTH 76(8):1016-1017, August 1986; Discussion 76:1460, December 1986.

Development of a decision aid for women choosing a method of birth control, by E. M. Wall. JOURNAL OF FAMILY PRACTICE 21(5):351-355, November 1985.

CONTRACEPTION—METHODS (continued)

Enhancement of antigonadotropin response to the beta-subunit of ovine luteinizing hormone by carrier conjugation and combination with the beta-subunit of human chorionic gonadotropin, by G. P. Talwar, et al. FERTILITY AND STERILITY 46(1):120-126, July 1986.

Family planning: beyond contraception . . . community health center in Jerusalem, by C. Kurtzman, et al. MCN 11(5):340-343, September-October 1986.

Frequency and adequacy in the use of contraceptive methods by women of Campinas, by A. Faúndes, et al. REVISTA PAULISTA DE MEDICINA 104(1):44-46, January-February 1986.

Immunological methods of birth control, by M. Sh. Verbitskii. VESTNIK AKADEMII MEDITSINSKIKH NAUK SSSR (1):28-36, 1986.

Modern aspects of contraception, by W. Moser. WIENER MEDIZINISCHE WOCHENSCHRIFT 136(11-12):286-298, June 30, 1986.

New advances in contraception and sterilization, by L. Iglesias Cortit. MEDICINA CLINICA 85(14):588-595, November 2, 1985.

Partnership, sexuality and contraception in mentally handicapped humans, by H. Krebs. FORTSCHRITTE DER MEDIZIN 103(30):740-743, August 15, 1985.

Perspectives of reproductive medicine, by E. Nieschlag. HAUTARZT 37(4):190-197, April 1986.

Practical aspects of clinical trials of contraceptive methods, by E. Weisberg. CLINICAL REPRODUCTION AND FERTILITY 4(2):139-147, April 1986.

Sexually transmitted diseases [letter], by H. W. Horne, Jr. FERTILITY AND STERILITY 46(1):157-158, July 1986.

When your patients ask about contraception for the middle years, by E. Trimmer. MIDWIFE, HEALTH VISITOR AND COMMUNITY NURSE 21(10):362, October 1985.

CONTRACEPTION—PSYCHOLOGY AND PSYCHIATRY
Contraception and the desire for pregnancy in the adolescent, by U. F. Colombo, et al. ANNALI DI OSTETRICIA GINECOLOGIA MEDICINA PERINATALE 106(6):352-358, November-December 1985.

Knowledge and practices of the community distributors of contraceptives in Honduras, by B. Janowitz, et al. BOLETIN DE LA OFICINA SANITARIA PANAMERICANA 101(1):48-57, July 1986.

Population of contraception, by S. L. Polchanova. FEL'DSHER I AKUSHERKA 51(5):38-42, May 1986.

Psychological factors related to post-abortion "subtle" contraceptive unreliability, by P. Lehtinen, et al. SCANDINAVIAN JOURNAL OF PSYCHOLOGY 26(3): 277-284, 1985.

Relationship of locus of control and contraception use in the adolescent population, by S. Visher. JOURNAL OF ADOLESCENT HEALTH CARE 7(3):183-186, May 1986.

CONTRACEPTION—PSYCHOLOGY AND PSYCHIATRY (continued)

Why some women fail to use their contraceptive method: a psychological investigation, by W. B. Miller. FAMILY PLANNING PERSPECTIVES 18(1):27-32, January-February 1986.

CONTRACEPTION—RESEARCH

Regression of pathologic changes induced by the long-term administration of contraceptive steroids to rodents, by G. Lumb, et al. TOXICOLOGIC PATHOLOGY 13(4):283-295, 1985.

Reversible immunosuppression of fertility in the rat following immunization by a liposome incorporated spermatozoal polypeptide fraction, by L. Mettler, et al. AMERICAN JOURNAL OF REPRODUCTIVE IMMUNOLOGY AND MICRO-BIOLOGY 9(2):56-61, October 1985.

Successful and unsuccessful contraceptors: a multivariate typology, by J. P. Hornick, et al. JOURNAL OF SOCIAL WORK AND HUMAN SEXUALITY 4(1-2):17-31, Winter 1985-1986.

Worldwide trends in funding for contraceptive research and evaluation, by L. E. Atkinson, et al. FAMILY PLANNING PERSPECTIVES 17(5):196-199+, September-October 1985.

CONTRACEPTION—VETERINARY

Long term reversible suppression of oestrus in bitches with nafarelin acetate, a potent LHRH agonist, by G. I. McRae, et al. JOURNAL OF REPRODUCTION AND FERTILITY 74(2):389-397, July 1985.

CONTRACEPTION AND COLLEGE STUDENTS

Assessing the need for education on sex and contraception among southern college freshmen, by Y. Iyriboz, et al. COLLEGE STUDENT JOURNAL 19:261-264, Fall 1985.

Cervical chlamydia trachomatis infection in university women: relationship to history, contraception, ectopy, and cervicitis, by H. R. Harrison, et al. AMERICAN JOURNAL OF OBSTETRICS AND GYNECOLOGY 153(3):244-251, October 1, 1985.

CONTRACEPTION AND PHYSICIANS

Catholic physician, the contraception issue and the three questions of ethics, by J. O'Donohoe. JOURNAL OF PASTORAL COUNSELING 18(1):34-46, 1983.

Contraception in female adolescents. Point of view of a pediatrician, by P. Berlier. REVUE FRANCAISE DE GYNECOLOGIE ET D'OBSTETRIQUE 81(5):275-277, May 1986.

What should the physician's role be in regulating fertility and sex behavior (a contribution for discussion), by A. Cernoch. CESKOSLOVENSKA GYNEKOL-OGIE 50(7):504-505, August 1985.

CONTRACEPTION AND RELIGION

Catholic physician, the contraception issue and the three questions of ethics, by J. O'Donohoe. JOURNAL OF PASTORAL COUNSELING 18(1):34-46, 1983.

Teen-age contraception (suit against DuSable High School birth control clinic in Chicago). CHRISTIANITY TODAY 103:1064, November 26, 1986.

CONTRACEPTION AND TEENS

Adolescent contraception: an update, by J. W. Kulig. PEDIATRICS 76(4 pt 2): 675-680, October 1985.

Advice for girls under 16 on contraception and pregnancy. LANCET 1(8478): 454, February 22, 1986.

American Academy of Pediatrics Committee on Adolescence: Sexuality, contraception, and the media. PEDIATRICS 78(3):535-536, September 1986.

Care of postpartum adolescents, by S. Fullar. MCN 11(6):398-403, November-December 1986.

Children, medical treatment and contraceptive agents. Is parental consent necessary?, by P. Bravender-Coyle. MEDICAL JOURNAL OF AUSTRALIA 144(8):416-419, April 14, 1986.

Comparative study (1964-1980) on knowledge and behavior in adolescents in the control of fertility, by N. Kapor-Stanulovic, et al. MEDICINSKI PREGLED 39(1-2):65-68, 1986.

Contraception and the desire for pregnancy in the adolescent, by U. F. Colombo, et al. ANNALI DI OSTETRICIA GINECOLOGIA MEDICINA PERINATALE 106(6):352-358, November-December 1985.

Contraception for the adolescent [letter]. POSTGRADUATE MEDICINE 79(4):44+, March 1986.

Contraception in female adolescents. Point of view of a pediatrician, by P. Berlier. REVUE FRANCAISE DE GYNECOLOGIE ET D'OBSTETRIQUE 81(5):275-277, May 1986.

Evaluation of a pregnancy prevention program for urban teenagers, by L. S. Zabin, et al. FAMILY PLANNING PERSPECTIVES 18(3):119-126, May-June 1986.

Influence of client-provider relationships on teenage women's subsequent use of contraception, by C. A. Nathanson, et al. AMERICAN JOURNAL OF PUBLIC HEALTH 75:33-38, January 1985.

Microbiology of the lower genital tact in postmenarchal adolescent girls: differences by sexual activity, contraception, and presence of nonspecific vaginitis, by M. A. Shafer, et al. JOURNAL OF PEDIATRICS 107(6):974-981, December 1985.

Paths to adolescent parenthood: implications for prevention, by L. H. Flick. PUBLIC HEALTH REPORTS 101(2):132-147, March-April 1986.

Perceptions of sexual responsibility: do young men and women agree?, by M. K. Sheehan, et al. PEDIATRIC NURSING 12(1):17-21, January-February 1986.

Relationship of locus of control and contraception use in the adolescent population, by S. Visher. JOURNAL OF ADOLESCENT HEALTH CARE 7(3):183-186, May 1986.

Role of health belief attitudes, sex education, and demographics in predicting adolescents' sexuality knowledge, by M. Eisen, et al. HEALTH EDUCATION QUARTERLY 13(1):9-22, Spring 1986.

CONTRACEPTION AND TEENS (continued)

Sex-education needs and interests of high school students in a rural New York county, by N. McCormick, et al. ADOLESCENCE 20(79):581-592, Fall 1985.

Supporting teenagers' use of contraceptives: a comparison of clinic services, by R. Herceg-Baron, et al. FAMILY PLANNING PERSPECTIVES 18(2):61-66, March-April 1986.

Teen pregnancy in New Orleans: factors that differentiate teens who deliver, abort, and successfully contracept, by E. Landry, et al. JOURNAL OF YOUTH AND ADOLESCENCE 15(3):259-274, June 1986.

Teen-age contraception (suit against DuSable High School birth control clinic in Chicago). CHRISTIANITY TODAY 103:1064, November 26, 1986.

Teenage girls in Malmö—study among 200 12-19-year-old girls visiting a Youth Conference in Malmö, Spring of 85, by M. Ivarsson, et al. JORDEMODERN 99(4):107-110, April 1986.

Teenagers and contraception [editorial], by J. D. Havard. BRITISH MEDICAL JOURNAL 292(6519):508-509, February 22, 1986.

Teenagers and contraception. Evaluation of the first year at the contraception guidance clinic in Sør-Varanger, by B. O. Eriksen, et al. TIDSSKRIFT FOR DE NORSKE LAEGEFORENING 105(23):1508-1510, August 20, 1985.

Teenagers talk about sex, pregnancy and contraception, by E. E. Kiser. FAMILY PLANNING PERSPECTIVES 17(2):83-90, March-April 1985.

Underage contraception, by L. Southgate. PRACTITIONER 229(1410):1067-1070, December 1985.

Who has the right to advise children on birth control?, by P. Gerber, et al. MEDICAL JOURNAL OF AUSTRALIA 144(8):419-423, April 14 1986.

CONTRACEPTION AND WOMEN
Contraception in female adolescents. Point of view of a pediatrician, by P. Berlier. REVUE FRANCAISE DE GYNECOLOGIE ET D'OBSTETRIQUE 81(5):275-277, May 1986.

CONTRACEPTIVE AGENTS
See also: Contraceptives

Antiprogestins; prospects for a once-a-month pill, by I. M. Spitz, et al. FAMILY PLANNING PERSPECTIVES 17(6):260-262, November-December 1985.

Birth control: what you need to know [pictorial], by D. Edmondson. PARENTS 61(10):156-158+, October 1986.

Birth control: what's now, what's next?, by P. Gadsby. GOOD HOUSEKEEPING 203(5):323, November 1986.

Children, medical treatment and contraceptive agents. Is parental consent necessary?, by P. Bravender-Coyle. MEDICAL JOURNAL OF AUSTRALIA 144(8):416-419, April 14, 1986.

Contraceptive agents and antithrombin III. New causes of thrombosis [letter], by U. Abildgaard, et al. TIDSSKRIFT FOR DEN NORSKE LAEGEFORENING 106(4):346-347, February 10, 1986.

CONTRACEPTIVE AGENTS (continued)

Contraceptives and the under 16s [letter], by C. Woodroffe, et al. BRITISH
MEDICAL JOURNAL 291(6054):1280, November 2, 1985.

Contraceptives: on hold. Liability fears are cutting off research, by M. Clark, et al.
NEWSWEEK 107(18):68, May 5, 1986.

Do oral contraceptive agents affect nutrient requirements—vitamin B-6?, by L. T.
Miller. JOURNAL OF NUTRITION 116(7):1344-1345, July 1986.

Facts about an implantable contraceptive: memorandum from a WHO meeting.
WHO BULLETIN 63(3):485-494, 1985.

Human seminal antiliquefying agents—a potential approach towards vaginal
contraception, by A. Mandal, et al. CONTRACEPTION 33(1):31-38, January
1986.

Investigation on the influence of steroidal contraceptives on milk lipid and fatty
acids in Hungary and Thailand. WHO Special Programme of Research, Development and Research Training in Human Reproduction, Task Force on
oral contraceptives, by M. Sas, et al. CONTRACEPTION 33(2):159-178,
February 1986.

Luteinizing hormone releasing hormone (LHRH): II. A new contraceptive agent,
by A. Rojanasakul, et al. JOURNAL OF THE MEDICAL ASSOCIATION OF
THAILAND 69(1):16-21, January 1986.

Next contraceptive revolution, by L. E. Atkinson, et al. FAMILY PLANNING PER-
SPECTIVES 18(1):19-26, January-February 1986.

Nonprescription contraceptives: increasing in popularity, by T. P. Reinders.
AMERICAN PHARMACY NS25(9):38-41, September 1985.

Oral contraceptive agents, by R. P. Shearman. MEDICAL JOURNAL OF AUS-
TRALIA 144(4):201-205, February 17, 1986.

Sex and contraceptive information for adolescents, by C. Lacoste. SOINS.
GYNECOLOGIE, OBSTETRIQUE, PUERICULTURE, PEDIATRIE (53):7-10,
October 1985.

Sexuality, contraception and health: birth control. LADIES HOME JOURNAL
103(8):54+, August 1986.

CONTRACEPTIVE AGENTS—FEMALE
See also: Contraceptives—Female

Comparative study of the metabolic effects of injectable and oral contraceptives,
by D. F. Liew, et al. CONTRACEPTION 33(4):385-394, April 1986.

Comparative study of Neo Sampoon, Ortho Vaginal Tablets and Emko Vaginal
Tablets in Accra, Ghana, by P. Lamptey, et al. CONTRACEPTION 32(5):445-
454, November 1985.

Contraception in hypertensive women using a vaginal ring delivering estradiol
and levonorgestrel, by F. Elkik, et al. JOURNAL OF CLINICAL ENDOCRIN-
OLOGY AND METABOLISM 63(1):29-35, July 1986; also in ARCHIVES DES
MALADIES DU COEUR ET DES VAISSEAUX 78(11):1717-1739, October
1985.

CONTRACEPTIVE AGENTS—FEMALE (continued)

Contraceptive development and clinical trials, by I. S. Fraser. CLINICAL REPRO-
DUCTION AND FERTILITY 4(1):75-85, February 1986.

Determination of the viscosity of vehicles for vaginal contraceptives with sodium
carboxymethylcellulose and Veegum HV, by M. Primorac, et al. PHARMAZIE
41(4):292, April 1986.

Effect of depo-provera and noristerat on some biochemical constituents of rat
uterus, by T. Bhowmik, et al. INDIAN JOURNAL OF EXPERIMENTAL
BIOLOGY 24(3):145-148, March 1986.

Effect of early postpartum use of the contraceptive implants, NORPLANT, on the
serum level of immunoglobulins of the mothers and their breastfed infants,
by K. A. Abdulla, et al. CONTRACEPTION 32(3):261-266, September 1985.

Effect of gossypol acetic acid on early pregnancy in rats, by N. G. Wang, et al.
YAO HSUEH HSUEH PAO 19(11):808-811, November 1984.

Effect of sodium lauryl sulphate on the viscosity of vehicles for vaginal contraceptives with sodium carboxymethylcellulose and Veegum HV, by M.
Primorac, et al. PHARMAZIE 41(4):293, April 1986.

Effect of vaginal contraceptive sponges on growth of toxic shock syndrome-
associated staphylococcus aureus in vitro, by P. G. Stumpf, et al. CON-
TRACEPTION 33(4):395-399, April 1986.

Effects of gossypol on the estrous cycle and ovarian weight in the rat, by Y. Gu, et
al. CONTRACEPTION 32(5):491-496, November 1985.

Effects of hormonal and nonhormonal contraceptives on lactation and incidence
of pregnancy, by S. Zacharias, et al. CONTRACEPTION 33(3):203-213,
March 1986.

Effects of long-acting injectable contraceptives on carbohydrate metabolism, by
K. Amatayakul, et al. INTERNATIONAL JOURNAL OF GYNAECOLOGY AND
OBSTETRICS 23(5):361-368, October 1985.

Fertility regulation in nursing women: VIII. Progesterone plasma levels and contraceptive efficacy of a progesterone-releasing vaginal ring, by S. Díaz, et al.
CONTRACEPTION 32(6):603-622, December 1985.

Flowers of hibiscus rosa-sinensis, a potential source of contragestative agent: II.
Possible mode of action with reference to anti-implantation effect of the
benzene extract, by A. K. Pal, et al. CONTRACEPTION 32(5):517-529,
November 1985.

Follow-up study of the efficacy and safety of injectable microencapsulated
megestrol acetate and a discussion on its contraceptive mechanism, by Z. Y.
Han, et al. INTERNATIONAL JOURNAL OF GYNAECOLOGY AND OBSTET-
RICS 23(3):207-211, June 1985.

Gonadotropin releasing hormone analogs for female contraception by inhibition
of ovulation, by S. J. Nillius. JOURNAL OF STEROID BIOCHEMISTRY
23(5B):849-854, November 1985.

Injectable contraceptives in developing countries [letter], by S. Nair. LANCET
1(8495):1440-1441, June 21, 1986.

CONTRACEPTIVE AGENTS—FEMALE (continued)

Intranasal peptide contraception by inhibition of ovulation with the gonadotropin-releasing hormone superagonist nafarelin: six months' clinical results, by J. A. Gudmundsson, et al. FERTILITY AND STERILITY 45(5):617-623, May 1986.

Mechanism of the contraceptive action of the triterpene glycosides from the rock jasmine androsace septentrionalis L, by M. N. Mats, et al. FARMAKOLOGIYA I TOKSIKOLOGIYA 49(2):38-39, March-April 1986.

Multiple actions of a novel vaginal contraceptive compound, ORF 13904, by R. G. Foldesy, et al. FERTILITY AND STERILITY 45(4):550-555, April 1986.

New contraceptive agent: various questions on p-sponges, by C. O. Börjeson. JORDEMODERN 98(10):326-329, October 1985.

New developments in oral, injectable and implantable contraceptives, vaginal rings and intrauterine devices [review], by E. Diczfalusy. CONTRACEPTION 33(1):7-22, January 1986.

Oestrogenic effects of the triphasic oral contraceptive agents [letter], by P. Baillie. SOUTH AFRICAN MEDICAL JOURNAL 68(10):706, November 9, 1985.

ORF 13904, a new long-acting vaginal contraceptive, by R. E. Homm, et al. CONTRACEPTION 32(3):267-274, September 1985.

Phase IV study of the injection Norigest in Pakistan, by A. Kazi, et al. CONTRACEPTION 32(4):395-403, October 1985.

Plasma levonorgestrel and progesterone levels in women treated with silastic covered rods containing levonorgestrel, by H. B. Croxatto, et al. CONTRACEPTION 31(6):643-654, June 1985.

Recent developments in female contraception: LHRH, by E. Vijayan. JOURNAL OF STEROID BIOCHEMISTRY 23(5B):827-831, November 1985.

Reply to comments on two articles dealing with the teratogenicity of cyproterone acetate (CA) and medroxyprogesterone acetate (MPA) [letter], by H. Spielmann. TERATOLOGY 32(2):319-320, October 1985.

Synthesis of d,1-15-methyl-17-phenyl-18,19,20-trinorprostagland in F2 alpha methyl ester and its 15-epimer, by Y. L. Wu, et al. CHUNG KUO I HSUEH KO HSUEH YUAN HSUEH PAO 7(2):145-149, April 1985.

Ultrasonic visualization of NORPLANT subdermal contraceptive devices, by R. J. Thomsen, et al. INTERNATIONAL JOURNAL OF GYNAECOLOGY AND OBSTETRICS 23(3):223-227, June 1985.

Use of contraceptive agents by women in the city of Frunze, by I. A. Abdyldaeva, et al. SOVETSKOE ZDRAVOOKHRONENIE (6):40-42, 1986.

Vaginal contraceptive activity of aryl 4-guanidinobenzoates (acrosin inhibitors) in rabbits, by J. M. Kaminski, et al. CONTRACEPTION 32(2):183-189, August 1985.

CONTRACEPTIVE AGENTS—FEMALE—COMPLICATIONS
Breast cancer and depot-medroxyprogesterone acetate. WHO Collaborative Study of Neoplasia and Steroid Contraceptives, by D. B. Thomas, et al. WHO BULLETIN 63(3):513-519, 1985.

CONTRACEPTIVE AGENTS—FEMALE—COMPLICATIONS (continued)

Concerns voiced on Depo Provera, by C. Sanders. RNAO NEWS 42(3):15+, Spring 1986.

Effect of norethisterone on the blood count and endometrial histology of Indian women, by C. Chaudhuri, et al. CONTRACEPTION 32(4):417-428, October 1985.

Galactorrhea in DMPA users: incidence and clinical significance, by D. Gongsakdi, et al. JOURNAL OF THE MEDICAL ASSOCIATION OF THAILAND 69(1):28-32, January 1986.

Indian Council of Medical Research. Task Force on Hormonal Contraception: Phase II randomized clinical trail with norethisterone oenanthate 50 mg alone and in combination with 5 mg or 2.5 mg of either estradiol valerate or cypionate as a monthly injectable contraceptive, by R. Baweja, et al. CONTRACEPTION 32(4):383-394, October 1985.

Invasive cervical cancer and depot-medroxyprogesterone acetate. WHO Collaborative Study of Neoplasia and Steroid Contraceptives, by D. B. Thomas, et al. WHO BULLETIN 63(3):505-511, 1985.

CONTRACEPTIVE AGENTS—FEMALE—ORAL—COMPLICATIONS
Hormonal contraception using depot preparations, by P. J. Keller. THERAPEUTISCHE UMSCHAU 43(5):395-399, May 1986.

CONTRACEPTIVE AGENTS—FEMALE—RESEARCH
Effect of depo-provera and noristerat on some biochemical constituents of rat uterus, by T. Bhowmik, et al. INDIAN JOURNAL OF EXPERIMENTAL BIOLOGY 24(3):145-148, March 1986.

CONTRACEPTIVE AGENTS—MALE
See also: Contraceptives—Male

Antifertility effects of embelin in male rats, by S. Agrawal, et al. ANDROLOGIA 18(2):125-131, March-April 1986.

Clinical trial of 19-nortestosterone-hexoxyphenylpropionate (Anadur) for male fertility regulation, by U. A. Knuth, et al. FERTILITY AND STERILITY 44(6):814-821, December 1985.

Contraception in male monkeys by intra-vas deferens injection of a pH lowering polymer, by S. K. Guha, et al. CONTRACEPTION 32(1):109-118, July 1985.

Contraceptive agents for men, by M. Primorac, et al. SRPSKI ARHIV ZA CELO-KUPNO LEKARSTVO 112(11-12):1197-1204, November-December 1984.

Effect of drug-vinyl copolymer delivery composites on the rat prostate, by M. Yoshida, et al. JOURNAL OF BIOMEDICAL MATERIALS RESEARCH 19(6):615-629, July-August 1985.

Effect of salicylazosulphapyridine (sulphasalazine) on male fertility [review], by A. Giwercman, et al. INTERNATIONAL JOURNAL OF ANDROLOGY 9(1):38-42, February 1986.

Effects of the male contraceptive agent gossypol on meiotic chromosomes of the male rat, by T. Bhagirath, et al. CYTOGENETICS AND CELL GENETICS 39(3):228-230, 1985.

CONTRACEPTIVE AGENTS—MALE (continued)

Gonadotropin releasing hormone (GnRH) agonists in male contraception, by R. S. Swerdloff, et al. MEDICAL BIOLOGY 63(5-6):218-224, 1986.

Hormonal effects of GnRH agonist in the human male: an approach to male contraception using combined androgen and GnRH agonist treatment, by R. S. Swerdloff, et al. JOURNAL OF STEROID BIOCHEMISTRY 23(5B):855-861, November 1985.

Male fertility regulation: recent advances, by G. M. Waites. WHO BULLETIN 64(2):151-158, 1986.

Present state of male contraception, by J. Zverina. CASOPIS LEKARU CES-KYCH 124(37):1157-1161, September 13, 1985.

Ribonucleotide reductase: an intracellular target for the male antifertility agent, gossypol, by G. A. McClarty, et al. BIOCHEMICAL AND BIOPHYSICAL RESEARCH COMMUNICATIONS 133(1):300-305, November 27, 1985.

Viability of mouse leydig cells in vitro following incubation with gossypol, by S. Pearce, et al. CONTRACEPTION 32(3):275-281, September 1985.

CONTRACEPTIVE AGENTS—MALE—COMPLICATIONS
Gossypol-hypokalaemia interrelationships, by S. Z. Qian. INTERNATIONAL JOURNAL OF ANDROLOGY 8(4):313-324, August 1985.

CONTRACEPTIVE AGENTS—MALE—RESEARCH
Effect of drug-vinyl copolymer delivery composites on the rat prostate, by M. Yoshida, et al. JOURNAL OF BIOMEDICAL MATERIALS RESEARCH 19(6):615-629, July-August 1985.

CONTRACEPTIVE AGENTS—RESEARCH
Antifertility effect of neem oil in female albino rats by the intravaginal and oral routes, by R. Lal, et al. INDIAN JOURNAL OF MEDICAL RESEARCH 83:89-92, January 1986.

Effects of gossypol on the estrous cycle and ovarian weight in the rat, by Y. Gu, et al. CONTRACEPTION 32(5):491-496, November 1985.

CONTRACEPTIVES—GENERAL
See also: Birth Control
            Contraception
            Contraceptive Agents
            Family Planning

Beware depo provera. HERIZONS 4(2):9, March 1986.

Birth control: what you need to know [pictorial], by D. Edmondson. PARENTS 61(10):156-158+, October 1986.

Birth control: what's now, what's next?, by P. Gadsby. GOOD HOUSEKEEPING 203(5):323, November 1986.

Contraception choices now. CHANGING TIMES 40:121-127, November 1986.

Contraception—his gain, your pain, by S. Schneider. MADEMOISELLE 92:116, April 1986.

CONTRACEPTIVES—GENERAL (continued)

Con(tra)ception: hormonal coin toss, by L. Davis. SCIENCE NEWS 130:5, July 5, 1986.

Contraception: what's ahead, by P. L. McIntosh. VOGUE 176:532, October 1986.

Contraceptive crisis, by A. E. Wilbur. SCIENCE DIGEST 94:54-61+, September 1986.

Contraceptive update, by C. Carver. CHATELAINE 59:44-45+, January 1986.

Depo provera approval unknown, by C. Clement. HEALTHSHARING 7(2):4, Spring 1986.

Etude de l'utilisation du Depo-provera; text in French and English. CANADIAN NURSE 82:8-9, June 1986.

Ford Foundation's work in population. FORD FOUNDATION REPORT August 1985, p. 53.

Good news about birth control bills, by M. Gray. MACLEAN'S 99:52b, September 22, 1986.

Illegitimacy—we ignore the roots, by S. Tyler. SAINT LOUIS 12(81):14, January 1986.

Is the old right now new?, by N. Thornton. SOCIAL ALTERNATIVES 5(4):6, November 1986.

Liability risks threaten medical supplies. FUTURIST 20:50, September-October 1986.

Matters of the heart: propranolol for birth control? AMERICAN JOURNAL OF NURSING 86:1096, October 1986.

Modern contraceptive practice in rural Appalachia, by G. A. Gairola, et al. AMERI-CAN JOURNAL OF PUBLIC HEALTH 76(8):1004-1008, August 1986.

More Robins sleaze. OFF OUR BACKS 16(4):14, April 1986.

Natural alternative, by N. Cameron. HERIZONS 4(6):39, September 1986.

Oral contraceptives and venous thromboembolism. AMERICAN JOURNAL OF NURSING 86:1044, September 1986; also in NURSES DRUG ALERT 10(9): 66, September 1986.

Pause that represses. SCIENCE DIGEST 94:15, August 1986.

Reproductive health. LADIES HOME JOURNAL 103:74+, May 1986.

Rights threatened, by P. Sheldrick. NEW DIRECTIONS FOR WOMEN 15(1):1, January 1986.

Risky business of birth control (liability suits), by C. Skrzycki. US NEWS AND WORLD REPORT 100:42-43, May 26, 1986.

School for scandal: birth control clinics, by J. Ruby. OFF OUR BACKS 16(11):2, December 1986.

CONTRACEPTIVES—GENERAL (continued)

Sex education laws and policies. STUDIES IN FAMILY PLANNING 16(4):219, July-August 1985.

Shielding greed, by C. Cooke. NATION 242(12):464, March 29, 1986.

Should she, or shouldn't she? Even the government is uncertain about Depo-provera, by T. Philip, et al. ALBERTA REPORT 13:18-19, September 29, 1986.

Social skills and responses in simulated contraceptive problem situations, by M. J. Hynes, et al. JOURNAL OF SEX RESEARCH 21(4):422-436, November 1985.

Spermicide and STDs. AMERICAN FAMILY PHYSICIAN 33:256, June 1986.

Spermicide information. SPARE RIB 165:51, April 1986.

Spermicides and birth defects. SCIENCE NEWS 130:399, December 20-27, 1986.

Surgeon General's warning (origin of word "condom"), by W. Safire. NEW YORK TIMES MAGAZINE December 14, 1986, p. 16.

Tabac et anovulants, c'est la guerre; with English summary, by D. Bergeron. CANADIAN NURSE 82:30-31, October 1986.

Vaginal spermicides and congenital disorders: the validity of a study [discussion], by R. N. Watkins, et al. JAMA 256:3095-3096, December 12, 1986.

Vending machines and the self-care concept, by J. L. Steinfirst, et al. JOURNAL OF AMERICAN COLLEGE HEALTH 34(1):37-39, August 1985.

Why your contraceptive can fail you, by A. Fischer. REDBOOK 166:34+, March 1986.

BANGLADESH
Characteristics of users of traditional contraceptive methods in Bangladesh, by M. Kabir, et al. JOURNAL OF BIOSOCIAL SCIENCE 18(1):23-33, January 1986.

BRAZIL
Contraceptive prevalence in the slums of Rio de Janeiro, by M. J. Wawer, et al. STUDIES IN FAMILY PLANNING 17(10:44-52, January-February 1986.

Side effects and discontinuation of oral contraceptive use in southern Brazil, by B. Janowitz, et al. JOURNAL OF BIOSOCIAL SCIENCE 18(3):261-271, July 1986.

CANADA
Contraceptive use in Canada, 1984, by T. R. Balakrishnan, et al. FAMILY PLANNING PERSPECTIVES 17(5):209-215, September-October 1985.

Reproductive factors, oral contraceptives and risk of malignant melanoma: Western Canada Melanoma Study, by R. P. Gallagher, et al. BRITISH JOURNAL OF CANCER 52(6):90-1907, December 1985.

CONTRACEPTIVES—GENERAL (continued)

CANADA (continued)
Will Canada ever see gays in condom ads?, by I. Timberlake. MARKETING 91:28, September 29, 1986.

CHINA
Patterns of contraceptive use in China, by D. K. Poston, Jr. STUDIES IN FAMILY PLANNING 17:17-27, September-October 1986.

COLOMBIA
Effect of child mortality on contraceptive use and fertility in Colombia, Costa Rica and Korea. POPULATION STUDIES 39(2):309, July 1985.

COSTA RICA
Effect of child mortality on contraceptive use and fertility in Colombia, Costa Rica and Korea. POPULATION STUDIES 39(2):309, July 1985.

DEVELOPING COUNTRIES
Assessment of burst strength distribution data for monitoring quality of condom stocks in developing countries, by M. J. Free, et al. CONTRACEPTION 33(3):285-299, March 1986.

Contraceptive use and annual acceptors required for fertility transition: results of a projection model, by J. Bongaarts. STUDIES IN FAMILY PLANNING 17:209-216, September-October 1986.

Injectable contraceptives in developing countries [letter], by S. Nair. LANCET 1(8495):1440-1441, June 21, 1986.

Teenage pregnancy in developed countries: determinants and policy implications, by E. F. Jones, et al. FAMILY PLANNING PERSPECTIVES 17(2): 53-62, March-April 1985.

EGYPT
Evaluation of the population and development program in Egypt, by J. M. Stycos, et al. DEMOGRAPHY 22(3):431-443, August 1985.

Oral contraceptive use and blood pressure in a German metropolitan population, by V. Cairns, et al. INTERNATIONAL JOURNAL OF EPIDEMIOLOGY 14(3):389-395, September 1985.

Rumor, misinformation and oral contraceptive use in Egypt, by J. DeClerque, et al. SOCIAL SCIENCE AND MEDICINE 23(1):83-92, 1986.

GHANA
Comparative study of Neo Sampoon, Ortho Vaginal Tablets and Emko Vaginal Tablets in Accra, Ghana, by P. Lamptey, et al. CONTRACEPTION 32(5):445-454, November 1985.

GREAT BRITAIN
Contraceptive advice: how the English differ from the Americans, by B. Qureshi. JOURNAL OF THE ROYAL SOCIETY OF HEALTH 106(3):77-79, June 1986.

Gillick judgment. Contraceptives and the under 16s: House of Lords ruling, by C. Dyer. BRITISH MEDICAL JOURNAL 291(6503):1208-1209, October 26, 1985.

CONTRACEPTIVES—GENERAL (continued)

GREAT BRITAIN (continued)
Study of the influence of ovulation stimulants and oral contraception on twin births in England, by F. Webster, et al. ACTA GENETICAE MEDICAE ET GEMELLOLOGIAE 34(1-2):105-108, 1985.

HUNGARY
Effect of the contraceptive pill on blood pressure: a randomized controlled trial of three progestogen-oestrogen combinations in Szeged, Hungary, by L. Kovacs, et al. CONTRACEPTION 33(1):69-71, January 1986.

Investigation on the influence of steroidal contraceptives on milk lipid and fatty acids in Hungary and Thailand. WHO Special Programme of Research, Development and Research Training in Human Reproduction, Task Force on oral contraceptives, by M. Sas, et al. CONTRACEPTION 33(2):159-178, February 1986.

INDIA
Impact of hormonal contraceptives vis-à-vis non-hormonal factors on the vitamin status of malnourishd women in India and Thailand. World Health Organization: Special Programme of Research, Development and Research Training in Human Reproduction. Task Force on Oral Contraceptives, by U. M. Joshi, et al. HUMAN NUTRITION. CLINICAL NUTRITION 40(3):205-220, May 1986.

India—right to life for females. INTERNATIONAL VIEWPOINT 94:22, March 10, 1986.

INDONESIA
Comparison of census and family planning program data on contraceptive prevalence, Indonesia, by K. Streatfield. STUDIES IN FAMILY PLANNING 16(6 pt 1):342-349, November-December 1985.

ITALY
Oral contraceptives in a southern Italian community, by M. A. Korovkin. CURRENT ANTHROPOLOGY 27:80-83, February 1986.

JAPAN
Condoms in Japan [letter], by B. Warming. NATURE 322(6074):10, July 3-9, 1986.

Contraceptive pill. Japan heads for legalization [news], by A. Anderson. NATURE 317(6040):760-761, October 31-November 6, 1985.

JORDAN
Family planning in Jordan: 1983 survey data, by A. Abdel-Aziz, et al. STUDIES IN FAMILY PLANNING 17(4):199-206, July-August 1986.

KOREA
Effect of child mortality on contraceptive use and fertility in Colombia, Costa Rica and Korea. POPULATION STUDIES 39(2):309, July 1985.

Evaluation of contraceptive history data in the Republic of Korea, by A. R. Pebley, et al. STUDIES IN FAMILY PLANNING 17(1):22-35, January-February 1986.

KUWAIT
Contraceptive use among women in Kuwait, by N. M. Shah, et al. INTERNATIONAL FAMILY PLANNING PERSPECTIVES 11(4):108-112, 1985.

CONTRACEPTIVES—GENERAL (continued)

MEXICO
Cost benefit analysis of the Mexican Social Security Administration's family planning program, by D. L. Nortman, et al. STUDIES IN FAMILY PLANNING 17(1):1-6, January-February 1986.

NIGERIA
Contraceptive knowledge and attitudes in urban Ilorin, Nigeria, by G. A. Oni. JOURNAL OF BIOSOCIAL SCIENCE 18(3):273-283, July 1986.

Control of reproduction: principle—Nigeria, by R. Pittin. REVIEW OF AFRICAN POLITICAL ECONOMY 35:40, May 1986.

Effects of women's education on postpartum practices and fertility in urban Nigeria, by G. A. Oni. STUDIES IN FAMILY PLANNING 16(6 pt 1):321-331, November-December 1985.

Sexual behavior, contraceptive practice, and reproductive health among Nigerian adolescents, by D. Nichols, et al. STUDIES IN FAMILY PLANNING 17(2):100-106, March-April 1986.

Use of contraceptives for birth spacing in a Nigerian city, by G. A. Oni, et al. STUDIES IN FAMILY PLANNING 17(4):165-171, July-August 1986.

PAKISTAN
Phase IV study of the injection Norigest in Pakistan, by A. Kazi, et al. CONTRACEPTION 32(4):395-403, October 1985.

PERU
Barriers to modern contraceptive use in rural Peru, by G. M. Tucker. STUDIES IN FAMILY PLANNING 17:308-316, November-December 1986.

PHILIPPINES
Demographic and contraceptive patterns among women in Northern Mindanao, the Philippines, by C. E. Tan, et al. SOCIAL BIOLOGY 31(3-4):232-242, Fall-Winter 1984.

PUERTO RICO
Contraceptive use and the need for family planning in Puerto Rico, by J. M. Harold, et al. FAMILY PLANNING PERSPECTIVES 18(4):185-188+, 1986.

SOUTH AFRICA
Factors associated with the perception of side-effects relating to the use of contraceptive methods . . . intra-uterine device, the hormonal pill and the injection, by G. Erasmus, et al. CURATIONIS 8(3):45-47, September 1985.

Study of factors related to contraceptive dropout: colored women in the metropolitan area of Capetown, by M. Strydom. CURATIONIS 8(2):44-45+, June 1985.

SUDAN
Crossover pill study among Sudanese women, by A. S. Gerais, et al. INTERNATIONAL JOURNAL OF GYNAECOLOGY AND OBSTETRICS 23(3): 229-233, June 1985.

THAILAND
Impact of hormonal contraceptives vis-à-vis non-hormonal factors on the

CONTRACEPTIVES—GENERAL (continued)

THAILAND (continued)
vitamin status of malnourishd women in India and Thailand. World Health Organization: Special Programme of Research, Development and Research Training in Human Reproduction. Task Force on Oral Contraceptives, by U. M. Joshi, et al. HUMAN NUTRITION. CLINICAL NUTRITION 40(3):205-220, May 1986.

Infant feeding practices, postpartum amenorrhea, and contraceptive use in Thailand, by J. Knodel, et al. STUDIES IN FAMILY PLANNING 16(6 pt 1):302-311, November-December 1985.

Investigation on the influence of steroidal contraceptives on milk lipid and fatty acids in Hungary and Thailand. WHO Special Programme of Research, Development and Research Training in Human Reproduction, Task Force on oral contraceptives, by M. Sas, et al. CONTRACEPTION 33(2):159-178, February 1986.

UNITED STATES
Contraceptive advice: how the English differ from the Americans, by B. Qureshi. JOURNAL OF THE ROYAL SOCIETY OF HEALTH 106(3):77-79, June 1986.

Contraceptive perceptions and method choice among young single women in the United States, by K. Tanfer, et al. STUDIES IN FAMILY PLANNING 17:269-277, November-December 1986.

Male birth-control pill to begin testing in United States. JET 71:28, November 10, 1986.

ZAIRE
Correlates and implications of breast-feeding practices in Bas, Zaire, by N. B. Mock, et al. JOURNAL OF BIOSOCIAL SCIENCE 18(2):231-245, April 1986.

Factors influencing the use of traditional versus modern family planning methods in Bas Zaire, by J. T. Bertrand, et al. STUDIES IN FAMILY PLANNING 16(6 pt 1):332-341, November-December 1985.

CONTRACEPTIVES—ADVERTISING
American Academy of Pediatrics supports contraceptive advertising. AMERICAN JOURNAL OF PUBLIC HEALTH 76:1442, December 1986.

Cold shower (contraceptive sponge marketing by VLI Corp.), by E. Paris. FORBES 138:129-130 November 17 1986.

Condom maker goes after women (marketing geared to women), by A. Lallande. VENTURE 8:82+, January 1986..

Rubber barons (rise in condom sales due to AIDS scare), by C. Leinster. FORTUNE 114:105-106+, November 24, 1986.

Social marketing of contraceptives, by W. P. Schellstede, et al. DRAPER FUND REPORT December 1986, pp. 21-26.

CONTRACEPTIVES—ATTITUDES
Age, gender, and ethnic differences in sexual and contraceptive knowledge, attitudes, and behaviors, by D. S. Moore, et al. FAMILY AND COMMUNITY HEALTH 8(3):38-51, November 1985.

CONTRACEPTIVES—ATTITUDES (continued)

Comparison of the effects of confluent vs. traditional contraceptive education on young people's knowledge, attitudes and behavior, by J. R. Daulk. DAI: A 47(3), September 1986.

Contraceptive diaphragm. Is it an acceptable method in the 1980s?, by G. T. Kovacs, et al. AUSTRALIAN AND NEW ZEALAND JOURNAL OF OBSTET-RICS AND GYNAECOLOGY 26(1):76-79, February 1986.

Contraceptive experience and attitudes to motherhood of teenage mothers, by B. Ineichen. JOURNAL OF BIOSOCIAL SCIENCE 18(4):387-394, 1986.

Contraceptive knowledge and attitudes in urban Ilorin, Nigeria, by G. A. Oni. JOURNAL OF BIOSOCIAL SCIENCE 18(3):273-283, July 1986.

Contributions of sex guilt and masturbation guilt to women's contraceptive attitudes and use, by D. L. Mosher, et al. JOURNAL OF SEX RESEARCH 21(1):24-39, February 1985.

Hypermasculinity and male contraceptive attitudes and behavior, by T. M. Exner. DAI: B 47(2), August 1986.

Oral contraceptives in a southern Italian community, by M. A. Korovkin. CUR-RENT ANTHROPOLOGY 27:80-83, February 1986.

Research on adolescent male attitudes about contraceptives, by P. M. Hewson. PEDIATRIC NURSING 12(2):114-116, March-April 1986.

Study of the perceptions of middle school girls regarding factors which influence their knowledge, attitudes and behaviors concerning the use or the non-use of contraceptives, by J. Hines-Harris. DAI: A 47(5), November 1986.

CONTRACEPTIVES—COMPLICATIONS
Contraceptive casualty? Spermicide lawsuit, by D. Begel. MULTINATIONAL MONITOR 7(14):14, October 1986..

Contraceptive sponges and toxic shock syndrome. AMERICAN FAMILY PHYSICIAN 34:234, July 1986.

Contraceptive steroids increase hepatic uptake of chylomicron remnants in healthy young women, by F. Berr, et al. JOURNAL OF LIPID RESEARCH 27(6):645-651, June 1986.

Contraceptives and pregnancy in melanoma patients, by K. Bork. HAUTARZT 36(9):542, September 1985.

Horrors of the Dalkon shield, by M. Lawton. PUBLIC CITIZEN 6(4):22, April 1986.

CONTRACEPTIVES—COUNSELING
Counseling on contraceptives: an unfilled need, by S. Steadman. AMERICAN PHARMACY NS25(9):42-46, September 1985..

CONTRACEPTIVES—EDUCATION
Age, gender, and ethnic differences in sexual and contraceptive knowledge, attitudes, and behaviors, by D. S. Moore, et al. FAMILY AND COMMUNITY HEALTH 8(3):38-51, November 1985.

CONTRACEPTIVES—EDUCATION (continued)

Comparison of the effects of confluent vs. traditional contraceptive education on young people's knowledge, attitudes and behavior, by J. R. Daulk. DAI: A 47(3), September 1986.

Contraceptive knowledge and attitudes in urban llorin, Nigeria, by G. A. Oni. JOURNAL OF BIOSOCIAL SCIENCE 18(3):273-283, July 1986.

CONTRACEPTIVES—FEMALE
See also: Contraception—Female

Adolescent facing contraception: methods, by M. R. Herrero Martin, et al. REVISTA DE ENFERMAGEN 9(95):40-48, June 1986.

Alcohol consumption, female sexual behavior and contraceptive use, by S. M. Harvey, et al. JOURNAL OF STUDIES ON ALCOHOL 47(4):327-332, July 1986.

Family planning. If the cap fits, by M. Renn. NURSING TIMES 82(5):22-24, January 29-February 4, 1986.

Local mechanical and chemical contraception. Coitus interruptus, by G. A. Hauser. THERAPEUTISCHE UMSCHAU 43(5):404-410, May 1986.

Pharmacokinetic and pharmacodynamic studies of vaginal rings releasing low-dose levonorgestrel, by B. L. Xiao, et al. CONTRACEPTION 32(5):455-471, November 1985.

CONTRACEPTIVES—FEMALE—COMPLICATIONS
Bacterial flora of the cervix in women using different methods of contraception, by M. Haukkamaa, et al. AMERICAN JOURNAL OF OBSTETRICS AND GYNE-COLOGY 154(3):520-524, March 1986.

Toxic shock syndrome, contraceptive methods, and vaginitis, by S. F. Lanes, et al. AMERICAN JOURNAL OF OBSTETRICS AND GYNECOLOGY 154(5): 989-991, May 1986.

CONTRACEPTIVES—FEMALE—BARRIER
Cervical cap, by E. Gollub. HEALTH PAC BULLETIN 16(6):22, August 1986.

Cervical cap: effectiveness, safety,and acceptability as a barrier contraceptive, by N. H. Lauersen, et al. MT. SINAI JOURNAL OF MEDICINE 53(4):233-238, April 1986.

Cervical cap moves toward FDA approval, by E. Gleick. NEW AGE March 1986, p. 11.

Cold shower (contraceptive sponge marketing by VLI Corp.), by E. Paris. FORBES 138:129-130 November 17 1986.

Contraception with the cervical cap: effectiveness, safety, continuity of use, and user satisfaction, by M. G. Powell, et al. CONTRACEPTION 33(3):215-232, March 1986.

Contraceptive diaphragm increase UTI risk. RN 49:68, August 1986.

Contraceptive diaphragm. Is it an acceptable method in the 1980s?, by G. T. Kovacs, et al. AUSTRALIAN AND NEW ZEALAND JOURNAL OF OBSTET-RICS AND GYNAECOLOGY 26(1):76-79, February 1986.

CONTRACEPTIVES—FEMALE—BARRIER (continued)

Diaphragm method contraceptors: implications for service organization and delivery . . . college women, by J. G. Zapka, et al. HEALTH EDUCATION QUARTERLY 12(3):245-257, Fall 1985.

Effect of vaginal contraceptive sponges on growth of toxic shock syndrome-associated staphylococcus aureus in vitro, by P. G. Stumpf, et al. CONTRACEPTION 33(4):395-399, April 1986.

Epidemiology of urinary tract infection: diaphragm use and sexual intercourse. Part 1, by B. Foxman, et al. AMERICAN JOURNAL OF PUBLIC HEALTH 75(11):1308-1313, November 1985.

Family planning: if the cap fits, by B. Spencer. NURSING TIMES 82(5):22-24, January 29-February 4, 1986.

Progress report on a study of the cervical cap, by J. Eliot, et al. JOURNAL OF REPRODUCTIVE MEDICINE 30(10):753-759, October 1985.

Relationship between weight change and diaphragm size change, by C. Kugel, et al. JOGN NURSING 15(2):123-129, March-April 1986.

Reliability of the vaginal diaphragm as a contraceptive method, by G. K. Döring, et al. GEBURTSHILFE UND FRAUENHEILKUNDE 46(1):33-36, January 1986.

Sponge story with holes, by S. O'Sullivan. SPARE RIB 161:42, December 1985.

Vaginal sponges and TSS. TRIAL 21(12):87-89, December 1985.

CONTRACEPTIVES—FEMALE—BARRIER—COMPLICATIONS
Barrier that can bother the bladder. EMERGENCY MEDICINE 18(6):81-82, March 30, 1986.

Diaphragm use and urinary tract infection [letter], by B. A. Peddie, et al. JAMA 255(13):1707, April 4, 1986.

Nightmare: women and Dalkon shield, by D. Williams. HARVARD WOMENS LAW JOURNAL 9:233, Spring 1986.

Toxic shock syndrome and the contraceptive sponge [editorial], by A. L. Reingold. JAMA 255(2):242-243, January 10, 1986.

Toxic shock syndrome and the vaginal contraceptive sponge, by G. Faich, et al. JAMA 225(2):216-218, January 10, 1986.

CONTRACEPTIVES—FEMALE—INJECTED
Comparative study of the metabolic effects of injectable and oral contraceptives, by D. F. Liew, et al. CONTRACEPTION 33(4):385-394, April 1986.

Social and demographic factors influencing the acceptability of injectable method for contraception in comparison with copper "T" I.U.D., by R. Goraya, et al. INDIAN JOURNAL OF MEDICAL SCIENCE 39(7):172-174, July 1985.

CONTRACEPTIVES—FEMALE—IUD
Copper T380A IUD approved by the USFDA. STUDIES IN FAMILY PLANNING 16:39, January-February 1985.

CONTRACEPTIVES—FEMALE—IUD (continued)

End of IUD marketing in the United States: what does it mean for American women?, by J. D. Forrest. FAMILY PLANNING PERSPECTIVES 18(2):52-55+, March-April 1986.

Epidemiological data, cytology and colposcopy in IUD (intrauterine device), E-P (estro-progestogens) and diaphragm users. Study of cytological changes of endometrium IUD related, by N. Fiore. CLINICAL AND EXPERIMENTAL OBSTETRICS AND GYNECOLOGY 13(1-2):34-42, 1986.

Factors associated with the perception of side-effects relating to the use of contraceptive methods . . . intra-uterine device, the hormonal pill and the injection, by G. Erasmus, et al. CURATIONIS 8(3):45-47, September 1985.

Intrauterine devices, by G. R. Thornton, Jr. TRIAL 22(11):44-48, November 1986.

Is lactation a risk factor of IUD- and sterilization-related uterine perforation? A hypothesis, by I. C. Chi, et al. INTERNATIONAL JOURNAL OF GYNAECOLOGY AND OBSTETRICS 22(4):315-317, August 1984.

IUD after 20 years [review]. FAMILY PLANNING PERSPECTIVES 17(6):244, November-December 1985.

IUD controversy: what does it mean for you? GLAMOUR 84:341-342, May 1986.

IUD insertion following induced abortion, by L. Querido, et al. CONTRACEPTION 31(6):603-610, June 1985.

Post-coital contraception by estrogen/progestagen combination or IUD insertion, by M. Luerti, et al. CONTRACEPTION 33(1):61-68, January 1986.

Postmenopausal removal of IUD, by R. M. Soerstrom. JAMA 255:3018, June 6, 1986.

Return to fertility after IUD removal for planned pregnancy, by L. Randic, et al. CONTRACEPTION 32(3):253-259, September 1985.

Searle quits IUD's. NEWSWEEK 107:60, February 10, 1986.

Searle: staring at some long days in court (suits involving intrauterine contraceptives), by E. Spragins, et al. BUSINESS WEEK February 17, 1986, p. 35.

Searle stops selling IUDs (copper-sever). FDA CONSUMER 20:4, April 1986.

Searle's troubles give Alza its big break (Progestasert intrauterine contraceptive system), by J. O. Hamilton. BUSINESS WEEK February 24, 1986, pp. 123-125.

Social and demographic factors influencing the acceptability of injectable method for contraception in comparison with copper "T" I.U.D., by R. Goraya, et al. INDIAN JOURNAL OF MEDICAL SCIENCE 39(7):172-174, July 1985.

CONTRACEPTIVES—FEMALE—IUD—COMPLICATIONS
Crime against women—A. H. Robins and Dalkon shield, by M. Mintz. MOBILIZER 5(2):1, Winter 1986.

Criminals by any other name (DalkonShield case), by R. Mokhiber. WASHINGTON MONTHLY 17:40-44, January 1986.

CONTRACEPTIVES—FEMALE—IUD—COMPLICATIONS (continued)

Dalkon doesn't do it, by J. Thomas. OFF OUR BACKS 16(2):8, February 1986.

Dalkon fiasco continues, by C. Clement. HEALTHSHARING 7(2):6, Spring 1986.

Dalkon shield, by P. M. Davis. DESIGN NEWS 41:262, December 2, 1985.

Dalkon shield: April 30 is deadline, by P. Abbott. PROTECT YOURSELF March 1986, p. 5.

Dalkon shield—just when you thought it was, by A. Reich. SIMPLY LIVING 2(11):17, 1986.

Dalkon shield outrage. PROGRESSIVE 50(3):40, March 1986.

Dalkon shields—the IUD is in the news again, by S. O'Sullivan. SPARE RIB 163:51, February 1986.

Farewell to the IUD, by B. Gladstone. NEW AGE 2(12):88, July 1986.

IUD removal causes pain, by P. De La Fuente. NEW DIRECTIONS FOR WOMEN 15(3):4, May 1986.

IUD taken off market, by J. Clark. NATIONAL NOW TIMES 18(8):6, February 1986.

IUD use and subsequent tubal ectopic pregnancy, by W.-H. Chow, et al. AMERI-CAN JOURNAL OF PUBLIC HEALTH 76:536-539, May 1986.

CONTRACEPTIVES—FEMALE—ORAL
Ability of women to recall their oral contraceptive histories, by A. Coulter, et al. CONTRACEPTION 33(2):127-137, February 1986.

Antacid does not reduce the bioavailability of oral contraceptive steroids in women, by J. V. Joshi, et al. INTERNATIONAL JOURNAL OF CLINICAL PHARMACOLOGY, THERAPY AND TOXICOLOGY 24(4):192-195, April 1986.

Beneficial and adverse side-effects of hormonal contraception [editorial], by R. J. Pepperell. MEDICAL JOURNAL OF AUSTRALIA 144(4):169-170, February 17, 1986.

Carbohydrate tolerance and serum lipid responses to type of dietary carbohy-drate and oral contraceptive use in young women, by P. B. Moser, et al. JOURNAL OF THE AMERICAN COLLEGE OF NUTRITION 5(1):45-53, 1986.

Catholic doctor who fought for the pill, by L. McLaughlin. DISCOVER 4:82+, February 1983.

Comparative study of the metabolic effects of injectable and oral contraceptives, by D. F. Liew, et al. CONTRACEPTION 33(4):385-394, April 1986.

Crossover pill study among Sudanese women, by A. S. Gerais, et al. INTERNA-TIONAL JOURNAL OF GYNAECOLOGY AND OBSTETRICS 23(3):229-233, June 1985.

Detection of ovulation by assay of the luteinizing hormone in the urine of ado-lescents, before prescribing oral contraceptives, by M. Blum, et al. REVUE

119

FRANCAISE DE GYNECOLOGIE ET D'OBSTETRIQUE 80(12):881-882, December 1985.

Development of a compulsive syndrome by ovulation inhibitors, by C. Calanchini. SCHWEIZER ARCHIV FUR NEUROLOGIE, NEUROCHIRURGIE UND PSYCHIATRIE 137(4):25-31, 1986.

Do oral contraceptive agents affect nutrient requirements—vitamin B-6?, by L. T. Miller. JOURNAL OF NUTRITION 116(7):1344-1345, July 1986.

Effect of the contraceptive pill on blood pressure: a randomized controlled trial of three progestogen-oestrogen combinations in Szeged, Hungary, by L. Kovacs, et al. CONTRACEPTION 33(1):69-71, January 1986.

Effect of cyclical hormonal changes in erythrocyte electrolyte transport mechanisms, by E. D. Gallery, et al. CLINICAL SCIENCE 70(3):263-269, March 1986.

Effect of hormonal contraception on blood protein levels, by P. Fassati, et al. CESKOSLOVENSKA GYNEKOLOGIE 51(5):328-331, June 1986.

Effect of a new oral antiandrogen-estrogen combination on the endometrium: histological and ultrastructural scanning electron microscopy study, by L. Fedele, et al. ACTA EUROPAEA FERTILITATIS 17(1):9-13, January-February 1986.

Effect of oral contraceptive steroids on the growth rate of human mammary epithelia in cell culture, by S. M. Longman. DAI: B 47(3),September 1986.

Effect of oral contraceptives on the apparent vitamin B6 status in some Sudanese women, by E. Y. Salih, et al. BRITISH JOURNAL OF NUTRITION 56:363-367, September 1986.

Effect of oral contraceptives on leukocyte phagocytic activity and plasma levels of prostaglandin E2 and thromboxane B2 in normal menstruating women, by J. A. Stratton, et al. AMERICAN JOURNAL OF REPRODUCTIVE IMMUNOLOGY AND MICROBIOLOGY 10(2):47-52, February 1986.

Effect of oral contraceptives on plasma and platelet lipid composition. Influence of the length duration of time of ingestion, by J. Aznar, et al. ACTA OBSTETRICIA ET GYNECOLOGICA SCANDINAVICA 65(1):33-40, 1986.

Effect of oral contraceptives on the rat brain and pituitary opioid peptides, by G. A. Tejwani, et al. PEPTIDES 6(3):555-561, May-June 1985.

Effect of oral contraceptives on serum prolactin: a longitudinal study in 126 normal premenopausal women, by P. L. Hwang, et al. CLINICAL ENDOCRINOLOGY 24(2):127-133, February 1986.

Effect of tumor promoting contraceptive steroids on growth and drug metabolizing enzymes in rat liver, by H. Ochs, et al. CANCER RESEARCH 46(3):1224-1232, March 1986.

Effects of oral contraceptives on cholesterol, by S. Roy. JOURNAL OF REPRODUCTIVE MEDICINE 31(6 suppl):549-558, June 1986.

Effects of oral contraceptives on fibrinolytic system among Japanese and American women, by M. Ogino. NIPPON SANKA FUJINKA GAKKAI ZASSHI 38(6):817-826, June 1986.

Effects of oral contraceptives on lipid metabolism, by R. M. Krauss. JOURNAL OF REPRODUCTIVE MEDICINE 31(6 suppl):549-550, June 1986.

Effects of pregnancy, postpartum lactation, and oral contraceptive use on the lipoprotein cholesterol/triglyceride ration, by R. H. Knopp, et al. METABOLISM 34(10):893-899, October 1985.

Effects on blood pressure of low dose oestroen and progestagen only oral contraceptives, by R. J. Weir, et al. JOURNAL OF HYPERTENSION 1(2): 100-101, December 1983.

Effects on the lipoprotein metabolism of an antiandrogen-estrogen oral contraceptive drug, by U. Larsson-Cohn, et al. ACTA OBSTETRICIA ET GYNECOLOGICA SCANDINAVICA 65(2):125-128, 1986.

Endometrial morphology during a normophasic and a triphasic regimen: a comparison, by P. Wynants, et al. CONTRACEPTION 33(2):149-157, February 1986.

Epidemiological data, cytology and colposcopy in IUD (intrauterine device), E-P (estro-progestogens) and diaphragm users. Study of cytological changes of endometrium IUD related, by N. Fiore. CLINICAL AND EXPERIMENTAL OBSTETRICS AND GYNECOLOGY 13(1-2):34-42, 1986.

Erythrocyte cation transport is sex-related and is modified by oral contraceptives, by G. S. Stokes, et al. CLINICAL AND EXPERIMENTAL HYPERTENSION 7(9):1199-1215, 1985.

Exposed: the bogus work of Prof. Briggs (contraceptive pill research), by B. Deer. SUNDAY TIMES September 28, 1986, pp. 27-28.

Factors associated with the perception of side-effects relating to the use of contraceptive methods . . . intra-uterine device, the hormonal pill and the injection, by G. Erasmus, et al. CURATIONIS 8(3):45-47, September 1985.

Female pelvic anatomy: MR assessment of variations during the menstrual cycle and with use of oral contraceptives, by S. McCarthy, et al. RADIOLOGY 160(1):119-123, July 1986.

Galactorrhea and serum prolactin levels in women using compound norgestrol, by L. J. Wang, et al. CHUNG HUA FU CHAN KO TSA CHIH 21(2):110-112+, March 1986.

Gonococcal pelvic inflammatory disease, oral contraceptives, and cervical mucus [letter], by M. Griffiths, et al. GENITOURINARY MEDICINE 61(1):67, February 1985.

Good news about cancer and the pill (breast cancer). NEWSWEEK 108:55, August 25, 1986.

Griseofulvin-oral contraceptive interaction [letter], by P. M. Catalano, et al. ARCHIVES OF DERMATOLOGY 121(11):1381, November 1985.

Hormonal contraception in diabetic women: acceptability and influence on diabetes control and ovarian function of a nonalkylated estrogen/progestogen compound, by S. O. Skouby, et al. CONTRACEPTION 32(1):23-31, July 1985.

Hospitalizations among black women using contraceptives, by J. E. Higgins, et al. AMERICAN JOURNAL OF OBSTETRICS AND GYNECOLOGY 153(3):280-287, October 1, 1985.

Immunoreactive renin, prorenim, and enzymatically active renin in plasma during pregnancy and in women taking oral contraceptives, by F. H. Derkx, et al. JOURNAL OF CLINICAL ENDOCRINOLOGY AND METABOLISM 63(4): 1008-1015, October 1986.

Impact of hormonal contraceptives vis-à-vis non-hormonal factors on the vitamin status of malnourishd women in India and Thailand. World Health Organization: Special Programme of Research, Development and Research Training in Human Reproduction. Task Force on Oral Contraceptives, by U. M. Joshi, et al. HUMAN NUTRITION. CLINICAL NUTRITION 40(3):205-220, May 1986.

Impairment of prednisolone disposition in women taking oral contraceptives or conjugated estrogens, by L. E. Gustavson, et al. JOURNAL OF CLINICAL ENDOCRINOLOGY AND METABOLISM 62(1):234-237, January 1986.

Imperialism and the pill (cultural and biological imperialism implicit in United States population control efforts), by T. Bethell. NATIONAL REVIEW 38:38-40, March 14, 1986.

Indicators of arterial blood pressure during hormonal contraception, by N. S. Trutko, et al. AKUSHERSTVO I GINEKOLOGIIA (9):56-57, August 1985.

Influence of a sequential-type oral contraceptive with ethinylestradiol-sulfonate soft gelatin capsules and norethisterone acetate on carbohydrate metabolism during the first twelve months, by S. Nikschick, et al. EXPERIMENTAL AND CLINICAL ENDOCRINOLOGY 85(3):257-262, June 1985.

Inhibition of tissue-type plasminogen activator in plasma of women using oral contraceptives and in normal women during a menstrual cycle, by J. Jespersen, et al. THROMBOSIS AND HAEMOSTASIS 55(3):388-389, June 30, 1986.

Interaction between antibiotic therapy and contraceptive medication, by R. Bainton. ORAL SURGERY, ORAL MEDICINE, ORAL PATHOLOGY 61(5): 453-455, May 1986.

Interaction of anticonvulsants and oral contraceptives in epileptic adolescents, by M. P. Diamond, et al. CONTRACEPTION 31(6):623-632, June 1985.

Keep taking the pill (we think). NEW SCIENTIST 111:21, September 25, 1986.

Lipid metabolism in hormonal contraception, by I. A. Manuilova, et al. AKUSHERSTVO I GINEKOLOGIIA (9):51-54, August 1985.

Liver parameters during administration of a combined contraceptive pill and its components, by J. Kulcsár-Gergely, et al. ACTA PHARMACEUTICA HUNGARICA 56(4):145-156, July 1986.

Low dose birth-control pills: lower risk. McCALLS 113:105, May 1986.

Macromolecular binding of prednisone in plasma of healthy volunteers including pregnant women and oral contraceptive users, by L. E. Gustavson, et al. JOURNAL OF PHARMACOKINETICS AND BIOPHARMACEUTICS 13(6): 561-569, December 1985.

Marked alterations in dose-dependent prednisolone kinetics in women taking oral contraceptives, by U. F. Legler, et al. CLINICAL PHARMACOLOGY AND THERAPEUTICS 39(4):425-429, April 1986.

Marvelon. A contraceptive pill with desogestrel, a new gestagenic substance, by I. C. Felding, et al. UGESKRIFT FOR LAEGER 147(42):3330-3332, October 14, 1985.

Marvelon—when the adverse effects become a marketing argument [letter], by V. Hansson. TIDSSKRIFT FOR DE NORSKE LAEGEFORENING 106(11):966-968, April 30, 1986.

Measurement of arterial smooth muscle cell mitogens in the blood of oral contraceptive users, by J. D. Bagdade, et al. ATHEROSCLEROSIS 56(2):149-155, August 1985.

Measurement of breast volume by ultrasound during normal menstrual cycles and with oral contraceptive use, by S. Malini, et al. OBSTETRICS AND GYNECOLOGY 66(4):538-541, October 1985.

Metabolic effects of oral contraceptives. A panel discussion. JOURNAL OF REPRODUCTIVE MEDICINE 31(6 suppl):569-572, June 1986.

New association of ethinylestradiol (0.035 mg) cyproterone acetate (2 mg) in the therapy of polycystic ovary syndrome, by L. Falsetti, et al. ACTA EUROPAEA FERTILITATIS 17(1):19-25, January-February 1986.

New developments in oral, injectable and implantable contraceptives, vaginal rings and intrauterine devices [review], by E. Diczfalusy. CONTRACEPTION 33(1):7-22, January 1986.

Norethisterone concentration in breast milk and infant and maternal plasma during ethynodiol diacetate administration, by I. D. Cooke, et al. CONTRACEPTION 31(6):611-621, June 1985.

Opioid regulation of pituitary gonadotropins and prolactin in women using oral contraceptives, by E. U. Snowden, et al. AMERICAN JOURNAL OF OBSTETRICS AND GYNECOLOGY 154(2):440-444, February 1986.

Oral contraceptive use and blood pressure in a German metropolitan population, by V. Cairns, et al. INTERNATIONAL JOURNAL OF EPIDEMIOLOGY 14(3): 389-395, September 1985.

Oral contraceptives and blood coagulation, by J. Bonnar, et al. JOURNAL OF REPRODUCTIVE MEDICINE 31(6 suppl):551-556, June 1986.

Oral contraceptives and diabetes, by G. Bargero, et al. MINERVA MEDICA 77(19):839-842, May 7, 1986.

Oral contraceptives and life expectancy, by J. A. Fortney, et al. STUDIES IN FAMILY PLANNING 17(3):117-125, May-June 1986.

CONTRACEPTIVES—FEMALE—ORAL (continued)

P-pills for women with acne/hirsutism [letter], by A. Røde, et al. TIDSSKRIFT FOR DEN NORSKE LAEGEFORENING 105(29):2099, October 20, 1985.

Paradoxic improvement of glucose intolerance in 8 females using estrogen-progestagen contraceptives containing norgestrel and ethinyl-estradiol, by P. Vexiau, et al. DIABETE ET METABOLISME 11(6):359-363, December 1985.

Patient record of the use of hormonal contraceptives—a possibility for better monitoring, by E. Canzler, et al. ZENTRALBLATT FUR GYNAEKOLOGIE 107(16):1017-1019, 1985.

Pharmacodynamic evaluation of the benzodiazepine-oral contraceptive inter-action, by P. D. Kroboth, et al. CLINICAL PHARMACOLOGY AND THERA-PEUTICS 38(5):525-532, November 1985.

Pharmacokinetics of oral contraceptive steroids in Egyptian women: studies with ovral, nordette and norminest, by I. el-Raghy, et al. CONTRACEPTION 33(4):379-384, April 1986.

Pill cleared of breast cancer role, by L. Davis. SCIENCE NEWS 130:100-101, August 16, 1986.

Pill cleared of causing breast cancer. NEW SCIENTIST 111:19, August 28, 1986.

Pill: the doctor's dilemma, by N. Timmins. TIMES March 8, 1986, p. 10.

Pill personality, by L. Murray. HEALTH 18:14, May 1986.

Pill 30 years on: a new perspective, by M. Potts. COMMUNITY MEDICINE 7(4): 241-247, November 1985.

Pill: what's right with it, by G. Blair. MADEMOISELLE 92:183-185+, August 1986.

Platelet and coagulation functions during triphasic oestrogen-progestogen treatment, by V. Bruni, et al. CONTRACEPTION 33(1):39-46, January 1986.

Post-coital contraception by estrogen/progestagen combination or IUD insertion, by M. Luerti, et al. CONTRACEPTION 33(1):61-68, January 1986.

Progestagenic activity and the mechanism of the contraceptive action of mecyge-prone, by G. V. Nikitina, et al. ARKHIV ANATOMII, GISTOLOGII I EMBRIOL-OGII 90(4):70-73, April 1986.

Progestogen-only pill [editorial], by P. W. Howie. BRITISH JOURNAL OF OB-STETRICS AND GYNAECOLOGY 92(10):1001-1002, October 1985.

Prospective study of drug use, smoking and contraceptives during early preg-nancy, by B. Sandahl. ACTA OBSTETRICIA ET GYNECOLOGICA SCANDINAVICA 64(5):381-386, 1985.

Prospective study of the metabolic effects of a low dose combined oral contra-ceptive, by D. F. Liew, et al. ASIA-OCEANIA JOURNAL OF OBSTETRICS AND GYNAECOLOGY 12(1):37-42, March 1986.

Protein C levels in late pregnancy, postpartum and in women on oral contra-ceptives, by R. Gonzalez, et al. THROMBOSIS RESEARCH 39(5):637-640, September 1, 1985.

CONTRACEPTIVES—FEMALE—ORAL (continued)

Randomized crossover comparison of two low-dose contraceptives: effects on serum lipids and lipoproteins, by W. März, et al. AMERICAN JOURNAL OF OBSTETRICS AND GYNECOLOGY 153(3):287-293, October 1, 1985.

Randomized cross-over comparison of two low-dose oral contraceptives upon hormonal and metabolic parameters: I. Effects upon sexual hormone levels, by H. Kuhl, et al. CONTRACEPTION 31(6):583-593, June 1985.

—: II. Effects upon thyroid function, gastrin, STH, and glucose tolerance, by H. Kuhl, et al. CONTRACEPTION 32(1):97-107, July 1985.

Randomized double-blind study of the effects of two low-dose combined oral contraceptives on biochemical aspects. Report from a seven-centered study. WHO Special Programme of Research, Development and Research Training in Human Reproduction. Task force on Oral Contraceptives. CONTRACEPTION 32(3):223-236, September 1985.

Relationship of self-concept and autonomy to oral contraceptive compliance among adolescent females, by E. U. Neel, et al. JOURNAL OF ADOLESCENT HEALTH CARE 6(6):445-447, November 1985.

Relative potency of progestins used in oral contraceptives, by L. J. Dorflinger. CONTRACEPTION 31(6):557-570, June 1985.

Renin-angiotensin system: oral contraception and exercise in healthy female subjects, by I. A. Huisveld, et al. JOURNAL OF APPLIED PHYSIOLOGY 59(6):1690-1697, December 1985.

Serum gonadotropi and ovarian steroid levels in women during administration of a norethindrone-ethinylestradiol triphasic oral contraceptive, by W. Y. Ling, et al. CONTRACEPTION 32(4):367-375, October 1985.

Study of factors related to contraceptive dropout: colored women in the metropolitan area of Capetown, by M. Strydom. CURATIONIS 8(2):44-45+, June 1985.

Study of the influence of ovulation stimulants and oral contraception on twin births in England, by F. Webster, et al. ACTA GENETICAE MEDICAE ET GEMELLOLOGIAE 34(1-2):105-108, 1985.

Sulpiride and the potentiation of progestogen only contraception, by M. R. Payne, et al. BRITISH MEDICAL JOURNAL 291(6495):559-561, August 31, 1985.

Surgery and the pill [letter], by P. H Dyson. BRITISH MEDICAL JOURNAL 291(6499):899, September 28, 1985.

Synphase—another triphasic oral contraceptive. DRUG AND THERAPEUTICS BULLETIN 23(20):79-80, October 7, 1985.

Synthesis of cyclopentylpropionic ester of norethisterone acetate as a long-acting contraceptive, by W. Chen, et al. YAO HSUEH HSUEH PAO 19(12): 935-937, December 1984.

Synthesis of gestodene, by H. Hofmeister, et al. ARZNEIMITTEL-FORSCHUNG 36(5):781-783, May 1986.

CONTRACEPTIVES—FEMALE—ORAL (continued)

Theophylline pharmacokinetics in adolescent females following coadministration of oral contraceptives, by G. Koren, et al. CLINICAL AND INVESTIGATIVE MEDICINE 8(3):222-226, 1985.

Triphasic oral contraception: metabolic effects in normal women and those with previous gestational diabetes, by S. O. Skouby, et al. AMERICAN JOURNAL OF OBSTETRICS AND GYNECOLOGY 153(5):495-500, November 1, 1985.

True or false?, by W. Cooper. GUARDIAN July 8, 1986, p. 8.

Twins on the pill. NEW SCIENTIST 110:27, May 8, 1986.

Unplanned pregnancies. AMERICAN FAMILY PHYSICIAN 33:212, May 1986.

Urinary excretion of melanocytic metabolites in fertile women, by R. Carstam, et al. ACTA DERMATO-VENEREOLOGICA 65(6):543-545, 1985.

Use and misuse of the term potency with respect to oral contraceptives, by J. W. Goldzieher. JOURNAL OF REPRODUCTIVE MEDICINE 31(6 suppl):533-539, June 1986.

Use of contraceptive agents by women in the city of Frunze, by I. A. Abdyldaeva, et al. SOVETSKOE ZDRAVOOKHRONENIE (6):40-42, 1986.

Use of oral contraceptives by women with epilepsy, by R. H. Mattson, et al. JAMA 256(2):238-240, July 11, 1986; Discussion 256:2961-2962, December 5 1986.

Uterine MR imaging: effects of hormonal stimulation, by B. E. Demas, et al. RADIOLOGY 159(1):123-126, April 1986.

Vaginal administration of a combined oral contraceptive containing norethis-terone acetate, by A. R. Souka, et al. CONTRACEPTION 31(6):571-581, June 1985.

Vitamin B-6 requirement and oral contraceptive use—a concern?, by J. E. Leklem. JOURNAL OF NUTRITION 116(3):475-477, March 1986.

Vitamin supplements to Indian women using low dosage oral contraceptives, by M. S. Bamji, et al. CONTRACEPTION 32(4):405-416, October 1985.

Weighting risks against benefits in contraceptive safety, by H. H. Akhter. NEW ERA NURSING IMAGE INTERNATIONAL 2(2):47-49, 1986.

CONTRACEPTIVES—FEMALE—ORAL—COMPLICATIONS
Alterations of cervical cytology and steroid contraceptive use, by G. Zarkovic. INTERNATIONAL JOURNAL OF EPIDEMIOLOGY 14(3):369-377, September 1985.

Another look at the pill and breast cancer [editorial]. LANCET 2(8462):985-987, November 2, 1985.

Assessment of psychological state associated with the menstrual cycle in users of oral contraception, by A. Marriott, et al. JOURNAL OF PSYCHOSOMATIC RESEARCH 30(1):41-47, 1986.

CONTRACEPTIVES—FEMALE—ORAL—COMPLICATIONS (continued)

Beneficial and adverse side-effects of hormonal contraception [editorial], by R. J. Pepperell. MEDICAL JOURNAL OF AUSTRALIA 144(4):169-170, February 17, 1986.

Benign liver tumors and oral contraceptives; diagnosis and treatment [letter], by O. S. Derksen, et al. NEDERLANDS TIJDSCHRIFT VOOR GENEESKUNDE 130(30):1372-1373, July 26, 1986.

Biological marker, strongly associated with early oral contraceptive use, for the selection of a high risk group for premenopausal breast cancer, by H. Olsson, et al. MEDICAL ONCOLOGY AND TUMOR PHARMACOTHERAPY 3(2):77-81, 1986.

Cancer of the liver and the use of oral contraceptives, by D. Forman, et al. BRITISH MEDICAL JOURNAL 292(6532):1357-1361, May 24, 1986.

Cancer risks and the contraceptive pill. What is the evidence after nearly 25 years of use?, by S. K. Khoo. MEDICAL JOURNAL OF AUSTRALIA 144(4):185-190, February 17, 1986.

Candidosis and oral contraception [letter], by D. G. Sylvester. PRACTITIONER 230(1414):299, April 1986.

Carbohydrate metabolism in women who used oral contraceptives containing levonorgestrel or desogestrel: a 6-month prospective study, by A. S. Luyckx, et al. FERTILITY AND STERILITY 45(5):635-642, May 1986.

Cardiovascular complications, lipoprotein metabolism and oral contraceptives, by C. Gagné. UNION MEDICALE DU CANADA 114(10):865-871, October 1985.

Case control study of breast cancer in relation to the use of steroid contraceptive agents, by C. Ellery, et al. MEDICAL JOURNAL OF AUSTRALIA 144(4):173-176, February 17, 1986.

Cerebral venous thrombosis and subarachnoid haemorrhage in users of oral contraceptives, by E. Chilvers, et al. BRITISH MEDICAL JOURNAL 292(6519):524, February 22, 1986.

Cervical cancer linked to pill. NEW SCIENTIST 112:16, November 20, 1986.

Chronic inflammatory bowel disease, cigarette smoking and use of oral contraceptives [letter], by J. H. Entrican, et al. BRITISH MEDICAL JOURNAL 292(6533):1464, May 31, 1986.

Chronic inflammatory bowel disease, cigarette smoking and use of oral contraceptives: findings in a large cohort study of women of childbearing age, by M. Vessey, et al. BRITISH MEDICAL JOURNAL 292(6528):1101-1103, April 26, 1986.

Clarification of causes of post-pill amenorrheal. ORVOSI HETILAP 127(18):1063-1064+, May 4, 1986.

Congenital abnormalities in the offspring of women who used oral and other contraceptives around the time of conception, by S. Harlap, et al. INTERNATIONAL JOURNAL OF FERTILITY 30(2):39-47, 1985.

CONTRACEPTIVES—FEMALE—ORAL—COMPLICATIONS (continued)

Contraception in women with diabetes mellitus, by L. Verschoor, et al. NEDER-LANDS TIJDSCHRIFT VOOR GENEESKUNDE 130(2):61-63, January 11, 1986.

Depo provera approval unknown, by C. Clement. HEALTHSHARING 7(2):4, Spring 1986.

Depo provera: drug associated with many dangers, by J. Manthorne. COM-MUNIQU'ELLES 12(1):12, January 1986.

Depo provera hearings. HEALTHSHARING 7(4):4, Fall 1986.

Depo-provera: is it a safe contraceptive?, by R. Maynard. CHATELAINE 59:94+, June 1986.

Drug interactions between oral contraceptive steroids and antibiotics, by M. L. Orme, et al. BRITISH DENTAL JOURNAL 160(5):169-170, March 8, 1986.

—[letter], by A. M. Brown, et al. BRITISH DENTAL JOURNAL 161(1):4, July 5, 1986.

Drug interactions in the use of steroid hormones, especially oral contraceptives, by H. M. Bolt. ARCHIVES OF GYNECOLOGY 238(1-4):717-723, 1986.

Drug interactions with oral contraceptive preparations, by G. M. Shenfield. MEDI-CAL JOURNAL OF AUSTRALIA 144(4):205-211, February 17, 1986.

Drug interactions with oral contraceptives, by P. F. D'Arcy. DRUG INTELLIGENCE AND CLINICAL PHARMACY 20(5):353-362, May 1986.

Drug interactions with the pill [letter], by M. A. Curran. MEDICAL JOURNAL OF AUSTRALIA 144(12):670-671, June 9, 1986.

Early oral contraceptive use and breast cancer risk [letter], by K. McPherson, et al. LANCET 1(8482):685-686, March 22, 1986.

Effect of female sex hormones on the incidence of disordered wound healing following tooth extraction, by A. Gänsicke, et al. ZAHNAERZTLICHE MUN-DEN UND KIEFERHEILKUNDE MIT ZENTRALBLATT 74(2):131-137, 1986.

Effect of hormonal contraceptives and caffeine on the Farnsworth-Munsell 100-hue Test, by M. Böhme, et al. ZENTRALBLATT FUR GYNAEKOLOGIE 107(21):1300-1306, 1985.

Effect of hormonal contraceptives on the coagulation system with special refer-ence to its inhibitors, by M. Misz, et al. ORVOSI HETILAP 126(43):2635-2640, October 27, 1985.

Effect of long-term hormonal contraception on plasma lipids, by J. P. Deslypere, et al. CONTRACEPTION 31(6):633-642, June 1985.

Effects of recent oral contraceptive use on the outcome of pregnancy, by P. N. Kasan, et al. EUROPEAN JOURNAL OF OBSTETRICS, GYNECOLOGY AND REPRODUCTIVE BIOLOGY 22(1-2):77-83, June 1986.

Embolic stroke in a woman with mitral valve prolapse who used oral contracep-tives, by E. H. Busch, et al. CHEST 90(3):454-455, September 1986.

CONTRACEPTIVES—FEMALE—ORAL—COMPLICATIONS (continued)

Endocervical neoplasia in long-term users of oral contraceptives: clinical and pathologic observations, by P. T. Valente, et al. OBSTETRICS AND GYNE- COLOGY 67(5):695-704, May 1986.

Epidemiology of oral contraceptives and the risk of breast cancer, by L. Webster. JOURNAL OF REPRODUCTIVE MEDICINE 31(6 suppl):540-545, June 1986.

Esophageal ulcer caused by the "pill", by G. Allmendinger. ZEITSCHRIFT FUR GASTROENTEROLOGIE 23(10):531-533, October 1985.

Evaluation of reports on the side effects of hormone contraceptives, by H. G. Neumann. ZEITSCHRIFT FUR AERZTLICHE FORTBILDUNG 79(24):1033- 1036, 1985.

Evidence for an increased risk of Crohn's disease in oral contraceptive users, by S. M. Lesko, et al. GASTROENTEROLOGY 89(5):1046-1049, November 1985.

Exogenous female sex hormones and birth defects, by A. P. Polednak. PUBLIC HEALTH REVIEWS 13(1-2):89-114, 1985.

Exogenous sex hormone exposure and the risk for major malformations, by E. J. Lammer, et al. JAMA 255:128-132, June 13, 1986.

Hemichorea and oral contraceptives, by A. Buge, et al. REVUE NEUROLOGI- QUE 141(10):663-665, 1985.

Hepatic adenoma and oral contraceptives: personal case, by G. B. Cassinelli. ANNALI ITALIANI DI CHIRURGIA 57(2):101-107, 1985.

Hepatic tumors and oral contraceptives: surgical management, by G. Gonzalez, et al. JOURNAL OF SURGERY AND ONCOLOGY 29(3):193-197, July 1985.

Hereditary uroporphyrinogen-decarboxylase deficiency predisposing porphyria cutanea tarda (chronic hepatic porphyria) in females after oral contraceptive medication, by F. Sixel-Dietrich, et al. ARCHIVES OF DERMATOLOGICAL RESEARCH 278(1):13-16, 1985.

Histochemical and immunohistochemical detection of putative preneoplastic liver foci in women after long-term use of oral contraceptives, by G. Fischer, et al. VIRCHOWS ARCHIV. CELL PATHOLOGY 50(4):321-337, 1986.

Histologic lesions caused by the use of oral contraceptives, by G. Oddi, et al. MINERVA GINECOLOGIA 38(7-8):541-544, July-August 1986.

Hormonal contraception and cancer, by J. Drife, et al. BRITISH JOURNAL OF HOSPITAL MEDICINE 35(1):25-29, January 1986.

Hormones and breast cancer [letter], by M. G. Burdette. JOURNAL OF THE FLORIDA MEDICAL ASSOCIATION 73(5):372-373, May 1986.

Increased euglobulin fibrinolytic potential in women on oral contraceptives low in oestrogen—levels of extrinsic and intrinsic plasminogen activators, prekaili- krein, factor XII and C1-inactivator, by J. Jespersen, et al. THROMBOSIS AND HAEMOSTASIS 54(2):454-459, August 30, 1985.

CONTRACEPTIVES—FEMALE—ORAL—COMPLICATIONS (continued)

Increased nevus estrogen and progesterone ligand binding related to oral contraceptives or pregnancy, by D. L. Ellis, et al. JOURNAL OF THE AMERICAN ACADEMY OF DERMATOLOGY 14(1):25-31, January 1986.

Inflammatory bowel disease and hormonal contraception, by T. Ritschard, et al. SCHWEIZERISCHE MEDIZINISCHE WOCHENSCHRIFT 116(18):594-597, May 3, 1986.

Inflammatory bowel disease in oral contraceptive users [letter], by B. M. Calkins, et al. GASTROENTEROLOGY 91(2):523-524, August 1986.

Ischemic strokes and oral contraception, by S. Godon-Hardy, et al. NEURO-RADIOLOGY 27(6):588-592, 1985.

Liver disorders related to oral contraceptives, M. Balázs, et al. ORVOSI HETILAP 127(29):1765-1770, July 20, 1986.

Liver tumours associated with contraceptive hormonal treatment, by B. Van Damme, et al. ACTA GASTROENTEROLOGICA BELGICA 48(4):404-409, July-August 1985.

Long term treatment with combined oral contraceptives and cigarette smoking associated with impaired activity of tissue plasminogen activator, by A. Kjaeldgaard, et al. ACTA OBSTETRICA ET GYNECOLOGICA SCANDI-NAVICA 65(3):219-222, 1986.

Long term use of oral contraceptives and cervical neoplasia: an association confounded by other risk factors?, by D. Hellberg, et al. CONTRACEPTION 32(4):337-346, October 1985.

Long term use of oral contraceptives and risk of invasive cervical cancer, by L. A. Brinton, et al. INTERNATIONAL JOURNAL OF CANCER 38(3):39-344, September 15, 1986.

Lymphocyte subsets in women on low dose oral contraceptives, by D. A. Baker, et al. CONTRACEPTION 32(4):377-382, October 1985.

Malignant epithelioid hemangioendothelioma of the liver in young women. Relationship to oral contraceptive use, by P. J. Dean, et al. AMERICAN JOURNAL OF SURGICAL PATHOLOGY 9(10):695-704, October 1985.

Mammographic breast pattern and oral contraception, by S. J. Leinster, et al. BRITISH JOURNAL OF RADIOLOGY 59(699):237-239, March 1986.

Metabolic effects of combined low-dose contraceptive tablets, by S. Zalányi, Jr., et al. ORVOSI HETILAP 127(9):511-514, March 2, 1986.

Mitral valve prolapse in women with oral contraceptive-related cerebrovascular insufficiency. Associated persistent hypercoagulable state, by M. B. Elam, et al. ARCHIVES OF INTERNAL MEDICINE 146(1):73-77, January 1986.

Modification of tear film break-up time by hormone contraceptives, by T. Christ, et al. FORTSCHRITTE DER OPHTHALMOLOGIE 83(1):108-111, 1986.

Oestrogenic effects of the triphasic oral contraceptive agents [letter], by P. Baillie. SOUTH AFRICAN MEDICAL JOURNAL 68(10):706, November 9, 1985.

On cohort effects in studies on oral contraceptive use and breast cancer [letter], by H. Olsson, et al. BRITISH JOURNAL OF CANCER 53(4):579, April 1986.

Oral contraceptive agents and coronary disease [letter], by L. Kjeldaas, et al. NORDISK MEDICIN 100(10):269, 1985.

Oral contraceptive use and breast cancer in young women, by O. Meirik, et al. LANCET 8508:650-655, 1986.

Oral contraceptive use and the risk of breast cancer, by The Cancer and Steroid Hormone Study of the Centers for Disease Control and the National Institute of Child Health and Human Development. NEW ENGLAND JOURNAL OF MEDICINE 315(7):405-411, August 14, 1986.

Oral contraceptive use and the risk of breast cancer in women with a "prior" history of benign breast disease, by V. B. Stadel, et al. AMERICAN JOURNAL OF EPIDEMIOLOGY 123(3):373-382, March 1986.

Oral contraceptive use has no adverse effect on the prognosis of breast cancer, by D. Rosner, et al. CANCER 57(3):591-596, February 1, 1986.

Oral contraceptives and antithrombin III [letter], by H. Stormorken. TIDSSKRIFT FOR DEN NORSKE LAEGEFORENING 105(32):2333, November 20, 1985.

Oral contraceptives and breast cancer [letter], by B. K. Armstrong. LANCET 1(8480):552-553, March 8, 1986.

Oral contraceptives and breast cancer: epidemiological evidence, by M. P. Vessey. IARC SCIENTIFIC PUBLICATIONS (65):37-48, 1985.

Oral contraceptives and breast cancer in young women, by B. V. Stadel, et al. LANCET 2(8462):970-973, November 2, 1985.

—[letter], by B. V. Stadel, et al. LANCET 1(8478):436, February 22, 1986.

Oral contraceptives and breast cancer: laboratory evidence, by P. Shubik. IARC SCIENTIFIC PUBLICATIONS (65):33-35, 1985.

Oral contraceptives and breast cancer: a national study, by C. Paul, et al. BRITISH MEDICAL JOURNAL 293(6459):723-726, 1986.

Oral contraceptives and breast cancer. A prospective cohort study, by R. J. Lipnick, et al. JAMA 255(1):58-61, January 3, 1986; Discussion 256:2346, November 7, 1986.

Oral contraceptives and breastfeeding: haematological effects on the infant, by H. Mandel, et al. ARCHIVES OF DISEASE IN CHILDHOOD 60(10):971-972, October 1985.

Oral contraceptives and cancer, by S. Holck, et al. ARCHIV FUR GESCHWULST-FORSCHUNG 56(2):155-167, 1986.

Oral contraceptives and cancers of the breast and of the female genital tract. Interim results from a case-control study, by C. LaVecchia, et al. BRITISH JOURNAL OF CANCER 54(2):311-317, August 1986.

Oral contraceptives and cardiovascular diseases, by R. Lara Ricalde, et al. GINE-COLOGIA Y OBSTETRICIA DE MEXICO 54:63-66, March 1986.

Oral contraceptives and cardiovascular diseases morbidity, by R. Lara Ricalde, et al. GINECOLOGIA Y OBSTETRICIA DE MEXICO 54:119-125, May 1986.

Oral contraceptives and cervical neoplasia: pooled information from retrospective and prospective epidemiologic studies, by S. Franceschi, et al. TUMORI 72(1):21-30, February 28, 1986.

Oral contraceptives and chlamydia infections [letter], by S. A. Gall. JAMA 255(1): 38-39, January 3, 1986.

Oral contraceptives and Crohn's disease [letter], by M. B. Albert, et al. GASTRO-ENTEROLOGY 90(4):1097-1098, April 1986.

Oral contraceptives and griseofulvin interactions [letter], by P. A. McDaniel, et al. DRUG INTELLIGENCE AND CLINICAL PHARMACY 20(5):384, May 1986.

Oral contraceptives and hepatocellular carcinoma, by J. Neuberger, et al. BRITISH MEDICAL JOURNAL 292(6532):1355-1357, May 24, 1986.

—[letter]. BRITISH MEDICAL JOURNAL 292(6532):1392-1393, May 24, 1986.

—[letter], by D. B. Petitti. BRITISH MEDICAL JOURNAL 293(6540):204, July 19, 1986.

Oral contraceptives and migraine headaches, by D. F. Archer, et al. JAMA 256:2394-2395, November 7, 1986.

Oral contraceptives and other risk factors for gallbladder disease, by B. L. Strom, et al. CLINICAL PHARMACOLOGY AND THERAPEUTICS 39(3):335-341, March 1986.

Oral contraceptives and prognosis of breast cancer in women aged 35 to 50, by D. H. Rosner, et al. JOURNAL OF SURGERY AND ONCOLOGY 30(1):52-59, September 1985.

Oral contraceptives and venous thromboembolism. NURSES DRUG ALERT 10(9):66, September 1986.

Oral contraceptives and venous thromboembolism: findings in a large prospective study, by M. Vessey, et al. BRITISH MEDICAL JOURNAL 292(6519): 526, February 22, 1986.

Oral contraceptives—time to take stock [editorial], by S. Shapiro. NEW ENG-LAND JOURNAL OF MEDICINE 315(7):450-451, August 14, 1986.

Peroral contraceptive agents and arterial hypertension, by A. Kokutsov, et al. VUTRESHNI BOLESTI 25(2):56-59, 1986.

Pill and cancer, by T. Rabe, et al. THERAPEUTISCHE UMSCHAU 43(5):372-387, May 1986.

Pill causes liver cancer—but not often. NEW SCIENTIST 110:19, May 29, 1986.

Pill does not cause "thrush", by F. Davidson, et al. BRITISH JOURNAL OF OBSTETRICS AND GYNAECOLOGY 92(12):1265-1266, December 1985.

Pill use and the risk of breast cancer, by F. Lesser. NEW SCIENTIST 108:26, November 7, 1985.

Possible cohort effects in studies on oral contraceptive use and breast cancer [letter], by M. G. Lê, et al. BRITISH JOURNAL OF CANCER 52(5):805-806, November 1985.

Rare form of benign tumor of the liver possibly related to the use of oral contraceptives: focal pediculated nodular hyperplasia, by J. Brouquet, et al. REVUE FRANCAISE DE GYNECOLOGIE ET D'OBSTETRIQUE 80(8-9):621-627, August-September 1985.

Relationship between urinary tract infection and oral contraceptive usage, by D. Tanphaichitra, et al. JOURNAL OF THE MEDICAL ASSOCIATION OF THAILAND 68(8):395-398, August 1985.

Reproductive factors, oral contraceptives and risk of malignant melanoma: Western Canada Melanoma Study, by R. P. Gallagher, et al. BRITISH JOURNAL OF CANCER 52(6):90-1907, December 1985.

Resting and exercise electrocardiographic abnormalities associated with sex hormone use in women. The Lipid Research Clinics Program Prevalence Study, by E. Barrett-Connor, et al. AMERICAN JOURNAL OF EPIDEMIOLOGY 123(1):81-88, January 1986.

Risk factors for uterine fibroids: reduced risk associated with oral contraceptives, by R. K. Ross, et al. BRITISH MEDICAL JOURNAL 293(6543):359-362, August 9, 1986.

Risk of hepatic vein thrombosis in relation to recent use of oral contraceptives. A case-control study, by D. Valla, et al. GASTROENTEROLOGY 90(4):807-811, April 1986.

Risks of contraception: the minipill, by E. Keller. THERAPEUTISCHE UMSCHAU 43(5):392-394, May 1986.

Risks of contraception: vascular diseases, by H. J. Genz, et al. THERAPEUTISCHE UMSCHAU 43(5):388-391, May 1986.

Screening examination of the liver directed at the incident of adenomas in women using hormonal contraceptives, by K. Axmann, et al. CESKOSLOVENSKA GYNEKOLOGIE 51(1):37-40, February 1986.

Serum prolac in levels in women using oral contraceptives (Gravistat), by W. Mikrut, et al. GINEKOLOGIA POLSKA 56(10):620-623, October 1985.

Side and site of deep vein thrombosis in women using oral contraceptives, by A. Kierkegaard. ACTA OBSTETRICA ET GYNECOLOGICA SCANDINAVICA 64(5):399-402, 1985.

Side effects and discontinuation of oral contraceptive use in southern Brazil, by B. Janowitz, et al. JOURNAL OF BIOSOCIAL SCIENCE 18(3):261-271, July 1986.

Side effects of oral contraceptive use in lactating women—enlargement of breast in a breast-fed child, by R. Madhavapeddi, et al. CONTRACEPTION 32(5):437-443, November 1985.

Sister chromatid exchange studies in women with long-term use of the oral contraceptive pills megestrol acetate compositas, by Q. Peng. CHUNG HUA FU CHAN KO TSA CHIH 20(5):309-310+, September 1985.

CONTRACEPTIVES—FEMALE—ORAL—COMPLICATIONS (continued)

Status of oral contraceptives as a risk factor in cerebrovascular diseases, by E. Auff, et al. WIENER KLINISCHE WOCHENSCHRIFT 98(10):304-310, May 16, 1986.

Sudden deafness and the contraceptive pill, by G. S. Hanna. JOURNAL OF LARYNGOLOGY AND OTOLOGY 100(6):701-706, June 1986.

Thrombosis due to permanent pacemaker and oral contraceptives, by M. F. Halub, et al. AMERICAN JOURNAL OF OBSTETRICS AND GYNECOLOGY 153(5):571-572, November 1, 1985.

Toxic shock syndrome, contraceptive methods, and vaginitis, by S. F. Lanes, et al. AMERICAN JOURNAL OF OBSTETRICS AND GYNECOLOGY 154(5): 989-991, May 1986.

Transient ischemic attack (T.I.A.) in a patient with non-thrombogenic hereditary protein C deficiency under oral contraceptives [letter], by F. Velasco, et al. THROMBOSIS AND HAEMOSTASIS 54(4):904, December 17, 1985.

Ultrasound demonstration of increased frequency of functional ovarian cysts in women using progestogen—only oral contraception, by Y. Tayob, et al. BRITISH JOURNAL OF OBSTETRICS AND GYNAECOLOGY 92(10):1003-1009, October 1985.

Unintended effects of oral contraceptives. I. Estrogen-related effects, by H. Kopera. WIENER MEDIZINISCHE WOCHENSCHRIFT 135(13-14):333-337, July 31, 1985.

—. II. Progesterone-caused effects, interactions with drugs, by H. Kopera. WIENER MEDIZINISCHE WOCHENSCHRIFT 135(17):415-419, September 1985.

Update on oral contraceptives, by M. Hanson, et al. JOURNAL OF REPRO-DUCTIVE MEDICINE 30(9 suppl):691-713, September 1985.

What does the micropill bring?, by M. Mall-Haefeli. THERAPEUTISCHE UMS-CHAU 43(5):365-371, May 1986.

CONTRACEPTIVES—FEMALE—ORAL—THERAPEUTIC USE
Oral contraceptive use modifies the manifestations of pelvic inflammatory dis-ease, by P. Wølner-Hanseen. BRITISH JOURNAL OF OBSTETRICS AND GYNAECOLOGY 93(6):619-624, June 1986.

Oral contraceptives, 1985 [letter], by P. F. Hall. CANADIAN MEDICAL ASSO-CIATION JOURNAL 134(1):16, January 1, 1986.

P-pills for women with acne/hirsutism [letter], by A. Røde, et al. TIDSSKRIFT FOR DEN NORSKE LAEGEFORENING 105(29):2099, October 20, 1985.

CONTRACEPTIVES—FEMALE—POSTCOITAL
Postcoital and postimplantation contraception, by V. I. Alipov, et al. AKUSHER-STVO I GINEKOLOGIIA (9):47-51, August 1985.

Postcoital contraception, by R. G. Fischer. PEDIATRIC NURSING 11(5):384, September-October 1985.

—, by V. Kliment, et al. CESKOSLOVENSKA GYNEKOLOGIE 51(2):103-105, 1986.

CONTRACEPTIVES—FEMALE—POSTCOITAL (continued)

—, by D. Sekulovic, et al. SRPSKI ARHIV ZA CELOKUPNO LEKARSTVO 113(5-6):485-492, May-June 1985.

Post-coital contraception by estrogen/progestagen combination or IUD insertion, by M. Luerti, et al. CONTRACEPTION 33(1):61-68, January 1986.

Postcoital contraception with PCA. DRUG AND THERAPEUTICS BULLETIN 23(25):97-98, December 16, 1985.

Pregnancy prophylaxis: parenteral postcoital estrogen, by C. L. Cook, et al. OB-STETRICS AND GYNECOLOGY 67(3):331-334, March 1986.

Steroid anti-hormones: anti-progesterone activity of RU 486 and its contra-gestational and other applications, by E. E. Baulieu, et al. BULLETIN DE L'ACADEMIE NATIONALE DE MEDECINE 169(8):1191-1199, November 1985.

CONTRACEPTIVES—FEMALE—POSTCOITAL—COMPLICATIONS
Risks of postcoital contraception using a d-norgestrel-ethinyl estradiol combina-tion, by H. Welti, et al. THERAPEUTISCHE UMSCHAU 43(5):438-440, May 1986.

CONTRACEPTIVES—FUNDING
Public funding of contraceptive, sterilization and abortion services, 1983, by R. B. Gold, et al. FAMILY PLANNING PERSPECTIVES 17:25-29, January-February 1985.

—, 1985, by R. B. Gold, et al. FAMILY PLANNING PERSPECTIVES 18:259-264, November-December 1986.

CONTRACEPTIVES—HISTORY
Contraception—with us and others, by R. Hallgren. JORDEMODERN 99(1-2):4-10, January-February 1986.

CONTRACEPTIVES—IMPLANTED
Implanted contraceptives. AMERICAN FAMILY PHYSICIAN 34:256, November 1986.

Under the skin (levonorgestrel contraceptive implants). SCIENTIFIC AMERICAN 255:78+, October 1986.

CONTRACEPTIVES—INJECTED
Beyond the pill: the WHO prepares to test a contraceptive vaccine, by D. Philip. ALBERTA REPORT 13:44-45, September 22, 1986.

Birth control vaccines, by J. A. Miller, et al. SCIENCE NEWS 129:365, June 7, 1986.

Contraceptive vaccine moves up from baboons to humans, by D. MacKenzie. NEW SCIENTIST 109:21, February 27, 1986.

Development of a contraceptive vaccine by purification of antigens from gametes, by S. Isojima, et al. AMERICAN JOURNAL OF REPRODUCTIVE IMMUNOL-OGY AND MICROBIOLOGY 10(3):90-92, March 1986.

Effects of long-acting injectable contraceptives on carbohydrate metabolism, by K. Amatayakul, et al. INTERNATIONAL JOURNAL OF GYNAECOLOGY AND OBSTETRICS 23(5):361-368, October 1985.

CONTRACEPTIVES—INJECTED (continued)

Factors associated with the perception of side-effects relating to the use of contraceptive methods . . . intra-uterine device, the hormonal pill and the injection, by G. Erasmus, et al. CURATIONIS 8(3):45-47, September 1985.

Identification of candidate antigens for the development of birth control vaccines. An international multi-centre study on antibodies to reproductive tract antigens, using clinically defined sera, by T. Hjort, et al. JOURNAL OF REPRODUCTIVE IMMUNOLOGY 8(4):271-278, December 1985.

Injectable contraceptives in developing countries [letter], by S. Nair. LANCET 1(8495):1440-1441, June 21, 1986.

Intravenous postcoital estrogen effectively prevents pregnancy. AMERICAN FAMILY PHYSICIAN 33:178, May 1986.

Introduction of the injectable contraceptive NET-EN into family planning clinics in Bangladesh, by S. S. Rahman, et al. WHO BULLETIN 63(4):785-791, 1985.

Phase IV study of the injection Norigest in Pakistan, by A. Kazi, et al. CONTRACEPTION 32(4):395-403, October 1985.

Prospects for developing vaccines to control fertility, by G. L. Ada, et al. NATURE 317:288-289, September 26-October 2, 1985.

Vaccine that may prevent pregnancy (work of Vernon Stevens and others). DISCOVER 7:13, May 1986.

CONTRACEPTIVES—INJECTED—COMPLICATIONS
Sister chromatid exchange in lymphocytes of peripheral blood in women injected with two steroid hormonal contraceptives, by Y. Shen. CHUNG HUA FU CHAN KO TSA CHIH 21(1):35-37+, January 1986.

CONTRACEPTIVES—INSURANCE
Contraceptives: on hold. Liability fears are cutting off research, by M. Clark, et al. NEWSWEEK 107(18):68, May 5, 1986.

CONTRACEPTIVES—KNOWLEDGE
Contraceptive knowledge and use of birth control as a function of sex guilt, by C. Berger, et al. INTERNATIONAL JOURNAL OF WOMEN'S STUDIES 8(1):72-79, January-February 1985.

CONTRACEPTIVES—LAWS AND LEGISLATION
Right of doctors in certain cases to prescribe contraceptives lawfully to children under the age of 16 without a parents consent [editorial]. ARCHIVES OF DISEASE IN CHILDHOOD 61(8):725-726, August 1986.

CONTRACEPTIVES—MALE
See also: Contraception—Male

Are male contraceptives forthcoming? BIOSCIENCE 36:287, April 1986.

Assessment of burst strength distribution data for monitoring quality of condom stocks in developing countries, by M. J. Free, et al. CONTRACEPTION 33(3):285-299, March 1986.

Can the condom make sex safe again?, by C. Sherman. MADEMOISELLE 92: 120, December 1986.

CONTRACEPTIVES—MALE (continued)

Condom maker goes after women (marketing geared to women), by A. Lallande. VENTURE 8:82+, January 1986..

Contraception—with us and others, by R. Hallgren. JORDEMODERN 99(1-2):4-10, January-February 1986.

High-tech birth control kills sperm with three volts. JET 71;30, December 1, 1986.

Hope for a male pill, by N. Underwood. MACLEAN'S 99:62f+, October 13, 1986.

Husbands' sex-role preferences and contraceptive intentions: the case of the male pill, by W. Marsiglio. SEX ROLES 12(5-6):655-663, March 1985.

Hypermasculinity and male contraceptive attitudes and behavior, by T. M. Exner. DAI: B 47(2), August 1986.

Ireland: clinic sued . . . condoms debates, by N. Bythe. OFF OUR BACKS 16(1): 10, January 1986.

Local mechanical and chemical contraception. Coitus interruptus, by G. A. Hauser. THERAPEUTISCHE UMSCHAU 43(5):404-410, May 1986.

Male birth-control pill to begin testing in United States. JET 71:28, November 10, 1986.

One step closer to a pill for men. NEW SCIENTIST 110:28, June 5, 1986.

Oral contraceptives, 1985 [letter], by P. F. Hall. CANADIAN MEDICAL ASSO-CIATION JOURNAL 134(1):16, January 1, 1986.

Research on adolescent male attitudes about contraceptives, by P. M. Hewson. PEDIATRIC NURSING 12(2):114-116, March-April 1986.

Will Canada ever see gays in condom ads?, by I. Timberlake. MARKETING 91:28, September 29, 1986.

CONTRACEPTIVES—MALE—BARRIER
Condoms and hepatitis B virus infection [letter], by G. Y. Minuk, et al. ANNALS OF INTERNAL MEDICINE 104(4):584, April 1986.

Condoms and the prevention of AIDS [letter]. JAMA 256(11):1442-1443, September 19, 1986.

Condoms in Japan [letter], by B. Warming. NATURE 322(6074):10, July 3-9, 1986.

Condoms prevent transmission of AIDS-associated retrovirus [letter], by M. Conant, et al. JAMA 255(13):1706, April 4, 1986.

Sex transmits AIDS. ECONOMIST 300:14, July 5, 1986.

Sheathed in profits, by H. McDonald. FAR EASTERN ECONOMIC REVIEW 131:47, January 2, 1986.

CONTRACEPTIVES—METHODS
Contraceptive methods available today. LADIES HOME JOURNAL 103:54+, August 1986.

CONTRACEPTIVES—METHODS (continued)

Contraceptive perceptions and method choice among young single women in the United States, by K. Tanfer, et al. STUDIES IN FAMILY PLANNING 17: 269-277, November-December 1986.

Factors affecting the choice of nonpermanent contraceptive methods among married women, by M. MacDowell, et al. SOCIAL BIOLOGY 31(3-4):222-231, Fall-Winter 1984.

Factors associated with the perception of side-effects relating to the use of contraceptive methods . . . intra-uterine device, the hormonal pill and the injection, by G. Erasmus, et al. CURATIONIS 8(3):45-47, September 1985.

High-tech birth control kills sperm with three volts. JET 71;30, December 1, 1986.

Social and demographic factors influencing the acceptability of injectable method for contraception in comparison with copper "T" I.U.D., by R. Goraya, et al. INDIAN JOURNAL OF MEDICAL SCIENCE 39(7):172-174, July 1985.

Why some women fail to use their contraceptive method: a psychological investigation, by W. B. Miller. FAMILY PLANNING PERSPECTIVES 18(1):27-32, January-February 1986.

CONTRACEPTIVES—ORAL

Adepal, by M. Parise, et al. SOINS. GYNECOLOGIE, OBSTETRIQUE, PUERICULTURE, PEDIATRIE (58):I-II, March 1986.

Antifertility effects of 2 alpha, 17 alpha-diethynyl, A-nor-androstane, 2 beta, 17 beta-dihydroxy, 2 beta-semisuccinate (AF-57), by Z. P. Gu, et al. CHUNG KUO YAO LI HSUEH PAO 6(2):121-124, June 1985.

Apoplectic leiomyomas of the uterus. A clinicopathologic study of five distinctive hemorrhagic leiomyomas associated with oral contraceptive usage, by J. L. Myles, et al. AMERICAN JOURNAL OF SURGICAL PATHOLOGY 9(11):798-805, November 1985.

Australia claims lead in race for unisex pill, by J. Ford. NEW SCIENTIST 110:21, May 8, 1986.

Bioavailability of ethinyloestradiol and levonorgestrel in patients with an ileostomy, by S. F. Grimmer, et al. CONTRACEPTION 33(1):51-59, January 1986.

Bowel preparation and the pill [letter], by W. E. Svensson. CLINICAL RADIOLOGY 36(3):340, May 1985.

Breast-feeding and the pill: do they mix? (folate deficiency in child). PREVENTION 38:124, November 1986.

Changes in blood coagulation during hormone contraception, by R. von Hugo, et al. GYNAEKOLOGISCHE RUNDSCHAU 25(suppl 2):138-141, 1986.

Cholelithiasis, pregnancy and contraceptive pills, by S. Evron, et al. HAREFUAH 109(7-8):204-206, October 1985.

Clinical assessment of a new triphasic oral contraceptive, by R. A. Apelo, et al. CLINICAL THERAPEUTICS 8(1):61-70, 1985.

CONTRACEPTIVES—ORAL (continued)

Clinical chemistry alterations in pregnancy and oral contraceptive use, by R. H. Knopp, et al. OBSTETRICS AND GYNECOLOGY 66(5):682-690, November 1985.

Contraception: no longer beyond the pill, by J. Seymour. NURSING TIMES 82(13):19-20, March 26-April 1, 1986.

Contraceptive and hormonal properties of achyranthes aspera in rats and hamsters, by V. Wadhwa, et al. PLANTA MEDICA (3):231-233, June 1986.

Contraceptive pill. Japan heads for legalization [news], by A. Anderson. NATURE 317(6040):760-761, October 31-November 6, 1985.

Contraceptive social marketing: lessons from experience. POPULATION REPORTS 13(3):773, July-August 1985.

Contraceptive sterilization in Puerto Rico, by C. W. Warren, et al. DEMOGRAPHY 23:351-365, August 1986.

Contraceptives: on hold. Liability fears are cutting off research, by M. Clark, et al. NEWSWEEK 107(18):68, May 5, 1986.

Current trends in the development of oral contraception, by V. V. Korkhov. FARMAKOLOGIYA I TOKSIKOLOGIYA 48(4):119-122, July-August 1985.

Do oral contraceptives prevent rheumatoid arthritis?, by D. J. del Junco, et al. JAMA 254:1938-1941, October 11, 1985; Discussion 256:215-216, July 11, 1986.

Effect of chronic administration of angravid on the guinea pig liver—some functional and morphological aspects, by I. Sliwinska. ACTA MEDICA POLONA 26(3-4):101-121, 1985.

Effect of combined ethinyl estradiol and norgestrel oral contraceptives on hepatic functions of albino rats, by B. Mandal, et al. ACTA PHYSIOLOGICA ET PHARMACOLOGICA BULGARICA 11(2):68-74, 1985.

Effect of norethisterone oxime on ovum transport and development, and on morphology of oviduct in rabbits, by D. Z. Li, et al. JOURNAL OF THE TONGJI MEDICAL UNIVERSITY 6(2):80-88, 1986.

Evaluation of the mutagenic properties of contraceptive hormonal preparations in monkeys, by Z. A. Dzhemilev, et al. VESTNIK AKADEMII MEDITSINSKIKH NAUK SSSR (3):45-47, 1986.

Gillick judgment. Contraceptives and the under 16s: House of Lords ruling, by C. Dyer. BRITISH MEDICAL JOURNAL 291(6503):1208-1209, October 26, 1985.

Interactions between ethanol and oral contraceptive steroids, by J. Hobbes, et al. CLINICAL PHARMACOLOGY AND THERAPEUTICS 38(4):371-380, October 1985.

Interactions may cause OC failures. RN 49:7, July 1986.

Issues in contraceptive development. POPULATION 15:1, May 1985.

CONTRACEPTIVES—ORAL (continued)

Lack of effect of sodium valproate on the pharmacokinetics of oral contraceptive steroids, by P. Crawford, et al. CONTRACEPTION 33(1):23-29, January 1986.

One step closer to a pill for men. NEW SCIENTIST 110:28, June 5, 1986.

Oral contraception, 1986. Currently available formulations, by R. Hale. JOURNAL OF REPRODUCTIVE MEDICINE 31(6 suppl):557-558, June 1986.

—. Endocrinology and pharmacology. A panel discussion. JOURNAL OF RE-PRODUCTIVE MEDICINE 31(6 suppl):565-568, June 1986.

—. Focus on Triphasil, by H. Ellsworth. JOURNAL OF REPRODUCTIVE MEDI-CINE 31(6 suppl):559-564, June 1986.

Oral contraceptive agents, by R. P. Shearman. MEDICAL JOURNAL OF AUS-TRALIA 144(4):201-205, February 17, 1986.

Oral contraceptives in a southern Italian community, by M. A. Korovkin. CUR-RENT ANTHROPOLOGY 27:80-83, February 1986.

Oral contraceptives: the state of the art, by R. B. Greenblatt. CLINICAL THERA-PEUTICS 8(1):6-27, 1985.

Possible effects of hormonal contraceptives on human mitotic chromosomes, by M. R. Pinto. MUTATION RESEARCH 169(3):149-157, March 1986.

Prevalence and trends in oral contraceptive use in premenopausal females ages 12-54 years, United States, 1971-1980, by R. Russell-Briefel, et al. AMERI-CAN JOURNAL OF PUBLIC HEALTH 75(10):1173-1176, October 1985.

Regression of pathologic changes induced by the long-term administration of contraceptive steroids to rodents, by G. Lumb, et al. TOXICOLOGIC PATHOLOGY 13(4):283-295, 1985.

Risk of postmolar invasive complications with oral contraceptive use [letter], by B. H. Yuen, et al. AMERICAN JOURNAL OF OBSTETRICS AND GYNECOL-OGY 153(8):924-926, December 15, 1985.

Rumor, misinformation and oral contraceptive use in Egypt, by J. DeClerque, et al. SOCIAL SCIENCE AND MEDICINE 23(1):83-92, 1986.

Spironolactone in combination with an oral contraceptive: an alternative treatment for hirsutism, by M. G. Chapman, et al. BRITISH JOURNAL OF OBSTETRICS AND GYNAECOLOGY 92(9):983-985, September 1985.

—[letter], by J. Guillebaud. BRITISH JOURNAL OF OBSTETRICS AND GYNAE-COLOGY 93(2):197-198, February 1986.

Structure elucidation of gestodene, by G. Cleve, et al. ARZNEIMITTEL-FOR-SCHUNG 36(5):784-786, May 1986.

There's no connection between cancer and OCs. RN 49:96, November 1986.

CONTRACEPTIVES—ORAL—COMPLICATIONS
Apoplectic leiomyomas of the uterus. A clinicopathologic study of five distinctive hemorrhagic leiomyomas associated with oral contraceptive usage, by J. L.

140

CONTRACEPTIVES—ORAL—COMPLICATIONS (continued)

Myles, et al. AMERICAN JOURNAL OF SURGICAL PATHOLOGY 9(11):798-805, November 1985.

Breast cancer and oral contraceptives [letter]. LANCET 2(8465):1180-1181, November 23, 1985.

—[review], by F. Clavel, et al. CONTRACEPTION 32(6):553-569, December 1985.

Contraceptive agents and antithrombin III. New causes of thrombosis [letter], by U. Abildgaard, et al. TIDSSKRIFT FOR DEN NORSKE LAEGEFORENING 106(4):346-347, February 10, 1986.

Controversies on progestogens and the metabolism of lipoproteins, by P. Fugère. UNION MEDICALE DU CANADA 115(2):78-79, February 1986.

Cutaneous melanoma and oral contraceptives: a review of case-control and cohort studies, by E. A. Holly. RECENT RESULTS IN CANCER RESEARCH 102:108-117, 1986.

Prescription contraceptives: countering the risks, by R. J. Ruggiero. AMERICAN PHARMACY NS25(9):32-37, September 1985.

Residual vascular risk of discontinued oral contraception. Role of antibodies to synthetic sex hormones, by V. Beaumont, et al. ATHEROSCLEROSIS 58(1-3):243-259, December 1985.

Resolution of a contraceptive-steroid-induced hepatic adenoma with subsequent evolution into hepatocellular carcinoma, by S. C. Gordon, et al. ANNALS OF INTERNAL MEDICINE 105(4):547-549, October 1986.

CONTRACEPTIVES—ORAL—THERAPEUTIC USE
Do oral contraceptives prevent rheumatoid arthritis? [letter], by J. M. Hazes, et al. JAMA 256(2):215-216, July 11, 1986.

Pituitary function and DHEA-S in male acne and DHEA-S, prolactin and cortisol before and after oral contraceptive treatment in female acne, by R. Palatsi, et al. ACTA DERMATO-VENEREOLOGICA 66(3):225-230, 1986.

Reduced estrogen ovulation inhibitor in acne therapy. Double-blind study comparing Diane-35 to Diane, by S. Aydinlik, et al. FORTSCHRITTE DER MEDIZIN 104(27-28):547-550, July 24, 1986.

CONTRACEPTIVES—POSTCOITAL—COMPLICATIONS
Biochemistry of human endometrium after two regimens of postcoital contraception: a dl-norgestrel/ethinylestradiol combination or danazol, by A. A. Kubba, et al. FERTILITY AND STERILITY 45(4):512-516, April 1986.

CONTRACEPTIVES—PSYCHOLOGY AND PSYCHIATRY
Assessment of psychological state associated with the menstrual cycle in users of oral contraception, by A. Marriott, et al. JOURNAL OF PSYCHOSOMATIC RESEARCH 30(1):41-47, 1986.

Contraceptive knowledge and use of birth control as a function of sex guilt, by C. Berger, et al. INTERNATIONAL JOURNAL OF WOMEN'S STUDIES 8(1):72-79, January-February 1985.

CONTRACEPTIVES—PSYCHOLOGY AND PSYCHIATRY (continued)

Contraceptives without consent? [letter], by F. Haggis. BRITISH JOURNAL OF PSYCHIATRY 147:91-92, July 1985.

Psychosocial aspects of contraceptive use, by C. Weiman. NURS RSA VER-PLEGING 1(5):21, June 1986.

CONTRACEPTIVES—RESEARCH
Beyond the pill: the WHO prepares to test a contraceptive vaccine, by D. Philip. ALBERTA REPORT 13:44-45, September 22, 1986.

Contraception in male monkeys by intra-vas deferens injection of a pH lowering polymer, by S. K. Guha, et al. CONTRACEPTION 32(1):109-118, July 1985.

Contraceptive and hormonal properties of achyranthes aspera in rats and hamsters, by V. Wadhwa, et al. PLANTA MEDICA (3):231-233, June 1986.

Contraceptive development and clinical trials, by I. S. Fraser. CLINICAL REPRODUCTION AND FERTILITY 4(1):75-85, February 1986.

Contraceptives: on hold. Liability fears are cutting off research, by M. Clark, et al. NEWSWEEK 107(18):68, May 5, 1986.

Development of a contraceptive vaccine by purification of antigens from gametes, by S. Isojima, et al. AMERICAN JOURNAL OF REPRODUCTIVE IMMUNOLOGY AND MICROBIOLOGY 10(3):90-92, March 1986.

Effect of chronic administration of angravid on the guinea pig liver—some functional and morphological aspects, by I. Sliwinska. ACTA MEDICA POLONA 26(3-4):101-121, 1985.

Effect of combined ethinyl estradiol and norgestrel oral contraceptives on hepatic functions of albino rats, by B. Mandal, et al. ACTA PHYSIOLOGICA ET PHARMACOLOGICA BULGARICA 11(2):68-74, 1985.

Effect of estrogen/progestin potency on clinical chemistry measures. The Lipid Research Clinics Program Prevalence Study, by C. E. Walden, et al. AMERICAN JOURNAL OF EPIDEMIOLOGY 123(3):517-531, March 1986.

Effect of gossypol acetic acid on early pregnancy in rats, by N. G. Wang, et al. YAO HSUEH HSUEH PAO 19(11):808-811, November 1984.

Effect of a new oral antiandrogen-estrogen combination on the endometrium: histological and ultrastructural scanning electron microscopy study, by L. Fedele, et al. ACTA EUROPAEA FERTILITATIS 17(1):9-13, January-February 1986.

Effect of norethisterone oxime on ovum transport and development, and on morphology of oviduct in rabbits, by D. Z. Li, et al. JOURNAL OF THE TONGJI MEDICAL UNIVERSITY 6(2):80-88, 1986.

Effect of oral contraceptive steroids on the growth rate of human mammary epithelia in cell culture, by S. M. Longman. DAI: B 47(3),September 1986.

Effect of oral contraceptives on the rat brain and pituitary opioid peptides, by G. A. Tejwani, et al. PEPTIDES 6(3):555-561, May-June 1985.

CONTRACEPTIVES—RESEARCH (continued)

Effect of oral contraceptives on serum prolactin: a longitudinal study in 126 normal premenopausal women, by P. L. Hwang, et al. CLINICAL ENDOCRINOLOGY 24(2):127-133, February 1986.

Effect of tumor promoting contraceptive steroids on growth and drug metabolizing enzymes in rat liver, by H. Ochs, et al. CANCER RESEARCH 46(3):1224-1232, March 1986.

Effects of the male contraceptive agent gossypol on meiotic chromosomes of the male rat, by T. Bhagirath, et al. CYTOGENETICS AND CELL GENETICS 39(3):228-230, 1985.

Evaluation of the mutagenic properties of contraceptive hormonal preparations in monkeys, by Z. A. Dzhemilev, et al. VESTNIK AKADEMII MEDITSINSKIKH NAUK SSSR (3):45-47, 1986.

Exposed: the bogus work of Prof. Briggs (contraceptive pill research), by B. Deer. SUNDAY TIMES September 28, 1986, pp. 27-28.

Hope for a male pill, by N. Underwood. MACLEAN'S 99:62f+, October 13, 1986.

Identification of candidate antigens for the development of birth control vaccines. An international multi-centre study on antibodies to reproductive tract antigens, using clinically defined sera, by T. Hjort, et al. JOURNAL OF REPRODUCTIVE IMMUNOLOGY 8(4):271-278, December 1985.

Influence of pregnancy, oophorectomy and contraceptive steroids on gall bladder concentrating function and hepatic bile flow in the cat, by G. Radberg, et al. GUT 27(1):10-14, January 1986.

Investigation on the influence of steroidal contraceptives on milk lipid and fatty acids in Hungary and Thailand. WHO Special Programme of Research, Development and Research Training in Human Reproduction, Task Force on oral contraceptives, by M. Sas, et al. CONTRACEPTION 33(2):159-178, February 1986.

Kangaroos bite the bullet. NEW SCIENTIST 109:21, March 6, 1986.

Male birth-control pill to begin testing in United States. JET 71:28, November 10, 1986.

Phase IV study of the injection Norigest in Pakistan, by A. Kazi, et al. CONTRACEPTION 32(4):395-403, October 1985.

Randomized crossover comparison of two low-dose contraceptives: effects on serum lipids and lipoproteins, by W. März, et al. AMERICAN JOURNAL OF OBSTETRICS AND GYNECOLOGY 153(3):287-293, October 1, 1985.

Randomized cross-over comparison of two low-dose oral contraceptives upon hormonal and metabolic parameters: I. Effects upon sexual hormone levels, by H. Kuhl, et al. CONTRACEPTION 31(6):583-593, June 1985.

—: II. Effects upon thyroid function, gastrin, STH, and glucose tolerance, by H. Kuhl, et al. CONTRACEPTION 32(1):97-107, July 1985.

Randomized double-blind study of the effects of two low-dose combined oral contraceptives on biochemical aspects. Report from a seven-centered study. WHO Special Programme of Research, Development and Research

143

CONTRACEPTIVES—RESEARCH (continued)

Training in Human Reproduction. Task force on Oral Contraceptives. CON-TRACEPTION 32(3):223-236, September 1985.

Reproductive engineering—social control of women, by R. Arditti. RADICAL AMERICA 19(6):9, November 1986.

Vaccine that may prevent pregnancy (work of Vernon Stevens and others). DIS-COVER 7:13, May 1986.

Vaginal contraceptive activity of aryl 4-guanidinobenzoates (acrosin inhibitors) in rabbits, by J. M. Kaminski, et al. CONTRACEPTION 32(2):183-189, August 1985.

Worldwide trends in funding for contraceptive research and evaluation, by L. E. Atkinson, et al. FAMILY PLANNING PERSPECTIVES 17(5):196-199+, September-October 1985.

CONTRACEPTIVES—SOCIOLOGY
Contributions of sex guilt and masturbation guilt to women's contraceptive atti-tudes and use, by D. L. Mosher, et al. JOURNAL OF SEX RESEARCH 21(1):24-39, February 1985.

Psychosocial aspects of contraceptive use, by C. Weiman. NURS RSA VER-PLEGING 1(5):21, June 1986.

Reproductive engineering—social control of women, by R. Arditti. RADICAL AMERICA 19(6):9, November 1986.

Social and demographic factors influencing the acceptability of injectable method for contraception in comparison with copper "T" I.U.D., by R. Goraya, et al. INDIAN JOURNAL OF MEDICAL SCIENCE 39(7):172-174, July 1985.

Social and environmental factors influencing contraceptive use among black adolescents, by D. P. Hogan, et al. FAMILY PLANNING PERSPECTIVES 17(4):165-169, July-August 1985.

CONTRACEPTIVES—STATISTICS
Demographic and contraceptive patterns among women in Northern Mindanao, the Philippines, by C. E. Tan, et al. SOCIAL BIOLOGY 31(3-4):232-242, Fall-Winter 1984.

Epidemiological data, cytology and colposcopy in IUD (intrauterine device), E-P (estro-progestogens) and diaphragm users. Study of cytological changes of endometrium IUD related, by N. Fiore. CLINICAL AND EXPERIMENTAL OB-STETRICS AND GYNECOLOGY 13(1-2):34-42, 1986.

Gallup survey uncovers birth control misconceptions. AMERICAN FAMILY PHYSICIAN 33:296+, April 1986.

CONTRACEPTIVES AND AGING
Contraception for the older woman [review], by E. Weisberg. CLINICAL REPRO-DUCTION AND FERTILITY 3(2):115-123, June 1985.

CONTRACEPTIVES AND BREASTFEEDING
Breast-feeding and the pill: do they mix? (folate deficiency in child). PREVEN-TION 38:124, November 1986.

CONTRACEPTIVES AND BREASTFEEDING (continued)

Breast feeding, fertility and child health: a review of international issues . . . the contraceptive effect of breast feeding, by M. J. Houston. JOURNAL OF ADVANCED NURSING 11(1):35-40, January 1986.

Contraception during lactation: considerations in advising the individual and in formulating programme guidelines, by M. H. Labbok. JOURNAL OF BIO-SOCIAL SCIENCE 9:55-66, 1985.

Contraceptive use, amenorrhea, and breastfeeding in postpartum women, by V. H. Laukaran, et al. STUDIES IN FAMILY PLANNING 16(6 pt 1):293-301, November-December 1985.

Correlates and implications of breast-feeding practices in Bas, Zaire, by N. B. Mock, et al. JOURNAL OF BIOSOCIAL SCIENCE 18(2):231-245, April 1986.

Effect of early postpartum use of the contraceptive implants, NORPLANT, on the serum level of immunoglobulins of the mothers and their breastfed infants, by K. A. Abdulla, et al. CONTRACEPTION 32(3):261-266, September 1985.

Effects of hormonal and nonhormonal contraceptives on lactation and incidence of pregnancy, by S. Zacharias, et al. CONTRACEPTION 33(3):203-213, March 1986.

Effects of pregnancy, postpartum lactation, and oral contraceptive use on the lipoprotein cholesterol/triglyceride ration, by R. H. Knopp, et al. METAB-OLISM 34(10):893-899, October 1985.

Fertility regulation in nursing women: VIII. Progesterone plasma levels and con-traceptive efficacy of a progesterone-releasing vaginal ring, by S. Díaz, et al. CONTRACEPTION 32(6):603-622, December 1985.

Norethisterone concentration in breast milk and infant and maternal plasma during ethynodiol diacetate administration, by I. D. Cooke, et al. CONTRACEPTION 31(6):611-621, June 1985.

Side effects of oral contraceptive use in lactating women—enlargement of breast in a breast-fed child, by R. Madhavapeddi, et al. CONTRACEPTION 32(5): 437-443, November 1985.

CONTRACEPTIVES AND COLLEGE STUDENTS
Contraception among female students in the University of Benin, by J. C. Chiwuzie, et al. JOURNAL OF THE ROYAL SOCIETY OF HEALTH 106(2):60-62, April 1986.

Contraception on campus (survey of college students). SOCIETY 23:3, May-June 1986.

Diaphragm method contraceptors: implications for service organization and de-livery . . . college women, by J. G. Zapka, et al. HEALTH EDUCATION QUARTERLY 12(3):245-257, Fall 1985.

Predicting contraceptive behavior among college students: the role of communi-cation, knowledge, sexual anxiety, and self-esteem, by J. M. Burger, et al. ARCHIVES OF SEXUAL BEHAVIOR 14(4):343-350, August 1985.

CONTRACEPTIVES AND ECONOMICS
Economy for women, by I. Karlsson. SOCIAL AFFAIRS 4:54, 1985.

CONTRACEPTIVES AND THE MENTALLY RETARDED

Contraception in the mentally handicapped, by L. Beck. FORTSCHRITTE DER MEDIZIN 103(30):739, August 15, 1985.

Partnership, sexuality and contraception in mentally handicapped humans, by H. Krebs. FORTSCHRITTE DER MEDIZIN 103(30):740-743, August 15, 1985.

CONTRACEPTIVES AND PARENTAL CONSENT
Children, medical treatment and contraceptive agents. Is parental consent necessary?, by P. Bravender-Coyle. MEDICAL JOURNAL OF AUSTRALIA 144(8):416-419, April 14, 1986.

Gillick defeated but have we seen last of her? SPARE RIB 161:43, December 1985.

Gillick judgment. Contraceptives and the under 16s: House of Lords ruling, by C. Dyer. BRITISH MEDICAL JOURNAL 291(6503):1208-1209, October 26, 1985.

Right of doctors in certain cases to prescribe contraceptives lawfully to children under the age of 16 without a parents consent [editorial]. ARCHIVES OF DISEASE IN CHILDHOOD 61(8):725-726, August 1986.

CONTRACEPTIVES AND PHYSICIANS
Availability of reproductive health services from United States private physicians, by M. T. Orr, et al. FAMILY PLANNING PERSPECTIVES 17(2):63-69, March-April 1985.

Catholic doctor who fought for the pill, by L. McLaughlin. DISCOVER 4:82+, February 1983.

On clinical judgement: modeling physicians' recommendations of contraceptives, by F. P. Shea. DAI: B 47(6), December 1986.

Pill: the doctor's dilemma, by N. Timmins. TIMES March 8, 1986, p. 10.

Right of doctors in certain cases to prescribe contraceptives lawfully to children under the age of 16 without a parents consent [editorial]. ARCHIVES OF DISEASE IN CHILDHOOD 61(8):725-726, August 1986.

CONTRACEPTIVES AND RELIGION
Catholic doctor who fought for the pill, by L. McLaughlin. DISCOVER 4:82+, February 1983.

CONTRACEPTIVES AND TEENS
Adolescent contraceptive behavior [review], by D. M. Morrison. PSYCHOLOG-ICAL BULLETIN 98(3):538-568, November 1985.

Comparison of the effects of confluent vs. traditional contraceptive education on young people's knowledge, attitudes and behavior, by J. R. Daulk. DAI: A 47(3), September 1986.

Contraceptive experience and attitudes to motherhood of teenage mothers, by B. Ineichen. JOURNAL OF BIOSOCIAL SCIENCE 18(4):387-394, 1986.

Contraceptive methods for adolescents, by Y. Salomon-Bernard. SOINS. GYNECOLOGIE, OBSTETRIQUE, PUERICULTURE, PEDITRIE (53):3, October 1985.

CONTRACEPTIVES AND TEENS (continued)

Contraceptive self-efficacy: a perspective on teenage girls' contraceptive behavior, by R. A. Levinson. JOURNAL OF SEX RESEARCH 22(3):347-369,
1986.

Contraceptive use in the chronically ill adolescent female: part I, by L. S. Neinstein, et al. JOURNAL OF ADOLESCENT HEALTH CARE 7(2):123-133,
March 1986.

Contraceptives and the under 16s [letter], by C. Woodroffe, et al. BRITISH
MEDICAL JOURNAL 291(6054):1280, November 2, 1985.

Detection of ovulation by assay of the luteinizing hormone in the urine of ado-
lescents, before prescribing oral contraceptives, by M. Blum, et al. REVUE
FRANCAISE DE GYNECOLOGIE ET D'OBSTETRIQUE 80(12):881-882,
December 1985.

Impact of sex education on sexual activity, contraceptive use and premarital pregnancy among American teenagers, by W. Marsiglio, et al. FAMILY PLANNING
PERSPECTIVES 18(4):151-154+, July-August 1985.

Interaction of anticonvulsants and oral contraceptives in epileptic adolescents, by
M. P. Diamond, et al. CONTRACEPTION 31(6):623-632, June 1985.

Is it legal to give birth control devices and information to a child under 16?, by L. S.
Dranoff. CHATELAINE 59:164, February 1986.

Principal decisional factors relating to contraceptive usage in adolescents, by D.
Moreau. NURSING PAPERS 17(4):54-70, Winter 1986.

Relationship of self-concept and autonomy to oral contraceptive compliance
among adolescent females, by E. U. Neel, et al. JOURNAL OF ADOLES-
CENT HEALTH CARE 6(6):445-447, November 1985.

Research on adolescent male attitudes about contraceptives, by P. M. Hewson.
PEDIATRIC NURSING 12(2):114-116, March-April 1986.

Right of doctors in certain cases to prescribe contraceptives lawfully to children
under the age of 16 without a parents consent [editorial]. ARCHIVES OF
DISEASE IN CHILDHOOD 61(8):725-726, August 1986.

Sex and contraceptive information for adolescents, by C. Lacoste. SOINS.
GYNECOLOGIE, OBSTETRIQUE, PUERICULTURE, PEDIATRIE (53):7-10,
October 1985.

Sexual behavior, contraceptive practice, and reproductive health among Nigerian
adolescents, by D. Nichols, et al. STUDIES IN FAMILY PLANNING 17(2):100-
106, March-April 1986.

Social and environmental factors influencing contraceptive use among black
adolescents, by D. P. Hogan, et al. FAMILY PLANNING PERSPECTIVES
17(4):165-169, July-August 1985.

Study of the perceptions of middle school girls regarding factors which influence
their knowledge, attitudes and behaviors concerning the use or the non-use
of contraceptives, by J. Hines-Harris. DAI: A 47(5), November 1986.

CONTRACEPTIVES AND TEENS (continued)

Supporting teenagers' use of contraceptives: a comparison of clinic services, by R. Herceg-Baron, et al. FAMILY PLANNING PERSPECTIVES 18(2):61-66, March-April 1986.

Teenage pregnancy in developed countries: determinants and policy implications, by E. F. Jones, et al. FAMILY PLANNING PERSPECTIVES 17(2):53-62, March-April 1985.

Teenagers talk about sex, pregnancy and contraception, by E. E. Kiser. FAMILY PLANNING PERSPECTIVES 17(2):83-90, March-April 1985.

Theophylline pharmacokinetics in adolescent females following coadministration of oral contraceptives, by G. Koren, et al. CLINICAL AND INVESTIGATIVE MEDICINE 8(3):222-226, 1985.

Youth in the 1980s: social and health concerns. POPULATION REPORTS 13(5):M350, November-December 1985.

CONTRACEPTIVES AND VITAMINS
Impact of hormonal contraceptives vis-à-vis non-hormonal factors on the vitamin status of malnourishd women in India and Thailand. World Health Organization: Special Programme of Research, Development and Research Training in Human Reproduction. Task Force on Oral Contraceptives, by U. M. Joshi, et al. HUMAN NUTRITION. CLINICAL NUTRITION 40(3):205-220, May 1986.

Vitamin B-6 requirement and oral contraceptive use—a concern?, by J. E. Leklem. JOURNAL OF NUTRITION 116(3):475-477, March 1986.

Vitamin supplements to Indian women using low dosage oral contraceptives, by M. S. Bamji, et al. CONTRACEPTION 32(4):405-416, October 1985.

CONTRACEPTIVES AND WOMEN
Condom maker goes after women (marketing geared to women), by A. Lallande. VENTURE 8:82+, January 1986.

Contraception among female students in the University of Benin, by J. C. Chiwuzie, et al. JOURNAL OF THE ROYAL SOCIETY OF HEALTH 106(2):60-62, April 1986.

Contraception for the older woman [review], by E. Weisberg. CLINICAL REPRODUCTION AND FERTILITY 3(2):115-123, June 1985.

Contraception in hypertensive women using a vaginal ring delivering estradiol and levonorgestrel, by F. Elkik, et al. JOURNAL OF CLINICAL ENDOCRINOLOGY AND METABOLISM 63(1):29-35, July 1986; also in ARCHIVES DES MALADIES DU COEUR ET DES VAISSEAUX 78(11):1717-1739, October 1985.

Contraception in women with diabetes mellitus, by L. Verschoor, et al. NEDERLANDS TIJDSCHRIFT VOOR GENEESKUNDE 130(2):61-63, January 11, 1986.

Contraceptive perceptions and method choice among young single women in the United States, by K. Tanfer, et al. STUDIES IN FAMILY PLANNING 17:269-277, November-December 1986.

CONTRACEPTIVES AND WOMEN (continued)

Contraceptive practices among female heroin addicts, by N. Ralph, et al. AMERICAN JOURNAL OF PUBLIC HEALTH 76(8):1016-1017, August 1986; Discussion 76:1460, December 1986.

Contraceptive steroids increase hepatic uptake of chylomicron remnants in healthy young women, by F. Berr, et al. JOURNAL OF LIPID RESEARCH 27(6):645-651, June 1986.

Contraceptive use among women in Kuwait, by N. M. Shah, et al. INTERNATIONAL FAMILY PLANNING PERSPECTIVES 11(4):108-112, 1985.

Contraceptive use in the chronically ill adolescent female: part I, by L. S. Neinstein, et al. JOURNAL OF ADOLESCENT HEALTH CARE 7(2):123-133, March 1986.

Demographic and contraceptive patterns among women in Northern Mindanao, the Philippines, by C. E. Tan, et al. SOCIAL BIOLOGY 31(3-4):232-242, Fall-Winter 1984.

Diaphragm method contraceptors: implications for service organization and delivery . . . college women, by J. G. Zapka, et al. HEALTH EDUCATION QUARTERLY 12(3):245-257, Fall 1985.

Economy for women, by I. Karlsson. SOCIAL AFFAIRS 4:54, 1985.

Factors affecting the choice of nonpermanent contraceptive methods among married women, by M. MacDowell, et al. SOCIAL BIOLOGY 31(3-4):222-231, Fall-Winter 1984.

Frequency and adequacy in the use of contraceptive methods by women of Campinas, by A. Faúndes, et al. REVISTA PAULISTA DE MEDICINA 104(1):44-46, January-February 1986.

Influence of client-provider relationships on teenage women's subsequent use of contraception, by C. A. Nathanson, et al. AMERICAN JOURNAL OF PUBLIC HEALTH 75:33-38, January 1985.

Reproductive engineering—social control of women, by R. Arditti. RADICAL AMERICA 19(6):9, November 1986.

Why some women fail to use their contraceptive method: a psychological investigation, by W. B. Miller. FAMILY PLANNING PERSPECTIVES 18(1):27-32, January-February 1986.

FAMILY PLANNING—GENERAL
See also: Birth Control
             Contraception
             Contraceptives

Actionmen, by M. Pownall. NURSING TIMES 81(49):16-17, December 4-10, 1985.

Bureaucratization of birth control: textual analysis of "background notes on birth planning", by N. Lundberg. RESOURCES FOR FEMINIST RESEARCH 15: 34-36, March 1986.

Can spouses be trusted? A look at husband/wife proxy reports, by R. Williams, et al. DEMOGRAPHY 22:115-123, February 1985.

Child care arrangements and fertility: an analysis of two-earner households, by E. L. Lehrer, et al. DEMOGRAPHY 22(4):499-513, November 1985.

Children and birth control [letter], by P. Gerber. MEDICAL JOURNAL OF AUSTRALIA 143(12-13):633-634, December 9-23, 1985.

Comparative study of behavioral qualities of only children and sibling children. CHILD DEVELOPMENT 57(2):357-361, April 1986.

Comparison of childfree and child-anticipated married couples, by S. R. Hoffman, et al. FAMILY RELATIONS 34:197-203, April 1985.

Comparisons of mothers of one child by choice with mothers wanting a second birth, by V. J. Callan. JOURNAL OF MARRIAGE AND THE FAMILY 47:155-164, February 1985.

Contraception in context, by R. M. Gillespie, et al. FRONTIERS 9(1):3-8 1986.

Contraceptive care and family planning: a correction [letter], by J. McCracken. JOURNAL OF THE ROYAL COLLEGE OF GENERAL PRACTITIONERS 36(285):179, April 1986.

Contraceptive care and family planning in an urban general practice, by J. S. McCracken. JOURNAL OF THE ROYAL COLLEGE OF GENERAL PRAC-TITIONERS 36(282):13-16, January 1986.

Contraceptive practices among female heroin addicts, by N. Ralph, et al. AMERICAN JOURNAL OF PUBLIC HEALTH 76(8):1016-1017, August 1986; Discussion 76:1460, December 1986.

Contributions of sex guilt and masturbation guilt to women's contraceptive atti-tudes and use, by D. L. Mosher, et al. JOURNAL OF SEX RESEARCH 21(1):24-39, February 1985.

Control of the reproductive function of the family and its determining factors, by A. A. Popov. SOVETSKOE ZDRAVOOKHRONENIE (7):36-39, 1985.

Copper T380A IUD approved by the USFDA. STUDIES IN FAMILY PLANNING 16:39, January-February 1985.

Decision to terminate childbearing: differences in preoperative ambivalence between tubal ligation women and vasectomy wives, by R. N. Shain, et al. SOCIAL BIOLOGY 31(1-2):40-58, Spring-Summer 1984.

Decline in maternal mortality and the consequent increase in fertility, by S. Mukerji. JOURNAL OF FAMILY WELFARE 31:22-33, December 1984.

Decomposing the black/white fertility differential, by C. St. John, et al. SOCIAL SCIENCE QUARTERLY 66:132-146, March 1985.

Desired fertility, the "up to God" response, and sample selection bias, by E. Jensen. DEMOGRAPHY 22(3):445-454, August 1985.

Diarrheal disease control and family planning: the status of women and commu-nity participation, by M. G. Wagner. TURKISH JOURNAL OF PEDIATRICS 28(2):141-143, April-June 1986.

FAMILY PLANNING—GENERAL (continued)

Differences in levels of fertility and mortality between Kerala and Uttar-Pradesh, by T. N. Kapoor. JOURNAL OF FAMILY WELFARE 31:3-14, December 1984.

Ectopic pregnancy and fertility control measures, by B. Palaniappan, et al. ASIA-OCEANIA JOURNAL OF OBSTETRICS AND GYNAECOLOGY 11(4):545-549, December 1985.

Family building in parents with Down's syndrome children, by A. R. Boon. JOURNAL OF EPIDEMIOLOGY AND COMMUNITY HEALTH 40(2):154-160, June 1986.

Family planning. SOINS. GYNECOLOGIE, OBSTETRIQUE, PUERICULTURE, PEDIATRIE (59):34-38, April 1986.

—, by J. L. Newman. FOCUS 36:6, Spring 1986.

Family planning. Accurate predictions, by M. Renn. NURSING TIMES 82(5):26-27, January 29-February 4, 1986.

Family planning before birth—and after, by J. Bermel. HASTINGS CENTER REPORT 16:2, June 1986.

Family planning. Fertility rights, by R. Shapiro. NURSING TIMES 82(5):24-28, January 29-February 4, 1986.

Family planning. If the cap fits, by M. Renn. NURSING TIMES 82(5):22-24, January 29-February 4, 1986.

—, by B. Spencer. NURSING TIMES 82(5):22-24, January 29-February 4, 1986.

Family planning: taking precautions, by C. Clifford. NURSING TIMES 82(38):55-56+, September 17-23, 1986.

Family planning under present conditions, by M. Bulajic, et al. SRPSKI ARHIV ZA CELOKUPNO LEKARSTVO 114(2):223-228, February 1986.

Family planning within primary health care, by G. de la Fuente Trigueros. REVISTA DE ENFERMAGEN 9(93):49-52, April 1986.

Fertility and adaptation: Indochinese refugees in the United States. INTERNATIONAL MIGRATION REVIEW 20(2):428-465, Summer 1986.

Fertility behaviour of female carriers of haemophilia, by S. S. D. Chaudhari, et al. JOURNAL OF INDIAN ANTHROPOLOGY 18:51-54, 1983.

Human rights of family planning, by R. J. Cook. NEW ERA NURSING IMAGE INTERNATIONAL 2(2):42-43, 1986.

Husbands' and wives' relative influence on fertility decisions and outcomes. POPULATION AND ENVIRONMENT 7(3):182, Fall 1984.

Impact of ethnicity. SOCIETY 23(1):38-40, November-December 1985.

Implementation and expansion of family planning services: questions and controversies, by A. M. Canesqui. REVISTA PAULISTA DE ENFERMAGEM 5(1):26-30, January-March 1985.

Incentives and disincentives in the Indian family welfare program, by J. K. Satia, et al. STUDIES IN FAMILY PLANNING 17(3):136-145, May-June 1986.

Infertility and infertility counselling, by U. Anand. JOURNAL OF FAMILY WELFARE 31:34-47, December 1984.

Integration of midwives of rural areas in family planning, by E. Calle Olmos, et al. REVISTA DE ENFERMAGEN 9(1):27-29, January 1986.

International family planning. HOUSTON JOURNAL OF INTERNATIONAL LAW 8:155-173, Autumn 1985.

—, by M. P. McPherson. DEPARTMENT OF STATE BULLETIN 86:43-45, March 1986.

Investing in children. WORLDWATCH PAPER June 1985, p. 64.

Market for health care information: an exploration of the use of available information by consumers, by B. J. Kay. JOURNAL OF AMBULATORY CARE MANAGEMENT 9(3):72-85, August 1986.

Outcome of pregnancy [letter], by R. Gray, et al. FERTILITY AND STERILITY 44(4):554-555, October 1985.

Parenthood by design, by J. Sleep. NURSING 3(2):71-74, February 1986.

Policy of persuasive compulsion in population control, by K. V. Oza. JOURNAL OF FAMILY WELFARE 31:61+, December 1984.

Postpartum sexuality and contraception, by J. Richters. HEALTHRIGHT 5(2):25-27, February 1986.

Preconceptional thinking. ORVOSI HETILAP 127(5):281-283, February 2, 1986.

Pregnancy during residency, by M. Sayres, et al. NEW ENGLAND JOURNAL OF MEDICINE 314(7):418-423, February 13, 1986.

Reproduction law—Part two, by B. M. Dickens. HEALTH MANAGEMENT FORUM 6(3):39-51, Autumn 1985.

Role of a sexuality division in a public health agency, by L. Lathrop. AARN NEWSLETTER 41(10):15-16, November 1985.

Sex preselection: realities, falsehoods and implications, by J. Kerin. HEALTHRIGHT 5:8-12, August 1986.

Some general principles and opportunities for specific strategies in health education, by A. J. Radford, et al. HYGIE 5(1):38-44, March 1986.

Stress is a good contraceptive, by R. Dunbar. NEW SCIENTIST 105:16-18, January 17, 1985.

Towards smaller families: the crucial role of the private sector. DRAPER FUND REPORT December 1986, pp. 1-32.

Towards a women's perspective on family planning, by V. Balasubrahamanyan. ECONOMIC AND POLITICAL WEEKLY 21:69-71, January 11, 1986.

FAMILY PLANNING—GENERAL (continued)

Traditional structures clash with new imperatives, by T. B. Kayembe. NEW ERA NURSING IMAGE INTERNATIONAL 2(2):44-46, 1986.

Trends in family planning in Croatia, by D. Stampar. LIJECNICKI VJESNIK 107(10):417-421, October 1985.

Use of contraceptive agents by women in the city of Frunze, by I. A. Abdyldaeva, et al. SOVETSKOE ZDRAVOOKHRONENIE (6):40-42, 1986.

Who stood to gain on the Dalkon Shield?, by J. Adams. NEW SCIENTIST 107:74-75, September 26, 1985.

AFRICA
Africa: the real problem [letter]. CANADIAN MEDICAL ASSOCIATION JOUR-NAL 133(12):1202+, December 15, 1985.

Family planning, by A. Kone-Diabi. WORLD HEALTH August-September 1986, pp. 10-12.

Family planning and child survival. AFRICA (180):61, August 1986.

Health and family planning in Africa, by J. Karefa-Smart. POPULI 13(2):20-29, 1986.

Sexually transmitted diseases in sub-Saharan Africa. A priority list based on Family Health International's Meeting, by M. J. Rosenbert, et al. LANCET 2(8499):152-153, July 19, 1986.

ASIA
South Asia's family planning schedule, by Y. Kureishi. INSIDE 10(47):47, November 1986.

AUSTRALIA
AFFPA guidelines, by Medical Task Force. Australian Federation of Family Planning Associations. HEALTHRIGHT 5:22-24, February 1986.

Overview: the history of contraception and abortion in Australia, by D. Wynd-ham. HEALTHRIGHT 5:9-11, November 1985.

BANGLADESH
Importance of family planning in reducing maternal mortality, by J. A. Fortney. STUDIES IN FAMILY PLANNING 18:109-114, March-April 1987.

Introduction of the injectable contraceptive NET-EN into family planning clinics in Bangladesh, by S. S. Rahman, et al. WHO BULLETIN 63(4): 785-791, 1985.

Performance of supply-oriented family planning policy in Bangladesh: an examination, by B. K. Paul. SOCIAL SCIENCE AND MEDICINE 22(6): 639-644, 1986.

CANADA
Canadian two-children families: factors influencing present and future family size. CANADIAN COUNSELLOR 19(3-4):152-160, July 1985.

CHINA
Family planning in China, by J. K. Kallgren. CURRENT HISTORY 85:269-272+, September 1986.

FAMILY PLANNING—GENERAL (continued)

CHINA (continued)
Family-planning policy improves, by X. Lin. BEIJING REVIEW 29:4-5, July 14 1986.

No slackening in family planning, by X. Yang. BEIJING REVIEW 29:6-7, March 10, 1986.

One-child family: international patterns and their implications for the People's Republic of China, by D. L. Poston, et al. JOURNAL OF BIOSOCIAL SCIENCE 18(3):305-310, July 1986.

Redirection of the Chinese family: ramifications of minimal reproduction, by H. Y. Tien. ASIAN PROFILE 14:305-313, August 1986.

Reducing China's one billion. MAZINGIRA 894):17, 1985.

Who lost China? (disagreement over family planning program). SCIENTIFIC AMERICAN 255:54D-55, November 1986.

Women's health care and the workplace in the People's Republic of China, by P. Elder, et al. JOURNAL OF NURSE-MIDWIFERY 31(4):182-188, July-August 1986.

CZECHOSLOVAKIA
Educational problems of marriage and planned parenthood in the Czecho-slovak SSR, by B. Buzek. ACTA UNIVERSITATIS PALACKIANAE OLOMUCENSIS FACULTATIS MEDICAE 107:385-390, 1984.

DEVELOPING COUNTRIES
Teenage pregnancy in developed countries: determinants and policy implica-tions, by E. F. Jones, et al. FAMILY PLANNING PERSPECTIVES 17(2): 53-62, March-April 1985.

Two-year study of organised family planning services in a developing country: experiences in Bendel State of Nigeria, by D. O. Ogbeide, et al. EAST AFRICAN MEDICAL JOURNAL 61(6):470-476, June 1984.

EGYPT
Evaluation of the population and development program in Egypt, by J. M. Stycos, et al. DEMOGRAPHY 22(3):431-443, August 1985.

Rumor, misinformation and oral contraceptive use in Egypt, by J. DeClerque, et al. SOCIAL SCIENCE AND MEDICINE 23(1):83-92, 1986.

ENGLAND
Confidentiality, the law in England, and sexually transmitted diseases, by M. D. Talbot. GENITOURINARY MEDICINE 62(4):270-276, August 1986.

FRANCE
Scientific warranty for sexual politics: demographic discourse on "repro-duction" (France 1945-1985), by N. Moreau-Bisseret. FEMINIST ISSUES 6(1):67-85, September 1986.

GHANA
Fertility and family planning in Accra, by G. B. Fosu. JOURNAL OF BIO-SOCIAL SCIENCE 18(1):11-22, January 1986.

FAMILY PLANNING—GENERAL (continued)

HONDURAS
Knowledge and practices of the community distributors of contraceptives in Honduras, by B. Janowitz, et al. BOLETIN DE LA OFICINA SANITARIA PANAMERICANA 101(1):48-57, July 1986.

INDIA
Comparison of 1970 and 1980 survey findings on family planning in India, by M. E. Khan, et al. STUDIES IN FAMILY PLANNING 16(6 pt 1):312-320, November-December 1985.

Family planning in Nepal from the user's and nonuser's perspectives, by S. R. Schuler, et al. STUDIES IN FAMILY PLANNING 17(2):66-77, March-April 1986.

India: NET-OEN trials stopped, by A. Henry. OFF OUR BACKS 16:12-13, October 1986.

INDONESIA
Comparison of census and family planning program data on contraceptive prevalence, Indonesia, by K. Streatfield. STUDIES IN FAMILY PLANNING 16(6 pt 1):342-349, November-December 1985.

Indonesia contraceptive prevalence survey report 1983: the results of surveys in five cities, University of Indonesia. US AGENCY FOR INTERNATIONAL DEVELOPMENT REPORT December 1984.

ISRAEL
Family planning: beyond contraception . . . community health center in Jerusalem, by C. Kurtzman, et al. MCN 11(5):340-343, September-October 1986.

Radio and family planning in Israel: letters to broadcastears, by R. Shtarkshall, et al. JOURNAL OF COMMUNICATION 35:69-81, Spring 1985.

JAMAICA
Lay concepts affecting utilization of family planning services in Jamaica, by C. P. MacCormack. JOURNAL OF TROPICAL MEDICINE AND HYGIENE 88(4):281-285, Augsut 1985.

JORDAN
Family planning in Jordan: 1983 survey data, by A. Abdel-Aziz, et al. STUDIES IN FAMILY PLANNING 17(4):199-206, July-August 1986.

MEXICO
Cost benefit analysis of the Mexican Social Security Administration's family planning program, by D. L. Nortman, et al. STUDIES IN FAMILY PLANNING 17(1):1-6, January-February 1986.

Politics of reproduction in a Mexican village, by C. H. Browner. SIGNS 11: 710-724, Summer 1986.

Psychosocial research and family planning services in Mexico, by M. Urbina Fuentes, et al. SALUD PULICA DE MEXICO 27(4):266-285, July-August 1985.

NEPAL
Proximate determinants of fertility in the Kathmandu Valley, Nepal: an anthro-

155

FAMILY PLANNING—GENERAL (continued)

NEPAL (continued)
pological case study, by J. L. Ross, et al. JOURNAL OF BIOSOCIAL SCI-
ENCE 18(2):179-196, April 1986.

NEW GUINEA
Reproductive decision-making in the Upper Ramu District, Papua New
Guinea: cognitive aspects of adaptive problem-solving, by L. Conton.
PAPUA NEW GUINEA MEDICAL JOURNAL 28(3):163-176, September
1985.

NICARAGUA
Nicaragua's women at war, by C. Gander. AFRICASIA 31:50, July 1986.

NIGERIA
Acceptance of contraceptive practice by grandmultiparae in Benin City,
Nigeria, by A. E. Omu, et al. INTERNATIONAL JOURNAL OF GYNAE-
COLOGY AND OBSTETRICS 24(2):145-150, April 1986.

Changing attitude and practice of men regarding family planning in Lagos,
Nigeria, by A. A. Olukoya. PUBLIC HEALTH 99(6):349-355, November
1985.

Family planning among Nigerian postsecondary female students, by I. C. A.
Oyeka. STUDIES IN FAMILY PLANNING 17(3):146-152, May-June
1986.

Offering an alternative to illegal abortion in Nigeria, by T. O. Odejide. NEW
ERA NURSING IMAGE INTERNATIONAL 2(2):39-42, 1986.

Physician attitudes and family planning in Nigeria, by D. L. Covington, et al.
STUDIES IN FAMILY PLANNING 17(4):172-180, July-August 1986.

Sexual behavior, contraceptive practice, and reproductive health among
Nigerian adolescents, by D. Nichols, et al. STUDIES IN FAMILY PLAN-
NING 17(2):100-106, March-April 1986.

Teaching medical students about family planning: experiences from a primary
health care course in Lagos, Nigeria, by A. A. Olukoya, et al. MEDICAL
EDUCATION 20(1):42-47, January 1986.

Two-year study of organised family planning services in a developing country:
experiences in Bendel State of Nigeria, by D. O. Ogbeide, et al. EAST
AFRICAN MEDICAL JOURNAL 61(6):470-476, June 1984.

PHILIPPINES
Evaluating the effects of optimally distributed public programs: child health
and family planning interventions (Laguna province), by M. R. Rosenzweig, et al. AMERICAN ECONOMIC REVIEW 76:470-482, June 1986.

PUERTO RICO
Contraceptive use and the need for family planning in Puerto Rico, by J. M.
Harold, et al. FAMILY PLANNING PERSPECTIVES 18(4):185-188+,
1986.

Family planning in Puerto Rico: progress toward the national health goals for
1990 (V), by J. G. Rigau Pérez. BOLETIN-ASOCIACION MEDICA DE
PUERTO RICO 78(2):55-60, February 1986.

FAMILY PLANNING—GENERAL (continued)

SENEGAL
Vanguard family planning acceptors in Senegal, by D. Nichols, et al. STUD-
IES IN FAMILY PLANNING 16(5):271-278, September-October 1985.

SINGAPORE
Eugenics on the rise: a report from Singapore, by C. K. Chan. INTERNA-
TIONAL JOURNAL OF HEALTH SERVICES 15(4):707-712, 1985.

Family size intentions and socioeconomic status in Singapore, 1974-1981.
STUDIES IN FAMILY PLANNING 16(4):199, July-August 1985.

Incentives and disincentives used to affect demographic changes in fertility
trends in Singapore, by K. Singh, et al. SINGAPORE MEDICAL JOUR-
NAL 27(2):101-107, April 1986.

SOUTH AFRICA
Study of factors related to contraceptive dropout: colored women in the
metropolitan area of Capetown, by M. Strydom. CURATIONIS 8(2):44-
45+, June 1985.

TAIWAN
Implications for adolecent sex education in Taiwan, by G. P. Cernada, et al.
STUDIES IN FAMILY PLANNING 17(4):181-187, July-August 1986.

THAILAND
Maintaining family planning acceptance levels through development incen-
tives in Northeastern Thailand, by J. Stoeckel, et al. STUDIES IN FAMILY
PLANNING 17(1):36-43, January-February 1986.

THIRD WORLD COUNTRIES
Fertility reduction policies and poverty in Third world countries: ethical issues,
by D. J. Hernandez. STUDIES IN FAMILY PLANNING 16:76-87, March-
April 1985.

UNITED STATES
Chlamydia trachomatis screening in family planning clinics in Wisconsin, by M.
L. Katcher, et al. WISCONSIN MEDICAL JOURNAL 85(1):27, January
1986.

Politics of adolescent pregnancy: a view of New York State, by A. F. Moran.
JOURNAL OF COMMUNITY HEALTH 11(1):19-22, Spring 1986.

Source of service and visit rate of family planning services: United States,
1982, by W. D. Mosher, et al. PUBLIC HEALTH REPORTS 101(4):405-
416, July-August 1986.

State laws and the provision of family planning and abortion services in 1985,
by T. Sollom, et al. FAMILY PLANNING PERSPECTIVES 17(6):262-266,
November-December 1985.

United States policy statement for the International Conference on Population. POPULATION AND DEVELOPMENT REVIEW 10(3):574-579,
1984.

ZAIRE
Factors influencing the use of traditional versus modern family planning
methods in Bas Zaire, by J. T. Bertrand, et al. STUDIES IN FAMILY
PLANNING 16(6 pt 1):332-341, November-December 1985.

FAMILY PLANNING—GENERAL (continued)

ZIMBABWE
Characteristics of new contraceptive acceptors in Zimbabwe, by T. Dow, et al.
STUDIES IN FAMILY PLANNING 17(2):107-113, March-April 1986.

FAMILY PLANNING—ATTITUDES
Assessment of knowledge and attitudes of high school students regarding family
planning—a need of the day, by R. Malhotra, et al. JOURNAL OF FAMILY
WELFARE 31:57-60, December 1984.

Attitude of girls towards marriage and a planned family, by R. Kumari. JOURNAL
OF FAMILY WELFARE 31:53-60, March 1985.

Changing attitude and practice of men regarding family planning in Lagos,
Nigeria, by A. A. Olukoya. PUBLIC HEALTH 99(6):349-355, November
1985.

Fertility reduction policies and poverty in Third world countries: ethical issues, by
D. J. Hernandez. STUDIES IN FAMILY PLANNING 16:76-87, March-April
1985.

Physician attitudes and family planning in Nigeria, by D. L. Covington, et al.
STUDIES IN FAMILY PLANNING 17(4):172-180, July-August 1986.

FAMILY PLANNING—ECONOMICS
Are block grants more responsive to state health needs? The case of the Federal
Family Planning Program (FY 76-81), by D. R. McFarlane. JOURNAL OF
HEALTH AND HUMAN RESOURCES ADMINISTRATION 8(2):147-167, Fall
1985.

1986-1987 budget: health assembly decides on zero growth. WHO CHRONI-
CLE 39(4):119, 1985.

Physician extender services in family planning agencies: issues in Medicaid reimbursement, by L. W. Mondy, et al. JOURNAL OF PUBLIC HEALTH
POLICY 7(2):183-189, Summer 1986.

FAMILY PLANNING—EDUCATION
Assessment of knowledge and attitudes of high school students regarding family
planning—a need of the day, by R. Malhotra, et al. JOURNAL OF FAMILY
WELFARE 31:57-60, December 1984.

Individual vs. group education in family planning clinics, by J. H. Johnson.
FAMILY PLANNING PERSPECTIVES 17(6):255-259, November-December
1985.

FAMILY PLANNING—HISTORY
Margaret Sanger: nurse and feminist, by M. Ruffing-Rahal. NURSING OUTLOOK
34(5):246-249, September-October 1986.

FAMILY PLANNING—LAWS AND LEGISLATION
Benefits vs burdens: the limitations of damages in wrongful birth, by J. H. Scheid.
JOURNAL OF FAMILY LAW 23(10:57-98, 1985.

State laws and the provision of family planning and abortion services in 1985, by
T. Sollom, et al. FAMILY PLANNING PERSPECTIVES 17(6):262-266,
November-December 1985.

FAMILY PLANNING—LITERATURE

POPLINE: a bibliographic demographic database, by A. W. Compton, et al. BEHAVIORAL AND SOCIAL SCIENCES LIBRARIAN 5(2):9-18, 1986.

FAMILY PLANNING—MORTALITY AND MORTALITY STATISTICS
Family planning and maternal mortality in the Third World [letter], by K. A. Harrison, et al. LANCET 1(8495):1441, June 21, 1986.

Family planning, maternal mortality, and literacy [letter], by G. Walker. LANCET 2(8499):162, July 19, 1986.

Importance of family planning in reducing maternal mortality, by J. A. Fortney. STUDIES IN FAMILY PLANNING 18:109-114, March-April 1987.

FAMILY PLANNING—NATURAL
Billings ovulation method [letter], by M. A. Wilson. SCIENCE 231(4740):783, February 21, 1986.

Conclusions and critical remarks on natural family planning, by L. Beck, et al. GYNAKOLOGE 18(4):234-236, December 1985.

Correlation of vaginal hormonal cytograms with cervical mucus symptoms as observed by women using the ovulation method of natural family planning, by R. S. Taylor, et al. JOURNAL OF REPRODUCTIVE MEDICINE 31(3):167-172, March 1986.

Lactation and postpartum infertility: the use-effectiveness of natural family planning (NFP) after term pregnancy, by L. I. Hatherley. CLINICAL REPRODUCTION AND FERTILITY 3(4):319-334, December 1985.

Natural alternative, by N. Cameron. HERIZONS 4(6):39, September 1986.

"Natural" control of fertility, by E. Basker. SOCIOLOGY OF HEALTH AND ILLNESS 8(1):3-25, March 1986.

Natural family planning. International developments, current status, future aspects, by C. A. Lanctot. GYNAKOLOGE 18(4):231-233, December 1985.

Natural family planning. Introduction and epidemiologic studies, by P. Frank, et al. GYNAKOLOGE 18(4):224-230, December 1985.

Natural methods of family planning, by E. Clubb. JOURNAL OF THE ROYAL SOCIETY OF HEALTH 106(4):121-126, August 1986.

Natural regulation of fertility, a responsibility of today's church?, by M. C. D'Ursel. LUMEN VITAE 41(2):205-215, 1986.

Ovulation prediction: a workable choice in fertility control?, by M. Westcott. HEALTHRIGHT 5(2):8-16, February 1986.

FAMILY PLANNING—NURSES AND NURSING
Nurse and her role as a family planning practitioner, by S. A. Samuel. NURSING JOURNAL OF INDIA 77(7):195-196, July 1986.

FAMILY PLANNING—PSYCHOLOGY AND PSYCHIATRY
Knowledge, science and clinical practice of psychiatry, by A. Balestrieri. RECENTI PROGRESSI IN MEDICINA 76(12):643-645, December 1985.

FAMILY PLANNING—PSYCHOLOGY AND PSYCHIATRY (continued)

Psychological counseling in unsuccessful family planning, by A. Lendvay, et al. ORVOSI HETILAP 127(26):1551-1555, June 29, 1986.

FAMILY PLANNING—RESEARCH
Individual and couple intentions for more children: a research note, by S. P. Morgan. DEMOGRAPHY 22:125-132, February 1985.

Prospects for developing vaccines to control fertility, by G. L. Ada, et al. NATURE 317:288-289, September 26-October 2, 1985.

FAMILY PLANNING—SOCIOLOGY
Commentary on Rothman's "the products of conception: the social context of reproductive choices", by M. Stacey. JOURNAL OF MEDICAL ETHICS 11: 193-195, December 1985.

Diarrheal disease control and family planning: the status of women and community participation, by M. G. Wagner. TURKISH JOURNAL OF PEDIATRICS 28(2):141-143, April-June 1986.

Family planning, maternal mortality, and literacy [letter], by G. Walker. LANCET 2(8499):162, July 19, 1986.

Family size intentions and socioeconomic status in Singapore, 1974-1981. STUDIES IN FAMILY PLANNING 16(4):199, July-August 1985.

Impact of social status, family structure and neighborhood on the fertility of black adolescents, by D. P. Hogan, et al. AMERICAN JOURNAL OF SOCIOLOGY 90:825-855, January 1985.

Psychosocial research and family planning services in Mexico, by M. Urbina Fuentes, et al. SALUD PULICA DE MEXICO 27(4):266-285, July-August 1985.

Search for gender differences on fertility-related attitudes: questioning the relevance of sociobiology theory for understanding social psychological aspects of human reproduction, by D. Granberg, et al. PSYCHOLOGY OF WOMEN QUARTERLY 9(4):431-437, December 1985.

Social and cultural aspects of family planning programmes, by S. Frankel. PAPUA NEW GUINEA MEDICAL JOURNAL 28(3):155-162, September 1985.

FAMILY PLANNING—STATISTICS
Comparison of 1970 and 1980 survey findings on family planning in India, by M. E. Khan, et al. STUDIES IN FAMILY PLANNING 16(6 pt 1):312-320, November-December 1985.

Developing current fertility indicators for foreign-born women from the Current Population Survey, by A. Bachu, et al. REVIEW OF PUBLIC DATA USE 12:185-196, October 1984.

Family planning: a population study of women aged 40-44 years, by J. J. Carroll. COMMUNITY MEDICINE 7(4):248-256, November 1985.

Incentives and disincentives used to affect demographic changes in fertility trends in Singapore, by K. Singh, et al. SINGAPORE MEDICAL JOURNAL 27(2):101-107, April 1986.

FAMILY PLANNING—STATISTICS (continued)

Indonesia contraceptive prevalence survey report 1983: the results of surveys in five cities, University of Indonesia. US AGENCY FOR INTERNATIONAL DEVELOPMENT REPORT December 1984.

Scientific warranty for sexual politics: demographic discourse on "reproduction" (France 1945-1985), by N. Moreau-Bisseret. FEMINIST ISSUES 6(1):67-85, September 1986.

FAMILY PLANNING AND COLLEGE STUDENTS
Family planning among Nigerian postsecondary female students, by I. C. A. Oyeka. STUDIES IN FAMILY PLANNING 17(3):146-152, May-June 1986.

Teaching medical students about family planning: experiences from a primary health care course in Lagos, Nigeria, by A. A. Olukoya, et al. MEDICAL EDUCATION 20(1):42-47, January 1986.

FAMILY PLANNING AND FEMINISM
Religion and reproductive freedom: towards a feminist ethic of rights and responsibility, by F. Kissling. FRONTIERS 9(1):13-16, 1986.

FAMILY PLANNING AND MALES
Black male sexuality, by R. Staples. CHANGING MEN 17:3, Winter 1986.

Changing attitude and practice of men regarding family planning in Lagos, Nigeria, by A. A. Olukoya. PUBLIC HEALTH 99(6):349-355, November 1985.

Prospect of parenthood for women and men, by M.-J. Gerson. PSYCHOLOGY OF WOMEN QUARTERLY 10:49-62, March 1986.

FAMILY PLANNING AND PHYSICIANS
Availability of reproductive health services from United States private physicians, by M. T. Orr, et al. FAMILY PLANNING PERSPECTIVES 17(2):63-69, March-April 1985.

Development and evaluation of a short-term training design for health professionals, by C. D. Brindis. MOBIUS 6(1):33-48, January 1986.

Physician attitudes and family planning in Nigeria, by D. L. Covington, et al. STUDIES IN FAMILY PLANNING 17(4):172-180, July-August 1986.

Physician extender services in family planning agencies: issues in Medicaid reimbursement, by L. W. Mondy, et al. JOURNAL OF PUBLIC HEALTH POLICY 7(2):183-189, Summer 1986.

FAMILY PLANNING AND POLITICS
Politics of reproduction in a Mexican village, by C. H. Browner. SIGNS 11:710-724, Summer 1986.

FAMILY PLANNING AND RELIGION
Family planning, by A. Kiura. AFER 28(3-4):215-227, June-August 1986.

Religion and reproductive freedom: towards a feminist ethic of rights and responsibility, by F. Kissling. FRONTIERS 9(1):13-16, 1986.

FAMILY PLANNING AND TEENS
Adolescent fertility; worldwide concerns. POPULATION BULLETIN 40(2):1, April 1985.

FAMILY PLANNING AND TEENS (continued)

Adolescent pregnancy-prevention program. A model for research and evaluation, by L. S. Zabin, et al. JOURNAL OF ADOLESCENT HEALTH CARE 7(2):77-87, March 1986.

Age variation in use of a contraceptive service by adolescents, by S. G. Philliber, et al. PUBLIC HEALTH REPORTS 100:34-39, January-February 1985.

Assessment of knowledge and attitudes of high school students regarding family planning—a need of the day, by R. Malhotra, et al. JOURNAL OF FAMILY WELFARE 31:57-60, December 1984.

Comparative study (1964-1980) on knowledge and behavior in adolescents in the control of fertility, by N. Kapor-Stanulovic, et al. MEDICINSKI PREGLED 39(1-2):65-68, 1986.

Healthworks—an adolescent assessment tool. The house, by K. Parker. CANADIAN NURSE 82(1):28-31, January 1986.

Impact of social status, family structure and neighborhood on the fertility of black adolescents, by D. P. Hogan, et al. AMERICAN JOURNAL OF SOCIOLOGY 90:825-855, January 1985.

Implications for adolecent sex education in Taiwan, by G. P. Cernada, et al. STUDIES IN FAMILY PLANNING 17(4):181-187, July-August 1986.

Motivations for adolescents' first visit to a family planning clinic, ed. by D. B. Schwartz, et al. ADOLESCENCE 21:535-545, Fall 1986.

Perceptions of sexual responsibility: do young men and women agree?, by M. K. Sheehan, et al. PEDIATRIC NURSING 12(1):17-21, January-February 1986.

Politics of adolescent pregnancy: a view of New York State, by A. F. Moran. JOURNAL OF COMMUNITY HEALTH 11(1):19-22, Spring 1986.

Role of health belief attitudes, sex education, and demographics in predicting adolescents' sexuality knowledge, by M. Eisen, et al. HEALTH EDUCATION QUARTERLY 13(1):9-22, Spring 1986.

School-based health clinics: a new approach to preventing adolescent pregnancy, by J. Dryfoos. FAMILY PLANNING PERSPECTIVES 17(2):70-82, March-April 1985.

Sex-education needs and interests of high school students in a rural New York county, by N. McCormick, et al. ADOLESCENCE 20(79):581-592, Fall 1985.

Strategies for evaluating a contraceptive service for teenagers, by J. E. Jones, et al. HEALTH CARE MANAGEMENT REVIEW 11(1):41-46, Winter 1986.

Supporting teenagers' use of contraceptives: a comparison of clinic services, by R. Herceg-Baron, et al. FAMILY PLANNING PERSPECTIVES 18(2):61-66, March-April 1986.

Teenage pregnancy and parenting: facts, myths and stigma, by M. A. Clark. HEALTHRIGHT 5(1):13-19, November 1985.

Teenage pregnancy in developed countries: determinants and policy implications, by E. F. Jones, et al. FAMILY PLANNING PERSPECTIVES 17(2):53-62, March-April 1985.

FAMILY PLANNING AND TEENS (continued)

Teenagers and contraception. Evaluation of the first year at the contraception guidance clinic in Sør-Varanger, by B. O. Eriksen, et al. TIDSSKRIFT FOR DE NORSKE LAEGEFORENING 105(23):1508-1510, August 20, 1985.

Teenagers talk about sex, pregnancy and contraception, by E. E. Kiser. FAMILY PLANNING PERSPECTIVES 17(2):83-90, March-April 1985.

FAMILY PLANNING AND WOMEN
Attitude of girls towards marriage and a planned family, by R. Kumari. JOURNAL OF FAMILY WELFARE 31:53-60, March 1985.

Comparisons of mothers of one child by choice with mothers wanting a second birth, by V. J. Callan. JOURNAL OF MARRIAGE AND THE FAMILY 47:155-164, February 1985.

Correlation of vaginal hormonal cytograms with cervical mucus symptoms as observed by women using the ovulation method of natural family planning, by R. S. Taylor, et al. JOURNAL OF REPRODUCTIVE MEDICINE 31(3):167-172, March 1986.

Current principles of regulation of the reproductive function in women, by I. A. Manuilova. AKUSHERSTVO I GINEKOLOGIIA (7):49-52, July 1985.

Diarrheal disease control and family planning: the status of women and community participation, by M. G. Wagner. TURKISH JOURNAL OF PEDIATRICS 28(2):141-143, April-June 1986.

Family planning: a population study of women aged 40-44 years, by J. J. Carroll. COMMUNITY MEDICINE 7(4):248-256, November 1985.

Nicaragua's women at war, by C. Gander. AFRICASIA 31:50, July 1986.

Prospect of parenthood for women and men, by M.-J. Gerson. PSYCHOLOGY OF WOMEN QUARTERLY 10:49-62, March 1986.

Towards a women's perspective on family planning, by V. Balasubrahamanyan. ECONOMIC AND POLITICAL WEEKLY 21:69-71, January 11, 1986.

Well woman care: whose responsibility?, by L. Jessopp, et al. JOURNAL OF THE ROYAL COLLEGE OF GENERAL PRACTITIONERS 35(279):490-491, October 1985.

FAMILY PLANNING CLINICS
Chlamydia trachomatis screening in family planning clinics in Wisconsin, by M. L. Katcher, et al. WISCONSIN MEDICAL JOURNAL 85(1):27, January 1986.

Criteria for selective screening for Chlamydia trachomatis infection in women attending family planning clinics, by H. H. Handsfield, et al. JAMA 255:1730-1734, April 4, 1986.

Ethics committee in a reproductive health clinic for mentally handicapped persons, by T. E. Elkins, et al. HASTINGS CENTER REPORT 16(3):20-22, June 1986.

Get beyond labels (controversy over federal funding of family planning clinics), by N. Amidei. COMMONWEAL 113:37-38, January 31, 1986.

FAMILY PLANNING CLINICS (continued)

Individual vs. group education in family planning clinics, by J. H. Johnson. FAMILY PLANNING PERSPECTIVES 17(6):255-259, November-December 1985.

Introduction of the injectable contraceptive NET-EN into family planning clinics in Bangladesh, by S. S. Rahman, et al. WHO BULLETIN 63(4):785-791, 1985.

Motivations for adolescents' first visit to a family planning clinic, ed. by D. B. Schwartz, et al. ADOLESCENCE 21:535-545, Fall 1986.

Nutrition within a family planning clinic, by A. C. Shovic. JOURNAL OF APPLIED NUTRITION 38:3-12, Spring-Fall 1986.

Papa don't preach (controversy surrounding school-based clinics). NATION 243(13):396-397, October 25, 1986.

Supporting teenagers' use of contraceptives: a comparison of clinic services, by R. Herceg-Baron, et al. FAMILY PLANNING PERSPECTIVES 18(2):61-66, March-April 1986.

Teenagers and contraception. Evaluation of the first year at the contraception guidance clinic in Sør-Varanger, by B. O. Eriksen, et al. TIDSSKRIFT FOR DE NORSKE LAEGEFORENING 105(23):1508-1510, August 20, 1985.

Who works in family planning clinics?, by F. Fisher, et al. BRITISH MEDICAL JOURNAL 291(6497):753-754, September 14, 1985.

FAMILY PLANNING COUNSELING
Unplanned pregnancy counselling, by V. Rivers. HEALTHRIGHT 5:20-22, November 1985.

FAMILY PLANNING PROGRAMS
Adolescent pregnancy-prevention program. A model for research and evaluation, by L. S. Zabin, et al. JOURNAL OF ADOLESCENT HEALTH CARE 7(2):77-87, March 1986.

Brainstorming: an application for programme planning in family welfare planning, by T. V. Kumaran. GEOGRAPHIA MEDICA 15:65-96, 1985.

Comparison of census and family planning program data on contraceptive prevalence, Indonesia, by K. Streatfield. STUDIES IN FAMILY PLANNING 16(6 pt 1):342-349, November-December 1985.

Cost benefit analysis of the Mexican Social Security Administration's family planning program, by D. L. Nortman, et al. STUDIES IN FAMILY PLANNING 17(1):1-6, January-February 1986.

Evaluating the effects of optimally distributed public programs: child health and family planning interventions (Laguna province), by M. R. Rosenzweig, et al. AMERICAN ECONOMIC REVIEW 76:470-482, June 1986.

Evaluation of contraceptive history data in the Republic of Korea, by A. R. Pebley, et al. STUDIES IN FAMILY PLANNING 17(1):22-35, January-February 1986.

Evaluation of a pregnancy prevention program for urban teenagers, by L. S. Zabin, et al. FAMILY PLANNING PERSPECTIVES 18(3):119-126, May-June 1986.

FAMILY PLANNING PROGRAMS (continued)

Family planning as a service. WORLD BANK WORLD DEVELOPMENT REPORT 1984, p. 127.

Family planning programs, by M. E. Gallen, et al. POPULATION REPORTS (31):J813-852, May-June 1986.

Fertility and family planning surveys [update]. POPULATION REPORTS (8): M289-M348, September-October 1985; 13(4):289, September-October 1985.

Ford Foundation's work in population. FORD FOUNDATION REPORT August 1985, p. 53.

Global accounting. ENVIRONMENT 27(6):6, July-August 1985.

Individual vs. group education in family planning clinics, by J. H. Johnson. FAMILY PLANNING PERSPECTIVES 17(6):255-259, November-December 1985.

Knowledge and practices of the community distributors of contraceptives in Honduras, by B. Janowitz, et al. BOLETIN DE LA OFICINA SANITARIA PANAMERICANA 101(1):48-57, July 1986.

Lactation amenorrhoea: an important present-day component of family planning programmes, by D. B. Jelliffe, et al. JOURNAL OF TROPICAL PEDIATRICS 31(5):240-241, October 1985.

Lay concepts affecting utilization of family planning services in Jamaica, by C. P. MacCormack. JOURNAL OF TROPICAL MEDICINE AND HYGIENE 88(4): 281-285, Augsut 1985.

Maintaining family planning acceptance levels through development incentives in Northeastern Thailand, by J. Stoeckel, et al. STUDIES IN FAMILY PLANNING 17(1):36-43, January-February 1986.

Multilevel dependence of contraceptive use on socioeconomic development and family planning program strength, by B. Entwisle, et al. DEMOGRAPHY 23(2):199-216, May 1986.

Multilevel effects of socioeconomic development and family planning programs on children never born, by B. Entwisle, et al. AMERICAN JOURNAL OF SOCIOLOGY 91:616-649, November 1985.

1984 report by the executive director of the United Nations Fund for Population Activities. UN FUND FOR POPULATION ACTIVITIES REPORT 1985.

1986-1987 budget: health assembly decides on zero growth. WHO CHRONICLE 39(4):119, 1985.

Physician extender services in family planning agencies: issues in Medicaid reimbursement, by L. W. Mondy, et al. JOURNAL OF PUBLIC HEALTH POLICY 7(2):183-189, Summer 1986.

Planned parenthood federation of America: its role as provider of information services, by G. A. Roberts. BEHAVORIAL AND SOCIAL SCIENCES LIBRARIAN 4(4):35-42, Summer 1985.

FAMILY PLANNING PROGRAMS (continued)

Policy agenda. WORLD BANK WORLD DEVELOPMENT REPORT 1984, p. 155.

Practice. Open all hours, by J. Seymour. NURSING MIRROR 161(16):22-24, October 16, 1985.

Public funding of contraceptive, sterilization and abortion services, 1983, by R. B. Gold, et al. FAMILY PLANNING PERSPECTIVES 17:25-29, January-February 1985.

—, 1985, by R. B. Gold, et al. FAMILY PLANNING PERSPECTIVES 18:259-264, November-December 1986.

Reducing China's one billion. MAZINGIRA 894):17, 1985.

Sex education laws and policies. STUDIES IN FAMILY PLANNING 16(4):219, July-August 1985.

Social and cultural aspects of family planning programmes, by S. Frankel. PAPUA NEW GUINEA MEDICAL JOURNAL 28(3):155-162, September 1985.

Source of service and visit rate of family planning services: United States, 1982, by W. D. Mosher, et al. PUBLIC HEALTH REPORTS 101(4):405-416, July-August 1986.

State laws and the provision of family planning and abortion services in 1985, by T. Sollom, et al. FAMILY PLANNING PERSPECTIVES 17(6):262-266, November-December 1985.

Two-year study of organised family planning services in a developing country: experiences in Bendel State of Nigeria, by D. O. Ogbeide, et al. EAST AFRICAN MEDICAL JOURNAL 61(6):470-476, June 1984.

Ultrasonography as a new important potential in improving family planning service, by M. H. Hamed et Affandi, et al. ULTRASOUND IN MEDICINE AND BIOL-OGY 2(suppl):99-100, 1983.

UNFPA executive director expresses "deep distress" at impending cut in United States contribution (disagreement concerning family planning program). UN CHRONICLE 22:53, September 1985.

UNFPA: what is it, what it does. UN FUND FOR POPULATION ACTIVITIES REPORT 1985.

Vanguard family planning acceptors in Senegal, by D. Nichols, et al. STUDIES IN FAMILY PLANNING 16(5):271-278, September-October 1985.

Who lost China? (disagreement over family planning program). SCIENTIFIC AMERICAN 255:54D-55, November 1986.

UNITED STATES
Screening for sexually transmitted diseases by family planning providers: is it adequate and appropriate?, by S. O. Aral, et al. FAMILY PLANNING PER-SPECTIVES 18:255-258, November-December 1986.

FERTILITY—GENERAL
Anti-fertility effect of passive immunization against progesterone is influenced by

166

genotype, by V. Rider, et al. JOURNAL OF ENDOCRINOLOGY 108(1):117-121, January 1986.

Are maternal fertility problems related to childhood leukaemia?, by H. A. van Steensel-Moll, et al. INTERNATIONAL JOURNAL OF EPIDEMIOLOGY 14(4):555-559, December 1985.

Artificial reproduction techniques, fertility regulation: the challenge of contemporary family law, by P. F. Silva-Ruiz. AMERICAN JOURNAL OF COMPARATIVE LAW 34(suppl):125-140, 1986.

Breast-feeding and fertility. JOURNAL OF BIOSOCIAL SCIENCE 9:1-173, 1985.

Breast feeding, fertility and child health: a review of international issues . . . the contraceptive effect of breast feeding, by M. J. Houston. JOURNAL OF ADVANCED NURSING 11(1):35-40, January 1986.

Cervicovaginal peroxidases: markers of the fertile period, by J. C. Tsibris, et al. OBSTETRICS AND GYNECOLOGY 67(3):316-320, March 1986.

Child care arrangements and fertility: an analysis of two-earner households, by E. L. Lehrer, et al. DEMOGRAPHY 22(4):499-513, November 1985.

Comment on Glenn Firebaugh's "population density and fertility", by E. Jensen. DEMOGRAPHY 23(20):283-284, May 1986.

Commodity aspirations in Easterlin's relative income theory of fertility, by D. A. Ahlburg. SOCIAL BIOLOGY 31(3-4):201-207, Fall-Winter 1984.

Comparison of fecundability with fresh and frozen semen in therapeutic donor insemination, by B. L. Bordson, et al. FERTILITY AND STERILITY 46(3):466-469, September 1986.

Comparisons of the potential utility of LHRH agonists and antagonists for fertility control, by B. H. Vickery. JOURNAL OF STEROID BIOCHEMISTRY 23(5B): 779-791, November 1985.

Decline in maternal mortality and the consequent increase in fertility, by S. Mukerji. JOURNAL OF FAMILY WELFARE 31:22-33, December 1984.

Decomposing the black/white fertility differential, by C. St. John, et al. SOCIAL SCIENCE QUARTERLY 66:132-146, March 1985.

Determinants of effective fecundability based on the first birth interval, by J. Kallan, et al. DEMOGRAPHY 23(1):53-66, February 1986.

Dietary potentiation of the antifertility effects of 5-thio-D-glucose in male rats, by W. L. Dills, Jr., et al. JOURNAL OF NUTRITION 116(5):900-915, May 1986.

Differential fertility and morphological constitution of spouses, by E. Kobyliansky, et al. ZEITSCHRIFT FUR MORPHOLOGIE UND ANTHROPOLOGIE 76(1): 95-105, 1985.

Differential fertilty by religious group in rural Sierra Leone, by M. Bailey. JOURNAL OF BIOSOCIAL SCIENCE 18(1):75-85, January 1986.

Effects of cesarean section on fertility and abortions, by E. Hemminki. JOURNAL OF REPRODUCTIVE MEDICINE 31(7):620-624, July 1986.

Effects of prostaglandin F2 alpha [letter], by A. R. Peters. VETERINARY RECORD 118(16):466-467, April 19, 1986.

Entry into marriage and parenthood by young men and women: the influence of family background, by R. T. Michael, et al. DEMOGRAPHY 22(4):515-544, November 1985.

Expectant treatment versus conservative treatment in the management of mild endometriosis, by P. C. Wong, et al. ASIA-OCEANIA JOURNAL OF OBSTETRICS AND GYNAECOLOGY 12(1):43-47, March 1986.

Fertility after nonsurgical treatment of ectopic pregnancy, by H. J. Carp, et al. JOURNAL OF REPRODUCTIVE MEDICINE 31(2):119-122, February 1986.

Fertility after varicocele ligation [letter], by R. Abdelmassih. FERTILITY AND STERILITY 44(4):562, October 1985.

Fertility and adaptation: Indochinese refugees in the United States. INTERNATIONAL MIGRATION REVIEW 20(2):428-465, Summer 1986.

Fertility behaviour of female carriers of haemophilia, by S. S. D. Chaudhari, et al. JOURNAL OF INDIAN ANTHROPOLOGY 18:51-54, 1983.

Fertility considerations and procreative alternatives in cancer care, by S. H. Kaempfer, et al. SEMINARS IN ONCOLOGY NURSING 1(1):25-34, February 1985.

Fertility considerations in the gynecologic oncology patient, by S. H. Kaempfer, et al. ONCOLOGY NURSING FORUM 13(1):23-27, January-February 1986.

Fertility decision making among young mothers, by S. K. Dunn. DAI: A 46(11): 3396A, May 1986.

Fertility in relation to the risk of breast cancer, by M. P. Vessey, et al. BRITISH JOURNAL OF CANCER 52(4):625-628, October 1985.

Fertility in young men and women after treatment for lymphoma: a study of a population, by D. J. King, et al. JOURNAL OF CLINICAL PATHOLOGY 38(11):1247-1251, November 1985.

Fertility, infertility and generation replacement, by W. D. Borrie. CLINICAL REPRODUCTION AND FERTILITY 4(1):55-64, February 1986.

Fertility regulation in nursing women: VIII. Progesterone plasma levels and contraceptive efficacy of a progesterone-releasing vaginal ring, by S. Díaz, et al. CONTRACEPTION 32(6):603-622, December 1985.

Fertility regulation—the present and the future. Status report by a Marsian from the planet called Earth, by E. Diczfalusy. CONTRACEPTION 32(1):1-22, July 1985.

Fertility rights, by L. B. Ackerman. SCIENCE 7:55-56, January-February 1986.

Impact of abortion on subsequent fecundity, by C. J. Hogue. CLINICAL OBSTETRICS AND GYNAECOLOGY 13(1):95-103, March 1986.

Induced abortion and fertility, by T. Frejka. FAMILY PLANNING PERSPECTIVES 17(5):230-234, September-October 1985.

Influence of salicylaldehyde and its analogs on the antispermatogenic effect of gossypol, by W. H. Wang, et al. YAO HSUEH HSUEH PAO 20(5):392-394, May 1985.

Integration of sample design for the National Survey of Family Growth, Cycle IV, with the National Health Interview Survey, by J. Waksberg, et al. VITAL HEALTH STATISTICS (96):1-38, December 1985.

Low forager fertility: demographic characteristic or methodological artifact?, by J. D. Early. HUMAN BIOLOGY 57(3):387-399, September 1985.

"Natural" control of fertility, by E. Basker. SOCIOLOGY OF HEALTH AND ILLNESS 8(1):3-25, March 1986.

Numerical simulation of the one-locus, multiple-allele fertility model, by A. G. Clark, et al. GENETICS 113(1):161-176, May 1986.

On the process of stabilization in the renewal model: approximations for the time to convergence, by W. Timischl. JOURNAL OF MATHEMATICAL BIOLOGY 24(1):71-79, 1986.

Polygyny-fertility hypothesis: a re-evaluation, by L. L. Bean, et al. POPULATION STUDIES 40(1):67-81, March 1986.

Population-genetical study of differential fertility in human (based on an example of habitual abortion). I. Approach to the problem and analysis of morpho-physiological and demographic traits, by IuP. Altukhov, et al. GENETIKA 22(7):1207-1212, July 1986.

Population genetics study of the differential fertility in urban populations, by A. N. Kucher, et al. GENETIKA 22(2):304-311, February 1986.

Post-partum fertility [review], by G. T. Kovacs. CLINICAL REPRODUCTION AND FERTILITY 3(2):107-114, June 1985.

Practical aspects on the estimation of the parameters in Coale's model for marital fertility, by G. Broström. DEMOGRAPHY 22(4):625-631, November 1985.

Prospects for fertility after chemotherapy or radiation for neoplastic disease, by M. D. Damwood, et al. FERTILITY AND STERILITY 45(4):443-459, April 1986.

Reformulation of the two-sex problem, by R. A. Pollak. DEMOGRAPHY 23(2): 247-259, May 1986.

Research on Pharmachim's ronidazole for its antifertility, embryotoxic and tera-togenic action, by E. Kozhukharov et al. VETERINARNO-MEDITSINSKI NAUKI 22(7):76-82, 1985.

Rural-urban differentials in fertility of South Indian women, by P. S. Rao, et al. INDIAN JOURNAL OF MEDICAL RESEARCH 83:401-403, April 1986.

Rural-urban differentials in marital fertility in four muslim populations, by S. Admad. JOURNAL OF BIOSOCIAL SCIENCE 17(2):157-166, 1985.

Selection for increased mutation rates with fertility differences between matings, by K. E. Holsinger, et al. GENETICS 112(4):909-922, April 1986.

Seminal plasma beta-human chorionic gonadotropin (beta-HCG): relationships with seminal characteristics and spermatozoal fertilizing capacity, by S. Y. Chan, et al. ANDROLOGIA 18(1):50-55, January-February 1986.

Sexuality and fertility among spinal cord and/or cauda equina injuries, by A. E. Comarr. JOURNAL OF THE AMERICAN PARAPLEGIA SOCIETY 8(4):67-75, October 1985.

Socio-economic status and fertility of couples examined for infertility, social status and fertility, by E. Bostofte, et al. ANDROLOGIA 17(6):564-569, November-December 1985.

Sperm antigens and autoantibodies: effects on fertility, by S. Shulman. AMERICAN JOURNAL OF REPRODUCTIVE IMMUNOLOGY AND MICROBIOLOGY 10(3):82-89, March 1986.

Sperm-agglutinating antibodies and decreased fertility in prostitutes, by W. B. Schwimmer, et al. OBSTETRICS AND GYNECOLOGY 30(2):192-200, August 1967.

Studies in antifertility agents. 50. Stereoselective binding of d- and 1-cent-chromans to estrogen receptors and their antifertility activity, by M. Salman, et al. JOURNAL OF MEDICINAL CHEMISTRY 29(9):1801-1803, September 1986.

Study of returning fertility after childbirth and during lactation by measurement of urinary oestrogen and pregnanediol excretion and cervical mucus production, by J. B. Brown, et al. JOURNAL OF BIOSOCIAL SCIENCE 9:5-23, 1985.

Time to break down taboos about infertility, by A. Templeton. NEW SCIENTIST 105:39, January 10, 1985.

Use of time to pregnancy to study environmental exposures, by D. D. Baid, et al. AMERICAN JOURNAL OF EPIDEMIOLOGY 124(3):470-480, September 1986.

AUSTRALIA
Ethnic differences in Australian fertility, by F. Yusuf. CLINICAL REPRODUCTION AND FERTILITY 4(2):107-116, April 1986.

BANGLADESH
Determinants of natural fertility in rural Bangladesh reconsidered, by R. Langsten. POPULATION STUDIES 39:153-162, March 1985.

Influence of female education, labor force participation, and age at marriage on fertility behavior in Bangladesh, by R. H. Chaudhury. SOCIAL BIOLOGY 31(1-2):59-74, Spring-Summer 1984.

Sex preference for children and its implications for fertility in rural Bangladesh, by R. Bairagi, et al. STUDIES IN FAMILY PLANNING 17:302-307, November-December 1986.

BOLIVIA
Human fertility and land tenure in highland Bolivia, by R. A. Godoy. SOCIAL BIOLOGY 31(3-4):290-297, Fall-Winter 1984.

FERTILITY—GENERAL (continued)

CANADA
Canadian fertility trends in perspective, by L. Needleman. JOURNAL OF BIO-
SOCIAL SCIENCE 18(1):43-56, January 1986..

CHINA
Marriage and fertility in China: a graphical analysis, by Z. Yi, et al. POPULA-
TION AND DEVELOPMENT REVIEW 11(4):721-736, December 1985.

COLOMBIA
Effect of child mortality on contraceptive use and fertility in Colombia, Costa
Rica and Korea. POPULATION STUDIES 39(2):309, July 1985.

COSTA RICA
Effect of child mortality on contraceptive use and fertility in Colombia, Costa
Rica and Korea. POPULATION STUDIES 39(2):309, July 1985.

EGYPT
Reflections on recent levels and trends of fertility and ortality in Egypt, by B.
Bucht, et al. POPULATION STUDIES 40(1):101-113, March 1986.

Seasonal fertility cycles in rural Egypt: behavioral and biological linkages, by
V. Levy. DEMOGRAPHY 23(1):13-30, February 1986.

GHANA
Fertility and family planning in Accra, by G. B. Fosu. JOURNAL OF BIO-
SOCIAL SCIENCE 18(1):11-22, January 1986.

INDIA
Child loss and fertility in rural Eastern Manhararhtra, by S. Chhabra, et al.
INDIAN JOURNAL OF PUBLIC HEALTH 29(1):55-58, January-March
1985.

Health, fertility, and society in India: microstudies and macrostudies [review
article], by B. D. Miller. JOURNAL OF ASIAN STUDIES 45:1027-1036,
November 1986.

Proceedings of the International Symposium on Gonadotropin Releasing
Hormone in Control of Fertility ond Malignancy. Hyderabad, India, 17-20
August 1984. JOURNAL OF STEROID BIOCHEMISTRY 23(5B):677-
873, November 1985.

IRELAND
Regulation of fertility in Belgrade, by M. Husar, et al. SRPSKI ARHIV ZA
CELOKUPNO LEKARSTVO 113(7):601-609, July 1985.

ISRAEL
How does fertility relate to religiosity: survey evidence from Israel, by S. Neuman, et al. SOCIOLOGY AND SOCIAL RESEARCH 70:178-180, January
1986.

KOREA
Effect of child mortality on contraceptive use and fertility in Colombia, Costa
Rica and Korea. POPULATION STUDIES 39(2):309, July 1985.

Evaluation of contraceptive history data in the Republic of Korea, by A. R.
Pebley, et al. STUDIES IN FAMILY PLANNING 17(1):22-35, January-
February 1986.

KUWAIT
Fertility levels, trends and differentials in Kuwait, by K. L. Kohli, et al. JOUR-
NAL OF BIOSOCIAL SCIENCE 18(2):197-208, April 1986.

MALAYSIA
Recent rise in Malay fertility: a new trend or a temporary lull in a fertility transition?, by C. Hirschman. DEMOGRAPHY 23(2):161-184, May 1986.

MEXICO
Effect of female education on marital fertility in different size communities of
Mexico, by J. Holian. SOCIAL BIOLOGY 31(3-4):298-307, Fall-Winter
1984.

Parity distribution and socioeconomic development in Mexico: implications of
the effects of subfecundity on the modernization/fertility relationship, by
K. Trent. SOCIAL BIOLOGY 31(3-4):208-221, Fall-Winter 1984.

NEPAL
Fertility at low and high altitude in Central Nepal, by I. F. Laurenson, et al.
SOCIAL BIOLOGY 32(1-2):65-70, Spring-Summer 1985.

Proximate determinants of fertility in the Kathmandu Valley, Nepal: an anthro-
pological case study, by J. L. Ross, et al. JOURNAL OF BIOSOCIAL SCI-
ENCE 18(2):179-196, April 1986.

NIGERIA
Effects of women's education on postpartum practices and fertility in urban
Nigeria, by G. A. Oni. STUDIES IN FAMILY PLANNING 16(6 pt 1):321-
331, November-December 1985.

Polygyny and fertility differentials among the Yoruba of western Nigeria, by J.
Ahmed. JOURNAL OF BIOSOCIAL SCIENCE 18(1):63-73, January
1986.

PAKISTAN
Effect of infant mortality on subsequent fertility in Pakistan and Sri Lanka, by
K. V. Rao, et al. JOURNAL OF BIOSOCIAL SCIENCE 18(3):297-303,
July 1986.

Fertility in Pakistan during the 1970s, by I. H. Shah, et al. JOURNAL OF BIO-
SOCIAL SCIENCE 18(2):215-229, April 1986.

PHILIPPINES
Breast-feeding and fertility among Philippine women: trends, mechanisms
and impact, by Z. C. Zablan. JOURNAL OF BIOSOCIAL SCIENCE 9:147-
158, 1985.

POLAND
Dermal ridge patterns and fertility in a Polish rural sample, by D. Z. Loesch, et
al. ANNALS OF HUMAN BIOLOGY 12(5):463-477, September-October
1985.

SCOTLAND
Victorian values and the fertility decline: the case of Scotland, by D. Kemmer.
CRITICAL SOCIAL RESEARCH 2(1):1-31, Winter 1986.

SINGAPORE
Dynamics of ageing in Singapore's population, by S. H. Saw. ANNALS OF

FERTILITY—GENERAL (continued)

SINGAPORE (continued)
THE ACADEMY OF MEDICINE, SINGAPORE 44(6):740-743, December
1985.

Fertility and eugenics: Singapore's population policies, by J. J. Palen. POP-
ULATION RESEARCH AND POLICY REVIEW 5(1):3-14, 1986.

SRI LANKA
Effect of infant mortality on subsequent fertility in Pakistan and Sri Lanka, by
K. V. Rao, et al. JOURNAL OF BIOSOCIAL SCIENCE 18(3):297-303,
July 1986.

Environmental and other factors influencing fertility in Sri Lanka, by D. F. S.
Fernando. JOURNAL OF BIOSOCIAL SCIENCE 18(2):209-214, April
1986.

SUDAN
Determinants of natural fertility in Sudan, by M. A. Khalifa. JOURNAL OF BIO-
SOCIAL SCIENCE 18(3):325-336, July 1986.

SURINAM
Recent fertility trends in Surinam, by H. E. Lamur. JOURNAL OF BIOSOCIAL
SCIENCE 18(1):57-62, January 1986.

UNITED STATES
Comment on Barbara Devaney's "an analysis of variations in United States
fertility and female labor force participation trends", by D. P. Smith.
DEMOGRAPHY 23(1):137-142, February 1986.

Differential fertility in the United States, 1980: continuity or change?, by H.
Wineberg, et al. JOURNAL OF BIOSOCIAL SCIENCE 18(3):311-324,
July 1986.

Economics and other determinants of annual change in United States fertility,
by W. R. Kennedy, et al. SOCIAL SCIENCE RESEARCH 13(3):250-267,
1984.

Expanding scope of the American Fertility Society, by E. E. Wallach. FER-
TILITY AND STERILITY 44(6):740-743, December 1985.

Reproductive impairments in the United States, 1965-1982, by W. D.
Mosher. DEMOGRAPHY 22(3):415-430, August 1985.

Trend and variation in the seasonality of United States fertility, 1947-1976, by
D. A. Seiver. DEMOGRAPHY 22:89-100, February 1985.

FERTILITY—FEMALE
Comment on Barbara Devaney's "an analysis of variations in United States fertility
and female labor force participation trends", by D. P. Smith. DEMOGRAPHY
23(1):137-142, February 1986.

Further report on the endocrinological profile of two synthetic estrogens with
antifertility properties, STS 456 and STS 593, by M. Koch, et al. EXPERI-
MENTAL AND CLINICAL ENDOCRINOLOGY 86(3):257-265, December
1985.

FERTILITY—FEMALE (continued)

Is there a connection between a woman's fecundity and that of her mother?, by C. M. Langford, et al. JOURNAL OF BIOSOCIAL SCIENCE 17(4):437-443, October 1985.

Observations on the fertility of hyperthyroid patients treated with radioactive iodine (1311) and their daughters, by P. Marinoni, et al. GIORNALE DI CLINICA MEDICA 66(9-10):307-311, September-October 1985.

Reproductive potential in adolescent girls with ambiguous genitalia, by D. K. Edmonds, et al. PEDIATRIC ANNALS 15(7):530-531+, July 1986.

Return to fertility after IUD removal for planned pregnancy, by L. Randic, et al. CONTRACEPTION 32(3):253-259, September 1985.

FERTILITY—MALE
Abnormal axonemes in sperm of fertile men, by D. G. Hunter, et al. ARCHIVES OF ANDROLOGY 16(1):1-12, 1986.

Chronic occupational lead exposure: the potential effect on sexual function and reproductive ability in male workers, by M. Cunningham. AAOHN JOURNAL 34(6):277-279, June 1986.

Clinical trial of 19-nortestosterone-hexoxyphenylpropionate (Anadur) for male fertility regulation, by U. A. Knuth, et al. FERTILITY AND STERILITY 44(6): 814-821, December 1985.

Effect of fertility, libido and sexual function of post-operative radiotherapy and chemotherapy for cancer of the testicle, by V. Levison. CLINICAL RADI-OLOGY 37(2):161-164, March 1986.

Effect of gossypol on spermatogenesis and fertility in man and mammals, by A. S. Sadykov, et al. ONTOGENEZ 16(4):346-357, July-August 1985.

Effect of salicylazosulphapyridine (sulphasalazine) on male fertility [review], by A. Giwercman, et al. INTERNATIONAL JOURNAL OF ANDROLOGY 9(1):38-42, February 1986.

Effects of Ramadhan fast on male fertility, by S. M. Abbas, et al. ARCHIVES OF ANDROLOGY 16(2):161-166, 1986.

Examination of the fertility of patients with malignant testicular cancer at the time of orchiectomy. The question of the opinion on cryopreservation, by W. Höppner, et al. ANDROLOGIA 18(4):398-405, July-August 1986.

Failure of high-dose sustained release luteinizing hormone releasing hormone agonist (buserelin) plus oral testosterone to suppress male fertility, by E. Michel, et al. CLINICAL ENDOCRINOLOGY 23(6):663-675, December 1985.

Fecundability rates from an infertile male population, by T. B. Hargreave, et al. BRITISH JOURNAL OF UROLOGY 58(2):194-197, April 1986.

Fertility after radiotherapy for testicular cancer, by S. D. Fossa. PROGRESS IN CLINICAL AND BIOLOGICAL RESEARCH 203:703-712, 1985.

Fertility and hormonal function in patients with a nonseminomatous tumor of the testis, by J. M. Nijman, et al. ARCHIVES OF ANDROLOGY 14(2-3):239-246, 1985.

Fertility in aging men, by H. R. Nankin. MATURITAS 7(3):259-265, September 1985.

Growing yams and men: an interpretation of Kimam male ritualized homosexual behavior, by J. P. Gray. JOURNAL OF HOMOSEXUALITY 11(3-4):55-68, Summer 1985.

Influence of neonatal injection of estradiol and testosterone on hypothalamo-hypophyseal-gonadal interrelationships and fertility in male rats, by V. G. Baranov, et al. NEUROSCIENCE AND BEHAVIORAL PHYSIOLOGY 15(5): 404-407, September-October 1985.

Long term followup of cosmetic appearance and genital function in boys with exstrophy: review of 53 patients, by H. G. Mesrobian, et al. JOURNAL OF UROLOGY 136(1 pt 2):256-258, July 1986.

Male fertility in factor XIII deficiency, by M. Frydman, et al. FERTILITY AND STERILITY 45(5):729-731, May 1986.

Morphologic study of microwave influence on male fertility. Influence of microwave irradiation on rat testes, by Y. X. Fang, et al. SSU-CHUAN I HSUEH YUAN HSUEH PAO 16(3):191-194, September 1985.

Morphometric analysis of spermatozoa in the assessment of human male fertility, by D. F. Katz, et al. JOURNAL OF ANDROLOGY 7(4):203-210, July-August 1986.

Prepubertal testicular torsion: subsequent fertility, by P. Puri, et al. JOURNAL OF PEDIATRIC SURGERY 20(6):598-560, December 1985.

Prostaglandins and male fertility, by M. Bygdeman, et al. ADVANCES IN PRO-STAGLANDIN AND THROMBOXANE AND LEUKOTRIENE RESEARCH 15:609-611, 1985.

Requirements for controlled therapeutic trials in male infertility, by H. W. Baker. CLINICAL REPRODUCTION AND FERTILITY 4(1):13-25, February 1986.

Studies of testicular function after treatment for testicular tumor. I. Fertilization of patients with testicular tumor before and after treatment, by A. Furuhata, et al. NIPPON HINYOKIKA GAKKAI ZASSHI 76(7):1022-1028, July 1985.

Testicular function and fertility in men with homozygous alpha-1 antitrypsin deficiency, by D. J. Handelsman, et al. ANDROLOGIA 18(4):406-412, July-August 1986.

Testicular vein ligation and fertility in men with varicoceles, by H. W. Baker, et al. BRITISH MEDICAL JOURNAL 291(6510):1678-1680, December 14, 1985.

FERTILITY—RESEARCH

Antifertility and mutagenic effects in mice from parenteral administration of di-2-ethylhexyl phthalate (DEHP), by D. K. Agarwal, et al. JOURNAL OF TOXI-COLOGY AND ENVIRONMENTAL HEALTH 16(1):71-84, 1985.

Antifertility effect of busulfan and procarbazine in male and female coyotes, by J. N. Stellflug, et al. BIOLOGY OF REPRODUCTION 33(5):1237-1243, December 1985.

Antifertility effect of polyvinylpyrrolidone-gossypol and gossypol in male rats, by Y. Wang, et al. CONTRACEPTION 32(6):651-660, December 1985.

Antifertility effects of embelin in male rats, by S. Agrawal, et al. ANDROLOGIA 18(2):125-131, March-April 1986.

Association between lameness and fertility in dairy cows, by S. Lucey, et al. VETERINARY RECORD 118(23):628-631, June 7, 1986.

Attitudes of women of reproductive age to in vitro fertilization and embryo research, by E. M. Aler, et al. JOURNAL OF BIOSOCIAL SCIENCE 18(2):155-167, April 1986.

Chronic low dose cyclophosphamide treatment of adult male rats: effect on fertility, pregnancy outcome and progeny, by J. M. Trasler, et al. BIOLOGY OF REPRODUCTION 34(2):275-283, March 1986.

Clinical and pathologico-anatomic findings in the bovine uterus after cesarean section and their significance for fertility, by R. Bouters. TIERARZTLICYHE PRAXIS 14(2):205-209, 1986.

Comparison of lamb production from indigenous and exotic x indigenous ewes in Indonesia, by I. C. Fletcher, et al. TROPICAL ANIMAL HEALTH AND PRODUCTION 17(3):127-134, August 1985.

Determinants of puberty in a seasonal breeder, by D. L. Foster, et al. RECENT PROGRESS IN HORMONE RESEARCH 42:331-384, 1986.

Dietary potentiation of the antifertility effects of 5-thio-D-glucose in male rats, by W. L. Dills, Jr., et al. JOURNAL OF NUTRITION 116(5):900-915, May 1986.

Does prolactin regulate prolificity in the ewe?, by V. O. Fuentes. VETERINARY RECORD 118(23):638, June 7, 1986.

Economics and other determinants of annual change in United States fertility, by W. R. Kennedy, et al. SOCIAL SCIENCE RESEARCH 13(3):250-267, 1984.

Effect of beta carotene supplementation on the beta carotene and vitamin A levels of blood plasma and some fertility indices of dairy cows, by S. Iwanska, et al. ARCHIV FUR TIERERNAHRUNG 35(8):563-570, August 1985.

Effect of delta 9-tetrahydrocannabinol in utero exposure on rat offspring fertility and ventral prostate gland morphology, by B. S. Ahluwalia, et al. JOURNAL OF ANDROLOGY 6(6):386-391, November-December 1985.

Effect of an enhanced natural radioactivity on mammal fertility, by A. Leonard, et al. SCIENCE OF THE TOTAL ENVIRONMENT 45:535-542, October 1985.

Effect of glyzophrol on fertility of female black rats (Rattus rattus), by S. Rani, et al. ACTA EUROPAEA FERTILITATIS 17(2):139-143, March-April 1986.

Effect of gossypol on spermatogenesis and fertility in man and mammals, by A. S Sadykov, et al. ONTOGENEZ 16(4):346-357, July-August 1985.

Effect of graded unilateral testicular biopsy on the reproductive capacity of male rats, by M. J. Cosentino, et al. JOURNAL OF UROLOGY 135(1):155-158, January 1986.

Effect of initial insemination and insemination interval on fertility in turkey hens, by D. R. McIntyre, et at. POULTRY SCIENCE 64(8):1549-1552, August 1985.

Effect of non-steroidal anti-inflammatory drugs on fertility of male rats, by W. Löscher, et al. JOURNAL OF REPRODUCTION AND FERTILITY 76(1):65-73, January 1986.

Effect of oviductal tissues from hens differing in fertility duration on the respiration of washed chicken spermatozoa, by E. E. Pierson, et al. POULTRY SCIENCE 65(3):598-600, March 1986.

Effect of progestagen, PMSG and time of insemination on fertility in ewes following intra-uterine insemination with frozen semen, by J. Eppleston, et al. AUSTRALIAN VETERINARY JOURNAL 63(4):124-125, April 1986.

Effect of salicylazosulphapyridine (sulphasalazine) on male fertility [review], by A. Giwercman, et al. INTERNATIONAL JOURNAL OF ANDROLOGY 9(1):38-42, February 1986.

Effect of sperm numbers per insemination following early or late initial inseminations in turkeys, by D. R. McIntyre, et al. POULTRY SCIENCE 65(7):1400-1404, July 1986.

Effect of zearalenone on the fertility of virgin dairy heifers, by G. A. Weaver, et al. AMERICAN JOURNAL OF VETERINARY RESEARCH 47(6):1395-1397, June 1986.

Effectiveness of genetic selection for prolificacy in pigs, by M. Bichard, et al. JOURNAL OF REPRODUCTION AND FERTILITY 33:127-138, 1985.

Effects of dietary protein and season on fertility of turkey semen stored 18 hours at 5 C, by T. J. Sexton. POULTRY SCIENCE 65(3):604-606, March 1986.

Effects of hyperprolactinaemia on reproduction in male mice, by M. Nonomura, et al. JOURNAL OF ENDOCRINOLOGY 107(1):71-76, October 1985.

Effects of (-) and (+) gossypol on the fertility of male rats, by N. G. Wang, et al. YAO HSUEH HSUEH PAO 19(12):932-934, December 1984.

Effects of total glycosides of tripterygium wilfordii on the reproductive organs of experimental animals. III. Dynamic observations on the reproductive organs and fertility in mice, by J. R. Zheng, et al. CHUNG KUO I HSUEH KO HSUEH YUAN HSUEH PAO 8(1):19-23, February 1986.

Emergence of the reproductive research enterprise: a sociology of biological, medical and agricultural science in the United States, 1910-1940, by A. E. Clark. DAI: A 47(2), August 1986.

Fecundity and longevity of houseflies after space flight, by R. E. Lee, Jr., et al. EXPERIENTIA 41(9):1191-1192, September 15, 1985.

Female rats in a laboratory display seasonal variation in fecundity, by T. M. Lee, et al. JOURNAL OF REPRODUCTION AND FERTILITY 77(1):51-59, May 1986.

Fertile mule in China and her unusual foal, by R. H. Rong, et al. JOURNAL OF THE ROYAL SOCIETY OF MEDICINE 78(10):821-825, October 1985.

Fertility and teratogenic studies of diethylene glycol monobutyl ether in rats and rabbits, by G. A. Nolen, et al. FUNDAMENTAL AND APPLIED TOXICOLOGY 5(6 pt 1):1137-1143, December 1985.

Fertility differences among male rabbits determined by heterospermic insemination of fluorochrome-labeled spermatozoa, by J. J. Parrish, et al. BIOLOGY OF REPRODUCTION 33(4):940-949, November 1985.

Fertility of mating in rats (Rattus norvegicus): contributions of androgen-dependent morphology and actions of the penis, by J. K. O'Hanlon, et al. JOURNAL OF COMPARATIVE PSYCHOLOGY 100(2):178-187, June 1986.

Fertility of the monorchid rat after partial resection of testes, by H. Hayashi, et al. ARCHIVES OF ANDROLOGY 14(2-3):267-269, 1985.

Fertility, reproduction, and postnatal survival in mice chronically exposed to isoflurane, by R. I. Mazze. ANESTHESIOLOGY 63(6):663-667, December 1985.

Fertility of sperm from t/+ mice; evidence that +-bearing sperm are dysfunctional, by P. Olds-Clarke, et al. GENETIC RESEARCH 47(1):49-52, February 1986.

Fertility study of rifaximin (L/105) in rats, by D. Bertoli, et al. CHEMIOTERAPIA 5(3):204-207, June 1986.

Fertility study on haloperidone acetate in rats, by S. Imoto, et al. JOURNAL OF TOXICOLOGICAL SCIENCES 10(suppl 1):71-81, August 1985.

Fetal surgery in the primate. III. Maternal outcome after fetal surgery, by N. S. Adzick, et al. JOURNAL OF PEDIATRIC SURGERY 21(6):477-480, June 1986.

Gonadal development and fertility of mice treated prenatally with dacmium during the early organogenesis stages, by P. P. Tam, et al. TERATOLOGY 32(3): 453-462, December 1985.

Gonadotropin-releasing hormone and prostaglandin F2 alpha for postpartum dairy cows: estrous, ovulation, and fertility traits, by M. Benmrad, et al. JOURNAL OF DAIRY SCIENCE 69(3):800-811, March 1986.

Improved fertility in dairy cows after treatment with selenium pellets, by T. J. McClure, et al. AUSTRALIAN VETERINARY JOURNAL 63(5):144-146, May 1986.

Influence of environmental temperature on prolificacy of pigs, by R. P. Wettemann, et al. JOURNAL OF REPRODUCTION AND FERTILITY 33:199-208, 1985.

Influence of light and photoperiodicity on pig prolificacy, by R. Claus, et al. JOURNAL OF REPRODUCTION AND FERTILITY 33:185-197, 1985.

Influence of monensin on fertility in rats, by M. Atef, et al. CLINICAL AND EXPERIMENTAL PHARMACOLOGY AND PHYSIOLOGY 13(2):113-121, February 1986.

Influence of neonatal injection of estradiol and testosterone on hypothalamo-hypophyseal-gonadal interrelationships and fertility in male rats, by V. G.

Baranov, et al. NEUROSCIENCE AND BEHAVIORAL PHYSIOLOGY 15(5): 404-407, September-October 1985.

Influencing prolificacy of sows by selection for physiological factors, by R. K. Johnson, et al. JOURNAL OF REPRODUCTION AND FERTILITY 33:139-149, 1985.

Lack of correlation between fertility and sperm numbers in male rats treated with histrelin, a potent LHRH agonist, by R. G. Foldesy, et al. JOURNAL OF ANDROLOGY 7(3):140-146, May-June 1986.

Lead exposure on critical days of fetal life affects fertility in the female mouse, by M. Wide. TERATOLOGY 32(3):375-380, December 1985.

Lifetime breeding studies in fully fed and dietary restricted female CFY Sprague-Dawley rats. 1. Effect of age, housing conditions and diet on fecundity, by A. M. Holehan, et al. MECHANISMS OF AGEING AND DEVELOPMENT 33(1): 19-28, December 1985.

Measurement of semen quality, fertility, and reproductive hormones to assess dibromochloropropane (DBCP) effects in live rabbits, by R. H. Foote, et al. FUNDAMENTAL AND APPLIED TOXICOLOGY 6(4):628-637, May 1986.

Nutrition and sow prolificacy, by F. X. Aherne, et al. JOURNAL OF REPRODUCTION AND FERTILITY 33:169-183, 1985.

Ontogeny of epididymal sperm reserves during the reproductive lifespan of rats after previous sexual experiences, by G. T. Taylor, et al. JOURNAL OF REPRODUCTION AND FERTILITY 77(20:419-423, July 1986.

Possible influence of strain differences on pregnancy initiation in laboratory rats, by D. Austin, et al. PHYSIOLOGY AND BEHAVIOR 37(4):621-625, 1986.

Potency of rat ejaculations varies with their order and with male age, by J. P. Toner, et al. PHYSIOLOGY AND BEHAVIOR 35(1):113-115, July 1985.

Preparation and properties of human chorionic gonadotropin antagonist for biological studies: antifertility effects in the female rat, by M. R. Sairam, et al. ACTA ENDOCRINOLOGICA 112(4):586-594, August 1986.

Prospective multicentre study to develop universal immunochemical tests for predicting the fertile period in women, by World Health Organisation Task Force on Methods for the Determination of the Fertile Period, Special Programme of Research, Development and Research Training in Human Reproduction. INTERNATIONAL JOURNAL OF FERTILITY 30(3):18-30, 1985.

Prospective serial study of the effects of radiotherapy on semen parameters, and hamster egg penetration rates, by R. H. Martin, et al. CLINICAL AND INVESTIGATIVE MEDICINE 8(3):239-243, 1985.

Relation between vitamin E supply and the fertility of laying hens, by A. Hennig, et al. ARCHIV FUR TIERERNAHRUNG 36(6):519-529, June 1986.

Relationship of nonreturn rates of dairy bulls to binding affinity of heparin to sperm, by J. L. Marks, et al. JOURNAL OF DAIRY SCIENCE 68(8):2078-2082, August 1985.

Relationship of the number of spermatozoa inseminated to fertility of turkey semen stored 6 h at 5 degrees C, by T. J. Sexton. BRITISH POULTRY SCIENCE 27(2):237-245, June 1986.

Reproductive capacity of male laboratory rats, by D. Austin, et al. PHYSIOLOGY AND BEHAVIOR 37(4):627-632, 1986.

Reproductive toxicity of marihuana smoke. A three-generation study in female Wistar rats, by N. V. Murthy, et al. WEST INDIAN MEDICAL JOURNAL 35(2): 130-134, June 1986.

Reproductive toxicity of 2,4-toluenediamine in the rat. 1. Effect on male fertility, by B. Thysen, et al. JOURNAL OF TOXICOLOGY AND ENVIRONMENTAL HEALTH 16(6):753-761, 1985.

Selection for postweaning gain in rats: II. Correlated response in reproductive performance, by J. G. Rios, et al. JOURNAL OF ANIMAL SCIENCE 63(1):46-53, July 1986.

Selection of breeds, strains and individual pigs for prolificacy, by C. Legault. JOURNAL OF REPRODUCTION AND FERTILITY 33:151-166, 1985.

Semen assessment, fertility and the selection of Hereford bulls for use in AI, by P. D. Wood, et al. JOURNAL OF REPRODUCTION AND FERTILITY 76(2): 783795, March 1986.

Semen fertility—an evaluation system for artificial insemination sires, technicians, herds, and systematic fixed effects, by R. W. Everett, et al. JOURNAL OF DAIRY SCIENCE 69(6):1630-1641, June 1986.

Semen production, sperm quality, and their heritabilities as influenced by selection for fertility of frozen-thawed semen in the chicken, by G. A. Anash, et al. POULTRY SCIENCE 64(9):1801-1803, September 1985.

Studies of hydroxypropylmethylcellulose acetate succinate on fertility in rats, by N. Hoshi, et al. JOURNAL OF TOXICOLOGICAL SCIENCES 10(suppl 2): 187-201, October 1985.

Study on the effect of (2"R)-4'-O-tetrahydropyranyladriamycin, a new antitumor antibiotic, on reproduction. I. Its effect on the fertility of rats, by M. Kurebe, et al. JAPANESE JOURNAL OF ANTIBIOTICS 39(2):463-476, February 1986.

Suprathreshold manipulations of testosterone and reproductive functioning in gonadally intact sexually experienced and inexperienced male rats, by G. T. Taylor, et al. PHYSIOLOGY AND BEHAVIOR 35(5):735-739, November 1985.

Systematic environmental, direct, and service sire effects on conception rate in artificially inseminated Holstein cows, by J. F. Taylor, et al. JOURNAL OF DAIRY SCIENCE 68(11):3004-3022, November 1985.

Testicular aspiration biopsy in evaluation of fertility of mink (Mustela vison), by C. Sundqvist, et al. JOURNAL OF REPRODUCTION AND FERTILITY 77(2): 531-535, July 1986.

Village production of West African dwarf goats and sheep in Nigeria, by J. E. Sumberg, et al. TROPICAL ANIMAL HEALTH AND PRODUCTION 17(3): 135-140, August 1985.

FERTILITY—RESEARCH (continued)

Zinc feeding and fertility of male rats, by K. Samanta, et al. INTERNATIONAL JOURNAL FOR VITAMIN AND NUTRITION RESEARCH 56(1):105-108, 1986.

FERTILITY—STATISTICS
Births, fertility, rhythms and lunar cycle. A statistical study of 5,927,978 births, by P. Guillon, et al. JOURNAL DE GYNECOLOGIE, OBSTETRIQUE ET BIOLOGIE DE LA REPRODUCTION 15(3):265-271, 1986.

Contraceptive use and annual acceptors required for fertility transition: results of a projection model, by J. Bongaarts. STUDIES IN FAMILY PLANNING 17:209-216, September-October 1986.

Effect of female education on marital fertility in different size communities of Mexico, by J. Holian. SOCIAL BIOLOGY 31(3-4):298-307, Fall-Winter 1984.

Estimation of fecundability from survey data, by N. Goldman, et al. STUDIES IN FAMILY PLANNING 16(5):252-259, September-October 1985.

Estimation of natural fertility: a micro approach, by E. M. Crimmins, et al. SOCIAL BIOLOGY 31(1-2):160-170, Spring-Summer 1984.

European survey of fertility and pregnancy in women with Crohn's disease: a case control study by European collaborative group, by J. F. Mayberry, et al. GUT 27(7):821-825, July 1986.

Fertility and mortality differences in relation to maternal body size, by M. R. Devi, et al. ANNALS OF HUMAN BIOLOGY 12(5):479-484, September-October 1985.

Fertility of workers. A comparison of logistic regression and indirect standardization, by T. B. Starr, et al. AMERICAN JOURNAL OF EPIDEMIOLOGY 123(3):490-498, March 1986.

Is the density-fertility relation a statistical artifact? A reply to Eric Jensen, by G. Firebaugh. DEMOGRAPHY 23(2):285-289, May 1986.

J. Y. Parlange, M. J. Guilfoyle, and R. E. Rickson's "mortality levels and family fertility goals", by S. Krishnamoorthy, et al. DEMOGRAPHY 22(4):633-637, November 1985.

Long term followup of cosmetic appearance and genital function in boys with exstrophy: review of 53 patients, by H. G. Mesrobian, et al. JOURNAL OF UROLOGY 136(1 pt 2):256-258, July 1986.

Motility and fertility of frozen bull spermatozoa in tris-yolk and milk extenders containing amikacin sulfate, by K. Ahmad, et al. JOURNAL OF DAIRY SCIENCE 68(8):2083-2086, August 1985.

Relative income, race, and fertility, by N. E. Johnson, et al. POPULATION STUDIES 39:99-112, March 1985.

FERTILITY AGENTS
Anovulation: etiology, evaluation and management, by S. L. Padilla, et al. NURSE PRACTITIONER 10(12):28-30+, December 1985.

Fertility regulating agents from traditional Chinese medicines, by Y. C. Kong, et al. JOURNAL OF ETHNOPHARMACOLOGY 15(1):1-44, January 1986.

FERTILITY AGENTS (continued)

Ovulation induction, by P. M. Smith. JOGN NURSING 14(6):37S-43S, November-December 1985.

Requirements for controlled therapeutic trials in male infertility, by H. W. Baker. CLINICAL REPRODUCTION AND FERTILITY 4(1):13-25, February 1986.

Scintigraphy of the bone marrow with 111In-citrin in polycythemia vera, by A. G. Prikhod'ko, et al. MEDITSINSKAIA RADIOLOGIIA 31(5):30-33, May 1986.

FERTILITY AGENTS—FEMALE
Sensitivity of the pituitary-ovarian system of animals to be nonhormonal preparation RL-S, by R. E. Lokhov, et al. VOPROSY MEDITSINSKAI KHIMII 32(3): 21-23, May-June 1986.

FERTILITY AND AGING
Age and fertility: how late can you wait?, by M. Menken. DEMOGRAPHY 22(4): 469-483, November 1985.

Age and infertility, by J. Menken, et al. SCIENCE 233(4771):1389-1394, September 26, 1986.

Calculation of age-specific fertility schedules from tabulation of parity in two censuses, by A. J. Coale, et al. DEMOGRAPHY 22(4):611-623, November 1985.

Dynamics of ageing in Singapore's population, by S. H. Saw. ANNALS OF THE ACADEMY OF MEDICINE, SINGAPORE 44(6):740-743, December 1985.

Fertility and parental age in Alzheimer disease, by J. A. White, et al. JOURNAL OF GERONTOLOGY 41(1):40-43, January 1986.

Fertility in aging men, by H. R. Nankin. MATURITAS 7(3):259-265, September 1985.

FERTILITY AND TEENS
Adolescent fertility; worldwide concerns. POPULATION BULLETIN 40(2):1, April 1985.

Reproductive potential in adolescent girls with ambiguous genitalia, by D. K. Edmonds, et al. PEDIATRIC ANNALS 15(7):530-531+, July 1986.

HYSTERECTOMY—GENERAL
Acute peripheral arterial occlusion associated with surgery for gynecologic cancer, by P. A. Townsend, et al. GYNECOLOGIC ONCOLOGY 25(1):108-114, September 1986.

Are preoperative antibiotics helpful in abdominal hysterectomy?, by C. C. Senior, et al. AMERICAN JOURNAL OF OBSTETRICS AND GYNECOLOGY 154(5): 1004-1008, May 1986.

Automatic suture stapling in abdominal hysterectomy, by E. Bendvold, et al. TIDSSKRIFT FOR DE NORSKE LAEGEFORENING 106(3):199, January 30, 1986.

Broad spectrum antibiotics as short term prophylaxis for elective abdominal hysterectomy: comparison of mezlocillin, cefazolin and placebo, by M. Hakim, et al. INTERNATIONAL JOURNAL OF GYNAECOLOGY AND OBSTETRICS 24(2):157-160, April 1986.

Cefotetan versus cefoxitin as prophylaxis in hysterectomy, by J. W. Orr, Jr., et al. AMERICAN JOURNAL OF OBSTETRICS AND GYNECOLOGY 154(4):960-963, April 1986.

Cervical carcinoma found incidentally in a uterus removed for benign indications, by P. B. Heller, et al. OBSTETRICS AND GYNECOLOGY 67(2):187-190, February 1986.

Cesarean and post-partum hysterectomy 1968-1983, by D. W. Sturdee, et al. BRITISH JOURNAL OF OBSTETRICS AND GYNAECOLOGY 93(3):270-274, March 1986.

Cesarean hysterectomy: indications, technique, and complications, by W. C. Plauché. CLINICAL OBSTETRICS AND GYNECOLOGY 29(2):318-328, June 1986.

Changes in bladder function in the woman undergoing radical hysterectomy for cervical cancer, by K. M. O'Laughlin. JOGN NURSING 15(5):380-385, September-October 1986.

Clinical aspects of perinatal hysterectomy, by Z. Slomko, et al. GINEKOLOGIA POLSKA 56(3):153-158, March 1985.

Clinical investigation on acupuncture combined anesthesia during the abdominal hysterectomy, by S. O. Xie, et al. CHEN TZU YEN CHIU 10(4):246-249+, 1985.

Comparison of recovery following hysterectomy and major cardiac surgery, by D. Gould, et al. JOURNAL OF ADVANCED NURSING 10(4):315-323, July 1985.

Comparison of the results of total hysterectomy with complete or partial suture of the vaginal stump, by V. Neglia. ANNALI DI OSTETRICIA GINECOLOGIA MEDICINA PERINATALE 106(4):221-224, July-August 1985.

Comparison of short and long courses of ampicillin for vaginal hysterectomy, by W. L. Benson, et al. JOURNAL OF REPRODUCTIVE MEDICINE 30(11):874-878, November 1985.

Comparison of water, electrolyte and nitrogen balance in the postoperative period after epidural or general anesthesia. A randomized study of patients undergoing hysterectomy, by S. M. Gregoretti. MINERVA ANESTESIOLO-GICA 51(3):87-91, March 1985.

Complete reconstruction of vagina after radical hysterectomy, by K. Ichinoe, et al. NIPPON SANKA FUJINKA GAKKAI ZASSHI 38(6):965-970, June 1986.

Complications in patients receiving both irradiation and radical hysterectomy for carcinoma of the uterine cervix, by A. J. Jacobs, et al. GYNECOLOGIC ON-COLOGY 22(3):273-280, November 1985.

Conditions for the transition of premorbid states into borderline forms of path-ology, by L. K. Khokhlov, et al. ZHURNAL NEVROPATOLOGII I PSIKHIATRII 85(11):1662-1665, 1985.

Continuous epidural anesthesia for elective cesarean hysterectomy, by D. H. Chestnut, et al. SOUTHERN MEDICAL JOURNAL 78(10):1168-1169+, October 1985.

Controlled, comparative study of moxalactam and cefazolin for prophylaxis of abdominal hysterectomy, by A. S. Berkeley, et al. SURGERY, GYNECOLOGY AND OBSTETRICS 161(5):457-461, November 1985.

Correlates of change in postmenopausal estrogen use in a population-based study, by M. Standeven, et al. AMERICAN JOURNAL OF EPIDEMIOLOGY 124(2):268-274, August 1986.

Cost and quality in the use of blood bank services for normal deliveries, cesarean sections, and hysterectomies, by R. H. Palmer, et al. JAMA 256(2):219-223, July 11, 1986.

Diagnosis of systemic polyartenritis nodosa following total abdominal hysterectomy and bilateral salpingo-oophorectomy: a case report, by C. M. Lombard, et al. INTERNATIONAL JOURNAL OF GYNECOLOGICAL PATHOLOGY 5(1):63-68, 1986.

Do you need these operations? [hysterectomy, breast surgery, D and C], by P. Dranov. HEALTH 18:24+, June 1986; Discussion 18:4, September 1986.

Doxycycline and cefamandole prophylaxis for premenopausal women undergoing vaginal hysterectomy, by D. L. Hemsell, et al. SURGERY, GYNECOLOGY AND OBSTETRICS 161(5):462-464, November 1985.

Early uterine body carcinoma: has post-operative vaginal irradiation any value?, by W. H. Bond. CLINICAL RADIOLOGY 36(6):619-623, November 1985.

Effect of cefmenoxime in protection against postoperative infection in common gynecological surgery, by T. Chimura, et al. JAPANESE JOURNAL OF ANTIBIOTICS 38(10):2809-2814, October 1985.

Effect of standard and low-molecular weight heparin fractions on fibrinolysis and platelet aggregation in patients undergoing hysterectomy [letter], by H. Bounameaux, et al. THERAPEUTISCHE UMSCHAU 55(2):298, April 30, 1986.

Effects of benzodiazepines as anaesthesia inducing agents on plasma cortisol level in elective hysterectomy, by A. Kertész, et al. ACTA MEDICA HUNGARICA 42(3-4):145-152, 1985.

Essay on elective hysterectomy and the treatment of uterine myoma, by S. Shinagawa, et al. NIPPON SANKA FUJINKA GAKKAI ZASSHI 38(7):1139-1143, July 1986.

Experimental evaluation of absorbable copolymer staples for hysterectomy, by R. R. Steckel, et al. OBSTETRICS AND GYNECOLOGY 68(3):404-410, September 1986.

FSH, LH, estradiol and testosterone levels after Seda-Presomen in women following hysterectomy with bilateral adnexotomy, by J. Stehlíková, et al. ACTA UNIVERSITATIS PALACKIANAE OLOMUCENSIS FACULTATIS MEDICAE 101:139-145, 1981.

Functional disorders of the lower urinary tract following a radical abdominal operation in cervical cancer, by G. Ralph, et al. GEBURTSHILFE UND FRAUENHEILKUNDE 45(9):625-629, September 1985.

Hysterectomies in New Zealand [letter], by B. Borman, et al. NEW ZEALAND MEDICAL JOURNAL 99(804):470, June 25, 1986.

Hysterectomy after caesarean section: the treatment of last resort for serious infection, by D. J. Tinga. EAST AFRICAN MEDICAL JOURNAL 63(5):362-364, May 1986.

Hysterectomy and sex of the gynecologist [letter], by G. Domenighetti, et al. NEW ENGLAND JOURNAL OF MEDICINE 313(23):1482, December 5, 1985.

Hysterectomy performed within one year after tubal sterilization, by J. S. Kendrick, et al. FERTILITY AND STERILITY 44(5):606-610, November 1985.

Hysterocolpectomy. The method of choice in genital prolapse in geriatric patients, by P. Hohlweg-Majert, et al. FORTSCHRITTE DER MEDIZIN 104(3): 27-28, January 16, 1986.

Increased incidence of menstrual abnormalities and hysterectomy preceding primary biliary cirrhosis, by A. J. Stellon, et al. BRITISH MEDICAL JOURNAL 293(6542):297-298, August 2, 1986.

Local metronidazole and PVP-iodine prevention before abdominal and vaginal hysterectomy, by R. J. Lellé, et al. GEBURTSHILFE UND FRAUENHEIL-KUNDE 46(2):102-104, February 1986.

Management of high-grade stage 1 adenocarcinoma of the endometrium: hysterectomy following low dose external beam pelvic irradiation, by D. S. Shimm, et al. GYNECOLOGIC ONCOLOGY 23(2):183-191, February 1986.

Management of intractable lymphocyst following radical hysterectomy, by Y. C. Choo, et al. GYNECOLOGIC ONCOLOGY 24(3):309-316, July 1986.

Mental retardation: a controversial indication for hysterectomy, by A. M. Kaunitz, et al. OBSTETRICS AND GYNECOLOGY 68(3):436-438, September 1986.

Meralgia paresthetica in women [letter], by H. R. Eskens. AMERICAN FAMILY PHYSICIAN 34(2):21, August 1986.

New trial for suit for unneeded hysterectomy. BOLETIN-ASOCIACION MEDICA DE PUERTO RICO 77(11):487, November 1985.

Non-resolution of pelvic sonographic abnormality after chemotherapy for persistent trophoblastic disease—a word of caution, by J. S. Woo, et al. EURO-PEAN JOURNAL OF OBSTETRICS, GYNECOLOGY AND REPRODUCTIVE BIOLOGY 22(3):153-156, July 1986.

Obstetric hysterectomy—an 11-year experience, by R. G. Thonet. BRITISH JOURNAL OF OBSTETRICS AND GYNAECOLOGY 93(8):794-798, August 1986.

Penetration of cefoperazone into the exudate of the retroperitoneal space after (semi-)radical hysterectomy, by S. Nozawa, et al. JAPANESE JOURNAL OF ANTIBIOTICS 39(3):686-692, March 1986.

Pilot prospective hysterectomy audit, by M. Lawrence, et al. AUSTRALIAN CLINICAL REVIEW 5(19):168-171, December 1985.

Post-cesarean hysterectomy. Clinico-statistical considerations, by S. Marsico, et al. MINERVA GINECOLOGIA 38(3):143-148, March 1986.

Pre- and postoperative changes in coagulation and fibrinolytic variables during abdominal hysterectomy under epidural or general anaesthesia, by S. Bredbacka, et al. ACTA ANAESTHESIOLOGICA SCANDINAVICA 30(3):204-210, April 1986.

Prognostic significance of interval from preoperative irradiation to hysterectomy for endometrial carcinoma, by R. Komaki, et al. CANCER 58(4):873-879, August 15, 1986.

Return to theatre—experience at the Mercy Maternity Hospital, Melbourne 1971-1982, by P. Ashton, et al. AUSTRALIAN AND NEW ZEALAND JOURNAL OF OBSTETRICS AND GYNAECOLOGY 25(3):159-169, August 1985.

Risk factor for tumor recurrence after radical hysterectomy for stage IB squamous cancer of cervix, by R. C. Nuss, et al. JOURNAL OF THE FLORIDA MEDICAL ASSOCIATION 72(9):768-770, September 1985.

Role of surgery in the strategy of primary local and regional treatment of stage I and II cancer of the endometrium, by L. Piana, et al. JOURNAL DE GYNECOLOGIE, OBSTETRIQUE ET BIOLOGIE DE LA REPRODUCTION 15(3): 347-354, 1986.

Ruptured tubal pregnancy six years after total vaginal hysterectomy, by J. P. Culpepper, 3d. JOURNAL OF THE MISSISSIPPI STATE MEDICAL ASSOCIATION 26(12):341-342, December 1985.

Series of 440 vaginal hysterectomies performed for non-prolapsed uterus, by Y. X. Zhang. CHUNG HUA FU CHAN KO TSA CHIH 20(5):294-297, September 1985.

Severe micturition disorder after a sling operation following radical hysterectomy, by H. Kölbl, et al. ZENTRALBLATT FUR GYNAEKOLOGIE 108(9):582-584, 1986.

Simple hysterectomy for stage Ia carcinoma of the uterine cervix, by N. Tsukamoto, et al. NIPPON GAN GHIRYO GAKKAI SHI 20(9):2041-2046, October 20, 1985.

Single dose intravenous tinidazole prophylaxis in abdominal hysterectomy, by G. R. Evaldson, et al. ACTA OBSTETRICIA ET GYNECOLOGICA SCANDINAVICA 65(4):361-365, 1986.

Successful intrauterine pregnancy after unilateral hysterectomy in a patient with uterus didelphys. A case report, by V. A. Catanzarite, et al. JOURNAL OF REPRODUCTIVE MEDICINE 31(2):133-135, February 1986.

Surgical treatment of women found to have invasive cervix cancer at the time of total hysterectomy, by J. W. Orr, Jr., et al. OBSTETRICS AND GYNECOLOGY 68(3):353-356, September 1986.

Treatment of cervical intraepithelial neoplasia III by hysterectomy without intervening conization in patients with adequate colposcopy, by J. R. van Nagell, Jr., et al. CANCER 56(12):2737-2739, December 15, 1985.

HYSTERECTOMY—GENERAL (continued)

Voiding dysfunction after radical abdominal hysterectomy, by H. C. Kuo, et al. TAIWAN I HSUEH HUI TSA CHIH 84(10):1137-1146, October 1985.

Volume reduction of the uterus during and soon after hysterectomy, by B. Ranney, et al. AMERICAN JOURNAL OF OBSTETRICS AND GYNECOLOGY 155(2):354-357, August 1986.

Wertheim's operation—a personal series of 55 cases, by M. C. Cheng. SINGA-PORE MEDICAL JOURNAL 26(6):443-447, October 1985.

Work capacity and social security of women after radical treatment of cervical cancer, by Iu. V. Artiushenko. AKUSHERSTVO I GINEKOLOGIIA (2):51-53, February 1986.

HYSTERECTOMY—COMPLICATIONS

Carcinoma of the residual stump. Cases of the First Obstetric-Gynecologic clinic of the University of Milan from 1955 to 1984, by R. Maggi, et al. ANNALI DI OSTETRICIA GINECOLOGIA MEDICINA PERINATALE 106(2):57-65, March-April 1985.

Case of prolapse of the vaginal vault after colpohysterectomy, by L. Bisbiglio, et al. MINERVA GINECOLOGIA 37(10):617-619, October 1985.

Cefoxitin single dose prophylaxis and/or T tube suction drainage for vaginal and abdominal hysterectomy (prospective randomized trial on 155 patients), by V. Scotto, et al. CLINICAL AND EXPERIMENTAL OBSTETRICS AND GYNE-COLOGY 12(3-4):75-81, 1985.

Cesarean hysterectomy: indications, technique, and complications, by W. C. Plauché. CLINICAL OBSTETRICS AND GYNECOLOGY 29(2):318-328, June 1986.

Changes in bladder function in the woman undergoing radical hysterectomy for cervical cancer, by K. M. O'Laughlin. JOGN NURSING 15(5):380-385, September-October 1986.

Changes in symptoms and colpo-cystourethrography in 35 patients before and after total abdominal hysterectomy: a prospective study, by B. M. Hansen, et al. UROLOGIA INTERNATIONALIS 40(4):224-226, 1985.

Changes in urethral closure pressure after radical hysterectomy for cervical cancer, by F. Christ, et al. ARCHIVES OF GYNECOLOGY 237(2):93-99, 1985.

Colpopexy by fashioning prosthetic ligaments in the treatment of prolapse of the vaginal dome after total hysterectomy, by C. A. Bonini, et al. MINERVA GINECOLOGIA 38(3):155-161, March 1986.

Complications of combined radical hysterectomy and pelvic radiation, by J. C. Remy, et al. GYNECOLOGIC ONCOLOGY 24(3):317-326, July 1986.

Complications of the surgical treatment of invasive cervical cancer, by T. Zaczek, et al. GINEKOLOGIA POLSKA 57(2):144-147, February 1986.

Computed tomography of vaginal cuff cyst: a late complication of hysterectomy, by M. C. Davis, et al. JOURNAL OF COMPUTOR ASSISTED TOMOGRAPHY 10(2):354-356, March-April 1986.

Effect of beta-adrenergic stimulation on the bladder and urethra following radical hysterectomy, by R. H. Kerr-Wilson, et al. GYNECOLOGIC ONCOLOGY 23(3):267-274, March 1986.

Experience of the Obstetrics and Gynecology Department of the 1st Workers Hospital in Sofia in preventing vaginal prolapse in vaginal hysterectomy, by T. Bobchev. AKUSHERSTVO I GINEKOLOGIIA 25(3):58-61, 1986.

Femoral neuropathy subsequent to abdominal hysterectomy. A comparative study, by J. A. Goldman, et al. EUROPEAN JOURNAL OF OBSTETRICS, GYNECOLOGY AND REPRODUCTIVE BIOLOGY 20(6):385-392, December 1985.

Hysterectomy complicated by perforation of a duodenal ulcer, by M. Powolny, et al. GINEKOLOGIA POLSKA 56(12):770-772, December 1985.

Is hysterectomy a risk factor for vaginal cancer?, by J. M. Herman, et al. JAMA 256(5):601-603, August 1, 1986.

Labor in twin pregnancy complicated by anuria caused by ligation of both ureters during hysterectomy in atonia, by A. Musierowicz, et al. GINEKOLOGIA POLSKA 56(11):707-711 November 1985.

Lymphatic pseudocysts as a complication of operations using the Wertheim-Meigs method, by J. Zeilinski, et al. GINEKOLOGIA POLSKA 57(2):122-128, February 1986.

Mini-doses of heparin in the prevention of microcirculatory disorders in patients operated on for uterine and ovarian cancer, by I. Sh. Nadiradze. VESTNIK AKADEMII MEDITSINSKIKH NAUK SSSR (7):58-61, 1985.

Ovarian failure phenomena after hysterectomy, by H. H. Riedel, et al. JOURNAL OF REPRODUCTIVE MEDICINE 31(7):597-600, July 1986.

Peritonitis of genital origin. 32 cases, by E. Tiret, et al. ANNALES DE CHIRUR-GIE 39(8):585-591, November 1985.

Post-hysterectomy urethral dysfunction: evaluation and management, by S. A. Farghaly, et al. BRITISH JOURNAL OF UROLOGY 58(3):299-302, June 1986.

Postoperative thrombosis of the inferior mesenteric artey, by N. P. Kondrat'ev. KHIRURGIIA (6):107-109, June 1985.

Postoperative uretero-vaginal fistula in a duplicated excretory system, by P. Cortellini, et al. ACTA BIOMEDICA DE L'ATENEO PARMENSE 56(3):143-148, 1985.

Prophylactic single-dose co-trimoxazole for prevention of urinary tract infection after abdominal hysterectomy, by R. Jaffe, et al. CHEMOTHERAPY 31(6): 476-479, 1985.

Short term prophylactic antibiotic for elective abdominal hysterectomy: how short?, by R. Gonen, et al. EUROPEAN JOURNAL OF OBSTETRICS, GYNECOLOGY AND REPRODUCTIVE BIOLOGY 20(4):229-234, October 1985.

HYSTERECTOMY—COMPLICATIONS (continued)

Supravaginal uterine amputation versus hysterectomy with reference to subjective bladder symptoms and incontinence, by P. Kikku. ACTA OBSTETRICIA ET GYNECOLOGICA SCANDINAVICA 64(5):375-379, 1985.

Topography of urologic injuries in abdominal hysterectomy. Therapeutic indications, by M. Arrabal Martín, et al. ARCHIVOS ESPANOLESE DE UROLOGIA 39(1):13-21, January-February 1986.

Ureteral lesions in gynecological surgery, by R. H. Bengió, et al. REVISTA DE LA FACULTAD DE CIENCIAS MEDICAS/UNIVERSIDAD NACIONAL DE CORDOBA 42(3):22-27, 1984.

Urodynamic changes in urethrovesical function after radical hysterectomy, by R. J. Scotti, et al. OBSTETRICS AND GYNECOLOGY 68(1):111-120, July 1986.

Urologic complications in women operated on for cervical cancer, by W. Lotocki. GINEKOLOGIA POLSKA 57(1):72-77, January 1986.

HYSTERECTOMY—ECONOMICS
Variations in hysterectomy costs by region. STATISTICS BULLETIN OF THE METROPOLITAN LIFE INSURANCE COMPANY 66(3):10-17, July-September 1985.

HYSTERECTOMY—METHODS
Abdominoplasty combined with gynecologic surgical procedures, by C. Voss, et al. OBSTETRICS AND GYNECOLOGY 67(2):181-185, February 1986.

Avoiding ureteral injury during total vaginal hysterectomy, by S. H. Cruikshank. SOUTHERN MEDICAL JOURNAL 78(12):1447-1450, December 1985.

Bladder wall mechanics and micturition before and after subtotal and total hysterectomy, by O. Lalos, et al. EUROPEAN JOURNAL OF OBSTETRICS, GYNECOLOGY AND REPRODUCTIVE BIOLOGY 21(3):143-150, March 1986.

Clinical and roentgenographic evaluation of the Cooper ligament suspension operation in treating vaginal vault prolapse (analysis of 24 cases), by W. Q. Shao. CHUNG HUA FU CHAN KO TSA CHIH 20(6):349-353+, November 1985.

Complications and results of Wertheim's operation performed for the treatment of uterine cancer, by J. Lansac, et al. JOURNAL DE CHIRURGIE 122(12):681-687, December 1985.

Determination of the volume of surgical intervention in cancer of the corpus uteri, by O. L. Smakhtina, et al. VOPROSY ONKOLOGII 32(3):86-88, 1986.

Evaluation of intrafascial hysterectomy by the Aldridge and Meredith methods modified by us, by J. Woyton. GINEKOLOGIA POLSKA 56(5-6):310-315, May-June 1985.

Hysterectomy. Methods of the Miami University Clinic, by H. E. Averette, et al. GYNAKOLOGE 19(2):70-78, June 1986.

Hysterocolpectomy in prolapse of the uterus in the elderly woman, by A. Lozano Elizondo, et al. GINECOLOGIA Y OBSTETRICIA DE MEXICO 53:171-173, June 1985.

HYSTERECTOMY—METHODS (continued)

Intramyometrial coring as an adjunct to vaginal hysterectomy, by S. R. Kovac. OBSTETRICS AND GYNECOLOGY 67(1):131-136, January 1986.

Methods for improving the efficacy of total hysterectomy performed at the Obstetrics and Gynecology Department of the 1st Workers Hospital in Sofia, by T. Bobchev. AKUSHERSTVO I GINEKOLOGIIA 25(3):61-66, 1986.

Operation of functional maintenance in myoma uteri, by K. Takahashi. NIPPON SANKA FUJINKA GAKKAI ZASSHI 38(6):971-975, June 1986.

Partial colpocleisis, by C. F. Langmade, et al. AMERICAN JOURNAL OF OB-STETRICS AND GYNECOLOGY 154(6):1200-1205, June 1986.

Preservation of the ovary [letter], by A. H. DeCherney, et al. FERTILITY AND STERILITY 45(5):738-741, May 1986.

Primary surgical therapy of uterine cancer, by B. U. Sevin. GYNAKOLOGE 19(2): 88-93, June 1986.

Prophylactic antibiotics in patients undergoing total vaginal or abdominal hysterectomy, by J. G. Tchabo, et al. INTERNATIONAL SURGERY 70(4):349-352, October-December 1985.

Prophylactic posterior culdoplasty [letter], by B. Piura. AMERICAN JOURNAL OF OBSTETRICS AND GYNECOLOGY 155(3):685-686, September 1986.

Results of the combined treatment of cervical cancer (surgical data of the District Satellite Hospital in Olsztyn 1975-1982), by T. Dobielinska-Eliszewska, et al. GINEKOLOGIA POLSKA 57(2):148-150, February 1986.

Surgical method of identifying the ureters during total vaginal hysterectomy, by S. H. Cruikshank. OBSTETRICS AND GYNECOLOGY 67(2):277-280, February 1986.

Total abdominal hysterectomy after radiation therapy for cervical cancer: use of omental graft for fistula prevention, by W. M. Petty, et al. AMERICAN JOUR-NAL OF OBSTETRICS AND GYNECOLOGY 154(6):1222-1226, June 1986.

Total abdominal hysterectomy. Perioperative patient care, by M. P. Wells, et al. AORN JOURNAL 42(3):368-373, September 1985.

Vaginal hysterectomy by means of morcellation, by P. Draca. EUROPEAN JOUR-NAL OF OBSTETRICS, GYNECOLOGY AND REPRODUCTIVE BIOLOGY 22(4):237-242, August 1986.

HYSTERECTOMY—NURSES AND NURSING
Patient care plan . . . abdominal hysterectomy, by C. Talbert. AD NURSE 1(3):26-29, May 1986.

HYSTERECTOMY—PSYCHOLOGY AND PSYCHIATRY
Analysis on the psychological implications of the intervention of hysterectomy for benign pathology, by A. Filiberti, et al. ANNALI DI OSTETRICIA GINECOLO-GIA MEDICINA PERINATALE 106(2):111-115, March-April 1985.

Cognitive methods of preparing women for hysterectomy: does a booklet help?, by L. Young, et al. BRITISH JOURNAL OF CLINICAL PSYCHOLOGY 24(pt 4):303-304, November 1985.

HYSTERECTOMY—PSYCHOLOGY AND PSYCHIATRY (continued)

Hidden problems after a hysterectomy, by D. Gould. NURSING TIMES 82(23):43-46, June 4-10, 1986.

Hysterectomy and tubal ligation, by M. Ryan, et al. ADVANCES IN PSYCHO-SOMATIC MEDICINE 15:180-198, 1986.

Personal control interventions: short- and long-term effects on surgical patients . . . coping with . . . hysterectomy, by J. E. Johnson, et al. RESEARCH IN NURSING AND HEALTH 8(2):131-145, June 1985.

Professional and lay social support for hysterectomy patients, by C. Webb. JOURNAL OF ADVANCED NURSING 11(2):167-177, March 1986.

Psychological effects of the preoperative informative session in patients undergoing hysterectomy, by R. Speranza, et al. MINERVA ANESTESIOLOGICA 52(3-4):67-73, March-April 1986.

Psychological meaning of mastectomy and surgical removal of the inner reproductive organs, by A. E. Bernstein. JOURNAL OF THE AMERICAN MEDICAL WOMEN'S ASSOCIATION 40(6):178-180, November-December 1985.

Psychological sequelae of hysterectomy, by Z. Jindrová, et al. CESKOSLOVEN-SKA GYNEKOLOGIE 51(6):415-419, July 1986.

Risk of psychological consequences in hysterectomy: a guide for normal clinical routine, by A. M. Cunio, et al. CHIRURGIA ITALIANA 38(2):201-205, April 1986.

HYSTERECTOMY—SOCIOLOGY
Professional and lay social support for hysterectomy patients, by C. Webb. JOURNAL OF ADVANCED NURSING 11(2):167-177, March 1986.

HYSTERECTOMY AND PHYSICIANS
Hysterectomy and sex of the gynecologist [letter], by G. Domenighetti, et al. NEW ENGLAND JOURNAL OF MEDICINE 313(23):1482, December 5, 1985.

PLANNED PARENTHOOD FEDERATION OF AMERICA
How planned parenthood won in Arkansas (ran two controversial commercials against abortion referendum). HUMAN EVENTS 46:5, November 22, 1986.

My church threw me out (executive director of Planned Parenthood of Rhode Island excommunicated by Catholic Church), ed. by M. Orth, et al. REDBOOK 167:14+, June 1986.

Planned parenthood federation of America: its role as provider of information services, by G. A. Roberts. BEHAVORIAL AND SOCIAL SCIENCES LIBRARIAN 4(4):35-42, Summer 1985.

Truth in advertising, please ("abortion rights" ads). AMERICA 154:1, January 4-11, 1986.

POPULATION CONTROL
Plato redivivus (eugenic program of *Republic* 5 and modern population control practices), by H. J. Vogt. THEOLOGISCHE QUARTALSCHRIFT 166(1):56-58, 1986.

PRO-CHOICE MOVEMENT

See also: Abortion Rights Groups

Patterns of collective action in the abortion conflict: an organizational analysis of the pro-choice movement, by S. Staggenborg. DAI: A 46(11):3495A, May 1986.

Pro-choice leader runs for president of Ontario NDP; interview of Pat Brighouse, by J. Rebick. CANADIAN DIMENSION 20:37-38, July-August 1986.

Pro-choice or pro-life, by J. South. NEW STATESMAN 110:10-12+, November 15, 1985.

Pro-choices cry foul: Saskatchewan feminists accuse a minister of making abortions difficult, by L. Cohen. ALBERTA REPORT 13:22, April 21, 1986.

Pro-life or pro-choice: is there a credible alternative?, by S. Andre. SOCIAL THEORY AND PRACTICE 12:223-240, Summer 1986.

Seeking common ground (pro-life and pro-choice partisans find ways to work together), by C. Bass, et al. CONNECTICUT MAGAZINE 49:58+, March 1986.

Strident scream: alarmed abortion patients tell all in a "pro-choice" film, by T. Gallagher, et al. ALBERTA REPORT 13:45, March 17, 1986.

PRO-LIFE MOVEMENT
Inside a right-to-life mind, by J. A. Hennessee. MADEMOISELLE 92:173+, April 1986.

Marketing anti-abortion as pro-life, by J. Allegretti. NATIONAL CATHOLIC REPORTER 19:3, January 21, 1983.

Maureen's choice: McTeer's new abortion job is disgusting to pro-lifers. ALBERTA REPORT 13:46-47, February 10, 1986.

Pro-choice or pro-life, by J. South. NEW STATESMAN 110:10-12+, November 15, 1985.

Pro-life or pro-choice: is there a credible alternative?, by S. Andre. SOCIAL THEORY AND PRACTICE 12:223-240, Summer 1986.

Pro-life price: Joe Borowski vows jail before he'll remove his sign, by B. Cansino. ALBERTA REPORT 12:24-25, October 14, 1985.

Pro-lifers give birth to phony abortion clinics, by M. Neuberger. WOMANEWS 8:1, September 1986.

Pro-lifers subpoena a mayor: but Calgary's Klein appeals to quash the ploy, by G. Siegfried. ALBERTA REPORT 13:35-36, August 18, 1986.

Profile groups press opposition to Upjohn's abortion drugs, by K. A. Lawton. CHRISTIANITY TODAY 30(10):37, July 11, 1986.

Prolife leaders say 1986 has been a very good year, by R. Frame. CHRISTIANITY TODAY 30:30-31, November 21, 1986.

Rethinking pro-life issues [editorial]. NATIONAL CATHOLIC REPORTER 19:12, January 21, 1983.

PRO-LIFE MOVEMENT (continued)

Right to life and the restoration of the American republic, by L. Lehrman. NATIONAL REVIEW 38:25-28, August 29, 1986.

Right-to-lifers don't let facts get in way, by E. Bader. GUARDIAN 38(38):3, June 25, 1986.

Row at (North Vancouver)Lions gate: pro-lifers vs. the AG, by S. Weatherbe. ALBERTA REPORT 13:41-42, May 12, 1986.

Seeking common ground (pro-life and pro-choice partisans find ways to work together), by C. Bass, et al. CONNECTICUT MAGAZINE 49:58+, March 1986.

Selling chastity—the sly new attack on your sexual freedom (prolife pregnancy-testing centers masquerading as abortion clinics), by S. Bolotin. VOGUE 176:482-483+, March 1986.

16500 fetuses intensify fight in which they have no stake, by P. Edmonds. NATIONAL CATHOLIC REPORTER 19:1+, January 21, 1983.

RIGHT TO LIFE MOVEMENT
    See: Pro-Life Movement

SEX AND SEXUALITY—GENERAL
    Age of sexual consent, by R. F. Kourany, et al. BULLETIN OF THE AMERICAN ACADEMY OF PSYCHIATRY AND THE LAW 14(2):171-176, 1986.

    Alcohol consumption, female sexual behavior and contraceptive use, by S. M. Harvey, et al. JOURNAL OF STUDIES ON ALCOHOL 47(4):327-332, July 1986.

    Alcohol use, sexual intercourse, and contraception: an exploratory study, by B. J. Flanigan, et al. JOURNAL OF ALCOHOL AND DRUG EDUCATION 31:6-40, Spring 1986.

    Beyond privacy: sexual and reproductive freedom [editorial]. GAY COMMUNITY NEWS 14(13):4, October 12, 1986.

    Black male sexuality, by R. Staples. CHANGING MEN 17:3, Winter 1986.

    Changing sexual attitudes among university students: a geographic comparison . . . before and after taking a sexuality course, by M. E. Taylor. HEALTH ED-UCATION 14(5):23-26, September-October 1983.

    Epidemiology of urinary tract infection: diaphragm use and sexual intercourse. Part 1, by B. Foxman, et al. AMERICAN JOURNAL OF PUBLIC HEALTH 75(11):1308-1313, November 1985.

    Feminist movements and changes in sex roles: the influence of technology, by J. J. Kronenfeld, et al. SOCIOLOGICAL FOCUS 19(1):47-60, 1986.

    Frank discussion: sex and the Sandinistas, by I. Laboy. GUARDIAN 38(33):17, May 21, 1986.

    Growing yams and men: an interpretation of Kimam male ritualized homosexual behavior, by J. P. Gray. JOURNAL OF HOMOSEXUALITY 11(3-4):55-68, Summer 1985.

SEX AND SEXUALITY—GENERAL (continued)

Hormones, mood and sexuality in lactating women, by E. M. Alder, et al. BRITISH JOURNAL OF PSYCHIATRY 148:74-79, January 1986.

Human sexuality and sex education information service and library, by L. Hallingby. BEHAVIORAL AND SOCIAL SCIENCES LIBRARIAN 4(4):43-48, Summer 1985.

Husbands' sex-role preferences and contraceptive intentions: the case of the male pill, by W. Marsiglio. SEX ROLES 12(5-6):655-663, March 1985.

Implications of treatment on sex knowledge, sex attitudes and contraception of sexual liberal/conservative males, by L. M. Haverstock. DAI: A 47(3), September 1986.

Medical sequelae of unorthodox sexual behaviour, by J. S. Black. AUSTRALIAN FAMILY PHYSICIAN 15(1):20-22+, January 1986.

Partnership, sexuality and contraception in mentally handicapped humans, by H. Krebs. FORTSCHRITTE DER MEDIZIN 103(30):740-743, August 15, 1985.

Postpartum sexuality and contraception, by J. Richters. HEALTHRIGHT 5(2):25-27, February 1986.

Predicting contraceptive behavior among college students: the role of communication, knowledge, sexual anxiety, and self-esteem, by J. M. Burger, et al. ARCHIVES OF SEXUAL BEHAVIOR 14(4):343-350, August 1985.

Premarital sex: attitudes and behavior by dating stage, by J. P. Roche. ADOLESCENCE 21(81):107-121, Spring 1986.

Qualitative and quantitative strategies for exploring the progress of sex education for the handicapped . . . college sexuality, by M. E. Taylor. HEALTH EDUCATION 16(3):16-19, June-July 1985.

Reflections: taking sex out of sex education; an alternative approach to teaching human sexuality, by R. L. Gibson. HEALTH VALUES 10(2):43-46, March-April 1986.

Sex and male responsibility, by P. Grant. GLAMOUR 84:314, March 1986.

Sexual scripts: permanence and change, by W. Simon, et al. ARCHIVES OF SEXUAL BEHAVIOR 15(2):97-120, April 1986.

Sexuality and fertility among spinal cord and/or cauda equina injuries, by A. E. Comarr. JOURNAL OF THE AMERICAN PARAPLEGIA SOCIETY 8(4):67-75, October 1985.

Sexuality, contraception and health: the sexual stages of marriage. LADIES HOME JOURNAL 103(8):51-53, August 1986.

Sexually transmissible infectious agents in sexually active and virginal asymptomatic adolescent girls, by R. C. Bump, et al. PEDIATRICS 77(4):488-494, April 1986.

Taking a sexual history, by B. Donovan. AUSTRALIAN FAMILY PHYSICIAN 15(3):258, March 1986.

SEX AND SEXUALITY—COLLEGE STUDENTS

Coitally active university students: sexual behaviors, concerns, and challenges, by C. A. Darling, et al. ADOLESCENCE 21(82):403-419, Summer 1986.

Moral reasoning, parental sex attitudes, and sex guilt in female college students, by S. Propper, et al. ARCHIVES OF SEXUAL BEHAVIOR 15(4):331-340, August 1986.

Relationship between the sexual attitudes of parents and their college daughters' or sons' sexual attitudes and sexual behavior, by W. L. Yarber, et al. JOURNAL OF SCHOOL HEALTH 56(2):68-72, February 1986.

Relationship of childhood sexual abuse with later psychological and sexual adjustment in a sample of college women, by M. E. Fromuth. CHILD ABUSE AND NEGLECT 10(1):5-15, 1986.

SEX AND SEXUALITY—SOCIOLOGY

Determinants of sexual and dating behaviors among adolescents, by M. D. Newcomb, et al. JOURNAL OF PERSONALITY AND SOCIAL PSYCHOLOGY 50(2):428-438, February 1986.

SEX AND SEXUALITY—TEENS

Adolescent contraception: an update, by J. W. Kulig. PEDIATRICS 76(4 pt 2): 675-680, October 1985.

Adolescent sexuality: elements and genesis, by M. S. Calderone. PEDIATRICS 76(4 pt 2):699-703, October 1985.

Adolescent sexuality in a therapeutic community: staff countertransference issues, by S. Schneider, et al. ADOLESCENCE 20(78):369-376, Summer 1985.

Adolescents' values, sexuality, and contraception in a rural New York county, by N. McCormick, et al. ADOLESCENCE 20(78):385-395, Summer 1985.

American Academy of Pediatrics Committee on Adolescence: Sexuality, contraception, and the media. PEDIATRICS 78(3):535-536, September 1986.

Biosocial foundations for adolescent female sexuality, by J. R. Udry, et al. DEMOGRAPHY 23(2):217-230, May 1986.

Children having children: teen pregnancies are corroding America's social fabric, by C. Wallis, et al. TIME 126(23):79-82+, December 9, 1985.

Cognitive development and aspects of adolescent sexuality, by V. A. Pestrak, et al. ADOLESCENCE 20(80):981-987, Winter 1985.

Coital and noncoital sexual behaviors of white and black adolescents, by E. A. Smith, et al. AMERICAN JOURNAL OF PUBLIC HEALTH 75(10):1200-1203, October 1985.

Contraceptive self-efficacy: a perspective on teenage girls' contraceptive behavior, by R. A. Levinson. JOURNAL OF SEX RESEARCH 22(3):347-369, 1986.

Counseling the sexually active teenager: reflections from pediatric practice, by K. R. Sladkin. PEDIATRICS 76(4 pt 2):681-684, October 1985.

Determinants of sexual and dating behaviors among adolescents, by M. D. Newcomb, et al. JOURNAL OF PERSONALITY AND SOCIAL PSYCHOL-OGY 50(2):428-438, February 1986.

Developmental theory and adolescent sexual behavior, by C. L. Howe. NURSE PRACTITIONER 11(2):65+, February 1986.

Disabled teenagers: sexual identification and sexuality counseling, by J. M. McKown. SEXUALITY AND DISABILITY 7(1-2):17-27, Spring 1984-Summer 1986.

Effects of sex education on adolescent behavior, by D. A. Dawson. FAMILY PLANNING PERSPECTIVES 18(4):162-170, July-August 1986.

Health problems and sexual activity of selected inner city, middle school students, by P. B. Smith, et al. JOURNAL OF SCHOOL HEALTH 56(7):263-266, September 1986.

Impact of sex education on sexual activity, contraceptive use and premarital pregnancy among American teenagers, by W. Marsiglio, et al. FAMILY PLANNING PERSPECTIVES 18(4):151-154+, July-August 1985.

Link between sexual maturation and "adolescent grieving" in parents of the dependent disabled, by S. Smith. SEXUALITY AND DISABILITY 6(3-4):150-154, Fall-Winter 1983.

Management of sexual issues in adolescent treatment programs, by G. M. Realmuto, et al. ADOLESCENCE 21(82):347-356, Summer 1986.

Microbiology of the lower genital tact in postmenarchal adolescent girls: differences by sexual activity, contraception, and presence of nonspecific vaginitis, by M. A. Shafer, et al. JOURNAL OF PEDIATRICS 107(6):974-981, December 1985.

On the effects of sex education: a response to those who would say it promotes teenage pregnancy, by D. D. Adame. HEALTH EDUCATION 16(5):8-10, October-November 1985.

Parent-child communication and adolescent sexual behavior, by S. F. Newcomer, et al. FAMILY PLANNING PERSPECTIVES 17(4):169-174, July-August 1985.

Paths to adolescent parenthood: implications for prevention, by L. H. Flick. PUBLIC HEALTH REPORTS 101(2):132-147, March-April 1986.

Perceptions of sexual responsibility: do young men and women agree?, by M. K. Sheehan, et al. PEDIATRIC NURSING 12(1):17-21, January-February 1986.

Pubertal development and friends: a biosocial explanation of adolescent sexual behavior, by E. A. Smith, et al. JOURNAL OF HEALTH AND SOCIAL BEHAVIOR 26(3):183-192, September 1985.

Public policy and adolescent sexual behavior in the United States, by M. L. Finkel, et al. SOCIAL BIOLOGY 30:140-150, Summer 1983.

Role of health belief attitudes, sex education, and demographics in predicting adolescents' sexuality knowledge, by M. Eisen, et al. HEALTH EDUCATION QUARTERLY 13(1):9-22, Spring 1986.

SEX AND SEXUALITY—TEENS (continued)

Sex and young people: leaving them alone to cope is not the answer, by M. Howard. JOURNAL OF THE MEDICAL ASSOCIATION OF GEORGIA 75(3):151-154 March 1986.

Sex, drugs, rock 'n' roll: are solutions possible? [commentary], by V. C. Strasburger. PEDIATRICS 76(4 pt 20:704-712, October 1985.

—: understanding common teenage behavior. An adolescent medicine symposium, October 20, 1984 and April 2-5, 1985 [introduction], by V. C. Strasburger. PEDIATRICS 76(4 pt 2):659-712, October 1985.

Sex education and sexual experience among adolescents, by F. F. Furstenberg, Jr., et al. AMERICAN JOURNAL OF PUBLIC HEALTH 75(11):1331-1332, November 1985.

Sexual activity in girls under 16 years of age, by S. L. Barron. BRITISH JOURNAL OF OBSTETRICS AND GYNAECOLOGY 93(8):787-793, August 1986.

Sexual behavior, contraceptive practice, and reproductive health among Nigerian adolescents, by D. Nichols, et al. STUDIES IN FAMILY PLANNING 17(2):100-106, March-April 1986.

Sexuality and the adolescent with cancer, by P. M. Klopovich, et al. SEMINARS IN ONCOLOGY NURSING 1(1):42-48, February 1985.

Targeting the adolescent male, by E. Pitt. JOURNAL OF COMMUNITY HEALTH 11(1):45-48, Spring 1986.

Teenagers talk about sex, pregnancy and contraception, by E. E. Kiser. FAMILY PLANNING PERSPECTIVES 17(2):83-90, March-April 1985.

Tragic costs of teen-age pregnancy, by C. Wallis. READERS DIGEST 128(768): 99-104, April 1986.

Youth in the 1980s: social and health concerns. POPULATION REPORTS (9):M349-M388, November-December 1985.

SEX EDUCATION
Importance of sex education topics: correlates with teacher characteristics and inclusion of topics in instruction, by W. L. Yarber, et al. HEALTH EDUCATION 15(1):36-41, January-February 1984.

New York City school system's family life education program, by S. Schecter. JOURNAL OF COMMUNITY HEALTH 11(1):54-57, Spring 1986.

Reflections: taking sex out of sex education; an alternative approach to teaching human sexuality, by R. L. Gibson. HEALTH VALUES 10(2):43-46, March-April 1986.

Role of a sexuality division in a public health agency, by L. Lathrop. AARN NEWSLETTER 41(10):15-16, November 1985.

Sex education and the educational administrator: a Canadian health educator's perspective, by K. A. Noble. HEALTH EDUCATION 17(3):20-23, June-July 1986.

Sex education and health education: the evolution of a graduate program, by M. V. Hamburg. HEALTH EDUCATION 16(4):7-10, August-September 1985.

SEX EDUCATION (continued)

Sex education bowl game, by C. Stivers. HEALTH EDUCATION 17(4):36, August-September 1986.

Sex education: fact or fiction?, by D. MacIntosh. CURATIONIS 8(4):24-26, December 1985.

Sex education laws and policies. STUDIES IN FAMILY PLANNING 16(4):219, July-August 1985.

Sex education mandates: are they the answer?, by L. D. Muraskin. FAMILY PLANNING PERSPECTIVES 18(4):171-174, July-August 1986.

Sexual responsibility: examining relationships, by H. R. Travis. HEALTH EDUCATION 17(4):34-35, August-September 1986.

Sexuality education: a more realistic view of its effects, by D. Kirby. JOURNAL OF SCHOOL HEALTH 55(10):421-424, December 1985.

Two o-clock: contraception. ECONOMIST November 15, 1986, pp. 41-42.

Using the forced choice ladder in sexuality education, by R. D. Gutierrez. HEALTH EDUCATION 17(4):39, August-September 1986.

SEX EDUCATION AND CHILDREN
Grim ABC's of AIDS: a government report says children must be told about the disease, by B. Kantrowitz, et al. NEWSWEEK 108(18):66-67, November 3, 1986.

SEX EDUCATION AND COLLEGE STUDENTS
Assessing the need for education on sex and contraception among southern college freshmen, by Y. Iyriboz, et al. COLLEGE STUDENT JOURNAL 19:261-264, Fall 1985.

Changing sexual attitudes among university students: a geographic comparison . . . before and after taking a sexuality course, by M. E. Taylor. HEALTH EDUCATION 14(5):23-26, September-October 1983.

Liberal studies . . . sex curricula in schools of nursing, by J. Kuczynski. NURSING TIMES 82(28):60-61, July 9-15, 1986.

Predicting contraceptive behavior among college students: the role of communi- cation, knowledge, sexual anxiety, and self-esteem, by J. M. Burger, et al. ARCHIVES OF SEXUAL BEHAVIOR 14(4):343-350, August 1985.

Qualitative and quantitative strategies for exploring the progress of sex education for the handicapped . . . college sexuality, by M. E. Taylor. HEALTH EDUCA- TION 16(3):16-19, June-July 1985.

Relationship between the sexual attitudes of parents and their college daughters' or sons' sexual attitudes and sexual behavior, by W. L. Yarber, et al. JOUR- NAL OF SCHOOL HEALTH 56(2):68-72, February 1986.

SEX EDUCATION AND THE HANDICAPPED
Qualitative and quantitative strategies for exploring the progress of sex education for the handicapped . . . college sexuality, by M. E. Taylor. HEALTH EDUCA- TION 16(3):16-19, June-July 1985.

Actions teach better than words: Teen Life Theater and role play in sex education, by P. Brick. HEALTH EDUCATION 17(1):47-50, February-March 1986.

"Are sperm different colors?" . . . working with young males in the area of sexuality education, by S. Norfleet. CHILDREN TODAY 14(6):14-17, November-December 1985.

Counseling the sexually active teenager: reflections from pediatric practice, by K. R. Sladkin. PEDIATRICS 76(4 pt 2):681-684, October 1985.

Disabled teenagers: sexual identification and sexuality counseling, by J. M. McKown. SEXUALITY AND DISABILITY 7(1-2):17-27, Spring 1984-Summer 1986.

Effects of formal sex education on adolescent intercourse, contraception and pregnancy in the United States, by D. A. Dawson. DAI: A 47(4), October 1986.

Effects of sex education on adolescent behavior, by D. A. Dawson. FAMILY PLANNING PERSPECTIVES 18(4):162-170, July-August 1986.

Grim ABC's of AIDS: a government report says children must be told about the disease, by B. Kantrowitz, et al. NEWSWEEK 108(18):66-67, November 3, 1986.

Impact of sex education on sexual activity, contraceptive use and premarital pregnancy among American teenagers, by W. Marsiglio, et al. FAMILY PLANNING PERSPECTIVES 18(4):151-154+, July-August 1985.

Implications for adolescent sex education in Taiwan, by G. P. Cernada, et al. STUDIES IN FAMILY PLANNING 17(4):181-187, July-August 1986.

On the effects of sex education: a response to those who would say it promotes teenage pregnancy, by D. D. Adame. HEALTH EDUCATION 16(5):8-10, October-November 1985.

Parent-child communication and adolescent sexual behavior, by S. F. Newcomer, et al. FAMILY PLANNING PERSPECTIVES 17(4):169-174, July-August 1985.

Public policy and public opinion toward sex education and birth control for teenagers, by P. A. Reichelt. JOURNAL OF APPLIED SOCIAL PSYCHOLOGY 16(2):95-106, 1986.

Services and educational approaches to adolescent pregnancy, by S. Harris. JOURNAL OF COMMUNITY HEALTH 11(1):31-34, Spring 1986.

Sex and young people: leaving them alone to cope is not the answer, by M. Howard. JOURNAL OF THE MEDICAL ASSOCIATION OF GEORGIA 75(3):151-154 March 1986.

Sex education and sexual experience among adolescents, by F. F. Furstenberg, Jr., et al. AMERICAN JOURNAL OF PUBLIC HEALTH 75(11):1331-1332, November 1985.

Sex-education needs and interests of high school students in a rural New York county, by N. McCormick, et al. ADOLESCENCE 20(79):581-592, Fall 1985.

SEXUALLY TRANSMITTED DISEASES

Confidentiality, the law in England, and sexually transmitted diseases, by M. D. Talbot. GENITOURINARY MEDICINE 62(4):270-276, August 1986.

Grim ABC's of AIDS: a government report says children must be told about the disease, by B. Kantrowitz, et al. NEWSWEEK 108(18):66-67, November 3, 1986.

Humoral immune responses in healthy heterosexual, homosexual and vasectomized men and in homosexual men with the acquired immune deficiency syndrome, by S. S. Witkin, et al. AIDS RESEARCH 1(1):31-44, 1983-1984.

Screening for sexually transmitted diseases by family planning providers: is it adequate and appropriate?, by S. O. Aral, et al. FAMILY PLANNING PERSPECTIVES 18:255-258, November-December 1986.

Sex transmits AIDS. ECONOMIST 300:14, July 5, 1986.

Sexually transmitted diseases [letter], by H. W. Horne, Jr. FERTILITY AND STERILITY 46(1):157-158, July 1986.

Sexually transmitted diseases in sub-Saharan Africa. A priority list based on Family Health International's Meeting, by M. J. Rosenbert, et al. LANCET 2(8499):152-153, July 19, 1986.

SEXUALLY TRANSMITTED DISEASES—PREVENTION
Condoms and the prevention of AIDS [letter]. JAMA 256(11):1442-1443, September 19, 1986.

Condoms prevent transmission of AIDS-associated retrovirus [letter], by M. Conant, et al. JAMA 255(13):1706, April 4, 1986.

Reducing the risk of acquiring AIDS . . . the condom, by M. S. Tillis. AAOHN JOURNAL 34(9):432-434, September 1986.

Rubber barons (rise in condom sales due to AIDS scare), by C. Leinster. FORTUNE 114:105-106+, November 24, 1986.

Sex transmits AIDS. ECONOMIST 300:14, July 5, 1986.

STERILIZATION—GENERAL
Contraceptive sterilization in Puerto Rico, by C. W. Warren, et al. DEMOGRAPHY 23:351-365, August 1986.

Contraceptive use in Canada, 1984, by T. R. Balakrishnan, et al. FAMILY PLANNING PERSPECTIVES 17(5):209-215, September-October 1985.

Current status of actions for wrongful life and wrongful birth, by S. Taub. LEGAL MEDICINE 1985, pp. 180-195.

Family planning: fertility rights, by R. Shapiro. NURSING TIMES 82(5):24-25, January 29-February 4, 1986.

Incentives and disincentives in the Indian family welfare program, by J. K. Satia, et al. STUDIES IN FAMILY PLANNING 17(3):136-145, May-June 1986.

Issues in contraceptive development. POPULATION 15:1, May 1985.

STERILIZATION—GENERAL (continued)

Last word on contraception. US NEWS AND WORLD REPORT 100:43, May 26, 1986.

Medico-legal risks of human voluntary sterilization, by P. LeQuinquis, et al. REVUE FRANCAISE DE GYNECOLOGIE ET D'OBSTETRIQUE 81(1):51-52, January 1986.

Modern contraceptive practice in rural Appalachia, by G. A. Gairola, et al. AMERICAN JOURNAL OF PUBLIC HEALTH 76(8):1004-1008, August 1986.

New advances in contraception and sterilization, by L. Iglesias Cortit. MEDICINA CLINICA 85(14):588-595, November 2, 1985.

Next contraceptive revolution, by L. E. Atkinson, et al. FAMILY PLANNING PERSPECTIVES 18(1):19-26, January-February 1986.

SIDS might influence sterilisation plans [letter], by S. Lurie. AUSTRALIAN FAMILY PHYSICIAN 14(10):1001, October 1985.

Sporicidal properties of mixtures of hydrogen peroxide vapor and hot air, by J. Wang, et al. FOOD TECHNOLOGY 40:60+, December 1986.

Sterilization trends [editorial], by K. Wellings. BRITISH MEDICAL JOURNAL 292(6527):1029-1030, April 19, 1986.

Unnatural selection—menace of hi-tech motherhood, by G. Corea. PROGRESSIVE 50(1):22, January 1986.

What you should know about sterilization (views of Johanna Perlmutter), by K. Stout. McCALLS 113:80, april 1986.

Whopper salmon. OCEANS 19:4, September-October 1986.

AUSTRALIA
Fruitful lessons from "sterile" arguments . . . compensation . . . negligence, by B. Piesse. AUSTRALIAN NURSES' JOURNAL 15(11):52-54, June 1986.

BANGLADESH
Bangladesh is coerced into sterilisation, by G. Vines. NEW SCIENTIST 107: 20-21, September 19, 1985.

BRITISH COLUMBIA
Creation of a haven for "human thoroughbreds": the sterilization of the feeble-minded and the mentally ill in British Columbia, by A. McLaren. CANADIAN HISTORICAL REVIEW 67:127-150, June 1986.

CANADA
Tubal sterilization in Manitoba, by M. M. Cohen. CANADIAN JOURNAL OF PUBLIC HEALTH 77(2):114-118, March-April 1986.

GERMANY
Connections between eugenics, sterilization and mass murder in Germany from 1933 to 1945, by F. Pfäfflin. MEDICINE AND LAW 5(1):1-10, 1986.

MEXICO
Female anticonception by voluntary surgery in the Ministery of Health, 1981-

STERILIZATION—GENERAL (continued)

MEXICO (continued)
1984, by R. Vernon, et al. SALUD PUBLICA DE MEXICO 27(6):492-506, November-December 1985.

NEPAL
Recent changes in the sociodemographic profile of sterilization acceptors in Nepal, by E. N. McIntosh, et al. INTERNATIONAL JOURNAL OF GYNAE-COLOGY AND OBSTETRICS 23(5):405-411, October 1985.

PUERTO RICO
Contraceptive sterilization in Puerto Rico, by C. W. Warren, et al. DEMOGRA-PHY 23:351-365, August 1986.

THAILAND
Tubotubal anastomosis for reversal of female sterilization in Thailand, by K. Limpaphayom. JOURNAL OF REPRODUCTIVE MEDICINE 31(7):601-604, July 1986.

UNITED STATES
California law governing the sterilization of developmentally disabled persons changes course: Conservatorship of Valerie N. WILLIAMETTE LAW RE-VIEW 22:622-629, Fall 1986.

Reproductive impairments in the United States, 1965-1982, by W. D. Mosher. DEMOGRAPHY 22(3):415-430, August 1985.

Sterilization of incompetents and the "late probate court" in California: how bad law makes hard cases, by B. A. Goldberg. PACIFIC LAW JOURNAL 18:1-30, October 1986.

Sterilization remark draws fire from black solons (comment directed to welfare mothers in Virginia). JET 70:12 June 9, 1986.

STERILIZATION—ATTITUDES
Childfree by choice: attitudes and adjustment of sterilized women, by B. M. DeVellis, et al. POPULATION AND ENVIRONMENT: BEHAVIORAL AND SOCIAL ISSUES 7(3):152-162, Fall 1984.

Psychosocial factors influencing American men and women in their decision for sterilization, by G. M. Burnell, et al. JOURNAL OF PSYCHOLOGY 120(2): 113-119, March 1986.

STERILIZATION—COMPLICATIONS
Acute salpingitis subsequent to tubal ligation, by A. J. Phillips, et al. OBSTET-RICS AND GYNECOLOGY 67(3 suppl):55S-48S, March 1986..

Endometriosis after tubal ligation, by H. N. Fakih, et al. JOURNAL OF REPRO-DUCTIVE MEDICINE 30(12):939-941, December 1985.

STERILIZATION—COUNSELING
Counseling women who request sterilization: psychodynamic issues and inter-ventions, by I. Kohn. SOCIAL WORK IN HEALTH CARE 11(2):35-60, Winter 1985-1986.

Court not bound to accept test of competent medical practice in deciding wheth-er contraceptive counselling is negligent, by D. Brahams. LANCET 2(8503): 407-408, August 16, 1986.

STERILIZATION—ECONOMICS

Public funding of contraceptive, sterilization and abortion services, 1983, by R. B. Gold, et al. FAMILY PLANNING PERSPECTIVES 17:25-29, January-February 1985.

— 1985, by R. B. Gold, et al. FAMILY PLANNING PERSPECTIVES 18:259-264, November-December 1986.

STERILIZATION—FAILURE
Pregnancy and unwanted children after failure of sterilization and voluntary termination of pregnancy. I. Disconcerting French and foreign jurisprudence, by J. H. Soutoul, et al. JOURNAL DE GYNECOLOGIE, OBSTETRIQUE ET BIOLOGIE DE LA REPRODUCTION 15(3):273-279, 1986.

STERILIZATION—FEMALE
See also: Sterilization—Tubal

Allergic reaction to Hulka clips, by W. T. Trathen, et al. OBSTETRICS AND GYNE-COLOGY 66(5):743-744, November 1985.

Childfree by choice; attitudes and adjustment of sterilized women, by B. M. DeVellis, et al. POPULATION AND ENVIRONMENT: BEHAVIORAL AND SOCIAL ISSUES 7(3):152-162, Fall 1984.

Comparative clinical trial of the tubal ring versus the Rocket clip for female sterilization, by C. Aranda, et al. AMERICAN JOURNAL OF OBSTETRICS AND GYNECOLOGY 153(7):755-759, December 1, 1985.

Counseling women who request sterilization: psychodynamic issues and interventions, by I. Kohn. SOCIAL WORK IN HEALTH CARE 11(2):35-60, Winter 1985-1986.

Decision to terminate childbearing: differences in preoperative ambivalene between tubal ligation women and vasectomy wives, by R. N. Shain, et al. SOCIAL BIOLOGY 31(1-2):40-58, Spring-Summer 1984.

Psychological aspects of female sterilisation—assessment of subsequent regret, by S. E. Clarkson, et al. NEW ZEALAND MEDICAL JOURNAL 98(786):748-750, September 11, 1985.

Psychosocial factors influencing American men and women in their decision for sterilization, by G. M. Burnell, et al. JOURNAL OF PSYCHOLOGY 120(2): 113-119, March 1986.

Regret after sterilization in women, by H. M. Verner, et al. NEDERLANDS TIJDSCHRIFT VOOR GENEESKUNDE 130(9):410-413, March 1, 1986.

Report on voluntary sterilisation with special reference to minors and women who are intellectually disabled, by L. Vick, et al. CLINICAL REPRODUCTION AND FAMILY 3(2):99-106, June 1985.

Socio-biological parameters in relation to permanent sterilisation of parents, by K. L. Gupta, et al. INDIAN JOURNAL OF PEDIATRICS 52(419):655-661, November-December 1985.

Surgical sterilization: ten years' experience, by L. J. Flores Revuelta, et al. GINECOLOGIA Y OBSTETRICIA DE MEXICO 53:163-165, June 1985.

STERILIZATION—FEMALE (continued)

Torsion of the fallopian tube—a late complication of sterilisation, by V. Sivane-saratnam. SINGAPORE MEDICAL JOURNAL 27(1):72-73, February 1986.

Uterine rupture following tubal implantation, by H. Scharp. ZENTRALBLATT FUR GYNAEKOLOGIE 107(18):1139-1140, 1985.

Voluntary female sterilization (comments following a judgment by the Superior Appellate Court 5/9/83), by P. Y. Poirier, et al. REVUE FRANCAISE DE GYNECOLOGIE ET D'OBSTETRIQUE 81(2):111-112, February 1986.

What to tell patients about sterilization, by F. Pool, et al. RN 49(5):55-56+, May 1986.

STERILIZATION—FEMALE—COMPLICATIONS
Allergic reaction to Hulka clips, by W. T. Trathen, et al. OBSTETRICS AND GYNE-COLOGY 66(5):743-744, November 1985.

STERILIZATION—INDUCED
What to tell patients about sterilization, by F. Pool, et al. RN 49(5):55-56+, May 1986.

STERILIZATION—LAWS AND LEGISLATION
California law governing the sterilization of developmentally disabled persons changes course: Conservatorship of Valerie N. WILLIAMETTE LAW REVIEW 22:622-629, Fall 1986.

Court not bound to accept test of competent medical practice in deciding wheth-er contraceptive counselling is negligent, by D. Brahams. LANCET 2(8503): 407-408, August 16, 1986.

Court on tubal sterilization in 1985, by J. H. Soutoul, et al. JOURNAL DE GYNE-COLOGIE, OBSTETRIQUE ET BIOLOGIE DE LA REPRODUCTION 14(5): 551-560, 1985.

Failed female sterilization and the law, by V. P. Argent. MEDICINE, SCIENCE AND THE LAW 25(2):136-142, April 1985.

Fruitful lessons from "sterile" arguments . . . compensation . . . negligence, by B. Piesse. AUSTRALIAN NURSES' JOURNAL 15(11):52-54, June 1986.

Mom who killed one child wants sterilization as plea bargain in 2nds' death (case of D. A. Williams). JET 70:38, August 4, 1986.

Nurse and the law. Fruitful lessons from "sterile" arguments, by B. Piesse. AUS-TRALIAN NURSES JOURNAL 15(11):52-54, June 1986.

Sterilization of incompetents and the "late probate court" in California: how bad law makes hard cases, by B. A. Goldberg. PACIFIC LAW JOURNAL 18:1-30, October 1986.

Sterilization remark draws fire from black solons (comment directed to welfare mothers in Virginia). JET 70:12 June 9, 1986.

Woman is sterilized to get a lesser sentence (case of D. A. Williams). JET 70:36, August 11, 1986.

STERILIZATION—MALE
Decision to terminate childbearing: differences in preoperative ambivalence

STERILIZATION—MALE (continued)

between tubal ligation women and vasectomy wives, by R. N. Shain, et al. SOCIAL BIOLOGY 31(1-2):40-58, Spring-Summer 1984.

Effects of vasectomy on the structure of the testicle in the cat, by J. Nuñez, et al. ACTAS UROLOGICAS ESPANOLAS 10(1):61-64, January-February 1986.

Effects of vasectomy on the testis [editorial], by C. J. Flickinger. NEW ENGLAND JOURNAL OF MEDICINE 313(20):1283-1285, November 14, 1985.

Non-operative procedure to induce male sterility, by M. C. Dandapat, et al. JOURNAL OF THE INDIAN MEDICAL ASSOCIATION 83(10):363-365, October 1985.

Pregnancies after sterilization, by D. Brahams. LANCET 1(8481):627, March 15, 1986.

Psychosocial factors influencing American men and women in their decision for sterilization, by G. M. Burnell, et al. JOURNAL OF PSYCHOLOGY 120(2): 113-119, March 1986.

Recanalisation of vas, by A. B. Singh, et al. JOURNAL OF THE INDIAN MEDICAL ASSOCIATION 83(9):303-305, September 1985.

Risks of male sterilization, by B. von Rütte. THERAPEUTISCHE UMSCHAU 43(5):434-437, May 1986.

Socio-biological parameters in relation to permanent sterilisation of parents, by K. L. Gupta, et al. INDIAN JOURNAL OF PEDIATRICS 52(419):655-661, November-December 1985.

Twenty year experience with vasovasostomy, by H. Y. Lee. JOURNAL OF UROLOGY 136(2):413-415, August 1986.

What to tell patients about sterilization, by F. Pool, et al. RN 49(5):55-56+, May 1986.

Who has a vasectomy reversal?, by L. Clarke, et al. JOURNAL OF BIOSOCIAL SCIENCE 18(3):253-259, July 1986.

Why does vasectomy reversal fail?, by M. G. Royale, et al. BRITISH JOURNAL OF UROLOGY 57(6):780-783, December 1985.

STERILIZATION—METHODS

Comparative clinical trial of the tubal ring versus the Rocket clip for female sterilization, by C. Aranda, et al. AMERICAN JOURNAL OF OBSTETRICS AND GYNECOLOGY 153(7):755-759, December 1, 1985.

Comparative review of female sterilisation—tubal occlusion methods, by P. H. Chick, et al. CLINICAL REPRODUCTION AND FERTILITY 3(2):81-97, June 1985.

Day case vaginal pomeroy tubectomy; a simplified technique, by A. Bashir. JPMA 35(10):301-306, October 1985.

Early puerperal laparoscopic sterilization—a new technique, by S. V. Parulekar, et al. JOURNAL OF POSTGRADUATE MEDICINE 31(3):167-169, July 1985.

STERILIZATION—METHODS (continued)

Fallopian tube sterilization with stainless steel clips (report of 1127 cases), by H. L. Huang, et al. CHUNG HUA FU CHAN KO TSA CHIH 20(6):373-374, November 1985.

Laparoscopic tubal ligation under local anesthesia, by D. Massouda, et al. JOURNAL OF THE TENNESSEE MEDICAL ASSOCIATION 79(2):75-76, February 1986.

Non-operative procedure to induce male sterility, by M. C. Dandapat, et al. JOURNAL OF THE INDIAN MEDICAL ASSOCIATION 83(10):363-365, October 1985.

Pathological changes in fallopian tubes following three different kinds of occlusive techniques in primates, by A. N. Gupta, et al. CONTRACEPTION 33(3): 245-255, March 1986.

Preventing pregnancy with tubal ties . . . clips [pictorial], by A. Spiropoulos. TODAY'S OR NURSE 8(1):13-15, January 1986.

Sterilization failures with bipolar tubal cautery [letter], by K. Hausner. FERTILITY AND STERILITY 46(1):150, July 1986.

Tubal ligation with local anaesthesia, by P. Barss. TROPICAL DOCTOR 15(4): 175-179, October 1985.

Tubo-ovarian histofunctional study in the rabbit after bilateral isthmus tubal sterilization and subsequent reanastomosis, by A. Baffoni, et al. MINERVA GINECOLOGIA 38(3):193-199, March 1986.

Value of routine dilation and curettage at the time of interval sterilization, by E. D. Lichter, et al. OBSTETRICS AND GYNECOLOGY 67(6):763-765, June 1986.

STERILIZATION—NURSES AND NURSING
Preventing pregnancy with tubal ties . . . clips [pictorial], by A. Spiropoulos. TODAY'S OR NURSE 8(1):13-15, January 1986.

STERILIZATION—PSYCHOLOGY AND PSYCHIATRY
Characteristics, perceptions and personalities of women seeking a reversal of their tubal sterilization, by S. Abraham, et al. MEDICAL JOURNAL OF AUSTRALIA 145(1):4-7, July 7, 1986.

Counseling women who request sterilization: psychodynamic issues and interventions, by I. Kohn. SOCIAL WORK IN HEALTH CARE 11(2):35-60, Winter 1985-1986.

Decision to terminate childbearing: differences in preoperative ambivalence between tubal ligation women and vasectomy wives, by R. N. Shain, et al. SOCIAL BIOLOGY 31(1-2):40-58, Spring-Summer 1984.

Female sterilization: can the woman who will seek reversal be identified prospectively?, by P. J. Taylor, et al. CLINICAL REPRODUCTION AND FERTILITY 4(3):207-215, June 1986.

Hysterectomy and tubal ligation, by M. Ryan, et al. ADVANCES IN PSYCHO-SOMATIC MEDICINE 15:180-198, 1986.

STERILIZATION—PSYCHOLOGY AND PSYCHIATRY (continued)

Married women and contraceptive sterilization: factors that contribute to pre-surgical ambivalence, by W. B. Miller, et al. JOURNAL OF BIOSOCIAL SCIENCE 17(4):471-479, October 1985.

Psychological adjustment to and recovery from laparoscopic sterilization and infertility investigation, by L. M. Wallace. JOURNAL OF PSYCHOSOMATIC RESEARCH 29(5):507-518, 1985.

Psychological aspects of female sterilisation—assessment of subsequent regret, by S. E. Clarkson, et al. NEW ZEALAND MEDICAL JOURNAL 98(786):748-750, September 11, 1985.

Psychosocial and psychophysiologic aspects of reproduction: the need for improved study design, by L. R. Ellsworth, et al. FERTILITY AND STERILITY 44(4):449-452, October 1985.

Regret after sterilization in women, by H. M. Vemer, et al. NEDERLANDS TIJDSCHRIFT VOOR GENEESKUNDE 130(9):410-413, March 1, 1986.

Regrets after tubal sterilization [editorial], by J. Couper-Smartt. MEDICAL JOURNAL OF AUSTRALIA 145(1):2-3, July 7, 1986.

Socio-biological parameters in relation to permanent sterilisation of parents, by K. L. Gupta, et al. INDIAN JOURNAL OF PEDIATRICS 52(419):655-661, November-December 1985.

STERILIZATION—RESEARCH

Absorbable or nonabsorbable suture material for microsurgical tubal anastomosis. Randomized experimental study on rabbits, by P. H. Scheidel, et al. GYNECOLOGIC AND OBSTETRIC INVESTIGATION 21(2):96-102, 1986.

Effects of the chemosterilant ornitrol on the nesting success of red-winged blackbirds, by D. Lacombe, et al. JOURNAL OF APPLIED ECOLOGY 23:773-779, December 1986.

Evaluation of a non-surgical technique for sterilising rams, by A. R. Mercy, et al. AUSTRALIAN VETERINARY JOURNAL 62(10):350-352, October 1985.

Laboratory evaluation of bisazir as a practical chemosterilan for the control of tsetse, Glossina spp. (diptera: glossinidae), by P. A. Langley, et al. BULLETIN OF ENTOMOLOGICAL RESEARCH 76:583-592, December 1986.

Pathological changes in fallopian tubes following three different kinds of occlusive techniques in primates, by A. N. Gupta, et al. CONTRACEPTION 33(3):245-255, March 1986.

STERILIZATION—SOCIOLOGY

Childfree by choice: attitudes and adjustment of sterilized women, by B. M. DeVellis, et al. POPULATION AND ENVIRONMENT: BEHAVIORAL AND SOCIAL ISSUES 7(3):152-162, Fall 1984.

Psychosocial and psychophysiologic aspects of reproduction: the need for improved study design, by L. R. Ellsworth, et al. FERTILITY AND STERILITY 44(4):449-452, October 1985.

Psychosocial factors influencing American men and women in their decision for sterilization, by G. M. Burnell, et al. JOURNAL OF PSYCHOLOGY 120(2):113-119, March 1986.

STERILIZATION—SOCIOLOGY (continued)

Recent changes in the sociodemographic profile of sterilization acceptors in Nepal, by E. N. McIntosh, et al. INTERNATIONAL JOURNAL OF GYNAE-COLOGY AND OBSTETRICS 23(5):405-411, October 1985.

STERILIZATION—STATISTICS

Laparoscopic tubal sterilization combined with removal of an intrauterine contraceptive device. A report of 49 cases, by J. S. Seiler. JOURNAL OF REPRODUCTIVE MEDICINE 31(5):339-342, May 1986.

Salpingoclasia by laparoscopy using silastic rings. Comparative analysis of 1,500 cases, by A. Kably Ambe, et al. GINECOLOGIA Y OBSTETRICIA DE MEXICO 53:341-344, December 1985.

STERILIZATION—TUBAL

Acute salpingitis subsequent to tubal ligation, by A. J. Phillips, et al. OBSTETRICS AND GYNECOLOGY 67(3 suppl):55S-48S, March 1986..

Changes in menstrual pattern following tubal ligation, by G. Rosales Estrada. GINECOLOGIA Y OBSTETRICIA DE MEXICO 53:167-169, June 1985.

Characteristics, perceptions and personalities of women seeking a reversal of their tubal sterilization, by S. Abraham, et al. MEDICAL JOURNAL OF AUSTRALIA 145(1):4-7, July 7, 1986.

Comparative clinical trial of the tubal ring versus the Rocket clip for female sterilization, by C. Aranda, et al. AMERICAN JOURNAL OF OBSTETRICS AND GYNECOLOGY 153(7):755-759, December 1, 1985.

Comparative review of female sterilisation—tubal occlusion methods, by P. H. Chick, et al. CLINICAL REPRODUCTION AND FERTILITY 3(2):81-97, June 1985.

Comprehensive review of female sterilisation—tubal occlusion methods, by P. H. Chick, et al. CLINICAL REPRODUCTION AND FERTILITY 3(2):81-97, June 1985.

Computed tomography of hydrosalpinx following tubal ligation, by K. Togashi, et al. JOURNAL OF COMPUTER ASSISTED TOMOGRAPHY 10(1):78-80, January-February 1986.

Counseling women who request sterilization: psychodynamic issues and interventions, by I. Kohn. SOCIAL WORK IN HEALTH CARE 11(2):35-60, Winter 1985-1986.

Court on tubal sterilization in 1985, by J. H. Soutoul, et al. JOURNAL DE GYNECOLOGIE, OBSTETRIQUE ET BIOLOGIE DE LA REPRODUCTION 14(5): 551-560, 1985.

Day case vaginal pomeroy tubectomy; a simplified technique, by A. Bashir. JPMA 35(10):301-306, October 1985.

Decision to terminate childbearing: differences in preoperative ambivalence between tubal ligation women and vasectomy wives, by R. N. Shain, et al. SOCIAL BIOLOGY 31(1-2):40-58, Spring-Summer 1984.

Early puerperal laparoscopic sterilization—a new technique, by S. V. Parulekar, et al. JOURNAL OF POSTGRADUATE MEDICINE 31(3):167-169, July 1985.

Effects of cortisol suppression by etomidate on changes in circulating metabolites associated with pelvic surgery, by S. Lacoumenta, et al. ACTA ANAESTHESIOLOGICA SCANDINAVICA 30(1):101-104, January 1986.

Effects of meclofenamate and acetaminophen on abdominal pain following tubal occlusion, by K. C. Huang, et al. AMERICAN JOURNAL OF OBSTETRICS AND GYNECOLOGY 155(3):625-629, September 1986.

Endometriosis after tubal ligation, by H. N. Fakih, et al. JOURNAL OF REPRODUCTIVE MEDICINE 30(12):939-941, December 1985.

Failed female sterilization and the law, by V. P. Argent. MEDICINE, SCIENCE AND THE LAW 25(2):136-142, April 1985.

Fallopian tube sterilization with stainless steel clips (report of 1127 cases), by H. L. Huang, et al. CHUNG HUA FU CHAN KO TSA CHIH 20(6):373-374, November 1985.

Family planning. Fertility rights, by R. Shapiro. NURSING TIMES 82(5):24-28, January 29-February 4, 1986.

Female anticonception by voluntary surgery in the Ministery of Health, 1981-1984, by R. Vernon, et al. SALUD PUBLICA DE MEXICO 27(6):492-506, November-December 1985.

Female sterilization: can the woman who will seek reversal be identified prospectively?, by P. J. Taylor, et al. CLINICAL REPRODUCTION AND FERTILITY 4(3):207-215, June 1986.

Halting St. Paul's tubals: an RC hospital says no to casual sterilization, by L. Cohen. ALBERTA REPORT 13:50, October 27, 1986.

Hysterectomy and tubal ligation, by M. Ryan, et al. ADVANCES IN PSYCHOSOMATIC MEDICINE 15:180-198, 1986.

Hysterectomy performed within one year after tubal sterilization, by J. S. Kendrick, et al. FERTILITY AND STERILITY 44(5):606-610, November 1985.

Laparoscopic sterilization in camps and institutional set-up, by P. N. Mhatre, et al. JOURNAL OF POSTGRAUDATE MEDICINE 31(1):20-23, January 1985.

Laparoscopic tubal ligation under local anesthesia, by D. Massouda, et al. JOURNAL OF THE TENNESSEE MEDICAL ASSOCIATION 79(2):75-76, February 1986.

Laparoscopic tubal sterilization combined with removal of an intrauterine contraceptive device. A report of 49 cases, by J. S. Seiler. JOURNAL OF REPRODUCTIVE MEDICINE 31(5):339-342, May 1986.

Laparoscopic tubal sterilization: methodologic progress by the use of a so-called coagulotome, by L. Moltz, et al. GEBURTSHILFE UND FRAUENHEILKUNDE 45(12):901-905, December 1985.

Luteal phase pregnancy and tubal sterilization, by G. S. Grubb, et al. OBSTETRICS AND GYNECOLOGY 66(6):784-788, December 1985.

STERILIZATION—TUBAL (continued)

Married women and contraceptive sterilization: factors that contribute to pre-surgical ambivalence, by W. B. Miller, et al. JOURNAL OF BIOSOCIAL SCI-ENCE 17(4):471-479, October 1985.

Married women's dissatisfaction with tubal sterilization and vasectomy at first-year follow-up: effects of perceived spousal dominance, by R. N. Shain, et al. FERTILITY AND STERILITY 45(6):808-819, June 1986.

Microsurgical reversal of sterilization: a six-year study, by M. M. Spivak, et al. AMERICAN JOURNAL OF OBSTETRICS AND GYNECOLOGY 154(2):355-361, February 1986.

Microsurgical tubal anastomosis, by G. Rosa, et al. REVISTA CHILENA DE OB-STETRICIA Y GINECOLOGIA 50(1):67-71, 1985.

Pathological changes in fallopian tubes following three different kinds of occlu-sive techniques in primates, by A. N. Gupta, et al. CONTRACEPTION 33(3): 245-255, March 1986.

Postpartum sterilization in a program of medical training, by J. G. Andrade Zamora, et al. GINECOLOGIA Y OBSTETRICIA DE MEXICO 54:148-151, June 1986.

Postpartum tubal ligation requires more bupivacaine for spinal anesthesia than does cesarean section, by E. I. Abouleish. ANESTHESIA AND ANALGESIA 65(8):897-900, August 1986.

Poststerilisation tubal pregnancy, by K. Jha, et al. JOURNAL OF THE INDIAN MEDICAL ASSOCIATION 83(20:70-71+, February 1985.

Preventing pregnancy with tubal ties . . . clips [pictorial], by A. Spiropoulos. TODAY'S OR NURSE 8(1):13-15, January 1986.

Psychological adjustment to and recovery from laparoscopic sterilization and infertility investigation, by L. M. Wallace. JOURNAL OF PSYCHOSOMATIC RESEARCH 29(5):507-518, 1985.

Psychosocial factors influencing American men and women in their decision for sterilization, by G. M. Burnell, et al. JOURNAL OF PSYCHOLOGY 120(2): 113-119, March 1986.

Rare events associated with tubal sterilizations: an international experience, by I. C. Chi, et al. OBSTETRICAL AND GYNECOLOGICAL SURVEY 41(1):7-19, January 1986.

Recurrent ectopic pregnancy after tubal sterilization, by M. R. Davis. OBSTET-RICS AND GYNECOLOGY 68(3 suppl):44S-45S, September 1986.

Regret after sterilization in women, by H. M. Verner, et al. NEDERLANDS TIJDSCHRIFT VOOR GENEESKUNDE 130(9):410-413, March 1, 1986.

Regrets after tubal sterilization [editorial], by J. Couper-Smartt. MEDICAL JOURNAL OF AUSTRALIA 145(1):2-3, July 7, 1986.

Reversibility after female sterilization, by W. Boeckx, et al. BRITISH JOURNAL OF OBSTETRICS AND GYNAECOLOGY 93(8):839-842, August 1986.

STERILIZATION—TUBAL (continued)

Salpingoclasia by laparoscopy using silastic rings. Comparative analysis of 1,500 cases, by A. Kably Ambe, et al. GINECOLOGIA Y OBSTETRICIA DE MEXICO 53:341-344, December 1985.

Socio-biological parameters in relation to permanent sterilisation of parents, by K. L. Gupta, et al. INDIAN JOURNAL OF PEDIATRICS 52(419):655-661, November-December 1985.

Sterilization approval and follow-through in Brazil, by K. J. Lassner, et al. STUDIES IN FAMILY PLANNING 17(4):188-198, July-August 1986.

Sterilization failures [letter], by R. J. Stock. AMERICAN JOURNAL OF OBSTETRICS AND GYNECOLOGY 154(4):970, April 1986.

Sterilization failures with bipolar tubal cautery [letter], by K. Hausner. FERTILITY AND STERILITY 46(1):150, July 1986.

Successful microsurgical reanastomosis program in a community hospital, by D. I. Galen, et al. JOURNAL OF REPRODUCTIVE MEDICINE 31(7):595-596, July 1986.

Surgical sterilization: ten years' experience, by L. J. Flores Revuelta, et al. GINECOLOGIA Y OBSTETRICIA DE MEXICO 53:163-165, June 1985.

Topical etidocaine during laparoscopic tubal occlusion for postoperative pain relief, by R. McKenzie, et al. OBSTETRICS AND GYNECOLOGY 67(3):447-449, March 1986.

Tubal ligation with local anaesthesia, by P. Barss. TROPICAL DOCTOR 15(4): 175-179, October 1985.

Tubal pregnancy following tubal sterilization, by E. Neeser, et al. GEBURTSHILFE UND FRAUENHEILKUNDE 45(10):702-705, October 1985.

Tubal sterilization in Manitoba, by M. M. Cohen. CANADIAN JOURNAL OF PUBLIC HEALTH 77(2):114-118, March-April 1986.

Tubo-ovarian histofunctional study in the rabbit after bilateral isthmus tubal sterilization and subsequent reanastomosis, by A. Baffoni, et al. MINERVA GINECOLOGIA 38(3):193-199, March 1986.

Uterine rupture following tubal implantation, by H. Scharp. ZENTRALBLATT FUR GYNAEKOLOGIE 107(18):1139-1140, 1985.

Value of routine dilation and curettage at the time of interval sterilization, by E. D. Lichter, et al. OBSTETRICS AND GYNECOLOGY 67(6):763-765, June 1986.

Voluntary female sterilization (comments following a judgment by the Superior Appellate Court 5/9/83), by P. Y. Poirier, et al. REVUE FRANCAISE DE GYNECOLOGIE ET D'OBSTETRIQUE 81(2):111-112, February 1986.

STERILIZATION—TUBAL—COMPLICATIONS

Allergic reaction to Hulka clips, by W. T. Trathen, et al. OBSTETRICS AND GYNECOLOGY 66(5):743-744, November 1985.

Bipolar tubal cautery failures [letter], by H. H. Sheikh. FERTILITY AND STERILITY 44(4):557, October 1985.

STERILIZATION—TUBAL—COMPLICATIONS (continued)

Complications of tubal sterilization, by W. E. Schreiner. THERAPEUTISCHE UMSCHAU 43(5):425-433, May 1986.

Computed tomography of hydrosalpinx following tubal ligation, by K. Togashi, et al. JOURNAL OF COMPUTER ASSISTED TOMOGRAPHY 10(1):78-80, January-February 1986..

Hormonal and menstrual changes following salpingoclasia, by F. Gaviño Gaviño, et al. GINECOLOGIA Y OBSTETRICIA DE MEXICO 54:136-140, June 1986.

Hydrosalpinx and tubal torsion: a late complication of tubal ligation, by L. D. Russin. RADIOLOGY 159(1):115-116, April 1986.

Is lactation a risk factor of IUD- and sterilization-related uterine perforation? A hypothesis, by I. C. Chi, et al. INTERNATIONAL JOURNAL OF GYNAECOLOGY AND OBSTETRICS 22(4):315-317, August 1984.

Laparoscopic sterilization with the Falope-ring technique in the puerperium, by M. Klaerke, et al. ACTA OBSTETRICIA ET GYNECOLOGICA SCANDINAVICA 65(2):99-101, 1986.

Rare events associated with tubal sterilizations: an international experience, by I. C. Chi, et al. OBSTETRICAL AND GYNECOLOGICAL SURVEY 41(1):7-19, January 1986.

Recurrent ectopic pregnancy after tubal sterilization, by M. R. Davis. OBSTETRICS AND GYNECOLOGY 68(3 suppl):44S-45S, September 1986.

Risks and benefits of laparoscopic sterilization, by S. Dueholm, et al. UGESKRIFT FOR LAEGER 147(47):3780-3783, November 18, 1985.

Torsion of the fallopian tube—a late complication of sterilisation, by V. Sivanesaratnam. SINGAPORE MEDICAL JOURNAL 27(1):72-73, February 1986.

Toxic shock syndrome, contraceptive methods, and vaginitis, by S. F. Lanes, et al. AMERICAN JOURNAL OF OBSTETRICS AND GYNECOLOGY 154(5): 989-991, May 1986.

STERILIZATION—VOLUNTARY

Childfree by choice: attitudes and adjustment of sterilized women, by B. M. DeVellis, et al. POPULATION AND ENVIRONMENT: BEHAVIORAL AND SOCIAL ISSUES 7(3):152-162, Fall 1984.

Counseling women who request sterilization: psychodynamic issues and interventions, by I. Kohn. SOCIAL WORK IN HEALTH CARE 11(2):35-60, Winter 1985-1986.

Report on voluntary sterilisation with special reference to minors and women who are intellectually disabled, by L. Vick, et al. CLINICAL REPRODUCTION AND FAMILY 3(2):99-106, June 1985.

Voluntary female sterilization (comments following a judgment by the Superior Appellate Court 5/9/83), by P. Y. Poirier, et al. REVUE FRANCAISE DE GYNECOLOGIE ET D'OBSTETRIQUE 81(2):111-112, February 1986.

STERILIZATION AND CRIMINALS

Adjudication. CRIMINAL LAW MONTHLY 5(5):13, October 1985.

STERILIZATION AND CRIMINALS (continued)

Creation of a haven for "human thoroughbreds": the sterilization of the feeble-
minded and the mentally ill in British Columbia, by A. McLaren. CANADIAN
HISTORICAL REVIEW 67:127-150, June 1986.

Sentencing—sterilization—child abuse. CRIMINAL LAW REPORTER: COURT
DECISIONS AND PROCEEDINGS 39(25):2483-2484, September 24, 1986.

Sterilization. CANADIAN NURSE 81:54, November 1985.

Sterilization and the retarded: who decides?, by S. Zwarun. CHATELAINE
59:57+, March 1986.

Woman is sterilized to get a lesser sentence (case of D. A. Williams). JET 70:36,
August 11, 1986.

STERILIZATION AND HOSPITALS
Halting St. Paul's tubals: an RC hospital says no to casual sterilization, by L.
Cohen. ALBERTA REPORT 13:50, October 27, 1986.

Successful microsurgical reanastomosis program in a community hospital, by D. I.
Galen, et al. JOURNAL OF REPRODUCTIVE MEDICINE 31(7):595-596, July
1986.

STERILIZATION AND THE MENTALLY RETARDED
California law governing the sterilization of developmentally disabled persons
changes course: Conservatorship of Valerie N. WILLIAMETTE LAW REVIEW
22:622-629, Fall 1986.

Creation of a haven for "human thoroughbreds": the sterilization of the feeble-
minded and the mentally ill in British Columbia, by A. McLaren. CANADIAN
HISTORICAL REVIEW 67:127-150, June 1986.

Mental retardation: a controversial indication for hysterectomy, by A. M. Kaunitz,
et al. OBSTETRICS AND GYNECOLOGY 68(3):436-438, September 1986.

Report on voluntary sterilisation with special reference to minors and women who
are intellectually disabled, by L. Vick, et al. CLINICAL REPRODUCTION AND
FAMILY 3(2):99-106, June 1985.

Sterilization and the retarded: who decides?, by S. Zwarun. CHATELAINE
59:57+, March 1986.

Sterilization of incompetents and the "late probate court" in California: how bad
law makes hard cases, by B. A. Goldberg. PACIFIC LAW JOURNAL 18:1-30,
October 1986.

Sterilization of the mentally disabled, by A. Gilmore. CANADIAN MEDICAL
ASSOCIATION JOURNAL 134(12):1390-1396, June 15, 1986.

Sterilization of the mentally retarded minor: the Re K. case, by C. A. P. Finch-
Noyes. CANADIAN JOURNAL OF FAMILY LAW 5:277-299, Fall 1986.

Sterilization of mentally retarded persons: reproductive rights and family privacy,
by E. S. Scott. DUKE LAW JOURNAL 1986:806-865, November 1986.

STERILIZATION AND PARENTAL CONSENT
Sterilization: can parents decide. EXCEPTIONAL PARENT 16(2):40-41, April
1986.

STERILIZATION AND PARENTAL CONSENT (continued)

Sterilization of the mentally retarded minor: the Re K. case, by C. A. P. Finch-Noyes. CANADIAN JOURNAL OF FAMILY LAW 5:277-299, Fall 1986.

STERILIZATION AND PHYSICIANS
Availability of reproductive health services from United States private physicians, by M. T. Orr, et al. FAMILY PLANNING PERSPECTIVES 17(2):63-69, March-April 1985.

Court not bound to accept test of competent medical practice in deciding whether contraceptive counselling is negligent, by D. Brahams. LANCET 2(8503): 407-408, August 16, 1986.

Provision of sterilization services by private physicians. FAMILY PLANNING PERSPECTIVES 17(5):216, September-October 1985.

STERILIZATION AND TEENS
Report on voluntary sterilisation with special reference to minors and women who are intellectually disabled, by L. Vick, et al. CLINICAL REPRODUCTION AND FAMILY 3(2):99-106, June 1985.

STERILIZATION AND WOMEN
Childfree by choice: attitudes and adjustment of sterilized women, by B. M. DeVellis, et al. POPULATION AND ENVIRONMENT: BEHAVIORAL AND SOCIAL ISSUES 7(3):152-162, Fall 1984.

Counseling women who request sterilization: psychodynamic issues and interventions, by I. Kohn. SOCIAL WORK IN HEALTH CARE 11(2):35-60, Winter 1985-1986.

Danger to pregnant women at the work site. Disagreement between employers and trade unions in the USA: sterilization or employment termination, by G. Schäcke. FORTSCHRITTE DER MEDIZIN 103(47-48):52-53, December 19, 1985.

Woman is sterilized to get a lesser sentence (case of D. A. Williams). JET 70:36, August 11, 1986.

STERILIZATION FAILURES
Bipolar tubal cautery failure [letter], by H. H. Sheikh. FERTILITY AND STERILITY 44(4):557, October 1985.

Sterilization failures [letter], by R. J. Stock. AMERICAN JOURNAL OF OBSTETRICS AND GYNECOLOGY 154(4):970, April 1986.

Sterilization failures with bipolar tubal cautery [letter], by K. Hausner. FERTILITY AND STERILITY 46(1):150, July 1986.

STERILIZATION REVERSAL
Absorbable or nonabsorbable suture material for microsurgical tubal anastomosis. Randomized experimental study on rabbits, by P. H. Scheidel, et al. GYNECOLOGIC AND OBSTETRIC INVESTIGATION 21(2):96-102, 1986.

Characteristics, perceptions and personalities of women seeking a reversal of their tubal sterilization, by S. Abraham, et al. MEDICAL JOURNAL OF AUSTRALIA 145(1):4-7, July 7, 1986.

Experience with microsurgical reversal of female sterilization, by D. L. Hill. MINERVA MEDICA 68(11):846-848, November 1985.

STERILIZATION REVERSAL (continued)

Female sterilization: can the woman who will seek reversal be identified prospectively?, by P. J. Taylor, et al. CLINICAL REPRODUCTION AND FERTILITY 4(3):207-215, June 1986.

I had my tubes untied, by T. Erickson. COSMOPOLITAN 194:221+, May 1983.

Microsurgical desterilizations. Reflections on 65 cases, by J. B. Dubuisson, et al. JOURNAL DE GYNECOLOGIE, OBSTETRIQUE ET BIOLOGIE DE LA RE-PRODUCTION 15(2):223-229, 1986.

Microsurgical reversal of sterilization: a six-year study, by M. M. Spivak, et al. AMERICAN JOURNAL OF OBSTETRICS AND GYNECOLOGY 154(2):355-361, February 1986.

Microsurgical tubal anastomosis, by G. Rosa, et al. REVISTA CHILENA DE OB-STETRICIA Y GINECOLOGIA 50(1):67-71, 1985.

New microsurgical methods for vasoepididymostomy, by G. Drawz, et al. URO-LOGIA INTERNATIONALIS 40(6):337-342, 1985.

Outcome of pregnancy following treatment of marital sterility, by P. Knorre, et al. ZENTRALBLATT FUR GYNAEKOLOGIE 108(3):175-181, 1986.

Peritoneal endometriosis in women requesting reversal of sterilization, by S. T. Dodge, et al. FERTILITY AND STERILITY 45(6):774-777, June 1986.

Proximal tubal surgery, by C. Racinet. REVUE FRANCAISE DE GYNECOLOGIE ET D'OBSTETRIQUE 80(11):831-835, November 1985.

Recanalisation of vas, by A. B. Singh, et al. JOURNAL OF THE INDIAN MEDICAL ASSOCIATION 83(9):303-305, September 1985.

Regret after sterilization in women, by H. M. Vemer, et al. NEDERLANDS TIJDSCHRIFT VOOR GENEESKUNDE 130(9):410-413, March 1, 1986.

Reversibility after female sterilization, by W. Boeckx, et al. BRITISH JOURNAL OF OBSTETRICS AND GYNAECOLOGY 93(8):839-842, August 1986.

Sperm analysis following vasectomy: when to perform a revasectomy?, by A. B. van Vugt, et al. NEDERLANDS TIJDSCHRIFT VOOR GENEESKUNDE 129(33):1579-1582, August 17 1985.

Sterilization reversal with additional use of fibrin glue (Beriplast). Preliminary report, by R. Baumann, et al. GEBURTSHILFE UND FRAUENHEILKUNDE 46(4):234-236, April 1986.

Successful microsurgical reanastomosis program in a community hospital, by D. I. Galen, et al. JOURNAL OF REPRODUCTIVE MEDICINE 31(7):595-596, July 1986.

Tubal reanastomosis in the rabbit with different suture materials, by C. Fernández del Castillo Ancira, et al. GINECOLOGIA Y OBSTETRICIA DE MEXICO 53:213-216, August 1985.

Tubo-ovarian histofunctional study in the rabbit after bilateral isthmus tubal sterilization and subsequent reanastomosis, by A. Baffoni, et al. MINERVA GINE-COLOGIA 38(3):193-199, March 1986.

STERILIZATION REVERSAL (continued)

Tubotubal anastomosis for reversal of female sterilization in Thailand, by K. Limpaphayom. JOURNAL OF REPRODUCTIVE MEDICINE 31(7):601-604, July 1986.

Twenty year experience with vasovasostomy, by H. Y. Lee. JOURNAL OF UROLOGY 136(2):413-415, August 1986.

Use of papaverine during vasovasostomy, by J. L. Marmar, et al. UROLOGY 28(1):56-57, July 1986.

Uterine rupture following tubal implantation, by H. Scharp. ZENTRALBLATT FUR GYNAEKOLOGIE 107(18):1139-1140, 1985.

Vasectomy and its reversal, by A. M. Belker. PRIMARY CARE 12(4):70-3717, December 1985.

Vasovasostomy: efficacy and cost containment by outpatient loupe magnification anastamosis, by F. A. Klein, et al. JOURNAL OF FAMILY PRACTICE 22(2): 176-177, February 1986.

Who has a vasectomy reversal?, by L. Clarke, et al. JOURNAL OF BIOSOCIAL SCIENCE 18(3):253-259, July 1986.

Why does vasectomy reversal fail?, by M. G. Royale, et al. BRITISH JOURNAL OF UROLOGY 57(6):780-783, December 1985.

VASECTOMY—GENERAL
Cell-mediated immunity to spermatozoal antigens after vasectomy: recent developments, by A. G. Tumbo-Oeri. EAST AFRICAN MEDICAL JOURNAL 62(6):372-378, June 1985.

Changes in seminiferous tubules after vasectomy, by R. Mehrotra, et al. INDIAN JOURNAL OF PATHOLOGY AND MICROBIOLOGY 28(4):371-378, October 1985.

Characteristics of vasectomies performed in selected outpatient facilities in the United States, 1980, by J. S. Kendrick, et al. JOURNAL OF REPRODUC-TIVE MEDICINE 30(12):936-938, December 1985.

Distribution of a seminal plasma-associated protein kinase inhibitor in normal, oligozoospermic, and vasctomized men, by J. F. Pliego, et al. BIOLOGY OF REPRODUCTION 34(5):885-893, June 1986.

Effect of neonatal vasectomy on testicular function, by I. Gerendai, et al. AN-DROLOGIA 18(4):353-359, July-August 1986.

Follow up study of 200 men after vaesctomy, by R. Milne, et al. HEALTH BULLE-TIN 44(3):137-142, May 1986.

Humoral immune responses in healthy heterosexual, homosexual and vasec-tomized men and in homosexual men with the acquired immune deficiency syndrome, by S. S. Witkin, et al. AIDS RESEARCH 1(1):31-44, 1983-1984.

Immunological consequences of vasectomy and consideration of some of their implications, by D. Blaustein, et al. ALLERGOLOGIA ET IMMUNOPATHOLO-GIA 14(2):95-99, March-April 1986.

Married women and contraceptive sterilization: factors that contribute to pre-surgical ambivalence, by W. B. Miller, et al. JOURNAL OF BIOSOCIAL SCI-ENCE 17(4):471-479, October 1985.

Married women's dissatisfaction with tubal sterilization and vasectomy at first-year follow-up: effects of perceived spousal dominance, by R. N. Shain, et al. FERTILITY AND STERILITY 45(6):808-819, June 1986.

Nature of the residual alpha-1,4-glucosidase activity in the seminal plasma of vasectomized men, by R. R. Tremblay, et al. ENZYME 34(1):33-38, 1985.

Pregnancies after sterilization, by D. Brahams. LANCET 1(8481):627, March 15, 1986.

Premedication with beta-blocking agents for vasectomy operations [letter], by I. S. Edwards. MEDICAL JOURNAL OF AUSTRALIA 144(12):670, June 9, 1986.

Present state of male contraception, by J. Zverina. CASOPIS LEKARU CES-KYCH 124(37):1157-1161, September 13, 1985.

Screening the vasectomy applicant: reassessing the importance of eligibility criteria, by J. Uhlman, et al. SOCIAL BIOLOGY 33:102-108, Spring-Summer 1986.

Serum lipid levels before and after vasctomy in men, by G. Zamora, et al. CON-TRACEPTION 32(20:149-161, August 1985.

Sperm analysis following vasectomy: when to perform a revasectomy?, by A. B. van Vugt, et al. NEDERLANDS TIJDSCHRIFT VOOR GENEESKUNDE 129(33):1579-1582, August 17 1985.

Sperm autoimmunity in vasctomized men and its relationship to atherosclerotic coronary artery disease, by S. C. Liu, et al. CLINICAL REPRODUCTION AND FERTILITY 3(4):343-348, December 1985.

Study of sperm antibodies in the sera of vasctomized males, by A. Murdia, et al. INDIAN JOURNAL OF PATHOLOGY AND MICROBIOLOGY 28(4):355-361, October 1985.

Sturgeon vas cautery—reusable and battery-powered, by S. S. Schmidt, et al. UROLOGY 27(3):273-274, March 1986.

To speak is not necessarily to be understood, by J. K. Avery. JOURNAL OF THE TENNESSEE MEDICAL ASSOCIATION 79(4):212, April 1986.

Twenty year experience with vasovasostomy, by H. Y. Lee. JOURNAL OF UROLOGY 136(2):413-415, August 1986.

Vasectomy, by H. Singh. QUARTERLY MEDICAL REVIEW 35(3):1-26, July 1984.

Vasectomy and its reversal, by A. M. Belker. PRIMARY CARE 12(4):70-3717, December 1985.

Vasectomy: what are community standards?, by R. K. Babayan, et al. UROLOGY 27(4):328-330, April 1986.

VASECTOMY—GENERAL (continued)

Was the vasectomy necessary after all?, by L. Nicholas. BRITISH MEDICAL JOURNAL 292(6520):604-605, March 1, 1986.

What to tell patients about sterilization, by F. Pool, et al. RN 49(5):55-56+, May 1986.

Why does vasectomy reversal fail?, by M. G. Royale, et al. BRITISH JOURNAL OF UROLOGY 57(6):780-783, December 1985.

VASECTOMY—COMPLICATIONS

Diet and vasectomy: effects on therogenesis in cynomolgus macaques, by T. B. Clarkson, et al. EXPERIMENTAL AND MOLECULAR PATHOLOGY 44(1):29-49, February 1986.

Effects of vasectomy on the structure of the testicle in the cat, by J. Nuñez, et al. ACTAS UROLÓGICAS ESPANOLAS 10(1):61-64, January-February 1986.

Effects of vasectomy on the testis [editorial], by C. J. Flickinger. NEW ENGLAND JOURNAL OF MEDICINE 313(20):1283-1285, November 14, 1985.

Quantitative pathologic changes in the human testis after vasectomy. A controlled study, by J. P. Jarow, et al. NEW ENGLAND JOURNAL OF MEDICINE 313(20):1252-1256, November 14, 1985.

Risk of myocardial infarction ten or more years after vaesctomy in men under 55 years of age, by L. Rosenberg, et al. AMERICAN JOURNAL OF EPIDEMIOLOGY 123(6):1049-1056, June 1986.

Risks of male sterilization, by B. von Rütte. THERAPEUTISCHE UMSCHAU 43(5):434-437, May 1986.

Spontaneous recanalization after vasctomy [review], by L. Gatenbeck, et al. LAKARTIDNINGEN 82937):3064-3065, September 11, 1985.

Vasal urinary fistula with retrograde reflux of urine after vasectomy, by K. M. Desai, et al. JOURNAL OF UROLOGY 135(5):1023-1024, May 1986.

Vasitis nodosa and spermatic granuloma of the skin: an histologic study of a rare complication of vasectomy, by K. Balogh, et al. JOURNAL OF CUTANEOUS PATHOLOGY 12(6):528-533, December 1985.

VASECTOMY—METHODS

Open-ended vasectomy: an assessment, by B. B. Errey, et al. FERTILITY AND STERILITY 45(6):843-846, June 1986.

Vasectomy failure and open-ended vasectomy [letter], by S. S. Schmidt. FERTILITY AND STERILITY 44(4):557-558, October 1985.

Vasectomy: a simple technique, by H. Singh. JOURNAL OF THE INDIAN MEDICAL ASSOCIATION 83(9):313-314, September 1985.

VASECTOMY—PSYCHOLOGY AND PSYCHIATRY

Decision to terminate childbearing: differences in preoperative ambivalence between tubal ligation women and vasectomy wives, by R. N. Shain, et al. SOCIAL BIOLOGY 31(1-2):40-58, Spring-Summer 1984.

Psychological and sexual problems following male sterilization, by L. Burgaard, et al. UGESKRIFT FOR LAEGER 148(12):734-738, March 17, 1986.

VASECTOMY—PSYCHOLOGY AND PSYCHIATRY (continued)

Psychosocial factors influencing American men and women in their decision for sterilization, by G. M. Burnell, et al. JOURNAL OF PSYCHOLOGY 120(2): 113-119, March 1986.

Socio-biological parameters in relation to permanent sterilisation of parents, by K. L. Gupta, et al. INDIAN JOURNAL OF PEDIATRICS 52(419):655-661, November-December 1985.

Who has a vasectomy reversal?, by L. Clarke, et al. JOURNAL OF BIOSOCIAL SCIENCE 18(3):253-259, July 1986.

VASECTOMY—RESEARCH
Blood supply in the testicle of the vasectomized rat, by J. Nuñez, et al. ACTAS UROLOGICAS ESPANOLAS 10(1):65-68, January-February 1986.

Diet and vasectomy: effects on therogenesis in cynomolgus macaques, by T. B. Clarkson, et al. EXPERIMENTAL AND MOLECULAR PATHOLOGY 44(1):29-49, February 1986.

Effect of flushing the vasa deferentia at the time of vasectomy on the rate of clearance of spermatozoa from the ejaculates of dogs and cats, by M. D. Frenette, et al. AMERICAN JOURNAL OF VETERINARY RESEARCH 47(2):463-470, February 1986.

Effects of vasectomy on the structure of the testicle in the cat, by J. Nuñez, et al. ACTAS UROLOGICAS ESPANOLAS 10(1):61-64, January-February 1986.

Enzyme-linked immunosorbent assay for measuring antisperm autoantibodies following vasectomy in Lewis rats, by J. C. Herr, et al. AMERICAN JOURNAL OF REPRODUCTIVE IMMUNOLOGY AND MICROBIOLOGY 11(3):75-81, July 1986.

Humoral and cell mediated immune responses to spermatozoal antigens in vasectomised diabetic monkeys, by N. Bansal, et al. INDIAN JOURNAL OF MEDICAL RESEARCH 83:293-297, March 1986.

Lectin staining of rat testis and epididymis after ligation of excurrent ducts at different levels, by T. Vanha-Perttula, et al. BIOLOGY OF REPRODUCTION 33(2):477-485, September 1985.

Plasma lipids in the vasectomized animal, by J. Nuñez, et al. ACTAS UROLOGICAS ESPANOLAS 10(1):69-72, January-February 1986.

Suppression of post-vasectomy cytotoxic sperm antibody formation in rats by a short-term pretreatment with cyclosporine, by J. Lovett, et al. AMERICAN JOURNAL OF REPRODUCTIVE IMMUNOLOGY AND MICROBIOLOGY 11(2):65-68, June 1986.

Sympathetic denervation of the rat vas deferens following unilateral vasectomy, by R. M. DeGaris, et al. CLINICAL AND EXPERIMENTAL PHARMACOLOGY AND PHYSIOLOGY 13(5):399-406, May 1986.

VASECTOMY AND PHYSICIANS
Vasectomies performed by private physicians, United States, 1980 to 1984, by J. S. Kendrick, et al. FERTILITY AND STERILITY 46(3):528-530, September 1986.

AUTHOR INDEX

Page numbers are given only for the first subject heading under which an entry appears. The first few words of the entry are given in order to assist in finding it on any given page.

Abbas, S. M.
  Effects of Ramadhan fast, 174
Abbott, P.
  Dalkon shield: April 30, 119
Abdel-Aziz, A.
  Family planning in Jordan, 112
Abdel-Hafez, S. K.
  Serodiagnosis of toxoplasma, 15
Abdelmassih, R.
  Fertility after varicocele ligation, 168
Abdulla, K. A.
  Effect of eary postpartum use, 145
Abdyldaeva, I. A.
  Use of contraceptive agents, 106
Abildgaard, U.
  Breast cancer and oral, 141
  Contraceptive agents and, 103
Abouleish, E. I.
  Postpartum tuba ligation, 210
Abraham, S.
  Characteristics, perceptions, 206
Abramson, A.
  Technique for mid-trimester, 48
Ackerman, L. B.
  Fertility rights, 81
Ada, G. L.
  Prospects for developing, 136
Adame, D. D.
  On the effects of sex ,199
Adamek, R. J.
  Sociology, ideology, and the, 22
Adams, J.
  Who stood to gain, 153
Adams, R.
  Man: an axiological analysis, 35
Adebayo, A.
  Opinions regarding abortion, 21

Admad,S.
  Rural-urban differentials in, 81
Adzick, N. S.
  Fetal surgery in the primate, 178
Agarwal, D. K.
  Antifertility and mutagenic, 175
Agrawal, S.
  Antifertility effects of embelin, 107
Aherne, F. X.
  Nurition and sow prolificacy, 179
Ahlburg, D. A.
  Commodity aspirations in, 167
Ahlers, D.
  Possible correlations between, 65
Ahluwalia, B. S.
  Effect of delta 9, 176
Ahmad, K.
  Motility and fertility of, 181
Ahmed, J.
  Polygyny and fertility, 172
Aikenhead, S.
  Abortion on the docket, 13
Ainsworth, M., 1
Aitken, R.
  Not killing, 21
Akhter, H. H.
  Weighting risks against, 126
Akmuradova, G.
  Use of heparin in the, 79
Akpokodje, J. U.
  Abortion of twins following, 24
Al-Awadi, S. A.
  Effect of consanguineous, 10
Albert, M. B.
  Oral contraceptives and, 132
Alder, E. M.
  Hormones, mood and, 194

220

Aler, E. M.
　Attitudes of women of, 88
Alipov, V. I.
　Postcoital and postimplanta..., 134
Allegretti, J.
　Marketing anti-abortion as, 192
Allen, M.
　Nurses speak out on teens, 50
Allen, W. E.
　Equine abortion and chloral, 22
Allmendinger, G.
　Esophageal ulcer caused by, 129
Alsheimer, B.
　AFP and HbF determination, 33
Altman, A. M.
　Midtrimester abortion with, 36
Altomonte, L.
　Thrombosis, recurrent abor..., 26
Altukhov, IuP.
　Population-genetical study of, 29
Amatayakul, K.
　Effects of long-acting, 105
Amidei, N.
　Get beyond labels, 42
Amortegul, A. J.
　Prevalence of chlamydia, 18
Amster, R.
　Typhoid fever complicating, 26
Anand, U.
　Infertility and infertility, 152
Anash, G. A.
　Semen production, sperm, 180
Andersen, P. K.
　Psychiatric admissions and, 37
Anderson, A.
　Contraceptive pill. Japan, 112
Anderson, D. E.
　Is abortion a civil right, 42
Anderson, J. W.
　Three abortion theorists: a, 22
Anderton, D. L.
　Adoption of fertility limitation, 87
Andorka, R.
　Social demography of, 85
Andrade Zamora, J. G.
　Postpartum sterilization in a, 210
Andre, S.
　Pro-life or pro-choice: is, 21
Andrews, L. B.
　Remaking conception and, 95
Angel, E.
　Immunohistochemical dem..., 32
Ann, M.
　Letter to my sisters, 11
Annas, G. J.
　Roe v Wade reaffirmed, 44
Antipenskaia, L. V.
　Importance of the marriage, 28

Apelo, R. A.
　Clinical assessment of a, 138
Appleyard, W. T.
　Outbreak of bovine abortion, 55
Aral, S. O.
　Screening for sexually, 166
Aranda, C.
　Comparative clinical trial of, 203
Aranda, C.
　Comparative clinical trial of, 205
Arber, S.
　Aftercare following miscarriage, 14
Archer, D. F.
　Oral contraceptives and, 132
Arditti, R.
　Reproductive engineering, 144
Argent, V. P.
　Failed female sterilization and, 204
Armon, P.
　Why I changed my, 70
Armstrong, B. K.
　Oral contraceptives and breast, 131
Arrabal Martín, M.
　Topography of urologic, 189
Arribas Gómez, I.
　Repeated abortion associated, 29
Artiushenko, Iu. V.
　Work capacity and social, 187
Asch, A.
　Uncertain futures, 12
Ashton, P.
　Return to theatre—experience, 186
Atad, J.
　Continuous extraovular, 7
Atef, M.
　Influence of monensin on, 178
Atkinson, L. E.
　Next contraceptive revolution, 89
　Worldwide trends in funding, 89
Auff, E.
　Status of oral contraceptives, 134
Austin, D.
　Possible influence of strain, 179
　Reproductive capacity of male, 180
Averette, H. E.
　Hysterectomy. Methods of the, 189
Avery, J. K.
　To speak is not, 217
Axmann, K.
　Screening examination of the, 133
Aydinlik, S.
　Reduced estrogen ovulation, 141
Aznar, J.
　Effect of oral contraceptives, 120
Babayan, R. K.
　Vasectomy: what are, 217
Bachu, A.
　Developing current fertility, 160

Bader, E.
  Abortion rights, 75
  Commitment greater than fear, 76
  Contraception and control, 95
  Fake clinic hauled into, 76
  Hierarchy's values don't value, 75
  100,000 march for women's, 78
  Right-to-lifers don't, 193
  Why not birth control, 93
Baffoni, A.
  Tubo-ovarian histofunctional, 206
Bagdade, J. D.
  Measurement of arterial, 123
Bagley, S. W.
  Risk factors for resuction, 37
Baid, D. D.
  Use of time to, 170
Bailey, M.
  Differential fertility by, 167
Baillie, P.
  Oestrogenic effects of the, 106
Bainton, R.
  Interaction between antibiotic, 122
Bairagi, R.
  Sex preference for children, 170
Baker, D., 1
Baker, D. A.
  Lymphocyte subsets in, 130
Baker, H. W.
  Requirements for controlled, 175
  Testicular vein ligation and, 175
Baker, J.
  Philosophy and the morality, 21
Balakrishnan, T. R.
  Contraceptive use in Canada, 89
Balasubrahamanyan, V.
  Towards a women's perspec..., 152
Balázs, M.
  Liver disorders related to, 130
Balestrieri, A.
  Knowledge, science and, 159
Balogh, K.
  Vasitis nodosa and spermatic, 218
Bamji, M. S.
  Vitamin supplements to Indian, 126
Banerjee, K., 1
Bansal, N.
  Humoral and cell mediatd, 219
Bansal, Y. P.
  Profil eof intra-partum, 79
Baranov, V. G.
  Influence of neonatal injection, 175
Bargero, G.
  Oral contraceptives and, 123
Barkhatova, T. P.
  Incipient spontaneous abortion, 58
  Threatened premature labor, 62

Barnett, W.
  Regional prospective study, 47
Barrett, C.
  Abortion controversy (Alberta, 13
Barrett-Connor, E.
  Resting and exercise electro..., 133
Barron, S. L.
  Sexual activity in girls, 197
Barss, P.
  Tubal ligation with local, 206
Bashir, A.
  Day case vaginal pomeroy, 205
Basker, E.
  "Natural" control of fertility, 81
Bass, C.
  Seeking common ground, 192
Bastos, A. da C.
  Medico-social aspects of, 96
Bateman, B. G.
  Pregnancy wastage asso..., 29
Baulieu, E. E.
  Steroid anti-hormones: anti, 135
Baumann, R.
  Sterilization reversal with, 215
Baweja, R.
  Indian Council of Medical, 107
Bean, L. L.
  Polygyny-fertility hypothesis, 169
Beard, R. W.
  Miscarriage or abortion, 36
Beaumont, V.
  Residual vascular risk of, 141
Beck, L.
  Conclusions and critical, 159
  Contraception in the mentally, 99
Beer, A. E.
  New horizons in the diagnosis, 29
Begel, D.
  Contraceptive casualty?, 115
Beifuss, J. T.
  Abortion ten years later, 59
Belcastro, P. A., 1
Belker, A. M.
  Vasectomy and its reversal, 216
Bendvold, E.
  Automatic suture stapling in, 182
Bengió, R. H.
  Ureteral lesions in gyne..., 189
Benmrad, M.
  Gonadotropin-releasing, 178
Benson, W. L.
  Comparison of short and, 183
Benvenuti, P.
  Abortion and the man. Psy..., 32
Berck, J.
  Bombers around town, 75
Berger, C.
  Contraceptive knowldge and, 136

Bergeron, D.
  Tabac et anovulants, c'est, 110
Beric, B.
  Abortion in the second trim..., 33
Berkeley, A. S.
  Controlled, comparative study, 184
Berlier, P.
  Contraception in female, 99
Berlinski, B.
  Usefulness of determining the, 62
Bermel, J.
  Family planning before birth, 80
Bernstein, A. E.
  Psychological meaning of, 191
Berr, F.
  Contraceptive steroids in..., 115
Bertoli, D.
  Fertility study of rifaximin, 178
Bertrand, J. T.
  Factors influencing the use, 114
Bethell, T.
  Imperialism and the pill, 83
Bhagirath, T.
  Effects of the male contracep.., 107
Bhowmik, T.
  Effect of depo-provera, 105
Bichard, M.
  Effectiveness of genetic, 177
Biehl, J.
  Abortion foes ruled out-of-order, 9
  Abortion rights win narow, 78
Binkin, N. J.
  Trends in induced legal, 38
Binns, D. St. Clair, 1
Birdsall, N., 1
Birgerson, L.
  Effects of epostane on, 7
Bisbiglio, L.
  Case of prolapse of the vaginal, 187
Bitsch, M.
  Rubella as the reason for, 47
Bizem, H.-R., 1
Black, C.
  Fund aids poor women, 77
Black, J. S.
  Medical sequelae of, 194
Blair, G.
  Pill: what's right with it, 124
Blakely, M. K.
  Souls on ice (frozen embryo, 22
Blaustein, D.
  Immunological consequences, 216
Blodgett, N.
  New RICO twist: damaged, 76
Bloshanskii, I. M.
  Vacuum-aspiration of uterine, 38
Blum, M.
  Detection of ovulation by, 119

Blumenthal, M.
  Clinic (male reaction), 51
Bobchev, T.
  Experience of the Obstetrics, 188
  Methods for improving the, 190
Bocklisch, H.
  Mycoplasma bovis abortion, 54
Boeckx, W.
  Reversibility after female, 210
Bohme Böhme, M.
  Effect of hormonal contra..., 128
Bolce, L.
  ERA and the abortion con..., 20
Bolotin, S.
  Selling chastity—the sly new, 21
Bolt, H. M.
  Drug interactions in the, 128
Bond, W. H.
  Early uterine body carcinoma, 184
Bongaarts, J., 2
  Contraceptive use and annual, 111
Bonini, C. A.
  Colpopexy by fashioning, 187
Bonnar, J.
  Oral contraceptives and blood, 123
Boon, A. R.
  Family building in parents, 151
Bopp, J.
  Examination of proposals, 42
Bordson, B. L.
  Comparison of fecundability, 167
Borella, P.
  Lead content in abortion, 11
Börjeson, C. O.
  New contraceptive agent, 106
Bork, K.
  Contraceptives and pregnancy, 115
Borman, B.
  Hysterectomies in New, 185
Borrie, W. D.
  Fertility, infertility and, 168
Borten, M.
  Early pregnancy interruption, 34
  Ectopic pregnancy among, 7
Bostofte, E.
  Socio-economic status and, 170
Boudaoud, S.
  Incidence of biological, 35
Bounameaux, H.
  Effect of standard and, 184
Bourgouin, P.
  Sonographic demonstration, 32
Bouters, R.
  Clinical and pathologico, 176
Bowers, N. A.
  Early pregnancy loss in the, 51
Bracken, M. B.
  Low birth weight in preg..., 23

Menarcheal age and habitual, 29
 Risk of late first and second, 26
Brackertz, M.
 Indication status of chromo..., 28
Brahams, D.
 Court not bound to accept, 202
 House of Lords rules, 42
 Pregnancies after sterilization, 205
Bräutigam, H. H.
 Complications of legal, 47
Bravender-Coyle, P.
 Children, medical treatment, 102
Bredbacka, S.
 Pre- and postoperative, 186
Brick, P.
 Actions teach better than, 199
Brindis, C. D.
 Development and evaluation, 161
Brinton, L. A.
 Long term use of oral, 130
Brodribb, S.
 Conference report: Feminist, 16
Brooks, R. J.
 Failure of strange females, 54
Broström, G.
 Practical aspects on the, 169
Broughton, E. S.
 Vaccination against leptospiral, 66
Brouquet, J.
 Rare form of benign, 133
Brown, A. M.
 Drug interactions between, 128
Brown, J. B.
 Study of returning fertility, 170
Browner, C. H.
 Politics of reproduction in, 155
Brügger, D.
 Preoperative cervix dilatation, 8
Bruni, V.
 Platelet and coagulation, 124
Brycz-Witkowska, J.
 Evaluation of karyotypes of, 57
Bucht, B.
 Reflections on recent levels, 84
Buckley, W. F.
 Dear Bob, you should, 42
Buge, A.
 Hemichorea and oral, 129
Bulajic, M.
 Family planning under, 151
Bulienko, S. D.
 Basis for the use of immuno..., 57
Bump, R. C.
 Sexually transmissible, 194
Burdette, M. G.
 Hormones and breast cancer, 129
Burgaard, L.
 Psychological and sexual, 218

Burger, J. M.
 Predicting contraceptive be..., 145
Burke, S.
 Protesters harass abortion clinic, 76
Burnell, G. M.
 Psychosocial factors, 202
Burnhill, M. S.
 Risk management in preg..., 39
 Treatment of women who have, 8
Bury, J. K.
 Teenage pregnancy, 97
Busch, E. H.
 Embolic stroke in a woman, 128
Buxton, D.
 Potential danger to pregnant, 65
Buzek, B.
 Educational problems of, 154
Byfield, L.
 Mr. Pawley's fetal mistake, 11
 Perils of apostasy: Maureen, 73
Byfield, T.
 Now if Paddy the publisher, 11
Bygdeman, M.
 Progesterone receptor block..., 37
 Prostaglandins and male, 175
Bythe, N.
 Ireland: clinic sued, 15
Cabrol, D.
 Induction of labour with, 48
Cadkin, A. V.
 Threatened abortion: sono..., 62
Cain, M., 1
Cairns, V.
 Oral contraceptive use and, 111
Calanchini, C.
 Development of a compulsive, 120
Calderone, M. S.
 Adolescent sexuality, 195
Calkins, B. M.
 Inflammatory bowel disease, 130
Callahan, D.
 Abortion: the new debate, 33
 How technology is refraining, 20
Callahan, J. C.
 Abortion, pluralism, feminism, 19
 Fetus and fundamental rights, 72
Callahan, S.
 Abortion and the sexual, 71
Callan, V. J.
 Comparisons of mothers of, 150
Calle Olmos, E.
 Integration of midwivs of, 152
Calzolari, E.
 Unusual translocation 46,XX,t..., 30
Cameron, I. T.
 Controlled release form of, 7
Cameron, N.
 Natural alternative, 81

Camp, S. L.
  What's new in contraception, 98
Campana, M.
  Role of chromosome aberra..., 29
Campbell, J.
  Women's media project, 75
Canesqui, A. M.
  Implementation and expansion, 151
Cansino, B.
  Pro-life price: Joe Borowski, 192
Canto de Cetina, T. E.
  Incomplete abortion: charac..., 19
Canzier, E.
  Patient record of the use, 124
Carney, W.
  Abortion tax deductions must, 67
Carp, H. J.
  Fertility after nonsurgical, 168
Carrick, P., 1
Carroll, J. J.
  Family planning: a population, 160
Carstam, R.
  Urinary excretion of melano..., 126
Carter, S. L.
  Morgan (Katzenbach, 43
Cartoof, V. G.
  Parental consent for abortion, 18
Carver, C.
  Contraceptive update, 109
Cassinelli, G. B.
  Hepatic adenoma and oral, 129
Castadot, R. G.
  Pregnancy termination: tech..., 36
Catalano, P. M.
  Griseofulvin-oral contraceptive, 121
Catanzarite, V. A.
  Successful intrauterine preg..., 186
Cernada, G. P.
  Implications for adolescent sex, 199
Cernoch, A.
  What should the physician's, 101
Chan, C. K.
  Eugenics on the rise, 157
Chan, S. Y.
  Seminal plasma beta-human, 170
Chandani, A.
  Doctors' attitude towards family, 91
Chapman, J.
  Political implications of attitudes, 14
Chapman, M. G.
  Spironolactone in combina..., 140
Chaudhari, S. S. D.
  Fertility behaviour of female, 151
Chaudhuri, C.
  Effect of norethisterone on, 107
Chaudhuri, P.
  Chlamydia trachomatis infection, 60

Chaudhury, R. H.
  Influence of female education, 82
Check, J. H.
  Decreased abortions in HMB, 59
  Risk of fetal anomalies, 59
Chen, W.
  Synthesis of cyclopentylpro..., 125
Cheng, M. C.
  Wertheim's operation—a, 187
Chestnut, D. H.
  Continuous epidural, 183
Chevrant-Breton, O.
  Contraception a year after, 45
Chhabra, S.
  Child loss and fertility, 171
Chi, I. C.
  Is lactation a risk factor, 212
  Rare events associated with, 210
Chick, P. H.
  Comparative review of female, 205
  Comprehensive review of, 208
Chilvers, E.
  Cerebral venous thrombosis, 127
Chimura, T.
  Effect of cefmenoxime in, 184
Chiwuzie, J. C.
  Contraception among female, 145
Cho, L.-J.
  Averting crisis in Asia?, 82
Choo, Y. C.
  Management of intractable, 185
Chow, W.-H.
  IUD use and subsequent, 119
Christ, F.
  Changes in urethral closure, 187
Christ, T.
  Modification of tear film, 130
Christensen, N. J.
  Cervical dilatation with sul..., 60
Christian, S. R., 2
Cicatelli, B.
  "Women, power, and sex, 75
Ciri, F.
  Various pharmacologic, 47
Clark, A. E.
  Emergence of the repro..., 177
Clark, A. G.
  Numerical simulation of the, 169
Clark, B. L.
  Frequency of infertility and, 25
Clark, D. A.
  Active suppression of host-vs, 53
Clark, J.
  IUD taken off market, 119
Clark, M.
  Contraceptives: on hold, 96
Clark, M. A.
  Teenage pregnancy and, 162

Clarke, L.
 Who has a vasectomy, 205
Clarkson, S. E.
 Psychological aspects of, 203
Clarkson, T. B.
 Diet and vasectomy: effects, 218
Claus, R.
 Influence of light and, 178
Clauvel, J. P.
 Spontaneous recurrent fetal, 30
Clavel, F.
 Breast cancer and oral, 141
Clement, C.
 Dalkon fiasco continues, 119
 Depo provera approval un..., 109
Clements, S.
 Abortion pill, 47
Cleve, G.
 Structure elucidation of, 140
Clifford, C.
 Family planning: taking pre..., 96
Clubb, E.
 Natural methods of family, 159
Coad, N. R.
 Evaluation of blood loss, 34
Coale, A. J.
 Calculation of age-specific, 182
Cohan, A. S.
 No legal impediment: access, 17
Cohen, L.
 Halting St. Paul's tubals, 209
 Pro-choice cry foul, 68
 Voice for the unborn: the, 13
Cohen, L. G.
 Selective abortion and the, 11
 Voice for the unborn: the, 45
Cohen, M. M.
 Tubal sterilization in Manitoba, 201
Collins, K. M.
 Outpatient termination of, 36
Colombo, U. F.
 Contraception and the desire, 100
Comarr, A. E.
 Sexuality and fertility among, 170
Compton, A. W.
 POPLINE: a bibliographic, 159
Conant, M.
 Condoms prevent transmis..., 137
Conton, L.
 Reproductive decision-making, 156
Cook, C. L.
 Pregnancy prophylaxis, 135
Cook, R. J.
 Human rights of family, 151
Cooke, C.
 Shielding greed, 110
Cooke, I. D.
 Norethisterone concentration, 123

Cooper, W.
 True or false?, 126
Cordier, M. P.
 Evaluation of 100 autopsies, 60
Corea, G.
 Unnatural selection—menace, 201
Corongiu, F.
 Is voluntary abortion to be, 46
Cortellini, P.
 Postoperative uretero-vaginal, 188
Cosentino, M. J.
 Effect of graded unilateral, 176
Coulter, A.
 Ability to women to, 119
Couper-Smartt, J.
 Regrets after tubal sterilization, 207
Couzinet, B.
 Termination of early pregnancy, 49
Covington, D. L.
 Physician attitudes and family, 156
Craine, S.
 Abortion rights actions sche..., 77
Crawford, P.
 Lack of effect of sodium, 140
Crichton, M. A.
 Sweeter side of life: a, 97
Crimmins, E. M.
 Estimation of natural fertility, 181
Crossman, R. C.
 Abortion: a case study in, 19
Crowley, W. F., Jr.
 Progesterone antagonism, 11
Croxatto, H. B.
 Plasma levonorgestrel and, 106
Cruikshank, S. H.
 Avoiding ureteral injury during, 189
 Surgical method of identi..., 190
Csécsei, K.
 Formatioin of amniotic bands, 25
Csongrády, A.
 Early placental abruption dia..., 80
Culliton, B. J.
 Mosher sues Stanford, 83
Culpepper, J. P., 3d
 Ruptured tuba pregnancy six, 186
Cundy, J. M.
 Use of an emulsion, 38
Cunio, A. M.
 Risk of psychological, 191
Cunningham, M.
 Chronic occupational lead, 174
Curran, M. A.
 Drug interactions with the, 128
Cvitanic, O. A.
 Inquiry into the moral pre..., 20
D'Adamo, A. F.
 Whither the womb?, 12

Damwood, M. D.
    Prospects for fertility after, 169
Danda, A. K., 2
Dandapat, M. C.
    Non-operative procedure to, 205
Darabi, K. P., 2
D'Arcy, P. F.
    Drug interactions with oral, 128
Darling, C. A.
    Coitally active university, 195
Darney, P. D.
    Preparation of the cervix, 37
Darshini, P.
    Rampant female foeticide, 15
Das, A. M.
    Acinetobacter calcoacepticus in, 63
    Yersinia enterocolitica asso..., 66
Das, C.
    Pregnancy interfering action, 36
Daulk, J. R.
    Comparison of the effects, 115
Davidson, F.
    Pill does not cause, 132
Davies, C.
    Tactic of legal reform, 44
Davies, F. G.
    Possible dioxin poisoning in, 23
Davies, M.
    Hypothesis: blocking factors, 31
Davis, L.
    Con(tra)ception: hormonal, 109
    Pill cleared of breast cancer, 124
Davis, M.
    Strasser on dependence, 12
Davis, M. C.
    Computed tomography of, 187
Davis, M. R.
    Recurrent ectopic pregnancy, 210
Davis, N. J., 2
Davis, P. M.
    Dalkon shield, 119
Dawson, D. A.
    Effects of formal sex education, 98
    Effects of sex education on, 196
Dawson, J.
    Ovine enzootic abortion, 55
Dean, P. J.
    Malignant epithelioid, 130
De Arce, M. A.
    Computer model for the study, 27
de Barella, A., 2
de Bellefeuille, P.
    Abortion of thinking, 45
De Blasi, P., Jr., 2
DeCherney, A. H.
    Preservation of the ovary, 190
    Resectoscopic management, 29

DeClerque, J.
    Rumor, misinformation and oral, 84
Deer, B.
    Exposed: the bogus work, 121
DeGaris, R. M.
    Sympathetic enervation of, 219
De La Fuente, P.
    IUD removal causes pain, 119
de la Fuente Trigueros, G.
    Family planning within primary, 151
del Junco, D. J.
    Do oral contraceptives prevent, 139
DeLong, W. J.
    Distinguishing between ovine, 63
Del Porto, G.
    Complex balanced trans..., 27
    Cytogenetic aspects of, 28
    Transferrin and infertility, 26
Demas, B. E.
    Uterine MR imaging: effects, 126
Demeny, P., 2
de Paiva, G.
    Problema populacional brasil..., 82
Derksen, O. S.
    Benign liver tumors and, 127
Derksen, R. H.
    Striking association between, 26
Derkx, F. H.
    Immunorective renin, prorenim, 122
Derrick, C., 2
Desai, K. M.
    Vasal urinary fistula with, 218
Deshpande, V.
    Place of elective cerclage, 59
Deslypere, J. P.
    Effect of long-term, 128
Despodova, Ts.
    Changes in the serum con..., 27
    Histomorphological, histoen..., 28
    Immunoglobulins in the serum, 28
    Our experience in treating, 31
Deutinger, J.
    Effect of induced abortion, 34
DeVellis, B. M.
    Childfree by choice: attitudes, 203
Devi, M. R.
    Fertility and mortality, 181
Diamond, E. J.
    Serum hormone patterns during, 66
Diamond, M. P.
    Interaction of anticonvulsants, 122
Díaz, S.
    Fertility regulation in nursing, 105
Dickens, B. M.
    Dilemma of wrongful birth, 34
    Prenatal diagnosis and, 21
    Reproduction law—Part two, 152

Diczfalusy, E.
    Fertility regulation—the, 168
    New developments in oral, 106
Diker, K. S.
    Ovine abortion associated with, 65
Dills, W. L., Jr.
    Dietary potentiation of the, 167
Dinto, K.
    Induced abortion and risk, 35
Djerassi, C.
    Abortion in the United States, 16
Dobielinska-Eliszewska, T.
    Results of the combined, 190
Dodge, S. T.
    Peritoneal endometriosis in, 215
Doerr, E.
    Answering silent scream, 69
Dognin, C.
    Problems caused by the, 46
Domennighetti, G.
    Hysterectomy and sex of the, 185
Donadio, S.
    Echographic monitoring of, 32
Donovan, B.
    Taking a sexual history, 194
Doppenberg, H. J.
    Pregnancy proceeding to, 40
Dorflinger, L. J.
    Relative potency of progestins, 125
Döring, G. K.
    Reliability of the vaginal, 117
Dosterom, N.
    Birth control and abortion, 15
Douglas, C.
    1986 election report, 71
Dow, T.
    Characteristics of new, 158
Draca, P.
    Vaginal hysterectomy by, 190
Dranoff, L. S.
    Is it legal to give birth, 147
Dranov, P.
    Do you need these, 184
Drawz, G.
    New microsurgical methods for, 215
Drife, J.
    Hormonal contraception and, 129
Dryfoos, J.
    School-based health clinics, 93
Dube, J. P.
    Toxoplasma-like sporozoa in, 66
Dubey, J. P.
    Epizootiologic investigations, 24
    Toxoplasma gondii-induced, 66
Dubrova, IuE.
    Genetic and clinical study, 28
Dubuisson, J. B.
    Microsurgical sterilizations, 215

Dudziak, U.
    Effects of artifical abortion, 39
Dueholm, M.
    Choice of contraception, 94
Dueholm, S.
    Risks and benefits of, 212
Dumez, Y.
    Method for first trimester, 48
Dunbar, R.
    Stress is a good, 152
Dunn, S. K.
    Fertility decision making among, 81
D'Ursel, M. C.
    Natural regulation of fertility, 92
Dworkin, S.
    Marching on Washington: I, 71
Dyer, C.
    Gillick judgment. Contracep..., 111
Dyson, P. H.
    Surgery and the pill, 125
Dzhemilev, Z. A.
    Evaluation of the mutagenic, 139
Dzhvebenava, G. G.
    Immunologic indices in hiabitual, 28
Early, J. D.
    Low forager fertility, 169
Eastell, R.
    Prolonged hypoparathyroidism, 25
Eddy, R. G.
    Pregnant women and chlamydia, 25
Edelman, P.
    Immunological disorders of, 28
Edmonds, D. K.
    Reproductive potential in, 174
Edmonds, P.
    16500 fetuses intensify fight, 193
Edmondson, D.
    Birth control: what you, 80
    Future of contraception, 96
Edwards, I. S.
    Premedication with beta, 217
Eiben, B.
    Rapid cytogenetic diagnosis of, 58
Eisen, M.
    Role of health belief, 102
Ek, B.
    Value of premedication and, 38
Elam, M. B.
    Mitral valve prolapse in, 130
Elder, J. K.
    Significance of leptospiral titres, 66
Elder, P.
    Women's health care and, 98
Eliot, J.
    Progress report on a, 117
Elkik, F.
    Contraception in hypertensive, 104

Elkins, T. E.
Attitudes of mothers of children, 20
Ethics committee in a, 163
Ellery, C.
Case control study of breast, 127
Ellis, D. L.
Increased nevus estrogen and, 130
Ellis, L. C.
Reduced progesterone and, 66
Ellis, W. A.
Bovine leptospirosis: some, 63
Isolation of leptospires from, 54
Leptospires in pig urogenital, 64
Prevalence of leptospira infec..., 65
Ellsworth, H.
Oral contraception, 1986, 140
Ellsworth, L. R.
Psychosocialand psycho..., 207
Ellsworth, L. R.
Psychosocial and psycho..., 207
el-Raghy, I.
Pharmacokinetics of oral, 124
Elujoba, A. A.
Anti-implantation activity of the, 7
Emson, H. E.
Victoria Gillick and the, 98
Engel, E.
Nature and significance of, 25
Engert, S.
West Germany—feminism and, 14
Entrican, J. H.
Chronic inflammatory bowel, 127
Entwisle, B.
Multilevel dependence of con..., 84
Multilevel effects of socio..., 81
Eppleston, J.
Effect of progestagen, 177
Erasmus, G.
Factors associaed with the, 118
Erickson, A.
Epidemiological study...I., 10
Epidemiological study...II. A, 10
Erickson, T.
I had my tubes untied, 215
Eriksen, B. C.
Prognostic value of ultrasound, 62
Eriksen, B. O.
Teenagers and contraception, 103
Errey, B. B.
Open-ended vasectomy: an, 218
Ervin, P., 2
Eskens, H. R.
Meralgia paresthetica in, 185
Espodova, Ts.
Changes in the serum levels, 27
Esrig, S. M.
Spontaneous abortion after, 26

Evaldson, G. R.
Does the hygroscopic pro..., 39
Single dose intravenous, 186
Everett, R. W.
Semen fertility—an evaluation, 180
Evron, S.
Cholelithiasis, pregnancy and, 138
Exner, T. M.
Hypermasculinity and male, 115
Faich, G.
Toxic shock syndrome and, 117
Fakih, H. N.
Endometriosis after tubal, 202
Falsetti, L.
New associationof ethiny..., 123
Fan, G. S.
Prevention and treatment of, 8
Fanchenko, N. D.
Characteristics of the en..., 27
Fang, Y. X.
Morphologic study of, 175
Farber, D. A.
Abortion economics, 67
Farghaly, S. A.
Post-hysterectomy urethral, 188
Faria, G.
Women and abortion: attitudes, 22
Farkas, M.
Induction of labour and, 49
Farley, G.
Sisters do it for themselves, 11
Farquharson, R. G.
Lupus anticoagulant: a place, 25
Fassati, P.
Effect of hormonal contra..., 120
Fater, A.
Woman's place is in the hospital, 8
Faúndes, A.
Frequency and adequacy in, 100
Faye, B.
Toxicity of calotropis procera, 55
Fedele, L.
Effect of a new oral, 120
Fee, E.
Abortion: the politics of necessity, 9
Feinstein, D. I.
Lupus anticoagulant, throm..., 25
Felding, I. C.
Marvelon. A contraceptive, 123
Fernández del Castillo Ancira, C.
Tubal reanastomosis in the, 215
Fernando, D. F. S.
Environmental and other factors, 86
Ferri, R. M.
Canadian abortion law, 13
Fiddes, T. M.
Phenotypic and functional, 29

Figà-Talamanca, I.
  Illegal abortion: an attempt, 23
Filiberti, A.
  Analysis on the psychological, 190
Finazzi, G.
  IgM gammopathy and the, 30
Finch-Noyes, C. A. P.
  Sterilization of the mentally, 213
Finkel, M. L.
  Public policy and adolescent, 18
Fiore, N.
  Epidemiological data, cytology, 118
Firebaugh, G.
  Is the density-fertility, 181
Fischer, A.
  Why your contraceptive can, 110
Fischer, G.
  Histochemical and immuno..., 129
Fischer, R. G.
  Postcoital contraception, 134
Fisher, F.
  Who works in family, 164
Flanigan, B. J.
  Alcohol use, sexual intercourse, 95
Fletcher, I. C.
  Comparison of lamb, 176
Flick, L. H.
  Paths to adolescent parent..., 87
Flickinger, C. J.
  Effects of vasectomy on, 205
Flores Revuelta, L. J.
  Surgical sterilization: ten, 203
Foldesy, R. G.
  Lack of correlation between, 179
  Multiple actions of a novel, 106
Foote, R. H.
  Measurement of semen, 179
Ford, J.
  Australia claims lead in, 82
Forman, D.
  Cancer of the liver, 127
Forrest, J. D.
  End of IUD marketing, 98
Fortin, R.
  Comparison of church state..., 72
Fortney, J. A.
  Importance of family planning, 153
  Oral contraceptives and life, 123
Fossa, S. D.
  Fertility after radiotherapy for, 174
Foster, D. L.
  Determinants of puberty in, 176
Fosu, G. B.
  Fertility and family planning, 84
Foulon, W.
  Chronic ureaplasma urealyticum, 80
Foxman, B.
  Epidemiology of urinary tract, 117

Fradd, C. R.
  Introduction to the history and, 13
Frame, R.
  Prolife leaders say 1986, 73
Frame, R. L.
  School-based health clinics, 87
Franceschi, S.
  Oral contraceptives and, 132
Francome, C., 2
Frank, P.
  Natural family planning, 159
Frankel, S.
  Social and cultural aspects, 160
Fraser, I. S.
  Contraceptive development, 105
  Techniques for termination of, 48
Frazier, H. C.
  Burns, abortions and dying, 9
Free, M. J.
  Assessment of burst strength, 111
Freedman, M. A.
  Comparison of complication, 17
Freeley, D.
  Abortion rights: contested, 77
Freeman, E.
  Influence of maternal attitudes, 20
Frejka, T.
  Induced abortion and fertility, 35
Frenette, M. D.
  Effect of flushing the, 219
Friedli, A.
  Preoperative dilatation of the, 37
Friedman, N.
  Immaculate contraception, 96
Fromuth, M. E.
  Relationship of childhood, 195
Frydman, M.
  Male fertility in factor, 175
Frydman, R.
  Transplacental passage of, 8
Fuchi, I.
  Midtrimester artificial abortion, 36
Fuchs, V. R.
  Expenditures for reproduction, 34
Fuentes, V. O.
  Does prolactin regulate, 176
Fugère, P.
  Controversies on progester..., 141
Fullar, S.
  Care of postpartum adolescents, 99
Furstenberg, F. F.
  Sex education and sexual, 197
Furuhata, A.
  Studies of testicular function, 175
Gadsby, P.
  Birth control: what's now, 80
Gagne Gagné, C.
  Cardiovascular complications, 127

Gairola, G. A.
  Modern contraceptive practice, 87
Galen, D. I.
  Successful microsurgical, 211
Gall, S. A.
  Oral contraceptives and, 132
Gallagher, R. P.
  Reproductive factors, oral, 110
Gallagher, T.
  Strident scream: alarmed, 192
Gallen, M. E.
  Family planning programs, 165
Gallery, E. D.
  Effect of cyclical hormonal, 120
Gander, C.
  Nicaragua's women at war, 156
Gans, L. P.
  Discriminat analysis as a, 88
Gänsicke, A.
  Effect of female sex hormones, 128
García Alonso, A.
  New trends in the, 60
Gardell, M. A.
  June, bioethics and the, 42
Gardner, S. L.
  Perinatal grief and loss, 51
Garfield, H.
  Privacy, abortion, and, 43
Gascon, D.
  Sida, ce que font, 81
Gasper, J. A.
  What can government do, 75
Gatenbeck, L.
  Spontaneous recanalization, 218
Gaviño, F.
  Hormonal and menstrual, 212
Genest, P.
  Influence of the length, 58
Gensler, H. J.
  Kantian argument against, 20
Genz, H. J.
  Risks of contraception, 133
Gerais, A. S.
  Crossover pill study a mong, 113
Gerasimovich, G. I.
  Clinical aspects and diagnosis, 55
Gerber, P.
  Children and birth control, 150
  Who has the right, 93
Gerendai, I.
  Effect of neonatal vasectomy, 216
Gerlis, L. M.
  Cardiac malformations in preg..., 57
Gerson, M.-J.
  Prospect of parenthood for, 161
Gessell, J. M.
  Problem of abortion: a, 21

Ghosh, A.
  Zinc deficiency is not a, 26
Gibson, R. L.
  Reflections: taking sex out, 194
Gillespie, R. M.
  Contraception in context, 96
Gilmore, A.
  Sterilization of the mentally, 213
Gilson, E.
  Who shall live?, 12
Ginsberg, F. D.
  Reconstructing gender in, 56
Girvin, B.
  Social change and moral, 15
Gitter, M.
  Experimental infection of preg..., 54
Giwercman, A.
  Effect of salicylazosulphapy.., 107
Gladstone, B.
  Farwell to the IUD, 119
Glantz, L. H.
  Abortion and the Supreme, 40
Glass, J.
  Heading our way: five-year, 81
Gleick, E.
  Cervical cap moves toward, 116
Glen, K.
  Understanding the abortion, 22
Göcke, H.
  Pathomorphology and genetics, 25
Godon-Hardy, S.
  Ischemic strokes and oral, 130
Godoy, R. A.
  Human fertility and land, 170
Goebel, P.
  Single abortion—multiple, 38
Gold, J.
  Abortion foes use clinical, 75
Gold, R. B.
  Public funding of contra...1983, 77
  Public funding of contra...1985, 77
Goldberg, B. A.
  Sterilization of incompetents, 202
Goldenring, J. M.
  Brain-life theory: towards a, 9
Goldman, E. B.
  Legal aspects of abortion, 46
Goldman, J. A.
  Femoral neuropathy subse..., 188
Goldman, N.
  Estimation of fecundability, 181
Goldstein, L. F.
  Examining abortion funding, 77
Goldzieher, J. W.
  Use and misuse of the, 126
Gollub, E.
  Cervical cap, 116

231

Gonen, R.
    Short term prophylactic, 188
Gongsakdi, D.
    Galactorrhea in DMPA users, 107
Gonzalez, G.
    Hepatic tumors and oral, 129
Gonzalez, R.
    Protein C levels in late, 124
Goode, P. T., 2
Goodman, E.
    Another abortion ruling, 41
Goraya, R.
    Social and demographic, 117
Gordon, L.
    Women's freedom, women's, 75
Gordon, S. C.
    Resolution of a contraceptive, 141
Gorman, M. J.
    Shalom and the unborn, 44
Gorton, T.
    Ireland—Sinn Fein debates, 15
Gosling, L. M.
    Selective abortion of entire, 66
Gould, D.
    Comparison of recovery, 183
    Hidden problems after, 191
Gow, H. B.
    Bombing clinics harms pro-, 75
Graber, C. V., 2
Gramick, J.
    Vatican's battered wives (nuns, 74
Granberg, D.
    Anomaly in political perception, 70
    Search for gender differences, 21
Grant, P.
    Sex and male responsibility, 88
Gray, J. P.
    Growing yams and men, 175
Gray, M.
    Good news about birth, 109
Gray, R.
    Outcome of pregnancy, 152
Graziani, M. P.
    Psychoreactivity in voluntary, 37
Greenblatt, R. B.
    Oral contraceptives: the state, 140
Greenhalgh, S., 2
Greenspoon, J. S.
    Cerebral infarction, lupus, 27
Gregoretti, S. M.
    Comparison of water, 183
Gregorini, G.
    Recurrent abortion with lupus, 29
Greig, A.
    Field studies on the efficacy, 54
Griffiths, M.
    Gonococcal pelvic inflamma..., 121

Grigorenko, P. P.
    Indices of steroid hormones and, 10
Grimes, D. A.
    Reversible contraception for the, 97
Grimmer, S. F.
    Bioavailability of ethinylo..., 138
Grisez, G.
    Infallibility and contraception, 91
Grubb, G. S.
    Luteal phase pregnancy and, 209
Gu, Y.
    Effects of gossypol on, 105
Gu, Z. P.
    Antifertility effects of 2 alpha, 138
Gudmundsson, J. A.
    Intranasal peptide contracep..., 106
Gudorf, C. E.
    To make a seamless garment, 12
Guha, S. K.
    Contraception in male monkeys, 99
Guillebaud, J.
    Spironolactone in combina..., 140
Guillon, P.
    Births, fertility, rhythms and, 181
Gupta, A. N.
    Pathological changes in, 206
Gupta, K. L.
    Socio-biological parameters in, 211
Gupta, K. L.
    Socio-biological parameters, 203
Gustavii, B.
    Miscarriage rate in women, 60
Gustavson, L. E.
    Impairment of prednisolone, 122
    Macromolecular binding of, 123
Gutlierrez, R. D.
    Using the forced choice, 198
Guttmacher, A. F., 2
Guy, M.
    Desire for a child, 80
Haas, G. G., Jr.
    Circulating antisperm anti..., 27
Hadjimichael, O. C.
    Abortion before first live birth, 23
Hadlow, V.
    Abortion and medical discipline, 8
Haggis, F.
    Contraceptives without con..., 142
Hakim, M.
    Broad spectrum antibiotics as, 182
Haldane, J. J.
    Ethics of life and death, 20
Hale, R.
    Oral contraception, 1986, 140
Hall, P. F.
    Oral contraceptives, 1985, 134
Hallett, G. L.
    Contraception and prescriptive, 91

Hallgren, R.
Contraception—with us and, 137
Hallingby, L.
Human sexuality and sex, 194
Halub, M. F.
Thrombosis due to permanent, 134
Hamburg, M. V.
Sex education and health, 197
Hamed et Affandi, M. H.
Ultrasonography as a new, 166
Hamilton, J. O.
Searle's troubles give Alza, 118
Han, Z. H.
Follow-up study of the, 105
Handelsman, D. J.
Testicular function and fertility, 175
Handsfield, H. H.
Criteria for selective screening, 94
Hanna, G. S.
Sudden deafness and the, 134
Hansen, B. M.
Changes in symptoms and, 187
Hansmann, I.
Cytogenetic analysis of early, 9
Hanson, M.
Update on oral contraceptives, 134
Hansson, V.
Marvelon—when the adverse, 123
Hardin, S. B.
Reflections on a miscarriage, 56
Hargreave, T. B.
Fecundability rates from an, 174
Harlap, S.
Congenital abnormalities in, 127
Harold, J. M.
Contraceptive use and the, 113
Harris, B. A., Jr.
Peripheral placental separation, 79
Harris, G. W., Jr.
Fathers and fetuses, 20
Harris, S.
Services and educational, 199
Harrison, H. R.
Cervical chlamydia trachomatis, 101
Harrison, K. A.
Family planning and maternal, 159
Harrison, R. F.
Treatment of habitual abortion, 31
Hart, L.
On the march for choice, 78
Hartnagel, T. F.
Public opinion and the, 21
Harvey, S. M.
Alcohol consumption, female, 116
Hatherley, L. I.
Lactation and postpatum, 159
Haukkamaa, M.
Bacterial flora of the cervix, 116

Hauser, G. A.
Local mechanical and chemical, 116
Hausner, K.
Sterilization failures with, 206
Havard, J. D.
Teenagers and contraception, 103
Haverstock, L. M.
Implications of treatment on, 99
Havlík, I.
Vaginal flora during supportive, 62
Havránek, F.
Population status and fertility, 97
Hayashi, H.
Fertility of the monorchid, 178
Hazes, J. M.
Do oral contraceptives prevent, 141
Healey, J. M.
Abortion 1986: state con..., 41
Hebert, C. C.
Spontaneous abortion and, 26
Hebert, C. C.
Spontaneous abortion and, 58
Heidam, L. Z.
Self-reported data on, 58
Heisterberg, L.
Sequelae of induced first, 40
Hellberg, D.
Long term use of oral, 130
Heller, P. B.
Cervical carcinoma found, 183
Hemingway, E.
Making the choie: 1927, 47
Hemminki, E.
Effects of cesarean section, 24
Henifin, M. S.
Wrongful life cases and, 47
Henker, B.
Abortion by the ballot box, 12
Hennessee, J. A.
Inside a right-to-life mind, 72
Hennig, A.
Relation between vitamin E, 179
Henry, A.
India: NET-OEN trials, 155
Henshaw, S. K.
Portrait of American women, 18
Herbert, S.
Case and comment: aiding, 80
Herceg-Baron, R.
Supporting teenagers' use of, 103
Herland, K.
Abortion coalition in Quebec, 13
Herman, J. M.
Is hysterectomy a risk, 188
Hermansen, J., 3
Hermsell, D. L.
Doxycycline and cefamandole, 184

Hernandez, D. J.
Fertility reduction policies and, 157
Herr, J. C.
Enzyme-linked immuno..., 219
Herreman, G.
Conference at the Salpêtriére, 24
Herrero Martin, M. R.
Adolescent facing contracep..., 99
Hervet, E.
Toward the disappearance of, 61
Hewson, P. M.
Research on adolescent male, 115
Hewson, P. M.
Research on adolescent, 137
Hewyard, C.
Abortion: a moral choice, 19
Higgins, J. E.
Hospitalizations among balck, 122
Hill, D. L.
Experience with microsurgical, 214
Hill, J. A.
Blood transfusions for recurrent, 30
Hillard, P. A.
Stitch in time . . . cervical, 12
Himmelstein, J. L.
Social basis of antifeminism, 22
Hines-Harris, J.
Study of the perception, 115
Hippler, R.
We are the majority, say, 19
Hirschman, C.
Recent rise in Malay, 172
Hjort, T.
Identification of candidate, 136
Ho, P. C.
Return of ovulation after, 61
Hobbes, J.
Interactions between ethanol, 139
Hoffacker, P.,3
Hoffman, S. R.
Comparison of childfree and, 150
Hofmeister, H.
Synthesis of gestodene, 125
Hogan, D. P.
Impact of social status, 160
Social and environmental, 144
Högberg, U.
Maternal deaths related to, 35
Hoge, D. R.
Interpreting change in American, 92
Hogue, C. J.
Impact of abortion on sub..., 39
Hohlweg-Majert, P.
Hysterocolpectomy. The, 185
Holck, S.
Oral contraceptives and, 131
Holden, C.
AID withholds U.N., 95

Holehan, A. M.
Lifetime breeding studies in, 179
Holian, J.
Effect of female education, 172
Hollstein, K.
Reform of Penal Code, 43
Holly, E. A.
Cutaneous melanoma and oral, 141
Holsinger, K. E.
Selection for increased, 169
Homans, H., 3
Homm, R. E.
ORF 13904, a new, 106
Hoppner   Höppner, W.
Examination of the fertility, 174
Hornaday, A.
Fetus as spaceman (views, 70
Horne, H. W., Jr.
Evidence of improved preg..., 59
Sexually transmitted diseases, 100
Hornick, J. P.
Successful and unsuccessful, 101
Hoshi, N.
Studies on hydroxypropyl..., 180
Houston, M. J.
Breast feeding, fertility and, 95
Hovey, G.
Supporting choice: Christian, 74
Howard, M.
Sex and young people, 197
Howard, T.
Abortion: the teenage patient, 33
Howdhury, S. I.
Equine herpesvirus type 1, 64
Howe, C. L.
Development theory and, 196
Howe, L. K., 3
Howie, P. W.
Progestogen-only pill, 124
Huang, H. L.
Fallopian tube sterilization, 206
Huang, K. C.
Effects of meclofenamate and, 209
Hughes, G. R.
Anticardiolipin syndrome, 30
Huisveld, I. A.
Renin-angiotensin system, 125
Hunter, D. G.
Abnormal axonemes in sperm, 174
Hurwitz, S. R.
Yolk sac sign: sonographic, 49
Husar, M.
Regulation of fertility in, 15
Hutti, M. H.
Exploratory study of the, 51
Hwang, P. L.
Effect of oral contraceptives, 120

Hyland, J. H.
Attempted conversion of twin, 33
Hynes, M. J.
Social skills and responses, 110
Ichinoe, K.
Complete reconstruction of, 183
Iglesias Cortit, L.
New advances in contracep..., 100
Imber, J. B., 3
Imoedemhe, D. A.
Intestinal injuries following, 39
Imoto, S.
Fertility study on haloperidone, 178
Ineichen, B.
Contraceptive experience and, 115
Ingerslev, H. J.
Fetal tibia retained in, 34
Isenalumhe, A. E.
Changing pattern of post-, 86
Ishii, M.
Clinical tests in obstetrics, 62
Ismach, J.
Second look at the pill, 99
Isojima, S.
Development of a contra..., 135
Ivarsson, M.
Teenage girls in Malmö, 103
Iwanska, S.
Effect of beta carotene, 176
Iyriboz, Y.
Assessing the need for, 101
Jack, M. S., 3
Jacobs, A. J.
Complications in patients, 183
Jaffe, R.
Fetal death in early pregnancy, 25
Prophylactic single-dose, 188
James, M.
Your hands: lethal or life, 39
Janowitz, B.
Knowledge and practices of, 100
Side effects and discon.., 110
Jaquith, C.
Nicaragua—debate on abortion, 15
Nicaragua—legalization of, 15
Jarallah, Y.
Is routine ultrasound before, 46
Jarow, J. P.
Quantitative pathologic, 218
Jelliffe, D. B.
Lactation amenorrhoea: an, 165
Jenish, D.
Henry's in the high court, 42
Jensen, E.
Comment on Glenn, 167
Desired fertility, the "up, 150
Jesaitis, E. K.
Abortion: a look at our Christian, 19

Jespersen, J.
Increased euglobulin fibri..., 129
Inhibition of tissue-type, 122
Jessopp, L.
Well woman care: whose, 163
Jha, K.
Poststerilisation tubal preg..., 210
Ji, Y. Y.
Production on monoclonal, 8
Jindrová, Z.
Psychological sequelae of, 191
Jirásek, J. E.
Immunologic factors and failed, 10
John, C. C.
Abortion: medical perspec..., 45
John, H. J., 3
Johnson, E. H.
Politics, power and prevention, 83
Johnson, J. E.
Personal control interventions, 191
Johnson, J. H.
Individual vs. group education, 89
Johnson, N. E.
Relative income, race, and, 181
Johnson, R. K.
Influencing prolificacy of sows, 179
Jonas, H. S.
On the abortion issue, 46
Jones, E. F., 3
Teenage pregnancy in, 111
Jones, J. E.
Strategies for evaluating a, 162
Jones, R. W.
Rules of practice in Paul, 21
Jongbloet, P. H.
Ageing gamete in relation to, 90
Jordan, S. M.
Moral community of persons, 20
Joshi, J. V.
Antacid does not reduce, 119
Joshi, U. M.
Impact of hormonal contra..., 112
Juhr, N. C.
Mycoplasma infection—factors, 54
Kabir, M.
Characteristics of users of, 110
Kably Ambe, A.
Salpingoclasia by laparoscopy, 208
Kaempfer, S. H.
Fertility considerations and, 168
Fertility considerations in, 168
Kafrissen, M. E.
Cluster of abortion deaths, 23
Kahn, K.
GLDC snubs Dukakis at, 70
Kaker, D. N., 3
Kallan, J.
Determinants of effective, 167

235

Kallgren, J. K.
  Family planning in China, 83
Kaminski, J. M.
  Vaginal contraceptive activity, 106
Kangas, G. L., 3
Kanhai, H. H.
  Selective termination in, 38
Kantrowitz, B.
  Grim ABC's of AIDS: a, 198
Kapoor, T. N.
  Differences in levels of, 151
Kapor-Stanulovic, N.
  Comparative study (1964, 162
Karefa-Smart, J.
  Health and family planning, 153
Kåregård, M.
  Incidence and recurrence rate, 79
Karesky, R. A.
  Comparison of two interven..., 51
Karlsson, I.
  Economy for women, 145
Kasai, R.
  Reproductive risk of para..., 29
Kasan, P. N.
  Effects of recent oral, 128
Katcher, M. L.
  Chlamydia trachomatis, 157
Katsulov, A.
  Abruptio placentae, 79
  Hormonal treatment of spon..., 57
Katz, D. F.
  Morphometric analysis of, 175
Kaunitz, A. M.
  Abortions that fail, 24
  Mental retardation: a con..., 185
Kay, B. J.
  Market for health care, 152
Kaye, C. I.
  Evaluation of chromosomal, 22
Kaye, T.
  Are you for RU-486, 71
Kayembe, T. B.
  Traditional structures clash, 153
Kazi, A.
  Phase IV study of, 106
Keirse, M. J.
  Safety of chorionic villus, 26
Keller, E.
  Risks of contraception: the, 133
Keller, P. J.
  Hormonal contraception using, 107
Kelly, J. J.
  Tracking the intractable: a, 18
Kelly, K.
  Consequences of treating the, 9
Kelly, P.
  Court upholds ortho damages, 88

Kemmer, D.
  Victorian values and the, 86
Kemp, J.
  Why abortion is a human, 22
Kendrick, J. S.
  Characteristics of vasectomies, 216
  Hysterectomy performed, 185
  Vasectomies performed by, 219
Kennedy, J. E.
  Abortion: toward a standard, 53
Kennedy, W. R.
  Economics and other, 173
Kenny, M., 3
Kenyon, E., 3
Kerin, J.
  Sex preselection: realities, 152
Kerr-Wilson, R. H.
  Effect of beta-adrenergic, 188
Kertész, A.
  Effects of benzodiazepines as, 184
Khachapuridz, N. V.
  Results of clinical use, 62
Khalifa, M. A.
  Determinants of natural, 173
Khan, A. R.
  Induced abortion in a rural, 12
Khan, B.
  Jerry Falwell meets the, 78
Khan, M. E.
  Comparison of 1970 and, 89
Khokhlov, L. K.
  Conditions for the transition, 183
Khoo, S. K.
  Cancer risks and the, 127
Kiel, F. W.
  Medical value of examining, 59
Kierkegaard, A.
  Side and site of deep, 133
Kikku, P.
  Supravaginal uterine, 189
Kim, I.-C., 3
King, D. J.
  Fertility in young men, 168
King, K. K.
  Bovine embryo transfer, 53
Kirby, D.
  Sexuality education: a more, 198
Kiriushchenkov, A. P.
  Acute endometritis and, 23
  Uterine myoma initiating a, 26
Kirkbride, C. A.
  Abortion in sheep caused, 52
  Porcine abortion caused by, 55
Kiser, E. E.
  Teenagers talk about sex, 75
Kissling, F.
  Religion and reproductive, 161

236

Kiupel, H.
  Haemophilus somnus infection, 54
Kiura, A.
  Family planning, 161
Kjaeldgaard, A.
  Long term treatment with, 130
Kjeldaas, L.
  Oral contraceptive agents, 131
Klaerke, M.
  Laparoscopic sterilization with, 212
Klein, F. A.
  Vasovasostomy: efficacy and, 216
Kliment, V.
  Postcoital contraception, 134
Kline, J.
  Induced abortion and the, 25
Klopovich, P. M.
  Sexuality and the adolescent, 197
Knodel, J.
  Infant feeding practices, post.., 114
Knopp, R. H.
  Clinical chemistry alterations in, 139
  Effects of pregnancy, post..., 121
Knorre, P.
  Outcome of pregnancy, 215
Knudsen, L. B.
  Deliveries and abortions, 45
  Legally induced abortion, 46
Knuth, U. A.
  Clinical tria of 19-, 107
Kobyliansky, E.
  Differential fertility and, 167
Koch, M.
  Further report on the, 173
Kohli, K. L.
  Fertility levels, trends and, 172
Kohn, I.
  Counseling women who, 202
Koinzer, G.
  Prevention of infection with, 37
Kokutsov, A.
  Peroral contraceptive agents, 132
Kölbl, H.
  Severe micturition disorder, 186
Komaki, R.
  Prognostic significance of, 186
Kondela, A.
  Isolation of Rift Valley fevor, 54
Kondrat'ev, N. P.
  Postoperative thrombosis of, 188
Kone-Diabi, A.
  Family planning, 153
Kong, Y. C.
  Fertility regulating agents, 181
Kopera, H.
  Unintended effects of oral...I, 134
  Unintended effects of oral...II, 134

Koren, G.
  Theophylline pharmaco..., 126
Korkhov, V. V.
  Current trends in the, 139
Korovkin, M. A.
  Oral contraceptives in a, 85
Kourany, R. F.
  Age of sexual consent, 193
Kovac, S. R.
  Intramyometrial coring as an, 190
Kovacs, G. T.
  Contraceptive diaphragm. Is it, 115
  Post-partum fertility, 169
Kovacs, L.
  Effect of the contraceptive, 112
Kozhukharov, E.
  Research on Pharmachim's, 169
Kramarskaia, N. B.
  Clinico-morphological aspects, 80
Krauss, R. M.
  Effects of oral contraceptives, 121
Krebs, H.
  Partnership, sexuality and, 100
Krishnamoorthy, S.
  J. Y. Parlange, 181
Kroboth, P. D.
  Pharmacodynamic evaluation, 124
Kronenfeld, J. J.
  Feminist movements and, 91
  Impact of birth control, 91
Krzeminski, A.
  Relation between various, 26
Kubba, A. A.
  Biochemistry of human, 141
Kubota, R.
  Abortion counseling, 32
Kucher, A. N.
  Population genetics study of, 29
Kuczynski, J.
  Liberal studies...sex, 198
Kugel, C.
  Relationship between weight, 117
Kuhl, H.
  Randomized cross-over...I, 125
  Randomized cross-over...II, 125
Kukharenko, V. I.
  Collagen synthesis in the cells, 24
Kuklík, M.
  Dermatoglyphic findings in, 28
Kulcsár-Gergely, J.
  Liver parameters during, 122
Kulig, J. W.
  Adolescent contraception: an, 102
Kulp, D.
  125,000 marck for women's, 78
Kumaran, T. V.
  Brainstorming: an application, 164

Kumari, R.
Attitude of girls towards, 158
Kuo, H. C.
Voiding dysfunction after, 187
Kurebe, M.
Study on the effect, 180
Kureishi, Y.
South Asia's family planning, 82
Kurtzman, C.
Family planning: beyond, 100
Kurz, W. S.
Genesis and abortion: an, 20
Kuznetsova, T. I.
Prevention of miscarriage, 59
Labarrere, C. A.
Primary chronic abortion, 29
Labbok, M. H.
Contraception during lactation, 145
Laboy, I.
Frank discussion: sex and, 193
Lacombe, D.
Effects of the chemosterilant, 207
Lacoste, C.
Sex and contraceptive, 104
Lacoumenta, S.
Effects of cortisol suppression, 209
Ladd, J.
Euthanasia, liberty, and religion, 72
Laferia, J. J.
Spontaneous abortion, 58
La Joie, K. S., 3
Lake, R. A.
Metaethical framework of, 20
Lal, R.
Antifertility effect of neem, 108
Lallande, A.
Condom maker goes after, 114
Lalos, O.
Bladder wall mechancis and, 189
Lammer, E. J.
Exogenous sex hormone, 129
Lamptey, P.
Comparative study of Neo, 104
Lamur, H. E.
Recent fertility trends in, 173
Lanctot, C. A.
Natural family planning, 159
Landry, E.
Teen pregnancy in New Orleans, 18
Landy, U.
Abortion counselling—a new, 32
Lanes, S. F.
Toxic shock syndrome, con..., 116
Lang, G.
Vancouver tribunal condemns, 13
Langford, C. M.
Is there a connection, 174

Langley, P. A.
Laboratory evaluation of, 207
Langmade, C. F.
Partial colpocleisis, 190
Langsten, R.
Determinants of natural, 170
Lanham, J. G.
Prostacyclin deficiency in a, 30
Lansac, J.
Complications and results, 189
Lara Ricalde, R.
Oral contraceptives..., 131
Oral contraceptives...morbidity, 132
Larsson-Cohn, U.
Effects on the lipoprotein, 121
Lassner, K. J.
Sterilization approval and, 211
Lathrop, L.
New pro-choice doctor, 70
Role of a sexuality, 152
Lauersen, N. H.
Cervical cap: effectiveness, 116
Laukaran, V. H.
Contraceptive use, amenor..., 89
Laurenson, I. F.
Fertility at low and, 172
La Vecchia, C.
Characteristics of women, 15
Lawrence, M.
Pilot prospective hysterec..., 185
Lawther, G., 3
Lawton, K. A.
Arguments over abortion, 41
High Court strikes down, 42
Profile groups press, 192
Lawton, M.
Horrors of the Dalkon, 115
Lazarus, A.
Psychiaric aspects of preg..., 37
Lê, M. G.
Possible cohort effects in, 133
Lee, E. T.
Rare late complication of first, 39
Lee, H. Y.
Twenty year experience with, 205
Lee, R. E., Jr.
Fecundity and longevity of, 177
Lee, T. M.
Female rats in a laboratory, 177
Legault, C.
Selectionof breeds, strains, 180
Legler, U. F.
Marked alteations is dose, 123
Lehrer, E. L.
Child care arrangements and, 150
Lehrman, L.
Right to life and the, 21

Lehtinen, P.
Psychological factors related, 37
Leibowitz, A.
Economic model of teenage, 17
Leinster, C.
Rubber barons (rise in, 114
Leinster, S. J.
Mammographic breast, 130
Leklem, J. E.
Vitamin B-6 requirement and, 126
Lellé, R. J.
Local metronidazole and PVP, 185
Lemle, L.
Conflict over a past abortion, 9
Lena, S. M.
Hypocrisy of abortion, 46
Lendvay, A.
Psychological counseling in, 160
Lennertz, J. E.
Human rights and institutional, 71
Leonard, A.
Effect of an enhanced, 176
Leoni, V.
Assay of polychlorobiphenyls, 22
LeQuinquis, P.
Medico-legal risks of human, 201
Lesko, S. M.
Evidence for an increased, 129
Leslie, N. J. S., 3
Lesser, F.
Pill use and the risk, 132
Levin, B.
Consum tet of homogeneity, 57
Levine, C.
Of fathers, fetuses, 43
Levinson, R. A.
Contraceptive self-efficcy, 147
Levison, V.
Effect of fertility, libido, 174
Levy, V.
Seasonal fertility cycles in, 171
Lewis, M. A., 4
Do contraceptive prices affect, 99
Li, D. Z.
Effect of norethisterone, 139
Liang, Z.-G.
Non-cross-reactivity of, 97
Lichter, E. D.
Value of routine dilation, 206
Liefeld, D. R.
Abortion and the two kingdoms, 8
Liew, D. F.
Comparative study of the, 104
Prospective study of the, 124
Light, R. U.
Africa and the limits to, 82
Limpaphayom, K.
Tubotubal anastomosis for, 202

Lin, C. C.
Cytogenetic studies in spon..., 13
Lin, X.
Family-planning policy, 154
Lind, T.
Human pregnancy failure, 24
Lindahl, B.
Identification of chorion villi, 32
Lindbohm, M. L.
Reproductive health of working, 58
Spontaneous abortions among, 23
Lindenthal, J. J.
Selected Jewish views of, 47
Lindermayer, V.
Abortion: how should women, 71
Lindsay, J.
Politics of population control, 85
Ling, W. Y.
Serum gonadotropi and, 125
Lipnick, R. J.
Oral contraceptives and breast, 131
Lippman, A.
Montreal Pregnancy Study: an, 13
Liu, S. C.
Sperm autoimmunity in, 217
Liyama, P.
25,000 in United States, 18
Loesch, D. Z.
Dermal ridge patterns and, 172
Löhr, K. F.
Trypanosoma evansi infection in, 66
Lokhov, R. E.
Sensitivity of the pituitary, 182
Lombard, C. M.
Diagnosis of systemic, 184
Longman, S. M.
Effect of oral contraceptive, 120
Lopes, P.
Partial termination of a, 36
López Elizondo, C.
Reflections on a miscarriage, 52
Loraine, J. A.
Contraception—the next 25, 83
Löscher, W.
Effect of non-steroidal, 177
Lotocki, W.
Urologic complications in, 189
Lotstra, H., 4
Lovett, J.
Suppression of post, 219
Low, C.
Cleric on a collision, 91
Flock at odds with its shepherds, 10
Lozano Elizondo, A.
Hysterocolpectomy in, 189
Lucas, M. H.
Immunofluorescence and cell, 54

Lucey, S.
  Association between lame..., 176
Luerti, M.
  Post-coital contraception by, 118
Luker, K., 4
Lumb, G.
  Regression of pathologic, 101
Lundberg, N.
  Bureaucratization of birth, 149
Luo, L. L.
  Study of the mechanism of, 8
Lurie, S.
  SIDS might influence, 201
Lushing, P.
  Abortion: a disputation, 9
Luyckx, A. S.
  Carbohydrate metabolism in, 127
MacCormack, C. P.
  Lay concepts affecting, 155
MacDowell, M.
  Factors affecting the choice, 96
Macintosh MacIntosh, D.
  Sex education: fact or, 198
MacKay, H. T.
  Safety of local versus, 38
MacKay, R.
  Spain—nation at war over, 16
MacKenzie, D.
  Contraceptive vaccine moves, 90
MacKenzie, I. Z.
  Prostaglandins in the fetal, 11
Madhavapeddi, R.
  Side effects of oral, 133
Maggi, R.
  Carcinoma of the residual, 187
Maguire, D. C.
  Catholicism and modernity, 72
Mahran, M.
  Use of ultrasound in the, 31
Makoi, Z.
  Impact of abortion policy on, 14
Malhotra, R.
  Assessment of knowledge, 158
Malini, S.
  Measurement of breast, 123
Mall-Haefeli, M.
  What does the micropill, 134
Mandal, A.
  Human seminal antiliquefying, 104
Mandal, B.
  Effect of combined ethinyl, 139
Mandel, H.
  Oral contraceptives and, 131
Manthorne, J.
  Depo provera: drug, 128
Manuilova, I. A.
  Current principles of regulation, 96
  Lipid metabolism in hormonal, 122

Mao, W. T.
  Preoperative cervical dilatation, 37
Mardesic, T.
  Abortion in early pregnancy, 9
Marinoni, P.
  Observations on the fertility, 174
Marks, J. L.
  Relationship of nonreturn, 179
Marmar, J. L.
  Use of papaverine during, 216
Marriott, A.
  Assessment of psychological, 126
Marshner, C., 4
Marsico, S.
  Post-cesarean hysterectomy, 186
Marsiglio, W.
  Husbands' sex-role preferences, 88
  Impact of sex education, 147
Martin, R. H.
  Prospective serial study of, 179
März, W.
  Randomized crossover com..., 125
Masel-Walters, L.
  For the "poor mute mothers", 10
Maslen, G.
  Downfall of absent profesor, 90
Massouda, D.
  Laparoscopic tubal ligation, 206
Mathiason, D.
  Terror and harrassment charged, 76
Mathie, W.
  Reason, revelation and, 43
Mats, M. N.
  Mechanism of the contracep..., 106
Mattson, R. H.
  Use of oral contraceptives by, 126
Mawyer, M.
  Supreme Court weighs, 44
Mayberry, J. F.
  European survey of fertility, 181
Maynard, R.
  Depo-provera: is it a, 128
Mazze, R. I.
  Fertility, reproduction, and, 178
McAuliffe, K.
  Startling fount of healing, 22
McBee, S.
  Call to tame the genie, 92
McCall, C.
  Denise's decision (teenager's, 74
McCarthy, S.
  Female pelvic anatomy: MR, 121
McClarty, G. A.
  Ribonucleotide reductase: an, 108
McClure, T. J.
  Improved fertility in dairy cows, 178
McCormack, E., 4

McCormick, B.
  Hospitals: new targets of, 68
McCormick, N.
  Adolescents' values, sexuality, 98
  Sex-education needs and, 98
McCracken, J.
  Contraceptive care and family, 45
McCracken, J. S.
  Contraceptive care and family, 96
McDaniel, P. A.
  Oral contraceptives and, 132
McDermott, R. J.
  Racial differences in the, 97
McDonald, H.
  Sheathed in profits, 137
McDonnell, K., 4
  Not an easy choice, 67
McFadyen, I. R.
  Missed abortion, and later, 49
McFarlane, D. R.
  Are block grants more, 158
McIntosh, E. N.
  Recent changes in the, 202
McIntosh, P. L.
  Contraception: what's ahead, 96
McIntyre, D. R.
  Effect of initial insemination, 177
  Effect of sperm numbers, 177
McIntyre, J. A.
  Antibody responses in, 27
  Characterization of maternal, 9
  Clinical value of research, 27
  Immunologic testing and, 31
  Laboratory and clinical aspects, 31
McKenzie, R.
  Topical etidocaine during, 211
McKnight, J.
  150,000 turn out for abortion, 78
McKown, J. M.
  Disabled teenagers: sexual, 196
McLaren, A.
  Creation of a haven for, 201
McLaughlin, L.
  Catholic doctor who fought, 119
McLeod, B.
  Propofol ("Diprivan") infusion, 37
McManus, S. P.
  Cytogenetics of recurrent, 57
McPherson, K.
  Early oral contraceptive use, 128
McPherson, M. P.
  International family planning, 84
McRae, G. I.
  Long term reversible sup..., 101
Meeker, D. L.
  Breed differences in return, 7
Mehrotra, R.
  Changes in seminiferous, 216

Meirik, O.
  Oral contraceptive use and, 131
Melton, G. B., 4
Menehan, K.
  Where have all the babies, 74
Menken, J.
  Age and infertility, 182
Menken, M.
  Age and fertility: how, 182
Mercy, A. R.
  Evaluation of a non-surgical, 207
Mesrobian, H. G.
  Long term followup of, 175
Mettler, L.
  Reversible immunosuppres.., 101
Metzger, D. A.
  Association of endometriosis, 24
Mhatre, P. N.
  Laparoscopic sterilization in, 209
Michael, R. T.
  Entry into marriage and, 80
Michalek, E.
  Self concept of women with, 30
Michel, E.
  Failure of high-dose, 174
Mikhailenko, E. T.
  Pathogenesis and correction, 62
Mikrut, W.
  Serum prolac in levels, 133
Mikulíková, L.
  Monitoring trophoblast-specific, 61
Milby, T. H.
  Natural law evolution, and the, 11
Miller, B. D.
  Health, fertility, and society, 85
Miller, C. D.
  Effects of socioeconomic, 86
Miller, J. A.
  Birth control vaccines, 135
Miller, L. T.
  Do oral contraceptive agents, 104
Miller, M. E.
  Teenage fertility, socioeco..., 90
Miller, W. B.
  Married women and contra..., 207
  Why some women fail, 101
Milne, R.
  Follow up study of 200, 216
Milner, C.
  Fort McMurray's choice, 13
Mintz, M.
  Crime against women—A.H., 118
Mintz, M. C.
  Abruptio placentae: apparent, 79
Minuk, G. Y.
  Condoms and hepatitis B, 137
Miodovnik, M.
  Elevated maternal glyco..., 57

Glycemic control and spon..., 25
Mirsky, J.
  Return of the baby, 83
Misz, M.
  Effect of hormonal contra..., 128
Mitchell, G.
  Bovine abortion associated, 53
Mitchell, P.
  Abortion—a personal approach, 9
Mitu, S.
  Influence of pregnancy, birth, 23
Mock, N. B.
  Correlates and implications of, 114
Moghadam, V.
  Feminists must humanize, 67
Mohamed, A. R.
  Enzyme activities in amniotic, 53
Mokhiber, R.
  Criminals by any other, 118
Moldanado, S. A.
  Trends in public attitudes, 22
Moltz, L.
  Laparoscopic tubal sterilization, 209
Mondy, L. W.
  Physician extender services in, 158
Montali, R. J.
  Equine herpesvirus type, 54
Moore, D. S.
  Age, gender, and ethnic, 114
Moore, P. D.
  Exploitation of animal mobility, 96
Morain, M.
  China's side, 83
  Directive language, 83
  International scene, 84
  Population update, 84
  Worldwide challenge, 84
Moran, A. F.
  Politics of adolescent, 157
Moreau, D.
  Principal decisional factors, 147
Moreau-Bisseret, N.
  Scientific warranty for sexual, 154
Morgan, S. P.
  Individual and couple, 160
Mori, T.
  Production of monoclonal anti..., 97
Morin, L.
  Right to live with pain, 37
Morrell, A.
  Labor union women join, 69
Morrison, D. M.
  Adolescent contraceptive, 146
Moser, P. B.
  Carbohydrate tolerance and, 119
Moser, W.
  Modern aspects of contracep.., 100

Mosher, D. L.
  Contributions of sex guilt, 115
Mosher, W. D.
  Religion and fertility in the, 87
  Reproductive impairments in, 173
  Source of service and visit, 87
Mott, S. C.
  Case of Brave New People:, 9
Mukerji, S.
  Decline in maternal mortality, 150
Mumford, S. D.
  Role of abortion in control, 24
Muraskin, L. D.
  Sex education mandates: are, 198
Murdia, A.
  Study of sperm antibodies, 217
Murphy, T. F.
  Acts and omissions doctrine and, 9
Murray, L.
  Pill personality, 124
Murthy, N. V.
  Reproductive toxicity of, 180
Musierowicz, A.
  Labor in twin pregnancy, 188
Musil, C. M.
  Non-negotiable demand, 11
Myles, J. L.
  Apoplectic leiomyomas of, 138
Nadiradze, I. Sh.
  Mini-doses of heparin in, 188
Nair, S.
  Injectable contraceptives in, 105
Nakayama, O.
  Analysis of nursing students', 19
Nakimova, Z. A.
  Features of the status of, 32
Nankin, H. R.
  Fertility in aging men, 175
Nathanson, C. A.
  Influence of client-provider, 102
Neaman, L. F., 4
Nebel, L.
  Malimplantation caused by, 32
Needleman, L.
  Canadian fertility trends in, 171
Neel, E. U.
  Relationship of self-concept, 125
Neeser, E.
  Tubal pregnancy following, 211
Neglia, V.
  Comparison of the results, 183
Neidhardt, A.
  Why me? Second trimester, 38
Neinstein, L. S.
  Contraceptive use in the 149
Nelson, D. M.
  Association of prolonged, pre... , 79

Nelson, J. R.
Live and let live and die when, 11
Nelson, P.
Moral discourse in the, 73
Neuberger, J.
Oral contraceptives and, 132
Neuberger, M.
Pro-lifers give birth, 76
Neuhaus, R. J.
Democratic morality, 70
Policy by pathology (high, 93
Neuman, S.
How does fertility relate, 85
Neumann, H. G.
Evaluation of reports on, 129
Neumeyer, H.
Prevention of habitual abortion, 30
Neustatter, A., 4
Newcomb, M. D.
Determinants of sexual and, 195
Newcomer, S. F.
Parent-child communication, 196
Newman, J. L.
Family planning, 151
Newmann, S.
Choice update—still ain't, 76
Ney, P.
Abortion [letter], 45
Ney, P. G.
Curious case of abortion, 9
Ngin, C.-S., 4
Nichols, D.
Sexual behavior, contra..., 147
Vanguard family planning ac..., 86
Nichols, L.
Was the vasectomy necessary, 218
Nichols, M. M.
Placental laceration and stillbirth, 79
Nieschlag, E.
Perspectives of reproductive, 100
Nightingale, Z.
Hunger must not be, 81
Nijman, J. M.
Fertility and hormonal function, 174
Nikitina, G. V.
Progestagenic activity and, 124
Nikonov, A. P.
Status of the kallikrein-kinin, 8
Nikschick, S.
Haptoglobin typing in abortion, 10
Influence of a sequential, 122
Nillius, S. J.
Gonadotrophin-releasing hor..., 99
Noble, K. A.
Sex education and the, 197
Nolen, G. A.
Fertility and teratogenic, 178

Nonomura, M.
Effects of hyperprolactin..., 177
Noonan, J. R., Jr., 4
Nordberg, O. S.
Why isn't contraception better, 98
Norfleet, S.
"Are sperm different colors?", 199
Nortman, D. L.
Cost benefit analysis of, 113
Nozawa, S.
Penetration of cefoperazone, 185
Ntrajan, P. K.
Cervical dilatation with pro..., 33
Nuñez, J.
Blood supply in the, 219
Effects of vasectomy on, 205
Plasma lipids in the, 219
Nurse, G. H.
Outbreak of toxoplasma gondii, 65
Nuss, R. C.
Risk factor for tumor, 186
Nuthall, J.
Unplanned pregnancy, 38
Nyberg, D. A.
Threatened abortion: sono..., 62
Oakely, A.
Miscarriage and its implications, 25
Oberweis, D.
Evaluation of the risk of, 57
Ochs, H.
Effect of tumor promoting, 120
Oddi, G.
Histologic lesions caused by, 129
Odejide, T. O.
Offering an alternative to, 16
O'Donohoe, J.
Catholic physician, the con..., 91
Ogbeide, D. O.
Two-year study of organised, 154
Ogino, M.
Effects of oral contraceptives, 121
Ogletree, J.
Preterm settles decade-long, 76
O'Hanlon, J. K.
Fertility of mating in rats, 178
Ohrstedt, R. J.
Abortion: focus on conflict, 71
Olasky, M.
Advertising abortion during, 16
Olasky, M. N.
Crossover in newspaper, 17
Opposing abortion clinics: a, 18
O'Laughlin, K. M.
Changes in bladder function, 183
Olds, C.
Fetus as a person, 20
Olds-Clarke, P.
Fertility of sperm from, 178

243

Oliver, G.
    Wrongful birth concept gains, 92
Olsson, H.
    Biological marker, strongly, 127
    On cohort effects in, 131
Olukoya, A. A.
    Changing attitude and practice, 156
    Teaching medical students, 156
Omu, A. E.
    Acceptance of contraceptive, 95
Oni, G. A.
    Contraceptive knowledge and, 113
    Effects of women's education, 113
    Use of contraceptives for, 98
Orme, M. L.
    Drug interactions between, 128
Orr, J. W., Jr.
    Cefotetan versus cefoxitin as , 183
    Surgical treatment of women, 186
Orr, M. T.
    Availability of reproduction, 70
Orth, M.
    My church threw me out, 17
Osebold, J. W.
    Congenital spirochetosis in, 24
Ostling, R. N.
    Church and state, 41
O'Sullivan, S.
    Dalkon shields—the IUD, 119
    Sponge story with holes, 117
Ottow, E.
    Synthesis of ent-17-(prop-1..., 8
Overall, C.
    New productive technology, 55
Oyeka, I. C. A.
    Family planning among, 156
Oza, K. V.
    Policy of persuasive com..., 152
Padilla, S. L.
    Anovulation: etiology, 181
Paige, C.
    Antiabortion movement and, 45
Pal, A. K.
    Flowers of hibiscus rosa-, 105
Palaniappan, B.
    Ectopic pregnancy and fertility, 151
Palatsi, R.
    Pituitary function and DHEA-S, 141
Palen, J. J.
    Fertility and eugenics, 173
Palmer, R. H.
    Cost and quality in the, 184
Paltrow, L.
    Amicus brief (Richard, 41
    Test-tube women: what, 12
Paris, E.
    Cold shower (contraceptive, 114

Paris, F. X.
    Value of an antiprogesterone, 8
Parise, M.
    Adepal, 138
Parker, K.
    Healthworks—an adolescent, 162
Parrish, J. J.
    Fertility differences among, 178
Parulekar, S. V.
    Accidental intra-myometrial, 39
    Early puerperal laparoscopic, 205
    Foetal bleeding in the first, 10
Paul, B. K.
    Performance of supply, 153
Paul, C.
    Oral contraceptives and breast, 131
Payne, M. R.
    Sulpiride and the potentiation, 125
Pearce, S.
    Viability of mouse leydig, 108
Pebley, A. R.
    Evaluation of contraceptive, 85
Peddie, B. A.
    Diaphragm use and urinary, 117
Pedersen, J. F.
    Prognostic significance of fetal, 61
Pedulla, D. M.
    Moral dilemma: two views, 21
Pellauer, M.
    On being pregnant, 21
Peng, Q.
    Sister chromatid exchange, 133
Penzhorn, B. L.
    Necrosis and abscessation of, 54
    Reconception of mares follow..., 23
Pepperell, R. J.
    Beneficial and adverse side, 119
Perez-Martinez, J. A.
    Bovine chlamydial abortion, 53
Persitz, E.
    HLA system and habitual, 28
Pestrak, V. A.
    Cognitive development and, 195
Peters, A. R.
    Effects of prostaglandin F2, 168
Petitti, D. B.
    Oral contraceptives and, 132
Petty, W. M.
    Total abdominalhysterectomy, 190
Pfäfflin, F.
    Connections between, 201
Philip, D.
    Beyond the pill: the WHO, 135
    Pricing the "burden" of a, 27
Philip, T.
    Should she, or shouldn't, 110
Philliber, S. G.
    Age variation in use of a, 162

Phillips, A. J.
  Acute salpingitis subsequent, 202
Phuapradit, W.
  Abortion: an attitude study, 16
Piana, L.
  Role of surgery in the, 186
Pickering, R. M.
  Pre-term foetal life times, 86
  Risks of preterm delivery, 40
Pierson, E. E.
  Effect of oviductal tissues, 177
Piesse, B.
  Fruitful lessons from "sterile", 201
  Nurse and the law, 204
Pinkerton, J. H.
  Fetal rights. The first, 34
Pinto, M. R.
  Possible effects of hormonal, 140
Pitt, E.
  Targeting the adolescent male, 197
Pittin, R.
  Control of reproduction, 16
Piura, B.
  Prophylactic posterior, 190
Plauché, W. C.
  Cesarean hysterectomy, 183
Pliego, J. F.
  Distribution of a seminal, 216
Poggi, S.
  Abortion rights withstand heat, 78
  Homophobia in what's left, 78
  Jimenez rally to target, 42
  Roe v Wade: 15 years, 44
Poirier, P. Y.
  Voluntary female sterilization, 204
Polchanova, S. L.
  Population of contraception, 100
Polednak, A. P.
  Exogenous female sex, 129
Pollak, R. A.
  Reformulation of the two-sex, 169
Ponsford, G.
  Policy-making: a CMA, 46
Pool, F.
  What to tell patients, 204
Popenoe, P. B., 4
Popov, A. A.
  Control of the reproductive, 150
Porter, R.
  "Secrets of generation, 31
Portuondo, J. A.
  Müllerian abnormalities in fertile, 25
Posluch, J.
  Possibilities of general, 36
Poston, D. K., Jr.
  Patterns of contraceptive use, 111
Poston, D. L.
  One-child family: International, 154

Potter, R. G.
  Fecundability and the fre..., 80
Potts, M.
  Pill 30 years on, 124
Powell, M. G.
  Contraception with the cervical, 116
Power, D. A.
  Maternal antibodies to paternal, 11
Pownall, M.
  Actionmen, 149
Powolny, M.
  Hysterectomy complicated by, 188
Prasad, R. S.
  New non-hormonal anti-...I., 7
  New non-hormonal anti-...II., 7
Prasad, S.
  Evaluation of intramuscular, 45
Prescott, J. W.
  Abortion of the silent scream, 19
Preston, S. H.
  Population growth and eco..., 84
Prikhod'ko, A. G.
  Scintigraphy of the bone, 182
Primorac, M.
  Contraceptive agents for men, 107
  Determination of the viscosity, 105
  Effect of sodium lauryl, 105
Procter, S. E.
  Cytogenetic analysis in 100, 16
Proctor, E.
  RCM supplement. "You can, 50
Proctor, E.
  "You can always try for, 52
Propper, S.
  Moral reasonging, parental, 195
Puri, P.
  Prepuberta testicular torsion, 175
Qian, G. Y.
  Evaluation of ultrasonography, 10
Qian, S. Z.
  Gossypol-hypokalaemia inter.., 108
Querido, L.
  IUD insertion following in..., 35
Qureshi, B.
  Contraceptive advice: how the, 111
Rabe, T.
  Pill and cancer, 132
Rachlin, J.
  Business as usual, 95
Racinet, C.
  Proximal tubal surgery, 215
Radberg, G.
  Influence of pregnancy, 143
Radford, A. J.
  Some general principles and, 152
Radikov, N.
  Serum concentrationof preg..., 49

Rády, M.
  Demonstration in Hungary of, 24
Rahman, S. S.
  Introduction of the injectable, 136
Rakhmatuilaeva, G. R.
  Role of hormonal disorders, 26
Ralph, G.
  Functional disorders of the, 184
Ralph, N.
  Contraceptive practices among, 87
Randic, L.
  Return to fertility after, 118
Rani, S.
  Effect of glyzophrol on, 176
Ranney, B.
  Volume reduction of the, 187
Rao, K. V.
  Effect of infant mortality, 172
Rao, P. S.
  Rural-urban differentials in, 169
Rao, R.
  India: move to stop sex-test, 14
Ray, A. C.
  Bovine abortion and death, 22
  Humanity, personhood, and, 20
Rayburn, W. F.
  Mid-gestational abortion for, 35
Reagan, R.
  Abortion and the conscience, 70
Realmuto, G. M.
  Management of sexual issues, 196
Rebick, J.
  Pro-choice leader runs for, 192
Reed, K. S.
  Involuntary pregnancy loss, 51
Refn, H.
  Ultrasonic scanning after, 40
Reich, A.
  Dalkon shield—just when, 119
Reichelt, P. A.
  Public policy and public, 87
Reidinger, P.
  Abortion: L.A. restrictions, 41
Reinders, T. P.
  Nonprescription contracep..., 104
Reingold, A. L.
  Toxic shock syndrome and, 117
Relkin, E.
  Using state constitutions to, 77
Remy, J. C.
  Complications of combined, 187
Renn, M.
  Family planning. Accurate, 151
  Family planning. If the, 116
Repa, B. K.
  Supreme Court preview, 44
Reskin, L. R.
  Lawyers are at odds, 71

Reynolds, T.
  Moral absolutism and abortion, 20
Reznikoff-Etievant, M. F.
  Idiopathic habitual abortions, 31
Rhoden, N. K.
  Should medical technology, 44
Richard, P. B.
  Teaching about abortion as, 22
Richards, A.
  Incidence of major abdominal, 23
Richards, G.
  How to get the poor, 83
Richters, J.
  Postpartum sexuality and, 97
Riddle, E. R. W., 5
Rider, V.
  Anti-fertility effect of, 167
Riedel, H. H.
  Ovarian failure phenomena, 188
Rienzo, B. A.
  Group discussion on contra..., 99
Rigall, N. J.
  Artificial birth control: an, 88
Rigau Pérez, J. G.
  Family planning in Puerto Rico, 156
Rios, J. G.
  Selection for postweaning, 180
Ritschard, T.
  Inflammatory bowel disease, 130
Rivers, V.
  Unplanned pregnancy, 164
Rivlin, M. E.
  Surgical management of diffuse, 56
Roberts, C.
  Cold hands, conception and, 95
Roberts, G. A.
  Planned parenthood, 165
Roche, J. P.
  Premarital sex: attitudes and, 194
Røde, A.
  P-pills for women with, 124
Roe, K. M., 5
Rojanasakul, A.
  Luteinizing hormone releasing, 104
Rolon, R.
  Nicaragua's minister of health, 15
Romagny, A.
  Contraception in female, 96
Rong, R. H.
  Fertile mule in China, 177
Rosa, G.
  Microsurgical tubal anasto..., 210
Rosales Estrada, G.
  Changes in menstrual pattern, 208
Rose, A.
  Abortion and the politics, 75
Rosenberg, L.
  Risk of myocardial infarction, 218

246

Rosenbert, M. J.
Sexually transmitted diseases, 153
Rosenzweig, M. R.
Evaluating the effects of, 86
Rosner, D.
Oral contraceptive use has, 131
Rosner, D. H.
Oral contraceptives and, 132
Ross, C. E.
Herd problem of abortions, 64
Ross, J. L.
Proximate determinants of, 156
Ross, R. K.
Risk factors for uterine, 133
Rothman, B. K.
Products of conception: the, 95
When a pregnant woman, 12
Roy, S.
Effects of oral contraceptives, 120
Royale, M. G.
Why does vasectomy reversal, 205
Rubin, E. R., 5
Ruby, J.
School for scandal: birth, 94
Ruffing-Rahal, M.
Margaret Sanger: nurse and, 158
Ruggiero, R. J.
Prescription contraceptives, 141
Rush, B.
Healing a hidden grief, 51
Rusheng, Y.
Population control urged, 82
Russell-Briefel, R.
Prevalence and trends in oral, 18
Russin, L. D.
Hydrosalpinx and tubal torsion, 212
Rust, M. E.
Abortion cases, 8
Ryan, M.
Hysterectomy and tubal, 191
Ryan, T.
Churches on abortion, 72
Rybalkina, L. D.
Risk of birth of children, 62
Rzadki, E. J.
Abortion: increasing the scope, 9
Sadovnick, A. D.
Fetal mortality in sibships, 10
Sadovsky, O.
Etiologic factors in habitual, 25
Sadykov, A. S.
Effect of gossypol on, 174
Safire, W.
Surgeon General's warning, 110
Safran, D.
Enflurane for the voluntary, 34
Sagara, Y.
Clinical management for abor..., 62

Sairam, M. R.
Preparation and properties of, 8
Salih, E. Y.
Effect of oral contraceptives, 120
Salman, M.
Studies in antifertility agents, 170
Salomon-Bernard, Y.
Contraceptive methods for, 99
Salov, I. A.
Diagnostic significance of, 49
Samanta, K.
Zinc feeding and fertility, 181
Samuel, S. A.
Nurse and her role as, 159
Sandahl, B.
Prospective study of drug, 124
Sanders, C.
Concerns voied on Depo, 107
Sangree, S.
Abortion in Nicaragua, 15
Sas, M.
Investigation on the influence, 104
Satia, J. K.
Incentives and disincentives in, 152
Sato, S.
Chondrifying fibrosarcoma in, 63
Sauerbrei, E. E.
Placental abruption and sub..., 80
Saw, S. H.
Dynamics of ageing in, 172
Sayres, M.
Pregnancy during residency, 152
Sazonov, A. M.
Flow-through method of, 55
Schäcke, G.
Danger to pregnant women, 214
Schaeffer, F., 5
Scharp, H.
Uterine rupture following tubal, 204
Schecter, S.
New York City school, 197
Scheid, J. H.
Benefits vs burdens: the, 158
Scheidel, P. H.
Absorbable or nonabsorbable, 207
Schellstede, W. P.
Social marketing of contra..., 114
Schlund, G. H.
Liability of the physician in, 27
Schmidt, F. H., 5
Schmidt, S.
Unholy water (abortionists who, 77
Schmidt, S. S.
Sturgeon vas cautery, 217
Vasectomy failure and open, 218
Schneider, S.
Abortion-clinic bombing: the, 16
Adolescent sexuality in a, 195

Contraception—his gain, you, 108
Schreiner, W. E.
    Complications of tubal, 212
Schuh, J.
    Bovine abortion caused by, 53
Schuler, S. R.
    Family planning in Nepal, 155
Schuyt, H. C.
    Abortions among dental, 22
Schwartz, D.
    Abortion rate in A.I.D., 59
Schwartz, D. B.
    Motivations for adolescents', 94
Schwimmer, W. B.
    Sperm-agglutinating, 170
Scialli, A. R.
    Reproductive toxicity of ovula..., 23
Sciorra, L. J.
    Translocation mosaicism in a, 30
Scott, E. S.
    Sterilization of mentally, 213
Scotti, R. J.
    Urodynamic changes in, 189
Scotto, V.
    Cefoxitin single dose prophy..., 187
Seaman, J. T.
    Chlamydia isolated from abor..., 63
Seiler, J. S.
    Laparoscopic tubal sterilization, 208
Seiver, D. A.
    Trend and variation in, 173
Sekulovic, D.
    Postcoital contraception, 135
Selassie, T.
    Rejected sex of Korea, 15
Seller, M. J.
    Effects of mid-trimester, 39
SenGupta, A.
    Choriocarcinoma following, 39
Senior, C. C.
    Are preoperative antibiotics, 182
Serville, F.
    Morphological study of the, 60
Sevin, B. U.
    Primary surgical therapy of, 190
Sexton, T. J.
    Effects of dietary protein, 177
    Relationship of the number, 180
Seymour, J.
    Contraception: no longer , 139
    Practice. Open all hours, 166
Shafer, M. A.
    Microbiology of the lower, 102
Shah, I. H.
    Fertility in Pakistan during, 172
Shah, N. M.
    Contraceptive use among, 112

Shain, R. N.
    Cross-cultural history of, 34
    Decision to terminate child..., 87
    Married women's dissatis..., 210
Shalev, E.
    Real-time ultrasound diagnosis, 61
Shao, W. Q.
    Clinical and roentgenographic, 189
Shapiro, R.
    Contraception: you can get, 96
    Family planning. Fertility, 151
    Family planning: fertility rights, 200
Shapiro, S.
    Oral contraceptives—time to, 132
Shapiro, T. M., 5
Sharma, S. C.
    Comparison of blood levels, 79
Shea, F. P.
    On clinical judgement, 146
Shearman, R. P.
    Oral contraceptive agents, 104
Sheehan, M. K.
    Perceptions of sexual, 92
Sheikh, H. H.
    Bipolar tubal cautery failure, 214
Sheldrick, P.
    Rights theatened, 109
Shen, Y.
    Sister chromatid exchange in, 136
Shenfield, G. M.
    Drug interactions with oral, 128
Sherman, C.
    Can the condom make, 136
Shimm, D. S.
    Management of high-grade, 185
Shinagawa, S.
    Essay on elective hysterec..., 184
Shovic, A. C.
    Nutrition within a family, 164
Shtarkshall, R.
    Radio and family planning, 85
Shubik, P.
    Oral contraceptives and breast, 131
Shulman, S.
    Sperm antigens and, 170
Shweni, P. M.
    Septic abortion complicated by, 56
Siegfried, G.
    Pro-lifers subpoena a mayor, 13
Siekmann, U.
    Chorioamniotic infections, 24
Silva-Ruiz, P. F.
    Artificial reproduction tech..., 88
Silver, E.
    India's unborn brides, 15
Simon, W.
    Sexual scripts: permanence, 194

Simons, J.
How conservative are British, 84
Simor, A. E.
Abortion and perinatal sepsis, 24
Simpson, J.
Finding a better way: excerpt, 10
Simpson, P.
I crossed over, 10
Sing, H.
Vasectomy: a simple, 218
Singh, A. B.
Recanalisation of vas, 205
Singh, H.
Vasectomy, 217
Singh, K.
Incentives and disincentives, 157
Singhania, L.
Chromosomal factors in, 24
Sivanesaratnam, V.
Torsion of the fallopian, 204
Sixel-Dietrich, F.
Hereditary uroporphyrinogen, 129
Skjeldestad, F. E.
Induced abortions and births, 16
Skjöldebrand, L.
Thyroxine-binding globulin in, 58
Skouby, S. O.
Hormonal contraception in, 122
Tripasic oral contraeption, 126
Skrzycki, C.
Risky business of birth, 81
Sladkin, K. R.
Counseling the sexually active, 195
Sleep, J.
Parenthood by design, 152
Sleptsova, S. I.
Methodology of epidemiological, 25
Sliwinska, I.
Effect of chronic administration, 139
Slobodian, L.
Choosing to abort: pro-life, 13
Slomko, Z.
Clinical aspects of perinatal, 183
Smakhtina, O. L.
Determination of the volume, 189
Smith, D. P.
Comment on Barbara, 173
Smith, E. A.
Coital and noncoital sexual, 195
Pubertal development and, 196
Smith, M. C.
Baccalaureate nursing students', 20
Smith, P. B.
Health problems and sexual, 196
Smith, P. M.
Ovulation induction, 182
Smith, S.
Link between sexual, 196

Snethlage, W.
Thrombocythaemia and recur..., 30
Snowden, E. U.
Opioid regulation of pituitary, 123
Snyder, R. V., 5
Soerstrom, R. M.
Postmenopausal removal of, 118
Solapurkar, M. L.
Has the MTP (Medical, 14
Soley, G. E.
To preserve and protect, 68
Sollom, T.
State laws and the provision, 18
Somell, C.
Cervical dilatation with mete..., 33
Somell, C.
Cervical dilatation with, 7
Sorenson, A. M.
Ethnicity and fertility: the, 92
Sophocles, A. M., Jr.
Birth control failure among, 9
Birth control failure (resulting, 95
Sorokina, M. I.
Status of immunological and, 56
Souka, A. R.
Vaginal administration of a, 126
Souriau, A.
Rapid detection of chlamydia, 66
South, J.
Pro-choice or pro-life, 14
Southgate, L.
Underage contraception, 103
Soutoul, J. H.
Court on tubal sterilization, 204
Pregnancy and unwanted, 14
Sowards, P. L.
Correlational and predictive, 51
Sozanski, L.
Effect of partusisten admin..., 59
Spadafora, M.
Perceived credibility of a, 36
Span, P.
Why smart women are, 93
Spätling, L.
Influence of different pro..., 35
Speckhard, A. C., 5
Specktor, M.
Minnesota judge strikes down, 17
Spencer, B.
Family planning. If the, 151
Speranza, R., 5
Psychological effects of the, 191
Spielmann, H.
Reply to comments on, 106
Spiropoulos, A.
Preventing pregnancy with, 206
Spitz, I. M.
Antiprogestins; prospects for, 103

Spitzer, R. J., 5
Spivak, M. M.
  Microsurgical reversal of, 210
Spragins, E.
  Searle: staring at some, 118
Srisuphan, W.
  Caffeine consumption during, 22
Stacey, M.
  Commentary on Rothman's, 160
Stadel, B. V.
  Oral contraceptives..., 131
  Oral contraceptives...[letter], 131
Stadel, V. B.
  Oral contraceptive use and, 131
Staggenborg, S., 5
  Coalition work in the, 78
  Patterns of collective action, 192
Stampar, D.
  Trends in family planning, 153
Stampe Sørensen, S.
  Midtrimester abortion by, 36
Standeven, M.
  Correlates of change in, 184
Staples, R.
  Black male sexuality, 161
Starr, T. B.
  Fertility of workers. A, 181
Steadman, S.
  Counseling on contraceptives, 115
Steckel, R. R.
  Experimental evaluation of, 184
Steel, J. M.
  Prepregnancy counseling and, 97
Stehlíková, J.
  FSH, LH, estradiol and 184
Steier, J. A.
  Human chorionic gonadotropin, 10
Steinbock, B.
  Legislation proposed to, 43
Steinfirst, J. L.
  Vending machines and the, 110
Stellflug, J. N.
  Antiferitlity effect of busulfan, 175
Stellon, A. J.
  Increased incidene of men..., 185
Stephens, J. D.
  Mid-trimester termination of, 60
Sternbach, N.
  Argentina "in democracy", 82
Sterzik, K.
  Beta-1-glycoprotein deter..., 61
Stetson, D. M.
  Abortion law reform in France, 14
Stewart, D. O.
  Roe v Wade reaffirmed, 44
Stivers, C.
  Sex education bowl game, 198

St. John, C.
  Decomposing the black, 150
Stock, J. G.
  Role of H2 receptor, 61
Stock, R. J.
  Sterilization failures, 211
Stoeckel, J.
  Maintaining family planning, 89
Stokes, G. S.
  Erythrocyte cation transport is, 121
Stormorken, H.
  Oral contraceptives and anti..., 131
Stout, K.
  What you should know, 201
Strasburger, V. C.
  Sex, drugs, rock, 197
  Sex, drugs, rock...under..., 197
Stratton, J. A.
  Effect of oral contraceptives, 120
Streatfield, K.
  Comparison of census and, 89
Strickland, D. M.
  Relationship between abortion, 26
Strickland, R. A.
  Banning abortion: an, 41
Strizhakov, A. N.
  Characteristics of the clinical, 79
Strobino, B.
  Characteristics of women, 27
  Vaginal spermicides and spon.., 23
Strohm, J.
  China: a nation in ferment, 83
Strom, B. L.
  Oral contraceptives and, 132
Strydom, M.
  Study of factors related to, 113
Stubblefield, P. G.
  Surgical techniques of uterine, 38
Stumpf, P. G.
  Effect of vaginal contraceptive, 105
Sturdee, D. W.
  Cesarean and post-partum, 183
Stycos, J. M.
  Evaluation of the population, 111
Sumberg, J. E.
  Village production of West, 180
Sumner, L. W.
  Moral theory and oral, 21
Sundqvist, C.
  Testicular aspiration biopsy, 180
Surkes, S.
  Plans for Rwanda, 86
Svensson, W. E.
  Bowel preparation and the, 138
Swanson-Kauffman, K. M.
  Caring in the instance of unex..., 50
  Combined qualitative metho..., 50

Swerdloff, R. S.
　Gonadotropin releasing hor..., 108
　Hormonal effects of GnRH, 108
Sylvester, D. G.
　Candidosis and oral contra..., 127
Sziachta, A.
　Analysis of abortions, 24
Tabor, A.
　Randomised controlled trial of, 26
Tado, S.
　Pregnancy and induced, 36
Taggert, M.
　Nurses ease pain in perinatal, 50
Takahashi, K.
　Operation of functional, 190
Takakuwa, K.
　Production of blocking anti..., 31
Talbert, C.
　Patient care plan, 190
Talbot, M. D.
　Confidentiality, the law in, 154
Talwar, G. P.
　Enhancement of antigonado... 100
Tam, P. P.
　Gonadal development and, 178
Tan, C. E.
　Demographic and contracep..., 113
Tanfer, K.
　Contraceptive perceptions, 114
Tannenbaum, T. N.
　Exposure to anesthetic gases, 23
Tanphaichitra, D.
　Relationship between urinary, 133
Taptunova, A. I.
　Effect of induced and, 34
Taskinen, H.
　Spontaneous abortions among, 58
Taub, S.
　Current status of actions for, 45
Taylor, G. F.
　Systematic environmental, 180
Taylor, G. T.
　Ontogeny of epididymal sperm, 179
　Suprathreshold manipulations, 180
Taylor, M. E.
　Changing sexual attitudes, 193
　Qualitative and quantitative, 194
Taylor, P. J.
　Female sterilization: can the, 206
Taylor, R. S.
　Correlation of vaginal hormonal, 159
Tayob, Y.
　Ultrasound demonstration of, 134
Tchabo, J. G.
　Prophylactic antibiotics in, 190
Tejwani, G. A.
　Effect of oral contraceptives, 120

Temkin, J.
　Pre-natal injury, homicide and, 14
Templeton, A.
　Time to break down, 170
Terry, N. P.
　"Alas! poor Yorick," I knew, 14
Tharapel, A. T.
　Recurrent pregnancy losses, 29
Thomas, D. B.
　Breast cancer and depot-, 106
　Invasive cervical cancer and, 107
Thomas, J.
　Dalkon doesn't do it, 119
Thomsen, R. J.
　Ultrasonic visualizatio of, 106
Thonet, R. G.
　Obstetric hysterectomy—an, 185
Thornton, G. R., Jr.
　Intrauterine devices, 118
Thornton, N.
　Is the old right now new?, 20
Thoulon, J. M.
　Ethical and legal...Medical, 45
Thouvenin, D.
　Ethical and legal...Legal, 45
Thysen, B.
　Reproductive toxicity of, 180
Tien, H. Y.
　Redirection of the Chinese, 83
Tierney, J.
　Fanisi's choice, 85
Tierney, T.
　State of the species, 85
Tillis, M. S.
　Reducing the risk of, 200
Timberlake, I.
　Will Canada ever see, 111
Timischi, W.
　On the process of, 169
Timmins, N.
　Pill: the doctor's dilemma, 124
　Right of doctors in, 146
Timothy, J.
　Late terminations of pregnancy, 60
Tinga, D. J.
　Hysterectomy after caesarean, 185
Tiret, E.
　Peritonitis of genital origin, 188
Togashi, K.
　Computed tomography of, 208
Tolchin, S. J.
　Impact of the Hyde, 42
Tollan, A.
　Contraception before and, 45
Tomásek, J.
　Termination of pregnancy in, 38
Tomlinson, R. V.
　Absorption and elimination, 7

251

Toner, J. P.
  Potency of rat ejaculations, 179
Toon, P. D.
  Acts and omissions doctrine, 33
Torry, D. S.
  Inhibitors of complement..., 28
Toth, A.
  Outcome of subsequent, 32
Toufexis, A.
  Birth control: vanishing options, 80
Townsend, P. A.
  Acute peripheral arterial, 182
Trasler, J. M.
  Chronic low dose cyclophos..., 176
Trathen, W. T.
  Allergic reaction to Hulka, 203
Travis, H. R.
  Sexual responsibility, 198
Tremblay, R. R.
  Nature of the residual, 217
Trent, K.
  Determinants of parity distri..., 90
  Parity distribution and, 172
Trichard, C. J.
  Mycoplasmas recovered from, 54
Trimmer, E.
  When your patients ask about, 100
Tripathy, S. N.
  Uterine rupture following, 40
Trupin, S.
  Relief of pain in first-trimester, 48
Trutko, N. S.
  Indicators of arterial blood, 122
Tsibris, J. C.
  Cervicovaginal peroxidases, 167
Tsukamoto, N.
  Simple hysterectomy for stage, 186
Tu, E. J. C.
  Age, period and cohort, 49
Tucker, G. M.
  Barriers to modern contra..., 113
Tumbo-Oeri, A. G.
  Cell-mediatd immunity to, 216
Tushnet, M.
  Comment on Tooley's Abortion, 20
Tyler, S.
  Illegitimacy—we ignore the, 81
Uchida, I. A.
  Detection and interpretation of, 10
Udry, J. R.
  Biosocial foundations for, 195
Uehling, M. D.
  Clinics of deception (pro, 72
Uhlman, J.
  Screening the vasectomy, 87
Umezawa, R.
  Battleground For McMurray, 13

Unander, A. M.
  Blood transfusioins generate, 31
  Transfusions of leukocyte-rich, 31
Underwood, N.
  Hope for a male pill, 137
Ungváry, G.
  On the embryotoxic effects, 23
Urbina Fuentes, M.
  Psychosocial research and, 155
Vaidya, S. S.
  Tricuspid valve endocarditis, 56
Valente, P. T.
  Endocervical neoplasia in, 129
Valette, A.
  Induced abortion: we could, 31
Valla, D.
  Risk of hepatic vein, 133
Valliance, T. R., 6
Van Damme, B.
  Liver tumours associated, 130
van der Lugt, B.
  Disappearance of human, 34
Van Dover, L. J. W., 6
Vanha-Perttula, T.
  Lectin staining of rat, 219
van nagell, J. R.
  Treatment of cervical intra..., 186
Vanoli, M.
  Histocompatibility in Italian, 28
Vanrell, J. A.
  Luteal phase defects in, 25
van Steensel-Moll, H. A.
  Are maternal fertility problems, 167
van Vugt, A. B.
  Sperm analysis following, 215
Vasileva, I.
  Importance of nutrition for, 57
Velasco, F.
  Transietn ischemic attack, 134
Vemer, H. M.
  Regret after sterilization in, 203
Ventura, S. J.
  Estimates of pregnancies and, 87
Verbitskii, M. Sh.
  Immunological mthods of birth, 89
Verma, K. K.
  Value of children, family, 82
Vernon, R.
  Female anticonception by, 202
Verschoor, L.
  Contraception in women with, 128
Vervest, H. A.
  Initial Dutch experiences with, 15
  Preliminary results with the, 37
Vessey, M.
  Chronic inflammatory bowel, 127
  Oral contraceptives and, 132

Vessey, M. P.
  Fertility in relation to, 168
  Oral contraceptives and breast, 131
Vexiau, P.
  Paradoxic improvement of, 124
Vick, L.
  Report on voluntary, 203
Vickery, B. H.
  Comparisons of the potential, 95
Vijayan, E.
  Recent developments in, 106
Vines, G.
  Bangladesh is coerced into, 201
Visher, S.
  Relationship of locus of control, 100
Vivier, C.
  Intense emotional reactions, 35
Vogt, H. J.
  Plato redivivus (eugenic pro..., 81
Vojtecky, M. A.
  Subtle differences on abortion, 61
von Gontard, A.
  Psychological sequelae of, 37
von Hugo, R.
  Changes in blood coagulation, 138
von Rütte, B.
  Risks of male sterilization, 205
von Sandersieben, J.
  Significance of the histologic, 66
von Voss, H.
  Abortion according to paragraph, 14
Voss, C.
  Abdominoplasty combined, 189
Wadhwa, V.
  Contraceptive and hormonal, 139
Wagner, C.
  United States—100,000 march, 79
Wagner, M. G.
  Diarrheal disease control and, 150
Wainer, J.
  Feelings about abortion: an, 20
  Second trimester abortion, 48
Waites, G. M.
  Male fertility regulation: recent, 108
Waksberg, J.
  Integration of sample design, 169
Walden, C. E.
  Effect of estrogen/progestin, 142
Walker, G.
  Family planning, maternal, 159
Walker, S.
  Familial complex autosomal, 28
Wall, E. M.
  Development of a decision, 93
Wallace, L. M.
  Psychological adjustment to, 207
Wallach, E. E.
  Expanding scope of the, 173

Wallis, C.
  Children having children: teen, 195
  Tragic costs of teen-age, 197
Wang, J.
  Sporicidal properties of, 201
Wang, J. F.
  Induced abortion: reported, 16
Wang, L. J.
  Galactorrhea and serum, 121
Wang, M. Z.
  Application of orthogonal, 7
Wang, N. G.
  Effect of gossypol acetic, 105
  Effects of (-) and (+), 177
Wang, W. H.
  Influence of salicyladehyde, 169
Wang, Y.
  Antifertility effect of polyvinyl..., 176
Warming, B.
  Condoms in Japan, 112
Warren, C. W.
  Contraceptive sterilization in, 139
  Seasonal variation in, 11
Watkins, R. N.
  Vaginal spermicides and, 110
Watson, W. J.
  Perinatal ethics [letter], 46
Wattenberg, B. J.
  Birth dearth (with dialogue), 80
Wattleton, F.
  Reproductive rights for, 43
Wawer, M. J.
  Contraceptive prevalence in, 110
Weatherbe, S.
  Row at (North Vancouver), 193
Weaver, G. A.
  Effect of zearalenone of the, 177
Webb, C.
  Professional and lay social, 191
Webster, F.
  Study of the influence, 112
Webster, L.
  Epidemiology of oral contra..., 129
Webster, M. A.
  Interruption of first trimester, 60
Wegmann, T. G.
  Self-sterility MHC polymorphism, 58
Weiman, C.
  Psychosocial aspects of con..., 142
Weir, R. J.
  Effects of blood pressure, 121
Weisberg, E.
  Contraception for the older, 96
  Practical aspects of clinical, 100
Weisman, C. S.
  Abortion attitudes and per..., 19
  Abortion attitudes and per..., 70

Weitz, R.
　　Summer on abortion, 12
Wellings, K.
　　Sterilization trends, 201
Wells, M. P.
　　Total abdominal hysterectomy, 190
Welti, H.
　　Risks of postcoital contra..., 135
Wennberg, R. N., 6
Westcott, M.
　　Ovulation prediction: a, 159
Westheimer, K.
　　Choice group says no, 78
　　Massachusetts to vote on, 17
Wettemann, R. P.
　　Influence of environmental, 178
Whicker, M. L., 6
White, J. A.
　　Fertility and parental age, 182
Wickwire, K. S., 6
Wide, M.
　　Lead exposure on critical, 179
Wiebe, E. R.
　　Retention of products of, 61
Wilbur, A. E.
　　Contraceptive crisis, 109
Wilde, G.
　　NOW backs investigation of, 69
Williams, D.
　　Nightmare: women and Dalkon, 117
Williams, E.
　　Adoption vs. abortion, 9
Williams, R.
　　Can spouses be trusted, 149
Willke, J. C.
　　Should abortion be legal?, 21
Wilsmore, A. J.
　　Ovine enzootic abortion: field, 65
Wilson, C.
　　Effects of waste anaesthetic, 68
Wilson, G. B.
　　Christian action: third approach, 72
Wilson, M. A.
　　Billings ovulation method, 159
Wilson, R. D.
　　Spontaneous abortion and, 58
Wimmer-Puchinger, B.
　　Adjustment to abortion in, 50
Wineberg, H.
　　Differential fertility in the, 173
Witkin, S. S.
　　Humoral immune responses, 200
Witt, E.
　　Court renews abortion, 42
Witte, S. T.
　　Abortion and early neonatal, 52
Wølner-Hanseen, P.
　　Oral contraceptive use, 134

Wong, P. C.
　　Expectant treatment versus, 168
Woo, J. S.
　　Non-resolution of pelvic, 185
Wood, P. D.
　　Semen assessment, fertility, 180
Woodroffe, C.
　　Contraceptives and the under, 104
Woyton, J.
　　Evaluation of intrafascial, 189
Wray, L.
　　RU 486—an antiprogestational, 97
Wu, Y. L.
　　Synthesis of d,1-15-, 106
Wu, Z. L.
　　Study of traumatic amenor..., 40
Wyatt, P. R.
　　Chorionic biopsy and increased, 33
Wynants, P.
　　Endometrial morphology, 121
Wyndham, D.
　　Overview: the history of, 12
Xiao, B. L.
　　Pharmacokinetic and pharma..., 116
Xie, S. O.
　　Clinical investigation on, 183
Yagami, Y.
　　Immunotherapy of habitual, 31
Yamazaki, K.
　　Influence of a genetic differ..., 54
Yang, X.
　　No slackening in family, 83
Yao, G. Y.
　　Experimental studies on, 34
Yarber, W. L.
　　Importance of sex education, 197
　　Relationship between the, 195
Yeh, M.
　　Study of in vivo and in vitro, 8
Yi, Z.
　　Marriage and fertility in, 83
Yoshida, M.
　　Effect of drug-vinyl, 107
Youlton, R.
　　XY transloction in a woman, 30
Young, L.
　　Cognitive methods of, 190
Yuen, B. H.
　　Occurrence of molar preg..., 36
　　Risk of postmolar invasive, 140
Yuill, B.
　　Disserting Catholics take pro-, 72
Yuille, M. A.
　　What is life?, 12
Yusuf, F.
　　Ethnic differences in, 170
Zabin, L. S.
　　Adolescent pregnancy, 162

Evaluation of a pregnancy, 92
Zablan, Z. C.
Breast-feeding and fertility, 172
Zacharias, S.
Effects of hormonal and, 105
Zacks, R.
New update: chane urged, 88
Zaczek, T.
Complications of the surgical, 187
Zalányi, S., Jr.
Metabolic effects of combined, 130
Zamora, G.
Serum lipid levels before, 217
Zapka, J. G.
Diaphragm method contra..., 117
Zarkovic, G.
Aterations of cervical cytology, 126
Zdravkovic, G.
Pregnancy with a malformed, 36
Zeilinski, J.
Lymphatic pseudocysts as a, 188
Zergollern, L.
Chromosome abnormalities, 27
Zhang, Y. X.
Series of 440 vaginal, 186
Zheng, J. R.
Effects of total glycosides, 177
Ziegler, J. G.
New life: God's call, 46
Zimmet, J. A.
Historical look at a con..., 88
Zverina, J.
Present state of male, 108
Zwarun, S.
Sterilization and the retarded, 213